EFFECTUAL PRAYER
NOURISHED
in the
HEART BY CHRIST

"Lord, teach us to pray." (Luke 11:1)

RICK D. BAWCOM

ISBN 979-8-88832-363-2 (paperback)
ISBN 979-8-88832-365-6 (hardcover)
ISBN 979-8-88832-364-9 (digital)

Christian Faith Publishing
832 Park Avenue
Meadville, PA 16335
www.christianfaithpublishing.com

Unless otherwise noted, all scripture references are from NKJV.

Printed in the United States of America

"To God my exceeding joy."
(Psalm 43:4)
To the Father, Son, and Holy Spirit:
kind and tender companions of my heart.
To my dear wife, Donna,
whose heart companionship in marriage, child-rearing,
and now grandparenting is my abiding joy.

CONTENTS

ACKNOWLEDGEMENTS

I want to thank God for weaving into my life several people who gave from their hearts to see this book come into being. First and before all other support is my wife and companion in life. She is my love, my sister, and my spouse, a genuine gift from God. Then there is my friend of fifty-one years, Rick French, who encouraged me to put this series into print and found the publisher. Kathi Mapledoarm, a dear sister in Christ, and her husband Jim, were faithful friends since the start of my ministry. She gave helpful feedback on the manuscript. Justin and Talitha Wilson, my son-in-law and daughter, devoted a year to my completing the book free of distractions. Without this support, it is doubtful this book would have come into being.

PREFACE

The way you think of prayer will influence the way you approach praying. If perceived as mere duty and obligation, there will be no relational joy experienced. However, if prayer is personally known and experienced as vital connection, an essential lifeline between your soul and your God through Jesus Christ, prayer moves into a different light, a new perspective, a living relationship. Prayer presents itself as God's gift and the only avenue to enjoy communion with the Godhead: Father, Son, and Holy Spirit. Think of it: actual connection and companionship between you and the Almighty! Understanding this relationship, purchased by Christ, is the purpose of the book you hold in your hands. I hope you read it slowly and meditatively.

The Lord Jesus found great delight in the presence of his Father. The bond of eternal love, satisfaction, and enriching fulfillment was evident in the atmosphere of his prayers. If you heard him, you would want him to teach you to pray. God the Father knew this about you. The disciples witnessed Christ praying, and it compelled them to ask, "Lord, teach us to pray." This little volume expounds his answer.

God created you and all mankind with the finite capacity to experience the joy of communion with him. What went wrong?

The world in which you live has been banished from the acceptable presence of God. Through inconceivable folly, the insane choice of our first parents to rebel against the divine will engulfed the human race in spiritual death. Though made in the image of God, the life of God has been removed from the soul of humanity. Revolt against our Creator's kindness is the plague of mankind. Alienation from divine goodness is now the natural condition of an ungrateful society.

A gaping void resides in the human soul. Hostile forces, defiant toward the Most High, rush in to entice the human race with unworthy replacements. The heart should be the chamber of God's adoring presence. Instead, it is an idol factory. The lust of the flesh, the lust of the eyes, and the pride of life give willing allegiance to the world's enticing substitutes. By default, the world owns no other god besides the ruler of darkness. It is held under the bewitching sway of their vowed enemy, the evil one. Now delusions and deceptions cloak the awareness of eternal reality and ultimate "face-to-face" confrontation with the Almighty.

What does the offended Godhead do with all this? From all eternity, God devised a way for mercy and grace to prevail in displays of astonishing love! This love of God intrudes as an alien power into the realms of darkness, death, and delusion. God designed the eternal plan of redemption through the work of his Son to accomplish two marvels: to bring individuals back to him and to give himself to them.

The death, burial, and resurrection of Jesus Christ opens the door for reconciliation with God. Nothing is more powerful for inflaming our souls with love to God than to know, sense, and taste divine love shed abroad in our hearts. Not just this. He creates a household, the family of God. God has decreed a new humanity, new creations in Christ Jesus, who are his beloved sons and daughters! This book is about enjoying this relationship purchased by Christ for his people.

As lovers of Christ, precious promises, divinely secured realities, are our new normal.

> If anyone loves me, he will keep my word;
> and my Father will love him, and we will come to
> him and make our home with him. (John 14:23)

This is the language of family! Paul speaks of the companionship we now have with the eternal Godhead.

> The grace of the Lord Jesus Christ, and the
> love of God, and the communion of the Holy

Spirit be with you all. Amen. (2 Corinthians 13:14)

Loved ones delight to be "with" one another.

In the history of redemption, sweet words of closeness and openness from God have been the norm. Hear what is held out to a person exercising faith, love, submission, and obedience to the Most High.

What great nation is there that has God so near to it, as the Lord our God is to us, for whatever reason we may call upon him? (Deuteronomy 4:7)

For since the beginning of the world men have not heard nor perceived by the ear, nor has the eye seen any God besides you, who acts for the one who waits for him. (Isaiah 64:4)

It is the same with us!

Everyone who asks receives, and he who seeks finds, and to him who knocks it will be opened. (Matthew 7:8)

This is because of the intimate relationship the Almighty has established with his people.

You are a chosen generation, a royal priesthood, a holy nation, his own special people, that you may proclaim the praises of him who called you out of darkness into his marvelous light; who once were not a people but are now the people of God, who had not obtained mercy but now have obtained mercy. (1 Peter 2:9–10)

A special people—not because of who we are but because of who and what God is in relationship with us. God tenderly determines to put his loving-kindness, mercy, grace, and hope in us. We confess with Jacob; we are not worthy of the least of God's mercies, nor of all the truth he has revealed to us (Genesis 32:10).

Each person in the holy Trinity is engaged as uniquely devoted to every believer. Eternal love and mercy invades the life, interrupts the course of human existence, and omnipotent (all-powerful) determination brings a dead soul to life. Then God loves his child as if he were the only child to love. Yet God loves all his people this way. Only an immense, immeasurable God could love like this. He does love like this.

We still live in the land of banishment and exile. A strange new reality emerges within our hearts: "we are not of this world." We become strangers in the place we once called home. We are travelers, pilgrims, no longer "earth dwellers." Paul tells us "our citizenship is in heaven" and our permanent address is "in Christ," who resides at the right hand of God the Father. Our thoughts and affections are set on things above (Colossians 3:2–4). In the pages ahead, we discuss how to navigate life in companionship with God.

The Bible is God's love letter sent from home. In it he opens his thoughts and affections to us. Prayer is our response in which we open our thoughts and affections to him. We worship him in praise with thanksgiving as prayerful expressions of heart and soul. Prayer is a humble lifting up of our heart and pouring our soul out to God in the name of Christ. It is our secure and affectionate utterance: "Abba, Father."

We live in a world of unrest, threats of dangerous flu viruses, embattled politics, and nuclear arsenals held by nations of hostility. Society is declining morally because of anti-Christian forces and a Christianity that has lost the power of relevance. Out-breakings of man's inhumanity to man spread like a plague. Barbaric cruelty is becoming more common.

The people of God, the church of the living God, are no match for the vicious forces of darkness. They are bent on the destruction of mankind and the obliteration of the image of God reflected in the human race. We desperately need to know how to pray and lay hold of God. Effectual fervent prayer has always been the need in the Christian community. Our wise, sovereign God knows how to get his people to really pray in their praying.

Here is a book of hope, divine love, and access to a peace that surpasses all human understanding. The pages ahead reveal Christ's shepherding leadership. His tender counsel will guide you into green pastures and still-water brooks, producing soul health and well-being. The invitation is to take the hand of Christ. Let him bring you into the acceptable presence of God the Father and enjoyment of the Holy Spirit's comforting companionship. Let the precious Savior, who is gentle and lowly, nurture you in effectual prayer.

It is a secure reality:

> He who dwells in the secret place of the Most High shall abide under the shadow of the Almighty. (Psalm 91:1)

> The Most High declares: "Because he has set his love upon me, therefore I will deliver him; I will set him on high, because he has known my name. He shall call upon me, and I will answer him; I will be with him in trouble; I will deliver him and honor him." (Psalm 91:14–13)

These precious promises are "yes" and "amen" in Christ Jesus, the Shepherd of your soul and the one who will teach you to pray.

INTRODUCTION

*Reality is a nuisance to those who want
to make it up as they go along.*

—Austin Farrer, Saving Belief, 1964

I love music! Phrases within lyrics capture certain realities of life. Often the expressions, linked with sentiment and emotion, plant themselves in the memory, almost without effort. Take a phrase like "make me wonderful in her eyes" or "let her look at me through the eyes of love." Creating playlists for different occasions and from various genres has become an enjoyable hobby of mine. One romantic song I found had this line: "companions of the heart." When I shared the phrase with my wife, she replied, "Oh, I love that phrase. Through all the seasons and trials we have gone through, we have become "companions of the heart." The words "companions of the heart" imply a longing to enjoy "deep-down togetherness"—our humanity craving the rich experience of healthy belongingness, companionship, and mutual value—two people enjoying each other's presence, input, and support. The atmosphere they enjoy includes loyalty, reliability, and unconditional devotion in the sojourn of life.

As I look back, my love for music began when I was eleven. In a box I found two albums, which were the only music in our home. One had patriotic songs of US history focused on men of honor and character. The other contained love songs by a popular singer of the day. When I had poison oak (which was often), I would sit for hours in front of a fan and listen to these two albums. I memorized the words and tunes. These songs were weaving beliefs and values into the fabric of who I was and how I saw life. Formed in my heart were values and what I came to esteem as genuine relational riches most desirable. This took place on a subconscious level.

Why was I so attracted to these albums? My dad left home at sixteen. His mother died when he was a young boy. The stepmother never liked him, which filled him with anger and bitterness. My dad's life was full of hostility. The poison took root in his soul, producing eruptions of malicious, venomous words. Experiences as these affected the way he saw the world and relationships. He drank a lot and engaged in extramarital affairs. In word and action, he made clear my standing: he did not want me. He saw me as a worthless inconvenience. I understood my dad had no desire to build a relationship with me or even know me. Hope in such a father-son relationship collapsed within my heart. On a gut level, my two-year-old soul knew.

Every child comes into the world with an inborn expectation of being the sparkle in someone's eye. We look for someone looking for us. A man I called "dad" never gave a thought to this, yet even a two-year-old child needs love and, if deprived, will bear the scars of neglect. This reality wove the values my father radiated into the fabric of my inner awareness. Ingrained beliefs like these take a long time to see with objectivity. They take even longer to correct within the belief and filter system of our subconscious. Dad left me with the sense I was not worth knowing and it is not safe to make your presence known.

Parents daily engrave beliefs into their children's hearts. Beliefs become self-views, a way of seeing. These form opinions about relationships. Views of the world around them emerge. Early impressions sprout and grow into sturdy "treelike" perspectives. These become the worldview etched upon a child's soul and become the default for what "seems" normal or the "way life is." My dad abandoned us when I was eight years old. My mom sought to do the best she could in raising us three boys by herself. She never remarried. She was lonely until the Holy Spirit molded her into a praying woman who deeply loved her heavenly Father.

Back to the albums. The patriotic songs spoke of being part of something bigger than myself—something important, where a person's character was noble, and honor played a vital role in self-respect. The songs of romance and love gave hope of being wanted, loved, and valued. Those words would not be in my eleven-year-old brain, yet they gave a vague hope of belongingness and the banishment of loneliness settled into my heart as a dream. Someday.

My early years had no connection with Christianity, religion, or the Bible. Mom went to church when I was twelve, but all I heard was noise and sounds upon dead ears. The years ahead had a little church attendance, but the spiritual deadness continued. In my high school days, I stopped going to church. Life made little sense. Subtle questions emerged on what life was all about, but I submerged them and lived for the moment. I lived "without Christ," "having no hope and without God in" the mess and delusions of the world. The world I faced was unstable and untrustworthy. I knew my vulnerability and tried to hide from its reality.

In the month I turned eighteen, Christ stopped me. He captured my attention and changed me forever. Words, which had no meaning before, became filled with life and relevance most personally. The scales came off my eyes; the veil lifted, which kept me blind to reality and the truth about myself. Sin, a genuine issue deserving God's wrath, and indignation became fearful realities. I sensed myself to be the "bull's-eye" of his righteous anger and deserved rejection. It was not just sin; it was me, "the sinner," coming to undeniable realism. The judgment of God, along with justified condemnation, stuck to my soul as a certainty I would face. However, it was God's kindness showing me the bad news about myself—my reality before him. Then he, in mercy and love, told me the good news of Christ's role as Savior of sinners. The concepts of Christ's death as a substitutionary sin bearer and words of mercy and grace came alive with attractive hope.

From December through August 1972, I wrestled with God's truth and my condition. My conscience and the question of approaching God became the greatest issues. Could I hope in his mercy and saving me—"the sinner"? Could acceptance be my honest expectation and undeserved privilege? He willingly answered for all my guilt.

The Holy Spirit implanted and shed abroad the love of God in my soul as I entrusted my life into Christ's saving care. Within my heart dawned a love that would never fail. "Oh, love, that will not let me go! I rest my weary soul on you." Divine love worked to cast out those fears rooted in my struggling doubts.

In February, I purchased a Bible and read from start to finish, completing it in one year. As passages stood out, I would underline them and think about them, asking God to help me understand what it meant. When I came to the Psalms, my heart broke with amazing hope in the large-hearted nature of the Almighty. Many texts stood out. Two passages, I remember, came with the warmth of divine affection; they were words of hope my soul clung to. I needed no effort to memorize them. It was as though the expressions reached out and embraced my heart. The Spirit engrafted these words into my soul. The personal reception and loving embrace of God over-whelmed me. My soul experienced the unconditional acceptance and full belonging with the Father.

> When my father and my mother forsake me, then the Lord will take me up. (Psalm 27:10, or "take me in" as in the ESV)

> A father of the fatherless, and a judge of the widows, is God in his holy habitation. (Psalm 68:5)

A living realness emerged in these words as if they were personal expressions of God the Father's heart and mind toward me. He made me believe he valued and wanted to know me. Faith was at work, prompted by love for him. These were invitational mercies and overtures of his love. Nothing was general—all were specific. I realized the relationship with the Father was a personal gift from Christ purchased and extended freely, wholeheartedly, and unconditionally. My soul sensed a "sparkle in the eye" of my heavenly Father—for me. Christ, sent by the Father, "loved me and gave himself for me." These relational experiences were more than reality. "Eternity" attached itself to everything and made all life make sense as preparation for an existence beyond this temporary world. A large part of the glory of the Gospel is the eternal God making a way to give us "himself" through the accomplishments of Christ.

Because of my experiences with my dad, I did not understand what a father was to be and do. I have known people who struggle with the word *father* because of their past familiarities with poor examples. Some had dads who inflicted pain of various kinds. For me, my dad was a hurting man who had no ability to think beyond himself. Through a growing acquaintance with my heavenly Father, I saw what a "real" father should be. This entire outlook was a sweet and kind gift of God certified by Christ's accomplishments.

We sometimes describe prayer as the "soul of a child pouring itself out into the heart of his heavenly Father." My reality was such an experience. Christ became a genuine companion to my soul. My relationship with Jesus Christ was as real and warm as the warmth of the sun. I longed to be a "companion" with his heart. This is what the angel to the church at Ephesus refers to as "your first love." Genuine believers want to walk close with God and enjoy deeper, richer experiences of life with Christ.

In the next few years, I fell in love with the Person and ministry of the Holy Spirit. The Spirit was never some impersonal power. Rather, he was one Individual of the holy Trinity. This divine Person brought the accomplishments of Christ to my soul with power and application. He worked life and personal enjoyment with the Savior into my soul's sensibilities. The Spirit's delight is to bring the Father and Son, with riches of an eternal provision in Christ, to a believer's heart. He stirred my soul to lay hold of these treasures as divine realities, freely gifted. I viewed faith as the hand of my soul, taking hold of the extended hand of my God through his truth and promises.

Oh, how I wish such experiences marked all my days! To speak of such "deep-down togetherness" with Christ, though most desirable, shows how far short I come. God often protects a young child in Christ during those early years; but then comes the spiritual warfare from within and without. I have experienced intimacy with Christ. He led me into the same with the Father and the Holy Spirit, yet my heart knows the gravitational pull—downward—and my inconsistencies stare me in the face. My sins have all too often kept me at a distance. How true, as an older writer expressed,

> Prayer will keep you from sinning, or sin
> will keep you from praying. (John Bunyan)

The words of Bernard of Clairvaux, written around AD 1150, speak of our longing:

> Our restless spirits yearn for thee,
> Where'er our changeful lot is cast,
> Glad when thy gracious smile we see,
> Blest when our faith can hold thee fast.

We also have to confess with Robert Robinson:

> Prone to wander, Lord, I feel it,
> Prone to leave the God I love;
> Here's my heart, O, take and seal it,
> Seal it for thy courts above.

Another hymn speaks of our security and conveys the rich reality of what we have in Christ. These are the words of Augustus Toplady. Written in the mid to late eighteenth century, they speak volumes of comfort to my heart along with multitudes of other followers of the Lamb:

> My name from the palms of His hands
> Eternity will not erase;
> Impressed on his heart, it remains
> In marks of indelible grace.
> Yes! I to the end shall endure,
> As sure as the earnest is given;
> More happy, but not more secure,
> The glorified spirits in heaven.

Oh, the riches of blood-bought privileges which are ours in Jesus Christ! He has secured our way into sweet and secure acceptance with the triune God. Our beloved Savior takes us by the hand and leads us into joy, inexpressible and full of glory. He takes us into the Father's tenderhearted embrace and full acceptance. Our Savior sends the Holy Spirit to make all his accomplishments effective in us. He makes our souls his home. His work includes making the present ministry of Christ toward us to be a lively present reality. In this way, he is with us as an ever-present help in time of need. Barnabas exhorted the disciples to "cleave to Christ with purpose of heart" (Acts 11:23). The Holy Spirit enables us to do so. What invitational mercies full of tenderness and securing reality. These are the ironclad guarantees of the Lord God Almighty.

What has Christ accomplished for us? An intimate relationship with each person of the Godhead! Does this sound attractive? The apostle Paul tells us the saints have a fellowship as rich and real as he describes in 2 Corinthians 13:14:

> The grace of the Lord Jesus Christ, and the
> love of God (the Father), and the communion of
> the Holy Spirit be with you all.

"Be with"—how? As a present reality and companionship, we are truly to enjoy. It is the heavenly air we are to breathe. We are the company our triune God keeps. Paul tells us: bask in the warmth of the Father's love, draw upon the sufficiency of Christ's grace as he becomes our strength to do what, by nature, we cannot. Know the companionship of the indwelling Holy Spirit, whose fellowship and personal assistance conveys all divine riches we have become partakers of in the Son of God. All such treasures, though spiritual, are yet substantial realities. These are more solid and enduring than the ground we stand on. For this earth will melt with fervent heat, but our union with the triune God will last for eternity. These are "solid joys and lasting pleasures."

These are great things, are they not? We are to desire great things greatly. How are we to enter actual enjoyment of these precious realities and privileges? The first essential step is to grow in an understanding of God's Word. His Word expresses his heart and mind through the pages of Scripture. These scriptures are to nourish our souls in these truths and many others to be discovered. The Bible is the "living word of God." His Word guides us into reality. Scripture delivers us from our delusions and the errors of human teaching. Read and study your Bible chiefly to understand and personally, intimately know the Lord. Second, we are to grow in the spirit of genuine prayer. True prayer is an abandonment of all other reliances. Prayer is a silent declaration of our dependence on God alone. This is where we, as children of God, learn to pour our souls into the embrace and heart of our Father. In prayer, we entrust our lives into the grip of our Savior's arms and skillful hands. By prayer, we enter the comforting capabilities of the Holy Spirit. If we prized these treasures enough to plead with God for their enjoyed experience, we would enjoy the responsiveness of our God all the more.

Will we enjoy rich closeness with God all the time? Sad to say, not in this life. I would tell my children life is like a canoe. Are we on course toward the destination all the time? No, mostly we are off course. It is the art of correction. We have to keep the destination in view and press on. So it is in the Christian life and in our communion with God. We get off course multiple times daily. What we need is the spiritual art of correcting our focus and pursuit. Keep closeness with God in view and press on.

Prayer is a large topic. This book is an attempt to open and expound only one essential part of prayer. The subject of prayer takes in a variety of experiences. We express thanksgiving and praise, worship, and communion. We engage in intercession for others. By praying, we bring our daily needs before our God and find strength in time of need. As long as we are in this world, by prayer, we fight in the spiritual warfare. There are different contexts of prayer. We have the private prayer of a child of God, family prayer, and corporate prayer. There are even days of national prayer.

In the prayers of the Bible, we find a style of praying often absent in the prayers of our day. What is it? Pleading with God. The subject of pleading may at first seem odd. I entreat you not to prejudge the subject before you take a walk with me through the pages of Scripture. It may surprise you how vital a role it plays in one's pursuit of communion/companionship with God and living the Christian life. Such praying weaves itself into our entire responsibility as praying people. In fact, pleading with God is an essential feature in what James describes as the "effectual fervent prayer of a righteous man." Our pleading is actual evidence we "desire great things greatly." Pleading is the spiritual energy of effectual fervent prayer.

No matter what we learn in the Bible, it will work no good in us unless God is at work (1 Corinthians 3:6–7). We may sow the seed of divine truth, we may water it, but God alone must give the increase. As Paul told Timothy, "meditate" on divine truth and "may God give you understanding" (2 Timothy 2:7). May we read and pray, pray and read with a dependence upon the Holy Spirit to breathe life into our souls and make us come alive to divine truth. As his Word penetrates our minds and hearts and watered by the Spirit's present ministry, look for growth. Should there be fruit to the good of your walk with God, to God alone be all glory and praise.

Rick D. Bawcom

God loves each one of his people as if there
was only one of them to love.

—John Blanchard

But when the kindness and the love of God our Savior toward man
appeared, not by works of righteousness which we have done, but
according to his mercy he saved us, through the washing of regeneration
and renewing of the Holy Spirit, whom he poured out on us abundantly
through Jesus Christ our Savior, that having been justified by his
grace we should become heirs according to the hope of eternal life.

—Titus 3:4–7

1

Why a Book on Pleading with God?

*As long as we continue living, we
must continue praying.*

—Matthew Henry

The death of our fourth daughter threatened to stab our hearts. Just five hours earlier, I picked Rachel up from her crib. In one week, she would experience her first birthday. Before I went to the office, my routine included taking her into Donna so she could nurse—a true "mother's delight" to snuggle with her baby.

The slight bump below her eye made me think an eye tooth was coming in. The other three girls were asleep, so I kissed my two girls goodbye and went off to work until lunch.

By 9:30 a.m., Donna called me with a touch of alarm in her voice. "You need to come home and look at Rachel's eye. That bump has swollen her eye shut! I'm worried."

In five minutes, I walked in the door. Sure enough, the lump swelled her eye shut, looking like the size of a golf ball. It was Friday, and the weekend was before us. To be honest, our discussion centered on the expense of an emergency visit on the weekend. We concluded I would stay and watch the girls, and Donna would talk to the doctor as he examined our daughter.

Thirty minutes later, she called. "Rick, I'm scared. Two doctors looked at her, and this is what they said: 'Take Rachel straight to the hospital. We will meet you there with an infectious disease specialist.'"

Our minds were spinning. Donna came home to pick me up, and we had a friend come watch the girls. Within twenty minutes, we walked into the hospital. To our shock, a nurse swooped Rachel from Donna's arms, and three doctors surrounded us. "It is a one-in-a-million chance. Four bacteria are in the air at all times. Should one of them enter the system, it will take over the body, and death is the result within a twenty-four-hour period. Our concern is how close it is to Rachel's eye. If it enters the liquid of the eye, it will go immediately to the brain and down the spinal column. In twelve hours, Rachel could die. Which bacteria it is, we do not know, so we have to give her antibiotics for all four."

Shock and numbness gripped us. We followed the nurse, half blinded by our tears. She took Rachel to a crib that looked like a mini jail. Bars and rails surrounded the crib so a child could not climb out. They strapped her down, placing a boardlike cloth-covered solid base under each limb. They found veins on each extremity and the heparin lock put in place. A jungle of tubes ran to four different dispensers of antibiotics.

Rachel cried and screamed. She looked at us with eyes full of questions. "Why are you letting this happen? Do something! Save me! Help me!" Any parent can relate to the feeling of helplessness, agony of heart, yet submitting to the unavoidable pain as the pathway to hope and health.

They said Donna could not nurse. Despite such a restriction of getting into the crib, she climbed in and sought to comfort Rachel in the only way she could. Distracting her from the terror, pain, and confusion, Donna let Rachel nurse!

Donna and I needed to be alone so we could pray. Unconscious of walking, we passed through a thick cloud of numbness and made it to our car. We held each other as we released a flood of tears, giving vent to unbelievable confusion, shock, and fear of the unknown.

I took Donna's hand and held it with the grip of love and effort to comfort. "Honey, at this moment, Christ has us and Rachel in his heart. At this second, he is praying for us. This has not come into our lives apart from the filter system of his great affection for us. We cannot trace out what he is doing, but we can trust what he is doing. He does all things well. He does all things with perfection and with eternal purposes."

The presence of Christ's soul near us in the car was comforting. We prayed with a reality of immediate access to the heart of God. Each person of the holy Trinity gave us their focused attention and caressed our souls with felt care. Oh, how the unconditional love of God filled our souls. Our need was to draw near to him and open our hearts. We had to express our fears and parental longings to our caring God, and we knew Christ was the Great Physician whose prayers are always successful.

"Oh, God, beloved Lord Jesus, we need you right now. Our daughter is in that hospital crib, alone and filled with fear. Please comfort her. We don't know what will happen. We are so helpless. We struggle. You are a help in time of trouble. This is a time of trouble, and we need your help. We trust you and long for what honors you more than anything else. We bow and yield our longings into your hand, into your heart. We want her to live. Lord Jesus, you prayed to remove the cup if possible but yielded your will to fulfill your Father's purpose. We come to you, our God, with this same spirit of yielding. Our belief is in you, but 'help our unbelief.' We trust you, and what you are doing, we know, will be right. Our confidence is that you are wise and will do nothing wrong. You are kind and tender and will do nothing unnecessary. You give life, and you take it. If you take our daughter, we will praise you. If you heal her and give her back to us, we will praise you with gratitude. Oh, but hold us through it all."

He held us. We prayed and pled with the Lord, and he responded with personal care. The comfort we received was a felt reality. The Lord Jesus took us and our daughter up in his consoling, capable arms. Rachel is living a vibrant and healthy life, full of affectionate devotion to her gracious God. For the next five years, we called her our "orangutan" because she would not let Donna go. She clung to her.

God takes his people through soul-wrenching events. Why? There are many answers to that question. We are to be certain God

3

would have us learn to cling to him with "purpose of heart" (Acts 11:23; 14:22). He also delights in showing himself mighty on our behalf as we walk in his ways and seek his face. God never works without purpose and plan. Our wisdom is to walk with him through it all.

There are many purposes in the works of God for every one of his children.

> Remember that the LORD your God led you all the way…to humble you and test you, to know what was in your heart, whether you would keep his commandments. So he humbled you, allowed you to hunger, and fed you…that he might make you know that man shall not live by bread alone, but man lives by every word that proceeds from the mouth of the LORD. (Deuteronomy 8:2–3)

Our Lord has a plan for us. Yes, it includes a steadfast hope and a future (Jeremiah 29:11). This plan includes much more—the development of our hearts, character, and authentic individuality. It includes growing and maturing in likeness to Christ. Our Father's goal includes the genealogy of hope: grace-infused faith giving birth to perseverance in love and attachment to him. Through this inward process, we enter trials or difficulties, which give birth to endurance, which engenders character, whose offspring is hope (Romans 5:1–5). In all this, we experience the fidelity of our God and the trustworthiness of his Word. This is the process of growth as believers, as followers of the Lamb.

Here are three areas we may count on God to focus in our lives as his children:

1. Growth in humility, which is also the genuine mind of Christ (Philippians 2:5). If God "come in the flesh" exhibited humility, where could we find an argument for exemption? We find the only place of "self-excuse" arises from ignorance of God and self. Humility embodies the "beati-

tudes" of our Lord's description of his people. You cannot have the "beatitudes" in the soul without humility. He who knows God will be humble. He who knows himself cannot be proud. Christ alone is our boast. Humility is likeness to Christ. Pride is likeness to Satan, who through his arrogance fell. The work of God in the soul pulverizes human pride (Jeremiah 9:23–24). When the wheat ripens, it bows.

2. Cultivating a down-to-earth spirituality rooted in a vital relationship with God. We hide nothing from God. He knows the truth about every one of us. This is true at every moment of our lives. God knows us better than we know ourselves. David needed God's help to know himself (Psalm 139:23–24). We have a remaining tendency to sin and to self-deception (Jeremiah 17:9–10). Our Father's focus is to make us a refreshingly real people.

3. Developing a maturing faith—tested, purified, and strengthened by grace alone. Spirit-wrought faith shows itself in confidence that God will take care of us (1 Peter 1:3–9; 5:6–7). As we grow closer to God, we come away from delusions and self-deceptions into reality. At the center of reality are the persons of the Trinity, who perfectly manifest harmony in their mutual love. This acts like a magnet to draw us in. We, too, must respond to it in our lives and actions. Our deepest desires will be to love God and to love what God loves. As we move toward maturity in Christ, we find enriching satisfaction, beauty, sanctifying pleasures which capture the heart. We taste and perceive the goodness and graciousness of God. "The things of earth grow strangely dim in the light of his glory and grace." Growth includes a steadier walking by faith and less by sight. Like true north draws the needle of the compass, we will set our affections on things above, not on the things of earth.

How will these God-authored activities show themselves in our lives? How do these fingerprints of Christ's workmanship manifest themselves? Through a deepening, enriching, and real prayer life—a prayer life which mirrors Christ and the mature saints recorded in the Bible. Biblical narratives are a kind gift and provision of God. We do ourselves a great injury if we neglect their study.

Consider Daniel. The Scriptures do not give all the details of his life and experiences. We know he lived in a context common to the Israelites of his day at the time of the Babylonian captivity. They do not tell us if his parents died or became part of the dispersed Israelites carried into other parts of the world. Babylonian soldiers may have intruded into the home and carried their young son away. Perhaps there was a time and place for the boys to report for deportation. We know his early years included vital instruction from the book of Proverbs and the first five books of the Bible. God's commands, precepts, and laws became etched on the tablets of his heart. Like Paul, he delighted in the law of God after the inward man (Romans 7:22). As John tells us, his redeemed state was clear in that the commandments were not burdensome to Daniel (1 John 5:3).

The character of the LORD drew his soul in believing devotion. His affections for the LORD mirrored those of David. He was not a man of mere head religion or external piety. Daniel was a young man who delighted in the LORD's law and relished the worship of his God. His delight was to do the will of God stated in his Word. The Psalms became a living expression of a genuine relationship with God. For Daniel, the Scriptures were the doorway into a rich communion with his God. Throughout the years of his captivity and service, he possessed and studied the scrolls of the Old Testament. He had hope in the LORD's faithfulness declared in the writings of Isaiah and Jeremiah, finding promises he sunk his soul's hope in.

Some have called the book of Daniel "the young man's guidebook" (it is also the young woman's guidebook). The book includes the quality essential in the formation of character. It sets true manliness on display. What is that quality? Strong courage to obey the LORD and walk in his ways no matter what comes. God's word engrafted into the heart will strengthen and sweeten the soul.

From a young age, Daniel learned to train his appetites. Whether he ate or drank or whatever else he did, he sought to do all to the glory and pleasure of his God. He knew the eroding powers of unprincipled desires which arose from remaining sin. He cultivated a healthy self-watch. Daniel drew the line of his dependence. He did not depend on his learning, training, or understanding. His dependence was on the LORD. Daniel grew in settled confidence in God that was real and personal. Throughout the book of Daniel, we read of his character, devotion, and prayer life. Daniel proved to be a solid young man of uncompromising conviction. God filled his soul with wisdom from above. God's wisdom is both approachable and attractive. Every attempt came upon him to brainwash his youthful vulnerability. Governmental programs were in place to squeeze him into a Babylonian identity or this world's mold. Notice they even removed his name and sought a realignment of who he was at his core. Yet at the end of his years, during the days of Cyrus and Darius, all kings call him Daniel!

There are noticeable characteristics of Daniel's prayer life. He knew a vital connection with the true and living God. A vibrant relationship with the LORD is a hallmark and track record of this man. God responded to him when he prayed. Daniel's trademark: an uncompromising principle of regular prayer in his daily routine. His enemies could count on his faithfulness, yet he maintained authenticity in his praying. Daniel knew what it was to pour his heart out to the LORD and plead with God (Daniel 2:17–18; 9:3–19). Ezekiel was contemporary with Daniel. He draws attention to three godly and powerful prayer warriors in difficult settings: Noah, Job, and Daniel (Ezekiel 14:14, 20).

Daniel lived in a dysfunctional society. He worked within a government at enmity with the true and living God. His life knew demands, busyness, and challenges which stretch the soul. He rubbed shoulders with superficial people. He interacted with shallow, carnal, self-seeking people. Treacherous enemies watched him closely and talked about him behind his back. Daniel walked in an environment hostile to genuine godliness. His world was under the sway of the evil one, and he battled against an adversarial social climate. He knew the sins of his own soul and the nation he loved.

What kept him from sinking? His own sin and the surrounding society made his "spiritual skin" crawl, yet he knew a real refuge.

The kingdom of his own soul raised the flag and banner of Christ's presence, promises, and rule. He was not his own! His entire life was the purchase of mercy, grace, and the coming sin bearer in whom he trusted like Abraham and Zachariah, by faith, in looking upon the one whom his sins pierced. His prayer life was a vital connection with his beloved God. Communion with God sustained him in a way only the Lord could see.

Daniel knew certain realities. Lukewarmness would suck the life out of his soul and destroy his walk with God. Careless praying produces careless living. Dull prayers reap a harvest of shallow experiences with the Lord. Inattentiveness to God's holy word provokes God's inattention to our prayers (Proverbs 28:9). The LORD's grace and his pleading with God are the only "life" preserving commodities he lived upon. When God said, "Seek my face," his whole soul responded, "Your face, O Lord, will I seek!" To this activity, Daniel would say in complete honesty, "This one thing I do!"

Daniel had a living and vivid connection with these historic promises given by God to his people.

> As for you, my son Solomon, know the God of your father, and serve him with a loyal heart and with a willing mind; for the Lord searches all hearts and understands all the intent of the thoughts. If you seek him, you will find him, but if you forsake him, he will cast you off forever. (1 Chronicles 28:9)

> Hear me, Asa, and all Judah and Benjamin. The Lord is with you while you are with him. If you seek him, you will find him; but if you forsake him, he will forsake you. (2 Chronicles 15:2)

> "And you will seek me and find me when you search for me with all your heart. I will be found by you," says the Lord, "and I will bring you back from your captivity, I will gather you

> from all the nations and from all the places where
> I have driven you," says the Lord, "and I will
> bring you to the place from which I cause you
> to be carried away captive." (Jeremiah 29:13–14)

Daniel was a humble man who believed God's word and embraced that word with great seriousness. They were the words of life in a dead and fallen world. As he prayed, he wove the promises of God into his entreaties. In every major event, Daniel exhibited the "fervent, effectual prayers of a righteous man." Daniel's prayers availed much. He knew what it was to plead with God. He was among the host who cries out day and night unto the Lord (Luke 18:7).

You hold in your hand a book on prayer. It focuses on pleading with God. Can you identify with the world Daniel lived in? Is it much like our world? Actually, the world, the flesh (our remaining sin), and the devil are the same at every stage of history. Faith alone is the victory that overcomes them. Our Lord makes it clear: the undeniable proof of the existence of faith is the existence of prayer—prayer that connects with life's realities, our Lord describes, as "crying to God day and night" (Luke 18:7). Christ asked this question after teaching on the incredible necessity of prayer: "Nevertheless, when the Son of Man comes, will he really find faith on the earth?" He began teaching a parable with this purpose: "That men always ought to pray and not lose heart" (v. 1). It is clear: no real prayer means no genuine faith. If there is genuine faith, there will be real prayer.

In the first year after my coming to faith in Christ, someone set a concept in my heart. It became established in my soul. "People attend Sunday morning because the church is popular. They come on Sunday night because the pastor is popular, but they come to the prayer meeting because the LORD is popular." This statement is an overgeneralization but embodies a sad reality. As A. W. Tozer mentioned, "It is difficult to get people to come to a gathering when God is the only attraction."

Why a book on pleading with God? Many of us feel like infants or toddlers in the practice of prayer. Intimidation marks many beaten-down souls accused of prayerlessness while those who expose this do not gently guide them into being prayerful. May you find nourishment, example, instruction, encouragement, and yes, a deep challenge, in these pages. May this book serve as a stimulant for your weakness, a remedy for sickness, and an inspiration to greater prayerfulness in our personal lives! Christ's people need encouragement, and the church needs revitalization in the activity of prayer modeled in the Scriptures. This is the argument for a book on pleading. It is the need of the hour for the majority of Christ's people.

Why a book on pleading with God? In 1 Chronicles 12:32, we read of the sons of Issachar "who understood the times, to know what Israel ought to do." We need such an understanding of our day. A clear perception of our wisest response to the times in which we live is a more earnest prayer life personally and as gathered assemblies of Christ. Paul warns of perilous times in the church in 2 Timothy 3:1–9. Paul charges us to a way of life far above our abilities.

> That you may become blameless and harmless, children of God without fault amid a crooked and perverse generation, among whom you shine as lights in the world. (Philippians 2:15)

The church will always exist in a culture like this.

> The entire world lies in the power of the evil one. (1 John 5:19)

Paul tells us Christ gives armor for the battle (Ephesians 6:10–20). In that passage, above everything mentioned, Paul stresses prayer as the most vital piece of our weaponry for the battle. Prayer is not the least we can do; it is the greatest. Our greatest need is to become skillful in calling upon God with effectual, fervent prayer that avails—much!

> And do this, knowing the time, that now it is high time to awake out of sleep; for now, our salvation is nearer than when we first believed. The

night is far spent, the day is at hand. Therefore, let us cast off the works of darkness, and let us put on the armor of light. Let us walk properly, as in the day, not in revelry and drunkenness, not in lewdness and lust, not in strife and envy. But put on the Lord Jesus Christ, and make no provision for the flesh, to fulfill its lusts. (Romans 13:11–14)

This will not happen without effectual and fervent prayer.

This is a book for the overwhelmed mother trying to walk with God in a demanding world. Here are words of help for the man who seeks to work hard, cultivate a genuine relationship with God, and lead his family in the ways of Christ. This is a book for a young person whose longing is to start life out right. Here is a book for young pastors whose passion is to assist the people of God in maturing and cultivating a genuine acquaintance with God. Here is a book for aged saints who long to leave a legacy of answered prayers. Along the way, I will give a word of encouragement to the people of God in an array of "real-life circumstances."

As you read this book, may Thomas Brooks's wise words form the lens through which you see:

> It is not he who reads the most, but he who meditates the most, makes the soundest, roundest, sweetest Christian.

If there is to be any benefit at all, we must receive it from the hand of Christ. Without him, we can do nothing. Remember, we can do all things through Christ who strengthens us.

> *To know how to speak to God is more important*
> *than knowing how to speak to men.*
>
> —Andrew Murray

2

Our Lord's Teaching on Prayer: He Expects Us to Plead (Part 1)

In God's name I beseech you,
let prayer nourish your soul as your
meals nourish your body.

—Francois Fenelon

The disciples enjoyed amazing privileges and opportunities to walk and talk with Christ. It was a slow realization for them to understand the incredible privilege. For three and a half years, they were companions with "God come in the flesh." As the embodiment of all the treasures of wisdom and knowledge, he lived with them and spoke words of grace and truth. He explained things to them with patience. In Christ Jesus, they had God in human flesh, Immanuel, as their companion, mentor, and helper.

The same is true for you and me in a greater way! Christ now dwells in the soul of a believer. The Holy Spirit inhabits a child of God, making him his "holy temple." He is present, available, and approachable in personal companionship. Christ always lives to carry you on his heart, and he lives within you as a believer: "Christ dwells in your heart by faith." His ear is open to your concerns. He experiences life with you. You take him everywhere. He never leaves or forsakes you. His supreme affections and skills all focus on you, your needs, and your well-being.

The Holy Spirit delights in his role in our redemption. He takes the gospel accounts of Christ's ministry and presses them as Christ's present personal care for you. The same Christ, caring for his sheep in the Gospels, lives in you to care for you. Those recordings of the life of Christ, with all the tender words and acts to people in need, describe the one who dwells in you through the person of the Spirit. The Holy Spirit thrills to make this care come alive in all the people of God. He invigorates hopeful cheer in the inner man, strengthens courage in the will, and energizes the conquering power of faith. How? By making known the actual presence of Christ. Moses "endured hardships as seeing him who is invisible." So also are we to do the same. The words "I will never leave you or forsake you" have personal force infused into them by the Holy Spirit. The Holy Spirit unites the believer's soul with the riches, provisions, strength, and grace of Christ. That is a vital part of his assisting ministry to us, and it is his delight.

If you could ask the Lord Jesus for insight on how to make it through the rest of your time on earth, what would he tell you? If you asked him for help to live with greater victory, what truth would he open? Would it surprise you if he spoke to you about your prayer life? Prayer is the avenue of access to divine fellowship and power. Praying is your response to the truths and message of God's word. Prayer is your connection to each person of the holy Trinity. The Lord Jesus would speak to you about the importance of prayer.

So, what about your present prayer life? Do you look upon prayer as Christ does? Do you desire Christ's personal direction for improving this vital activity? Can you "do" the Christian life without this? Paul knew how insufficient he was.

> Not that we are sufficient of ourselves to
> think of anything as being from ourselves, but
> our sufficiency is from God. (2 Corinthians 3:5)

Paul did not think he was sufficient of himself to think a good thought or do a good deed to the pleasure of God, nor did Paul believe he could live the Christian life without a vital connection to Christ. He had a conviction and felt need he actually lived by—to draw strength and grace from the Lord Jesus. We cannot do this without prayer! Paul lived with a continual acquaintance with his soul's poverty. Yet "blessed" (truly happy) "are the poor in spirit." It moves the weak to cry to the strong for strength. Paul was expressing the reality of Christ's statement "Without me, you can do nothing." Paul knew where his sufficiency came from. We will touch on this again.

Look at Luke 11:1:

> Now Jesus was praying in a certain place, and when he finished, one of his disciples said to him, "Lord, teach us to pray."

"Lord, we want to know God as you do. We want to pray as you do. There is something so real, so personal and attractive in the way you pray. Help us pray like that." This disciple asked a significant question. Remember, he is a brother who wanted help in an area common to all believers. What a kind display and proof our heavenly Father knows what things we need before we ask. We need guidance in this area, and our Savior provides it. Who better to teach us to pray than the one who perfectly prays clothed with our humanity? He is our Great High Priest who excels in prayer. He is the very one that has and even now prays for us! This is the appointed way for faith to thrive. It is an active faith which overcomes the world and leads us in victory! Prayer is the way to make it to our journey's end. Faith, exercised in prayer, is the way to vanquish all enemies.

Let's look at our Lord's answer to this disciple in verses 2–13. He tells us what to pray for and how to pray. The teaching comes in four parts. We need all four parts:

- Part 1 verses 2–4, gives the wide content of prayer. This is a directory for prayer.
- Part 2 verses 5–8, our Lord addresses the need for persevering in prayer.

- Part 3 verses 9–10, we are to pray with assurance of success as the expression of living, active faith.
- Part 4 verses 11–13, pray with assurance of your tender Father's wise response.

The account in Luke is shorter than Matthew, found in 6:6–13. Matthew records some introductory cautions along with petitions and praises not found here. We are not to pray like the Pharisees, who put on a performance. We are not to think our many words make good prayers. Avoid empty repetition of phrases or expressions that come from mere habit. Our purpose in this book is not a treatment of the model prayer; rather, to draw attention to the flow of thought in our Lord's instruction. His answer is for all his disciples.

Part 1 verses 2–4, gives the wide content of prayer. This is a directory for prayer.

So he said to them, "When you pray, say, 'Our Father in heaven, hallowed be your name. Your kingdom come. Your will be done on earth as it is in heaven. Give us day by day our daily bread and forgive us our sins, for we also forgive everyone who is indebted to us. And do not lead us into temptation, but deliver us from the evil one.'"

First, Christ tells his disciples prayer is a "family" matter (v. 2). We come as people adopted and integrated into the divine "family." We draw near to our Father as members of the "household of God" as his "dear children." Look how Paul quotes God giving us this identity in 2 Corinthians 6:18:

"I will be a Father to you, and you shall be my sons and daughters," says the Lord Almighty.

Born of the Spirit, he moves us to cry out "Abba, Father" (Romans 8:15–16). We are not merely added to God's household.

The Holy Spirit creates the "nature" of a child of God within us. Our Lord stresses prayer is foremost about our new family relationship into which the Spirit adopts and births us!

Why is this important for us to realize? Rightly understood, this will breathe confidence into our souls. God will provide for his children, protect his children, and hear his children when they speak to him. A relationship is a living reciprocal dialogue. Respect and deep acquaintance are essential qualities of actual connection between persons—even between a finite person and an infinite person. Mutual "heart acquaintance" shows a quality relationship. God wants us to be companions of the heart with him. The Lord Jesus opens this eternal connection and brings us into its enjoyments. "In this manner, therefore, pray" is the warmth of welcome and invitational hospitality of the Godhead to build that reciprocal tie of eternal kinship. Our Lord tells us he and the Father will make their home with us, make known their delight to spend time in intimate conversation! (John 14:19–23). This should make us bow in humility and rise with amazement and praise but genuinely enter and cultivate a life of prayer. The realization and enjoyment of this relationship comes through the Scriptures, the living word of God, and prayer.

We are his, and he is ours! The honor of our God, the furtherance of his kingdom, and the actualization of his will become the supreme priority of our lives. Notice that these include our own eternal redemption! Deliverance from the wrath of God and incorporation into the family of God accomplish the honoring of his name, the furtherance of his kingdom, and the fulfilling of his will. Eternal values come into view. They are worth living for. Some saints in history found them worth dying for (Hebrews 11).

Second, Christ gives a sweeping panorama of all that concerns us in this life (vv. 3–4). Bring it all to your Father. Matthew says, "In this manner," "pray like this," not reiterate these words. Our Lord does not give a rigid form to duplicate. When Christ prays, he never repeated these words, the disciples and apostles did not repeat them, and he did not expect us to. Here he gives a helpful guide in forming our own prayers. It is not a form but freely opening our hearts to God that Christ teaches and desires. The priority of our Father's glory and his will in our lives and in the world is a must. We are to keep first things first. Then he touches upon the categories of our actual needs and stresses free expression of all that concerns us. Matthew and Luke emphasize simplicity, conciseness, mental clarity, and spiritual comprehensiveness. Matthew captures the atmosphere of wonder, love, and praise.

Christ says your Father's glory and will are of utmost importance. In worship and gratitude, express genuine concern for "our Father's" purposes to happen. Have the Lord before us as our God at all times, which is a heart embrace of the first commandment. This perspective of eternal priority is living with eternity's values in view. This is the heart of seeking first God's kingdom and righteousness. What is the triune God's response to such a heart?

> All these things you need will be added to you. (Matthew 6:31–33)

Yes, there is an actual battle, yet there is a real responsive relationship in this wonderful connection you have with the Father. Our triune God is present to help us navigate through the struggles of life. These struggles include daily provision, forgiveness, relationship challenges, divine protection from sin and the evil one throughout our earthly sojourn.

We are to pray, convinced he takes personal interest and care in and for us and our every need. From daily necessities to daily forgiveness, we bring it all to him. Our God communicates an invitational assurance nothing can separate us from him and his love. Nothing escapes his awareness and care.

> Casting all your care upon Him, for He cares for you. (1 Peter 5:7)

Your cares matter to him! Share them with him. Thus, we are to pour out our hearts to him at all times, for God is a refuge for every individual child of his (Psalm 62:8). We live in a hostile world lying under the sway of the evil one (1 John 5:19). We daily run into temptations from within and without. Our wisdom is to make God our companion in this warfare. The very "name of the LORD is a strong tower." Our safety is to run into this tower by prayer. God with us, realized in prayer, we break through all obstacles in the way by pleading. We come to him for personal communication. We come for safety, instruction, guidance, and the supply of our needs. In this "directory of prayer," our Lord is saying, "Take your Father's hand, and walk through life together as his child. Face life together, and relate everything to him." When we say, "Our Father," he responds, "Yes, my sons and daughters."

It is that moment by moment relating all your life to God, walking together. This is the atmosphere Christ would have all his people experience. When you read, "so and so walked with God," here is the vital makeup of what it is. This is the heart of "praying without ceasing." It is a shared life we live with God. Will it be easy? Obviously not. Therefore, our Lord addresses the need for energy being exerted in our praying. The Lord's response to this disciple did not stop at this point. The rest of the instruction, through verse 13, highlights the need for energy, confidence, and assured success in our praying. Pleading with God captures the remaining of our Lord's instruction on prayer.

The subject of pleading with God is not "the key" to prayer or formula to get what you want. It is not punching the right combination of numbers and the vault of heaven opens. When we descend to form or formula seeking, there is no relationship; rather, a form of assumed manipulation. This can take place slowly, but the result is viewing God as a utility, which makes God, in our motives and values, exist merely to meet our needs. To be honest, we all fall into a tendency of "hoping for a formula" to get what we sense we need or want instead of forging forward in faith to know and walk with God. Pleading speaks of focused energy in a secure relationship; however, we all want an easier way even though it is to our detriment.

Our God wants us to pursue a "relationship" (Ephesians 2:19; 5:1). If we drift into the "formula seeking," we no longer pursue genuine closeness. We fall into a detached, lifeless exercise of religious "duty," hoping we can tap into a way of successful praying.

We shift our focus on "doing it right" instead of drawing near to a person. Our concern becomes "getting what we want." A relationship is not the longed-for focus anymore. We slide toward "external" performance. We can develop our own form of "Protestant Rosary." Our devotion becomes mental. Then the Christian life and prayer become as exciting as watching paint dry. So the temptation is to shift to surface experiences, external excitements, shallow praying, put on a smile, and distract ourselves with activity and entertainment. We become more concerned about our kingdom instead of God's. We pray general prayers and are happy with ourselves and our performance. To ward off feelings of guilt, we focus on what makes us feel good. We slowly become comfortable and would have it no other way. We resent anything that disturbs this.

Part 2 verses 5–8, our Lord addresses the need for persevering in prayer.

> And He said to them, "Which of you shall have a friend (neighbor), and go to him at midnight and say to him, 'Friend, lend me three loaves; for a friend of mine has come on his journey, and I have nothing to set before him'; and he will answer from within and say, 'Do not trouble me; the door is now shut, and my children are with me in bed; I cannot rise and give you?' I say to you, though he will not rise and give him because he is his friend, yet because of his persistence he will rise and give him as many as he needs."

Later on, in this same gospel account, our Lord will speak a parable to the "end we ought always to pray and not lose heart" or faint (Luke 18:1). Here in Luke 11, Jesus stresses the same point. This story (Luke 11) speaks of a guest who was a friend from afar, arrives at a man's home unannounced. They had no communication system to call ahead. He is weary, needing a meal and a place to lay his head. The host, surprised and unprepared, had a shortage of food in the house, which hindered meeting the humanitarian need of his guest. Therefore, he goes to his neighbor-friend to help him out. The reluctant neighbor refuses to inconvenience himself with the need. There was an attempt at indifference. The man with the guest will not let his neighbor return to his bed in peace. Rather, he persists in knocking and asking until the needed supply comes forth.

Christ teaches his disciples to be like the man at the door. In prayer, don't give up so easily. There are times it appears God is indifferent or reluctant to meet our needs! Be honest. We have felt or thought this. This is more of a common experience with the people of God. Would you not agree? How often do we judge the Lord by our own feeble sense and limited understanding? We are prone to get discouraged and not pray in a way of perseverance. We give up and assume God does not care. Our foolishness makes us mind readers of our Father, and we draw wrong conclusions.

Yet notice Christ's praise for persevering in expressing and pressing our need: "Yet…he will rise and give him whatever he needs." Why? Because he would not give up, and the door kept shaking and booming from the force of his blows. He made it clear: "You will not leave me in my need. You will do something about it. You will not go to bed until I know the supply of my need to do this man right." Christ is teaching us to bring energy and determination in our praying! We are to come to God this way. Remember, our Lord is teaching us to pray.

The parable referred to in Luke 18 concerns a widow and an unjust judge. Though unwilling to meet her need, because of her continual pestering, he granted her request. She would not let him go until he acted on her behalf. She had a felt need he could not and would not feel, nor did he care to, and she would not leave until he did something about it. Our Lord tells us we are to pray like this. However, there is a difference. We are to pray with assurance our Father is not an indifferent neighbor! Nor is he an unjust judge who couldn't care less about our concerns. Christ would not have us take counsel from our feelings, fears, or shortsightedness. The Lord Jesus does not want us to get frustrated with God and conclude, "Well, if he doesn't conform to my time expectations, he doesn't care about me." Doesn't that sound childish? Our Lord does not want us to force our time frame upon the Almighty. Internal perspectives have gone wrong when we act like little sovereigns in our tiny universe, demanding things go as we see fit. Where is the desire for the Father's will being done? Where is the "not my will but your will be done"?

Rather, he would have us lay hold of our God, who hears and answers the prayers of his children. He would have us not let him go until he blesses us. Our heavenly Father already has the disposition to hear and respond. Look at what our Savior says in Luke 18:7:

> And shall God not avenge his own elect
> who cry out day and night to him, though he
> bears long with them?

With God our Father, he bears long with us and will answer our prayers. With us, we are to fit the description of a person who "cries out to him day and night!" Our Lord teaches us to be a persevering people in prayer and learn to cry out or plead with God instead of giving up. That's what our Lord wants. That's what he is teaching his disciples.

Christ is teaching us this lesson:

"My disciples, don't be content merely to mouth prayers. Know your need. Sense it in a way that moves and motivates you to lay hold of your God. If you know and feel your poverty of soul, it will arouse you to find my fullness infused within your being. Pray with an argument. Know the Bible, and use its promises and statements of God's expressed character and will. Pray with persistence. Pray with intensity when you need to. Get your needs met. I want you to plead in your praying. Put your heart and energy of soul into praying. Prize God's involvement. Mean business with the Almighty." Beloved, if we do not receive this part of Christ's teaching on prayer, we do ourselves harm. Remember, Christ is still answering the request "teach us to pray."

God values our presence with him. God loves desperate people who want him, need him, and will not go on without him. He loved it when Moses said, "Don't command me to go unless you go with me!" He wants us to come and enjoy him in an atmosphere of genuine delight—mutual delight in one another. (Zephaniah 3:17; Psalm 37:4: put these verses together and see your reality as a child of God.) His intention is for us to experience communion and companionship, which is far more important than a transaction to meet a need. Let "need" be an opportunity to get together with your heavenly Father. Prayer is always more than asking God to run errands for us. We are to love the giver far more than the gift. Christ says in Luke 11 and 18, "Pray in such a way you give your God no rest until he gives you rest in answering your prayers."

We sometimes think we have to wait long for God to meet our needs. There is more to it. Listen to these words from Isaiah 30:18:

> Therefore, the LORD will wait, that he may be gracious to you; and therefore he will be exalted, that he may have mercy on you. For the LORD is a God of justice, blessed are all those who wait for him.

God's timing is perfect. The Lord is waiting for the perfect time and way of response. He values our valuing him by spending time in his presence. Why? So we may commune with him, basking in his presence with a firm conviction "the judge of all the earth does right." He answers at the right time, with perfect knowledge of everything which concerns us. Value him and his presence far more than getting a request met. Let this be a motivating force to persevere in prayer: "I love spending time with my God."

You might say, "Who thinks like this?" Answer: each person of the holy Trinity!

Sometimes, to my shame, I have come to God with a need; but all my focus was upon the need, and I glanced toward God. This is so far from the desire of his heart. What would more delight the heart of God is for us to draw near in love, praise, and adoration. Delight ourselves in him. Magnify him. Express our gratitude for who he is and who he is to us. Then with him, take up the need together.

Acknowledge, "Oh, my gracious God, what is this in the light of your massive skill and capabilities? Yet it is an issue pressing me. You gave me your own Son. Will you not, with him, give me everything else I need? May you take this up with your power and wisdom. Work on behalf of my well-being. Meet this need, and fulfill the words of your commitment to your dependent child. I have no one else to go to and no other place to put my trust. Remember the words you have given me—words of promise upon which you have made me hope" (Philippians 4:6–7; Romans 8:32; Psalm 119:49; Matthew 7:7). This is pleading with biblical reasoning and argument. Our Lord makes it clear: "My teaching and desire are for you to pray in this manner."

Dear brethren, do you get the heart of this? Is pleading in prayer coming into focus? Can you see yourself forming arguments from what you read in God's Word and using them in drawing near to God with earnest desires to experience God's response to you?

This is the pathway to develop Christian character.

This is the way we seek our Father in meeting the needs arising in our lives.

This is our wise heavenly Father, our gracious Lord Jesus, our beloved Holy Spirit—all companions tutoring us in Christian graces. I hope this is becoming attractive to you and motivating for a sweeter prayer life.

It is all part of his plan for our good. Do you get the sense of what God wants from us? The Godhead and his children are to be colaborers and companions in life? That's right. This is a vital reality of what it is to "walk with God." We are to "work out our own salvation with fear and trembling, for it is God who works in us to will and to do of his own good pleasure" (Philippians 2:12–13). Our working and God's works are to be concurrent workings and interdependent necessities. They are to be confluent realities. We are to be colaborers with God in our own well-being and spiritual progress. God will not read the Bible for you, and you are not to read the Bible without him. Just like the children of Israel going into the Promised Land, they could never do it without God. God would not do it without them. It was a mutual activity. So is the Christian life. God works from his purposed decree the treasury of his love, kindness, and grace. We work, drawing all our strength and enablement from the treasury in Christ, freely given to us because of his role as our Great High Priest. This is abiding in and drawing from Christ, who is our source of strength and ability.

Do this in an atmosphere of "family ties with the Almighty." Persist in presenting your needs, and don't let him go until he blesses you. Press this relationship and its enjoyments to his heart. Show how much you value it by the sweat of your soul in pursuing it. As James Denney writes, "The kingdom of God is not for the well-meaning but for the desperate."

Can you enter these expressions of prayer? Are these longings found in your soul? "O Lord, you said you want me to know you, to love you, and to walk with you. I long for this. I need you to walk with me. My heart aches for you to make your presence and help a real, experienced joy in my soul. Do not leave me to myself. Lord, I seek your strength so I can seek your face. I long to grow and develop Christian character. Oh, make me make progress in Christlikeness. Without you, I can't do this. Will you not get more praise from me if you do this? When I grow in likeness to your Son, my Father, it will delight your heart. Oh, my God, get delight this way!"

Remember Aaron and Hur, who held up the hands of Moses (Exodus 17:12)? As long as Moses held his staff high in the air, Joshua was victorious; but his hands grew weary, so Aaron and Hur came to hold them up. This gave life and victory on the battlefield for the people of God. Christ is telling us something very important. If we want life and victory on the battlefield of life, we must be a praying people. If we want a lively and rich prayer life, we also have an Aaron and Hur to hold up our petitions. What are they? Perseverance and importunity.

When the Lord Jesus teaches on prayer, he places stress on our steadfast continuance in prayer. He further presses us to be importunate in prayer. What is importunity in prayer? It is to be persistent, demanding, even unrelenting until he gives an answer! Now he may remove the burden or strengthen the back, but he will answer his children.

*Before we can pray, "Thy kingdom come," we must
be willing to pray, "My kingdom go."*

—Alan Redpath

Prayer is the sweat of the soul.

—Martin Luther

3

Our Lord's Teaching on Prayer: He Expects Us to Plead (Part 2)

These inward trials I employ, from self,
and pride, to set you free; and break your schemes
of earthly joy, that you may find your all in me.

—John Newton

Don't touch Christianity unless you mean business.
I promise you a miserable existence if you do.

—Henry Drummond

The flu had hit our family hard. When you have ten children, it drags on. Our son, only three, developed a fever. I laid him beside our bed to watch how warm he got. After an hour, he grew stiff and convulsed. When I picked him up, he was rigid and burning with fever. Donna ran a cool bath. We put him in to bring down the temperature.

When he was back to normal, we ran him to the hospital. The emergency doctors made it clear he had more than the flu. Something serious was wrong. However, they did not know what. A series of tests had to happen. Then came the doctors' decision to do a spinal tap. They asked me to hold him while they poked him in the spine!

My son could not understand why so much pain was being inflicted on his body. He screamed and twisted. Then he looked at me and said, "Dad, why are you letting them do this?" My heart broke. The look on his face haunts me to this day and produces tears. I looked at the doctors and said, "This is too much! You can't do this and expect me to hold my son." They stopped. While writing this, the tears flow freely. Would my son see me as the cause of his pain?

It turned out the spinal tap was unnecessary. Some tests came back. He had reflux, a condition where urine from the bladder backs up to the kidneys. This was because the valves within the ureters failed. These are tubes which go from the kidneys to the bladder. The fever came from a bacterial infection. Because of this, he lost one-third of one kidney and two-thirds of the other. A short time later, he had surgery which repaired the valves. I was with him every moment I could.

We prayed for the children as the flu hit our home. Prayer quickly moved from general petitions to specific entreaties at the throne of grace for a miraculous act of God on behalf of our son. From the moment our son's fever spiked until the postsurgery visit, our family sought the LORD with increased intensity for God's intervening mercies. We went from asking to seeking and from seeking to knocking at heaven's door. My wife and I still bring the matter of his health before the throne of grace. He is doing fine but must be careful about his diet and lifestyle.

What have we seen from the teaching of our Lord on prayer?

Part 1 verses 2–4, gives the wide content of prayer. This is a directory for prayer.

Part 2 verses 5–8, our Lord addresses the need for persevering in prayer.

Now, in this third section, our Lord takes us a step further. He teaches us to pray with assurance. We are to have a confident belief we are not praying in vain. This is living faith and living by faith. Pray with assurance of the things hoped for being granted. Pray with a realization of substantial confidence that your Father will meet your needs. You confidently wait for their arrival (Hebrews 11:1; 2 Corinthians 5:7).

Part 3 verses 9–10, we are to pray with assurance of success as the expression of living, active faith.

Christ teaches we may need increased intensity as we pray from a felt sense of need. This is like the story of the visiting friend and neighbor just referred to; however, this section takes us a step further. We are to express our determination to find God's help in the needs we experience in life. There is more. We are to do so with a divinely warranted assurance we shall receive! Increased intensity, mixed with the confidence of God's guaranteeing success in our prayers, should infuse strength in our belief as we pray. Notice how our Savior speaks of guaranteed success. There is a "matter of fact" sense in our Lord's words: "If you do this, I assure you it will be successful, and you will have the divine response. Ask in faith, nothing wavering. Don't be unstable in this. Exercise yourselves to be strong in your confidence in God's responsiveness to you. He will respond, and you will get what you need."

"And I tell you, ask, and it will be given you; seek, and you will find knock, and it will be opened to you." Ask, seek, and knock imply an increased intensity. "Show a determination to make the breakthrough to find his help and response in time of need." Success is ours in such an approach. "For everyone who asks receives and the one who seeks finds and to the one who knocks, it will be opened." Pray and, as needed, increase your intensity and determination, but keep your eye on the God of all hope. You shall reap if you do not faint (Luke 18:1; Galatians 6:9).

These are kind and encouraging words from your Savior. They declare your God is a giving God and already predisposed to respond and meet your needs.

For your Father knows the things you have
need of before you ask him. (Matthew 6:8)

> If you lack wisdom, ask God for it, ask in
> faith and it will be given. (James 1:5)

Be confident. It will be given. Prize getting the wisdom you need, and search for it more than others search for hidden silver or gold (James 1; Proverbs 2). Do not think of putting God to work while you sit idle. Perhaps God will give wisdom as you go digging in his word for it! Remember, the entire Christian life is a mutual pursuit of you and your triune God facing life together. This is communion, fellowship, and companionship.

If you make the effort to go all the way to heaven, to the throne of grace, you will not come away empty-handed. There are promises given to you by God which cover every need you have in life and in your journey to heaven. Do you believe this? All these promises are "yea and amen in Christ Jesus" (2 Corinthians 1:20). Paul said, with confidence,

> My God will supply all your need according
> to his riches in glory by Christ Jesus. (Philippians
> 4:19)

There is no room for debate or doubt in this matter.

A reality check—often we have not the answers because we simply do not ask or we say a prayer with no genuine faith or confidence in God's openheartedness and openhandedness or we ask and do not receive because we are all consumed with selfish desires. We don't get what we want fast enough, and the fleshly response is "Well, I guess God does not care." "Oh, it is too much of a bother." We may have an unspoken desire to put God to work while we take our ease or just get on with our lives (James 4:3). Such selfishness spells death in any relationship of depth or quality. How many marriages fall apart because one spouse is all consumed with "self" and everyone else exists for their benefit? Our God will never fit into that category.

I have had many conversations with my children and foster children about the difference between "takers" and "givers" in life. God is a giver of sweet gifts. His people are givers of grateful praise. God is not a taker, and his people are not to be takers. His children are receivers, but the Spirit fills them with amazement over God's kindness and generosity. The relationship is foremost; answered prayer is secondary. Do we hold this priority? Yet answered prayer is essential! There is tenderness in Christ's words—a genuine openhearted representation of assured success in response to our intentional and focused prayers. May we not twist them to mean something different.

> Now this is the confidence that we have in Him, that if we ask anything according to His will, He hears us. (1 John 5:14)

This is so simple. Where do the complications come from? What is the source of our bewilderments and, at times, our frustrations with answered prayer?

Mark it down: when God doesn't seem to be answering prayer in the way we expect, then we must trust there's something he knows that we do not. This is simple to understand. It is not always easy to embrace.

When the cause is God's wise sovereignty and fatherly wisdom, we must "trust and obey, for there's no other way to be happy in Jesus but to trust and obey."

> The secret things belong to the LORD our God, but those things which are revealed belong to us—that we may do all the words of this law. (Deuteronomy 29:29)

Our God is always accomplishing infinitely more than we could possibly imagine. Embrace this: our Father's care and wisdom are perfect. Isaiah 30:18 says he waits to be gracious, his delays are not denials, and he will respond. Ask the Holy Spirit to weave into your heart David's disposition and counsel.

> Wait on the LORD; be of good courage, and he shall strengthen your heart; wait, I say, on the LORD! (Psalm 27:14)

The Almighty will not hand the reigns of rule over to you. Bless the Lord for this. Therefore, know and conclude you are knocking at the right door! On the other side of the door is one who cares for you.

Drink in the words of this precious hymn of instruction and consolation:

> What e'er my God ordains is right: he never
> will deceive me; he leads me by the proper path; I
> know he will not leave me: I take, content, what
> he has sent; his hand can turn my griefs away,
> and patiently I wait his day. (Samuel Rodigast,
> 1675)

When the cause lies with us and there are too many possibilities to list, pray for the Spirit's light and a teachable disposition.

> The commandment is a lamp, and the law
> a light; reproofs of instruction are the way of life.
> (Proverbs 6:23)

> The ear that hears the rebukes of life will
> abide among the wise. He who disdains instruc-
> tion despises his own soul, but he who heeds
> rebuke gets understanding. The fear of the LORD
> is the instruction of wisdom, and before honor is
> humility. (Proverbs 15:31–33)

Embrace these principles as guide rails through life's journey.

A few paragraphs above, the apostle James addresses three possible reasons for unanswered prayer: (1) We think about it but do not actually ask. (2) We ask but with little or no genuine faith. (3) We ask from the motivating spring of selfish desires. Later James shows if undealt with, this opens the door to worldliness—a greater danger than many realize.

We can go deeper. No one walks around with a list of their blind spots! When we say, "Well, I don't see anything God might see in me to hinder prayer!" Obviously we have drifted from knowing ourselves as we ought.

> If God would mark iniquity no one could
> stand before him! (Psalm 130:4)

What we do not see must be pointed out by a faithful friend. There is nothing new under the sun, even in the slippery tendencies of our hearts (Jeremiah 17:9–10). Your God knows you better than you know yourself. Ask him to search you and bring to your awareness any hindrance (Psalm 139:23–24; Psalm 66:18; Isaiah 59:1–2; Philippians 3:15).

There were two terrible errors the prophets continually confronted within the nation of Israel. The roots of these delusions grew from misconceptions of the God of Israel. Sadly, the majority of Israelites made shipwreck of their faith. It is wise and prudent to guard our hearts against drifting down these paths of delusional views of God. So, what are they?

1. That God is subject to moods, has needs, can be deceived and manipulated. God says to the errant Israelites who never really knew him: "If I were hungry, I would not tell you; for the world is mine, and all its fullness. You hate instruction and cast my words behind you. You called evil good and good evil. These things you have done, and I kept silent; you thought that I was altogether like you; but I will rebuke you, and set them in order before your eyes" (Psalm 50:12, 17, 21).

2. That God was difficult to please, prone to require unrealistic devotion and sacrifices, and needed to be appeased. The man with one talent had this view of God: "I knew you to be a hard man" (Matthew 25:25). This harsh view of God was the soul plague of Micah's day. "Will the LORD be pleased with thousands of rams, ten thousand rivers of oil? Shall I give my firstborn for my transgression, the fruit of my body for the sin of my soul?" (Micah 6:7). It was like

they said, "Oh, what does it take to please God, get him off our backs, and get what we want?"

It was to this terrible mindset Micah responds with such beauty and simplicity:

> No, no! It is so simple and sweet. "He has shown you, O man, what is good; and what does the LORD require of you but to do justly, to love mercy, and to walk humbly with your God?" These are not complex concepts to a humble, teachable heart.

The expression "walk humbly" in the original implies to "humble yourself" (i.e., Get off your high horse of self-importance, humble yourself to a life you are not worthy of, and enter the precious, gracious invitation to walk with God!) The people in Micah's day had no heart for this.

The only real remedy against these errors is the saving knowledge of Christ and, through him, God the Father (John 17:3). We all have the seeds of such errors within us through our remaining sin. It is our wisdom and safety to own this reality. We are to keep our hearts against drifting into such views of God. We do so by the Spirit's help to grow and mature in personal acquaintance with our triune God.

> The entrance of his word gives light. (Psalm 119:130)

> Let us resolve by God's grace, that however poor and feeble our prayers may seem to be, we will pray on. (J. C. Ryle)

*Part 4 verses 11–13, pray with assurance of
your tender Father's wise response.*

The point in this last section is, again, to persevere in prayer. We are actively to wait on the Lord. Our Father will respond.

> For since the beginning of the world, men have not heard nor perceived by the ear, nor has the eye seen any God besides you, who acts for the one who waits for him. (Isaiah 64:4)

> Wait on the Lord; be of good courage, and he shall strengthen your heart; wait, I say, on the Lord! (Psalm 27:14)

Now Christ highlights a particular type of assurance in our waiting. Our God is the God of hope, and we are to be confident confiders in him. Our Savior stresses the atmosphere of family security and assurance. Christ wants us to come to him, and our Father convinced he will meet our genuine need with fatherly wisdom and perfect appropriateness.

Over the last ten years, Donna and I had the privilege of having forty-eight foster children in our home. At different times, some children would be fearful about life. Both of us understood this from the core of our own being. The first principle we communicated to these children is "you are safe." We valued and cared about them individually in our home.

Our communication in their times of fear: "You know we care about you and want what is good for you? You are safe to talk to us. We will be here for you and do all we can to help you through this time."

There has always been a genuine response: "Yes, I know that. Thank you. It means a lot to me."

How much more should we "know that" as our Father brought us into his household and family, not as foster children, but sons and daughters, his actual blood-bought Spirit-birthed, and adopted children! We are eternally his, and he is ours. He cares and will do all that is good, most acceptable, and perfect for us (Romans 12:1–2)!

Christ is telling us to be confident in our Father's appropriate gifts. Your needs are important. Your Father gives with an open heart and open hand and with perfect wisdom. He is not an indifferent neighbor or an unjust judge who couldn't care less about our needs. Everything affecting us affects his heart. Everything in our lives filters through Christ's intercession for us and fellow feeling with us (Hebrews 4:14–16). Isaiah tells us, "In all their afflictions, it afflicted him [Christ]" (Isaiah 63:9). When Saul of Tarsus persecuted the saints, Christ stopped him and asked, "Why are you persecuting me?" The Father, Son, and Holy Spirit are in this life with us!

Our Father will never trick us or mock our requests.

> If a son asks for bread from any father among you, will he give him a stone? Or if he asks for a fish, will he give him a serpent instead of a fish? Or if he asks for an egg, will he offer him a scorpion? If you then, being evil, know how to give good gifts to your children, how much more will your heavenly Father give the Holy Spirit to those who ask him? (Luke 11:11–13)

Notice the teaching of our Lord concludes with assurance our heavenly Father as the supreme expression of his love, provision, and response to our prayers will assuredly give the Holy Spirit to those who ask.

How does this strike you? What thoughts does it stir up? Does it seem a climactic crescendo landing flat? Does it seem confusing? Is there a slight sense of "How does this relate to my needs?" This shows a breakdown in thinking as God thinks.

Apart from the work of the Spirit, there would be no new birth, no salvation, no Christian living, and there could be no prayer (the very thing Christ is teaching). The believer has all the resources he needs for life and prayer in the person and personal work of the Holy Spirit alone. We need the Spirit for genuine prayer, and our Father will give the Spirit's help and influence for this purpose. Our Lord is saying, "Do you want to pray? You cannot do so without the Holy Spirit. Your Father will give the personal help of the Spirit. Just go to him and ask." Notice how Paul speaks of the Spirit's personal help.

> Likewise, the Spirit also helps in our weaknesses. For we do not know what we should pray for as we ought, but the Spirit himself makes intercession for us with groanings which cannot be uttered. Now he who searches the hearts knows what the mind of the Spirit is, because he makes intercession for the saints according to the will of God. (Romans 8:26–27)

There will be more on this later.

This answer comes full circle to the original approach we make to our Father. Our calling upon God the Father with affection results from the Spirit's influence. Our childlike tenderness arises from the Holy Spirit's work within (Romans 8:14–17). It is, by the "Spirit, we cry Abba, Father." He works within us to desire the glory of our Father's name. The Father works his will on earth as in heaven, and we would have it no other way. Why? Because the Holy Spirit infuses this perspective, priority, and value as we grow in a knowledge of the Scriptures through the Spirit's help. The Holy Spirit is the author of our delight in the Father's honor, kingdom, and will.

Throughout the history of redemption, no one expressed saving faith apart from the Holy Spirit. The Spirit enabled them to live and pray as believers in their God. It was the Holy Spirit who made Daniel and David who they were despite their natural inadequacies and failings. The privilege of New Testament times is the further revealing of each person of the holy Trinity. They highlighted their individual roles in our redemption in Ephesians 1. Salvation brings us into a personal communion with each divine person of the Trinity. The Spirit authors that communion (2 Corinthians 13:14). Old Testament saints had this; however, we have it with God's spotlight bringing it to great clarity. Why? For our soul-enriching joy.

There is a helpful saying I heard years ago: "The New Testament is in the Old contained. The Old Testament is in the New explained." It is the nature of progressive revelation. This work of the Spirit was anticipated as it moved into the attention and focus of the New Testament and the forming of new covenant communities, local churches. It highlights the wondrous privilege we have as believers.

> I will put my Spirit within you and cause you to walk in my statutes, and you will keep my judgments and do them. (Ezekiel 36:27)

Notice how Paul expresses this:

> Clearly you are an epistle of Christ, ministered by us, written not with ink but by the Spirit of the living God, not on tablets of stone but on tablets of flesh, that is, of the heart. (2 Corinthians 3:3)

The meeting of every need we have comes from the Spirit's personal care to us and within us. In his divine person, he loved us with an everlasting love. In his loving-kindness, he drew us and made us new creations in Christ Jesus through the new birth. What he began, he will complete. Our safekeeping and progress in grace, our growth in Christlikeness and perseverance in the faith result through the Spirit's stewardship of our lives. The Father, for his eternal purposes of love, gives us to Christ to redeem. Christ gives us to the Spirit to mature and keep. The Spirit makes all the accomplishments and provisions of Christ real to us and in us. Here is the holy Trinity at work for our eternal joy.

From the new birth and our growth in grace to profiting in the Scriptures, these arise from the Holy Spirit. The draining of lifeblood from our remaining sin is a work of the Holy Spirit in the mortification of sin (Romans 8:13). Our ability to pray or experience joy, peace, and hope cannot be apart from the Spirit (Romans 15:13). Our triumphing over our circumstances to have joy in the Lord, which is our strength, is from the Spirit. All these flow from the gift and ministry of the Holy Spirit. Who gives us such a wonderful internal minister? Our heavenly Father and victorious Lord Jesus as the gift of their eternal love and affection.

Do we need the Word of God to produce life in us?

Do we need wisdom to walk through life's perplexities, challenges, and trials?

Do we need divine guidance in decisions or navigating difficulties?

Do we need strength in our lives to be content, take up responsibilities, or obey the Lord?

Do we long to grow more like Christ?

Do we need more wonder, love, and praise as we gaze upon the unsearchable riches of Christ?

Do you want the purchased provisions of Christ made real to your soul?

Do you desire Christ's accomplishments to have liveliness and practical relevance?

Do you long to live by Christ's strength and grace?

Do you want to behave yourself wisely in life's circumstances?

Do you want to pray more genuinely and successfully?

All these needs and so many more only come through the loving, personal work of the Holy Spirit. He delights in our reliance upon him and our enjoyment of communing fellowship with him. Do you open your heart to God the Father, God the Son, and God the Holy Spirit? They are all engaged to secure us and meet our moment-by-moment needs. They delight in comforting us. It is a Trinitarian work to get us to glory so we will be with them forevermore. This is our one true God. He is our God who hears and answers prayer. Our God is our constant companion in life through every event and every felt need. For all this to dwell in us with "realness" results from the Spirit's ministry. Do you now see why our Lord concludes his teaching on prayer with the Father giving the Spirit to those who ask?

The answer to the disciple's request "teach us to pray" points to a missing element in the praying of our day. Why do we so often stop after the simple content of prayer? After the Lord Jesus tells us the content of prayer, the strong emphasis is on the determination that in praying, we really pray. He knew the trials we would face without and within. Christ expects his people to know God and plead with God in prayer. Of the four sections to Christ's answer on how to pray, two of them emphasize an earnestness, unrelenting determination, and perseverance (i.e., pleading). As we expound pleading, we will see this more and more. There is an essential thread woven throughout our Lord's teaching. This is true in all his instructions on prayer. It sheds light on the way the people of God would approach the Almighty in times of need and great perplexity. We will find this earnest seeking God in the activity of the saints throughout history.

When God intends great things for his people, he first stirs them up to seek and pray for them.

We should have seasons marked by more earnest approaches to the throne of grace and the face of God.

We should experience times of intense pleading.

We ought to plead with the Lord Jesus to take up the needs of his bride, accosted and molested by the evil one.

Ministers are to be examples to the people on how to lay hold of God. How will the next generation learn to pray earnestly and effectively unless they experience and witness it?

In the assemblies of our Lord Jesus, where are the cries in the courts of heaven: "O Lord, how long? Oh, Lord, do not tarry. Come down and revive your people. Stir your people up to a more earnest walking with you. Deliver us from dry externalism. Give that heart experience of your authority and presence. Our gracious Lord, make us salt and light in this dark and unsavory world. Do not leave us to our own church life, like a religious business; break in upon us and fill us with holy awe and restore your glory in our midst. Lord Jesus, walk in the midst of this lampstand (Revelation 1) and make your authority and presence known. Shepherd your sheep in this place."

> The church use to be a lifeboat, now it's a
> cruise ship. (Leonard Ravenhill)

Would we see an alteration in the church's condition? Would we influence this "perverse generation" more if we knew this pleading with God? What is happening in our culture? Our world is drifting more and more into a no-truth, no-meaning, no-certainty mantra. It dominates society and even creeps into the churches. To lose a grip on God's word produces "everyone doing what is right in their own eyes." Pragmatism has more authority than "Thus says God's word." The true end of life is to not live to ourselves but to him who died for us! These words are widely known but rarely lived. Confusion of opinions does not own God as its author. Are we too busy doing our "church thing" that we miss the ineffective witness and perceived irrelevance of the church to society and modern culture?

Progressive "Christianity" is more and more popular. "Live your truth" is the main reason the world is such a mess. It removes the foundation of sound teaching and the "faith once for all delivered to the saints." This false teaching is more appealing to the younger generations, who are steering away from sound biblical teaching. What can capture souls to the authority of God's precious Word? To speak of "sound doctrine" pushes them away. The real important matters are pragmatic: how they feel and what makes people happy or feel good about themselves.

Years ago, society lamented the destruction of the family. Now they attempt to redefine it. Divorce in the church is as great as outside the church. God would have the home be the center of life from which we go out into the world. Now, many go out of the home to find and have a life. Depression is at epidemic levels in women, men, and teens. Do we long for divine answers to these and many other problems? It would enhance our influence as salt and light if we gave God no rest until he made us more real and honest in our role on the earth. How will the next generation learn to pray if we go on with little token prayers in the assemblies of God's people? Would we see a difference if we learned:

The art and skill of holy pleading with God?

Our beloved Savior expects us to be a pleading people! May the thought of letting him down tear at our hearts, motivate our souls, and invigorate our prayer life. He took our sins upon himself that we would no longer live to ourselves but to and for him who so loved us. Our citizenship is in heaven, and we are no longer "earth dwellers." Show this in our prayers. Show it in pleading as he taught us and expects from us.

Cold prayers always freeze before they reach heaven.

—Thomas Brooks

4

A Definition of Pleading (Part 1)

*The church upon its knees would
bring heaven upon the earth.*

—E. M. Bounds

*When problems get Christians praying,
they do more good than harm.*

—John Blanchard

If you look up the term *pleading* in a dictionary, it would express variations on these themes: to appeal earnestly, to implore, to beseech, to entreat, to beg, to offer persuasive reasons or arguments for or against something. Pleading is an appeal to another. It could be a person or a group of people.

These definitions help get a sense of what it is to plead with God. Dictionaries are great tools, but they are not the word of God. So let's look at this word in the Bible.

Going to various passages, we find a personal element in pleading. The person pleading seeks to stir up an awareness of a pressing need. The pleader looks for compassion to secure a remedy. It is a remedy from the only one who can help. Need grips the one who pleads. He sees actions someone could and must take. The "pleader" sees the action as a righteous and legitimate result of a request for a worthy cause.

Keep this in mind: pleading does not equal a flood of emotion nor a Niagara of words. We must not confuse pleading with hoping our unhappy case will impress God, nor that our tears, earnestness, or pitiful portrayals will somehow move God to "feel sorry for us" and, therefore, take action. It is not a victim feeling or whining before God. Unbelievers used these tactics before false gods like Baal. Our Lord warned us of such carnal praying and fleshly reliances. This would be to put our faith in our performances.

We will find pleading is sometimes not even found in words; rather, the look upon the face and actions of the soul. Our tears, sighs, and groanings have a pleading language our heavenly Father hears.

> Hear my prayer, O Lord, and give ear to my cry; do not be silent at my tears; for I am a stranger with you, a sojourner, as all my fathers were. (Psalm 39:12)

They form wordless pleas or arguments for God's involvement. Think of what John Bunyan said: "Better let your heart be without words than your words without heart." In our confusion, our Father is perfectly perceptive, aware, and capable of reading our hearts. He is always in perfect harmony with our needs even when we are not.

When God kindly blessed my wife and me with children, she would sometimes say, "Oh, that's her 'I need to burp' cry or that's her 'change my diaper' cry. No, Rick, that's her 'I'm hungry' cry."

"Oh, honey, she wants attention. Just pick her up."

Mothers are adept at understanding "baby babble and crying." Any mother, so in tune with her baby, can make sense of such "communication." It is the same with our gracious Father, our beloved Savior, and our caring Holy Spirit. Remember, communication is about 7 percent words, 38 percent tone, and 55 percent posture and physical expression.

Four ingredients which make up genuine pleading with God appear as we see how the Bible uses the word:

1. It is an urgent request.

a) Example from the parable in Luke 11:5–10: Jesus told the story of the friend who came at midnight and the resistant neighbor being approached for needed supplies. In Israel's culture, this action was appropriate and expected. It was part of the hospitable and humanitarian requirements God gave his people:

> You shall open your hand wide to your brother, to your poor and your needy, in your land. (Deuteronomy 15:11)

There were general principles of care for others woven into the social fabric of the nation of Israel, which expressed their wise value when embraced and implemented. It was to be the compassionate heart of God reflected in the lives of his people.

> Whoever shuts his ears to the cry of the poor
> will also cry himself and not be heard. (Proverbs 21:13)

Therefore, when confronted with rejection, indifference, and denial from his neighbor, instead of defeat and dejection, it drew up the energy of urgency and determination. This story shows a man being moved to plead, to entreat, and to press the uprightness of the demand as a form of human kindness and humanitarian sensitivity. The urgency of need produced urgency at the door and persistence in the knocking. When a righteous cause was obvious, there was no room to take no for an answer. This man said, "No, this weary traveler will not go to bed hungry!" This is a vital part of what our Lord wants us to understand in this story. Miss this, and you miss the teaching of our Savior. This is the purpose of the parable-story—to show what we should do in our prayers when a righteous cause or urgent need arises in our lives. Remember, this is still our Lord teaching us to pray. He has simply moved from what to pray to how to pray.

Christ says, "You want to know how to pray? Pray this way! Pray, making urgent requests. As needs arise, there will be occasions of earnest knocking. Don't forget I have ordained that it should be so. However, when you sense a denial, do not give up. I am speaking about this so you will not give up. Value drawing near to me. Open your heart and concerns to me. Do not settle for what you think is a 'no.' Just like this man, refuse to settle for no. If this does not happen in your involvement in prayer, you don't understand my instruction and divine will concerning prayer amid life's realities."

b)   Example of my daughter. One evening, I went over to a neighbor's house with my daughter, Charity. As we rounded the corner and approached the house, his dog came running straight toward my little girl. She cried out in fear and terror. I swung her up into my arms as the dog lunged for her, scraping her leg and making it bleed. In her fear, she looked with urgency for me to protect her. There was urgent pleading in her voice, eyes, and pulsations of body. "Daddy, help me. Protect me!" With no words, there was an urgency in her soul and fear in her eyes communicating a pleading to me for rescue. Any father would have done all he could to respond and protect his little girl. When I returned home, the neighbor came over with an overwhelming concern for her. He even told us the amount of his liability insurance! I assured him my daughter would be alright, and she was. Our heavenly Father cares infinitely more for each of his sons and daughters. Connect this with the next example.

c)   Example of Peter. When Peter walked on the water with Jesus, he took his eyes off the Lord and locked them on the waves; he felt his danger and sank. He cried out, "Lord, save me!" (Matthew 14:30). Fear filled Peter with a sense of urgency for the Lord to deliver him from sinking and drowning. This was an urgent plea arising from a felt need. Peter's actions and urgent cries to Jesus show pleading in his eyes, voice, and soul.

d) Example from carnal and selfish people. There is a sad use of the word *plead* found in Mark 5:17: "Then they pleaded with Him to leave their region." The situation was this: Christ entered the country of the Gadarenes, and the man living in the tombs, sometimes referred to as the "madman" of Gadara, came out to him. Demons filled this man—unclean spirits, who tormented him unmercifully. Our Lord, filled with compassion for an anguish-stricken soul (as he always is), cast the unclean spirit out. However, just before he did so, the unclean spirit asked if they could possess the nearby herd of swine, an illegal business in Israel. The Lord Jesus allowed this departure, and about two thousand swine perished in the water, ruining the swine business in the region. When the owners and townspeople heard what happened, they "pleaded with him to leave their region."

What an amazing real-life story. Here people had the Lord of glory come into their region, and yet they preferred swine more than the Savior! Sad to say, we see this same reality repeatedly in our day. Notice they felt the urgency of business profits disappearing, the ruination of their investments; desperate to get rid of the cause of their plight and financial anguish, it moved them to "plead with him to leave their region."

These real-life stories should help us get a feel for the concept of pleading. It is a deeply felt sense of need attached to urgency to get a remedy. Someone must find solutions. Intervention is essential, and there is no alternative. This is the biblical use of the phrase "to plead"—to implore.

2. It is an appeal from felt helplessness.

To plead is to express a painful sense of real trouble from which we see no escape. This produces touching and moving entreaties, pitiful cries for help. These are statements or actions designed to arouse empathy, sympathy, and tender compassion in one or ones who can bring remedy, solution, or deliverance. The word communicates a felt vulnerability, which presses the heart to despair unless intervention comes. Again, a display of this can be in actions without words.

a) Example of the woman with an issue of blood.

> Now a certain woman had a flow of blood for twelve years, and had suffered many things from many physicians. She spent all she had and was no better, but grew worse. When she heard about Jesus, she came behind Him in the crowd and touched His garment. For she said, "If only I may touch his clothes, I shall be made well."
>
> Immediately the fountain of her blood was dried up, and she felt in her body she was healed of the affliction. Jesus, immediately knowing in Himself power had gone out of Him, turned around in the crowd and said, "Who touched my clothes?"
>
> But His disciples said to Him, "You see the multitude thronging you, and you say, 'Who touched me?'" [Christ was saying, "Oh, no, some anguished heart reached out to me in faith. I not only felt it, but I sensed my responsiveness to human need mixed with Spirit-wrought faith in my capabilities. I must identify this soul for her heart's life-changing encouragement. She needs to know I know her. I am one who will always invite her to trust my care and abilities, both now and forever."]
>
> And He looked around to see her who had done this thing. But the woman, fearing and trembling, knowing what had happened to her, came and fell down before Him and told Him

the whole truth. And He said to her, "Daughter, your faith has made you well. Go in peace and be healed of your affliction." (Mark 5:25–34)

What an amazing and touching account. Her internal world comprised desperation, pain, loneliness, and she felt the threat of being penniless. Life had dashed so many of her hopes upon the rocks of life's tragic moments. As she passed through every agonizing event, a settled sense of helplessness closed in on her, suffocating any sense of hope. Now she hears of the Lord Jesus passing her way. She had to get to him. She had no other hope. Embarrassed, she would not lift her voice or make a sound. She felt herself to be an unclean outcast of society, but if she could but touch the hem of his garment! There was a powerful wordless pleading going on in her soul: "Help me, Lord. Life has killed all my dreams and now all my hopes as well, but I must get to you. I believe you are a help to the helpless. I have nowhere else to go and no one else to trust."

Such a pleading, entreating, hoping heart our Savior could not—no, would not—ignore! Notice the way he addresses her:

And he said to her, "Daughter, your faith has made you well. Go in peace and be healed of your affliction."

"Daughter!" Family affection, care, identity, and delight expressed to her and in her. Sweet words of inclusion and belong-ingness. Invitational belongingness to him and his Father. He could not let her go without drawing attention to her triumphant actions rooted in a firm belief in the Savior and Helper of those who "feel" their needs—the only true and eternal friend of sinners. He draws attention to her after her healing, which changed her entire social standing in the community. No longer an unclean outcast, much like the lepers, now an admired, humble triumphant follower of Christ. She expressed humble boldness that day, and it changed her life for time and eternity.

Dear child of God, did you know your Father and Savior want you to experience this kind of responsiveness and compassion from them as you trust and seek them in your life? Our greatest folly is to act like we have no need and everything is just fine. That is delusional in the light of our reality. Rather, our wisdom is to be in touch with the enormity of our continual need of Christ's presence and help in our lives. These historical accounts are to help us see the true and real Christ who carries us on his heart every day and for the rest of our earthly journey (Hebrews 4:14–16; 7:25).

b)   Example of King Jehoshaphat and the people of Judah. We find a graphic and touching occasion of pleading with the LORD in the days of King Jehoshaphat. It includes the entire assembly of Judah and Jerusalem. Here is an example of the way God's people should experience corporate pleading in prayer (2 Chronicles 20:1–30). This was a time of gut-wrenching, heart-wrenching helplessness that was deeply felt.

The nations of Ammon, Moab, and Mount Seir united to attack Judah. The armies were overwhelming. By the time the king heard of it, the armies were too close and would soon be upon them. Jehoshaphat painfully knew their plight and vulnerability. "So Judah gathered together to ask help from the Lord; and from all the cities of Judah, they came to seek the Lord" (2 Chronicles 20:4–23). If God did not act, they would die or become slaves.

As we read this, notice the arguments. God's character, past actions, his chosen relationships, and promises are the arguments and foundation for their pleadings. They also put on display physical arguments for God to act. If God was true to his own standards, he could not be silent and stand still.

Then Jehoshaphat stood in the assembly of Judah and Jerusalem in the house of the Lord before the new court and said,

O Lord God of our fathers, are you not God
in heaven and do you not rule over all the king-

doms of the nations and in your hand, is there not power and might so no one can withstand you? Are you not our God who drove out the inhabitants of this land before your people Israel and gave it to the descendants of Abraham, your friend forever? And they dwell in it and have built you a sanctuary in it for your name [now he quotes Solomon when he dedicated the temple, and Solomon was quoting Moses, who was quoting God] saying, "If disaster comes upon us—sword, judgment, pestilence, or famine—we will stand before this temple and in your presence (for your name is in this temple) and cry out to you in our affliction and you will hear and save." And now, here are the people of Ammon, Moab, and Mount Seir—whom you would not let Israel invade when they came out of the land of Egypt, but they turned from them and did not destroy them—here they are, rewarding us by coming to throw us out of your possession which you have given us to inherit. O our God, will you not judge them? For we have no power against this great multitude coming against us, nor do we know what to do, but our eyes are upon you.

Now all Judah, with their little ones, their wives, and their children, stood before the Lord.

Then the Spirit of the Lord came upon Jahaziel, the son of Zechariah, the son of Benaiah, the son of Jeiel, the son of Mattaniah, a Levite of the sons of Asaph, in the assembly's midst. And he said,

Listen, all you of Judah and you inhabitants of Jerusalem, and you, King Jehoshaphat! Thus says the Lord to you: "Do not be afraid nor dismayed because of this great multitude, for the battle is not yours, but God's. Tomorrow go

down against them. They will surely come up by
the Ascent of Ziz, and you will find them at the
end of the brook before the Wilderness of Jeruel.
You will not need to fight in this battle. Position
yourselves, stand still and see the salvation of the
Lord, who is with you, O Judah and Jerusalem!"
Do not fear or be dismayed; tomorrow go out
against them, for the Lord is with you.

Jahaziel communicated the word of God to them, and they
believed it!

(It is important to notice God never told them the specific
things he was going to do. He gave a promise. They were to believe it
and obey the Lord as far as he gave them light and direction. When
they took that step, only then would they see the works of God as he
kept his word and promise.)

And Jehoshaphat bowed his head with his face to the ground,
and all Judah and the inhabitants of Jerusalem bowed before the
Lord, worshiping the Lord. Then the Levites of the children of the
Kohathites and of the children of the Korahites stood up to praise the
Lord God of Israel with voices loud and high.

So they rose early in the morning and went out into the Wilderness
of Tekoa; and as they went out, Jehoshaphat stood and said,

Hear me, O Judah and you inhabitants of
Jerusalem: believe in the Lord your God, and he
shall establish you; believe his prophets, and you
shall prosper.

And when he had consulted with the people, he appointed
those who should sing to the Lord and who should praise the beauty
of holiness as they went out before the army and were saying, "Praise
the Lord, for his mercy endures forever."

Now when they sang and praised God, the
Lord set ambushes against the people of Ammon,

Moab, and Mount Seir, who had come against
Judah; and they were defeated. For, the people of
Ammon and Moab stood up against the inhabitants of Mount Seir to utterly kill and the LORD
destroyed them. And when they had made an end
of the inhabitants of Seir, they helped to destroy
one another. (2 Chronicles 20:1–30)

Notice a few important parts of the story. God draws attention to holy pleading throughout this passage. The king recognized the impossibility of defending themselves; they were helpless.
Jehoshaphat, with the people, pours out his heart before the Lord as
a mouthpiece for the people. They came as one voice, one heart, and
one cry just as we are to do as churches which call upon the Lord
Jesus (Acts 4:24—oh, that we might see this again in the churches).
They were there with their little ones, their wives, and their children,
representing the most helpless and vulnerable in Judah. Why? God
commands we defend the widow, the poor, the needy, and the vulnerable. It is an argument for God to act. God's Word condemns us
if we turn a deaf ear to the needs and cries of such. How could God,
who gave the command, violate his own word? All this is a vivid
display of Judah's cry and pleading for help for God's intervention to
save the helpless.

Jehoshaphat uses God's own promises: "If disaster comes upon
us—sword, judgment, pestilence, or famine—we will stand before
this temple and in your presence (for your name is in this temple)
and cry out to you in our affliction, and you will hear and save."
They hold God to be true to his promises and words—the very
words he caused his people to hope upon. This entire event expresses
helplessness and vulnerability yet one harmonious plea and trust in
the Lord from the gathered assembly of God's own people. They call
upon him to rise and save in a desperate time. They rely upon God's
character and promises.

What was the result? This is an amazing story of faith in the face
of pending disaster. They gathered to sing the praises of the Lord in
the wilderness. When their enemies were coming upon them, they

sang: "Praise the LORD, for his mercy endures forever." When they sang, the Lord put the enemies to confusion and in-fighting, in which they were all destroyed. God accomplished an amazing deliverance on their behalf. God fought for the helpless. He heard and answered their plea expressed in word and action. It was essential that the people came before the Lord to plead. How many mercies and divine interventions do we lose because we do not plead?

I remember many times, walking by my mother's room and hearing her crying out to the Lord. She felt her vulnerability and helplessness to provide for us three boys not just food and clothing but training and guidance in life. She would seek the Lord for her fatherless children who needed the influence of a man. The voice of my mother's prayers still sounds in my ears. I think any mother, especially single mothers, could feel what my mom felt in those days of her helplessness. My own children were witnesses to her pleading prayers. They still speak of it to this day. May our children hear our wrestling before the Lord and communicating powerful pleas for divine interventions.

> *Oh, how greatly has the man advanced who has*
> *learned not to be his own, not to be governed by his*
> *own reason, but to surrender his mind to God!*

—John Calvin

> *God doesn't want our success; he wants us. He doesn't*
> *demand our achievements; he demands our obedience.*

—Charles Colson

5

A Definition of Pleading (Part 2)

The true measure of God's love is that he loves without measure.

—Anon

At the heart of prayer and pleading, we find a sincere soul taking God at his word. Why? Because of the character of God. We can do this because God is faithful and perfectly reliable. At one time, it was a common compliment of reliable character: "His word is his bond." This is, without fail, true of God. It is the foundation of our confidence in faith and prayer. God is as "good as his word." Paul tells us we...

> Have hope of eternal life which God, who cannot lie, promised before time began. (Titus 1:2)

Abraham embraced this with his whole being. Our gracious God sets Abraham before us as a great example of faith, belief in God's promises, friendship with God, and pleading with God. This is the testimony given concerning Abraham:

> He was called the friend of God. (James 2:23)

However, when we read the Genesis account, we find Abraham a struggling man who made mistakes, sinful errors of judgment, and even fearful as "unbelief" threatened to creep into his heart! Abraham was not a super saint. He was a failing, sometimes stumbling individual who wrestled with sin like us all. Do not lose sight that he was a real man who lived on earth, and God saved him by grace. When told of a coming child, he and Sarah were excited. The delay was unbearable, and they sinfully tried to take matters into their own hands: Hagar and Ishmael were the result. Abraham lied about Sarah being his wife not just once—twice!

In Genesis 15, we find Abraham afraid of local nations retaliating against him but, most of all, struggling with God's promise of a child. It was in this condition God comes to him in a vision: "Do not be afraid, Abram. I am your shield, your exceedingly great reward." Abraham opens his heart struggles to the Lord, tells God of another alternative for an heir—Eliezer of Damascus! The Lord renews his promise to Abraham concerning his own child with Sarah. Then we have the rich testimony, repeated in the New Testament, Abraham "believed in the LORD, and he accounted it to him for righteousness" (Genesis 15:6).

Take this to heart. In this condition, God comes with the scoop shovel of grace, picks Abraham up, and the Holy Spirit infuses grace into his soul, enabling him to break through doubt and fear. He believed God! Then God declares, "See my friend, my child Abraham. He believes my promise. All my people will do this." In this way, Abraham is "the father of us all."

> He did not waver at the promise of God through unbelief, but was strengthened in faith, giving glory to God, and being fully convinced that what he had promised he was also able to perform. (Romans 4:16–25)

Notice "he was strengthened in faith." God will do this for you and me.

Our triune God says the same to us. "I will help you with faith, trust, prayer, pleading, and with everything you face. Keep your eyes on me. If you need help with that, just ask me. I will give you everything you need to make it through your life's journey. I want you to make the journey with me as your strength and help. Walk with me like Abraham, my friend, did."

As you learn to pray and plead with God, take Abraham's example to heart. The same grace and Holy Spirit will be there for you as a help to enable you. He is the same God. You may boldly say, "The Lord is my helper."

What have we come to see as a definition of pleading so far?

1. It is an urgent request.
2. It is an appeal from felt helplessness.

In this chapter, we consider two more important parts of its use in the Scriptures which form our definition of pleading with God.

3. It is a legal request for righteous judgment.

God told Abraham his intentions to destroy Sodom and Gomorrah because of their great wickedness. Abraham was entreating the Lord concerning Sodom in Genesis 18 because of his nephew Lot. Abraham had not been in the cities but had some hope Lot would have influenced others concerning the true and living God. In his famous pleading with the Lord, Abraham used arguments of fifty righteous people down to ten:

> "You will not destroy the righteous with the
> wicked, will you?" He says, "Shall not the judge
> of all the earth do right?" (Genesis 18:25)

Abraham saw God as Judge of all the earth—one committed to legal righteousness and moral uprightness. He did not see all that God saw concerning these cities. The point I would like you to notice is this: the Lord heard and responded to Abraham's pleading. He delivered Lot and destroyed the cities, notorious for their wickedness.

This illustration helps us understand the phrase "to plead." This is the pleading you would find in a court of law. Perhaps when you heard the word *plead*, you thought of courtroom activity. In the Bible, people and God himself use it this way. Most people are familiar with the courtroom scene of an advocate speaking to the judge or jury, arguing the case for true justice. You might even think of Christ, our advocate, who pleads on our behalf. His arguments are his own accomplishments satisfying justice, shedding his blood for our sins. Now, as our High Priest, ever living to pray for us, he is doing so right now as you read.

a) Example of David. David used this word. The occasion was King Saul, through fear and jealousy, hunting for David to kill him. It became clear to this sweet psalmist of Israel there was no legitimate cause or valid reason for the king to act this way. David began to long for God to take King Saul and himself to court and make a determination between them. David would not lift his hand against God's anointed. The opportunity to kill the king presented itself within a cave. David refused to act on it. Shortly, as Saul left the cave, David confronts Saul. Hear what David said:

> As the proverb of the ancients says, "Wickedness proceeds from the wicked." But my hand shall not be against you. After whom has the king of Israel come out? Whom do you pursue? A dead dog? A flea? Therefore let the Lord be a judge, and judge between you and me, and see and plead my case, and deliver me out of your hand. (1 Samuel 24:13–15)

You can hear David's heart being poured out to the Lord and King Saul. He felt the urgency and danger of his circumstances. He knew his vulnerability and helplessness before King Saul. David felt the only course of hope was for God to take them into his courtroom for a hearing and make a determination between them. David felt the futility of pleading with the king any more. His hope was for God to take up his case and plead his cause.

b) Example of God himself. Our God pleads with people. Does this surprise you? It happens through the combined influence of Scripture, the work of the Holy Spirit, and the work of conscience. Sometimes God did this through prophets.

This theme of courtroom pleading shows up again and again throughout the pages of Scripture. There are too many passages, so we have to be selective. Here are a few:

> Do not rob the poor because he is poor, nor oppress the afflicted at the gate; for the Lord will plead their case, and plunder the soul of those who plunder them. (Proverbs 22:22–23)

> Do not remove the ancient landmark, nor enter the fields of the fatherless; for their Redeemer is mighty; he will plead their cause against you. (Proverbs 23:10–11)

That is an amazing statement. Who would ever want the God of heaven and earth, our creator and sustainer and ultimate judge, to be the one who pleads against us?

Let us remember, with all the horrible crimes against humanity, the terrible shootings and murders, the oppressing of the vulnerable and needy, the horrible slaughter of the silent screams from the womb, the genocide that has taken place in history—God does not forget these acts or the cries of desperation and pain. He will address them if not in this life, then in the courtroom of heaven on that last day of account. The verdict will be eternal.

c) Example of the inexcusable neglect of the people. God declares a grievous sin within the covenant community of his people. We all should take this to heart and consider the way God thinks. What is it? When there is an absence of people to pray and plead. That's right. When God's own people do not plead, it offends God. It's like a spiritual lethargy, dullness, or disconnect overtakes the people. Hear how God sees it in this passage as Isaiah and Ezekiel represent it:

> And there is no one who calls on your name, who stirs himself up to take hold of you; for you have hidden your face from us and have consumed us because of our iniquities. (Isaiah 64:7)

> So I sought for a man among them who would make a wall, and stand in the gap before me on behalf of the land, that I should not destroy it; but I found no one. (Ezekiel 22:30)

Do you hear the longing in the prophet's heart as he represents the heart of God? Where are the people, in the light of present circumstances, that would "stir himself up to take hold of God"? Remember Jacob wrestling with God and not letting him go until he blessed him. God loves it when people come to him in this manner. With reverence? Yes. With humility and godly fear? Yes. But with holy determination to see the works of God on behalf of his people in times of need.

The enemy of God, humanity, and the church is coming in like a flood in our day. "Oh our God, we see the abominations of the land, the sins of society, and the growing hatred for your church. Our souls mourn and grieve because of the spiritual pollutions that flow in the land. We need you and your omnipotent interventions. Our souls long to see your workings. We do not know your eternal decree, but we see the despising of your name everywhere and the ignoring of your holy person. O God, we see your church treated as an irrelevant thing, a relic of past ages, simply a weak people needing a crutch. Where are you, O God? Come down and take up the terrible state of the church, society, and a God-neglecting population."

This is more serious than we think. Sometimes in the history of God's people, when no one was pleading for what was righteous and just it displeased the Lord, an atmosphere of calling good evil and evil good had turned divine morality on its head. We see the same issue in our day. One of the few things needed for evil to triumph is for good people to do nothing or for his people to neglect pleading with him for interventions. Hear the mind of God in this matter:

> No one calls for justice, nor does any plead for truth. They trust in empty words and speak lies; they conceive evil and bring forth iniquity. (Isaiah 59:4)

God is never an idle spectator. God himself will plead his case in judgment. This will shut every mouth as all guilty appear before the LORD with no recourse.

> The Lord stands up to plead, and stands to judge the people. (Isaiah 3:13)

Pleading is a legal request for righteous judgment to be exacted. "O God, let not the wicked triumph. Set up a defense for your cause and people. Convert them from the error of their ways. As with Saul of Tarsus, change them into Pauls."

We have one last important aspect of pleading. It is a precious way to conclude this chapter.

4. It is an affectionate appeal to arise and take up your responsibility.

> Now I plead with you, brethren, by the name of our Lord Jesus Christ, you all speak the same thing, and there be no divisions among you, but you be perfectly joined together in the same mind and in the same judgment. (1 Corinthians 1:10)

The word Paul uses has two concepts woven together:

a)   It is calling a person to one's side, to summon somebody over, to draw close, as in having a private conversation.

b)   Then it suggests calling on someone to hear your words of exhortation, entreaty, comfort, or instruction and act upon them, put them into action.

In the years of being parents, my wife and I have many vivid memories of such communications with our own children. One evening, I was speaking to my thirteen-year-old, explaining the meaning of "Honor your father and your mother." The fifth commandment was the topic for family devotions over several evenings. The scene is still fresh in my memory even though this took place over thirty years ago. I was entreating my thirteen-year-old daughter, Hannah, to have a heart of obedience to God's command, which reflected God's will for her. My effort was to bring her heart to the will of God, who gave her life, breath, and being.

Here is what I said: "You know honey, when I read these words, it is important for you to understand something about me. From my youngest days, my dad made me feel I was not worth the ground I stood on. So when it says, 'Honor your father,' I actually don't feel worthy of honor. Yet it is not me saying this to you as much as God telling you what your responsibility is before him. Now the same God who tells you to honor your father also tells me to teach you to do so. He tells me to obey him in many other ways. So, it may help for you to know we are both commanded by God to be obedient to him. We fulfill different roles right now, but we need hearts and wills to embrace his commands. Let's have this response which delights to do what God commands, from the heart, out of love for him."

She later told me the way I approached the subject meant a great deal to her and made the embrace of the command sweeter and easier. It was one of those tender moments between a dad and daughter. I still prize it to this day along with so many others. Just recently, she told me she used the same approach with her children.

Notice the approach with my daughter. I drew her alongside my heart and softly appealed for her to embrace her God-given responsibility. This is what Paul was doing. Did he call upon them to obey the command of the Sovereign King and Head of the church? Yes. Was it urgent that they obey? Yes. Look at how he appealed to their hearts and consciences. He communicated with wonderful tenderness and a representative of Christ. This is how Paul was pleading with them in the passage quoted above.

Three more passages give us this tender flavor of the Word:

> We then, as workers together with him also plead with you not to receive the grace of God in vain. (2 Corinthians 6:1)

> And now I plead with you, lady, not as though I wrote a new commandment to you, but one which we have had from the beginning: that we love one another. (2 John 1:5)

Both Paul and John were making tender appeals to the minds, hearts, consciences, and choices of these people to be genuine and obedient to what they knew would please the Lord, who saved them. Imitate the example of Christ in his own love by loving one another. Behind these words are the astonishing actions of Christ washing John's feet in that upper room—the example of our sovereign Lord and great Creator stooping to serve his people's needs. This draws from our souls the expression "Hallelujah, what a Savior." John 13 contains the humble service of the majestic Savior stooping to meet the needs of his people. He then states,

> Do you see what I have done? It came from the love in my heart for you. Do the same. Have humble love in your heart toward your brethren. Make sure they actually sense it. Demonstrate it, not just in words, but in deeds and in truth.

Again, I believe you can sense the tenderness of Paul's heart as he wrote to the people of God in Corinth:

> Now I, Paul, myself, am pleading with you by the meekness and gentleness of Christ. (2 Corinthians 10:1)

Paul places himself face-to-face with his unscrupulous opponents at Corinth. Paul highlights the qualities which belong to Christ: the meekness and gentleness he showed throughout his life and ministry. All his disciples or followers, which belonged to him, are to imitate their Savior, Lord, and Shepherd (Matthew 11:29; Isaiah 42:2; Romans 12:1).

Paul captures the disposition of Christ toward his own people:

> But we were gentle among you, just as a nursing mother cherishes her own children. So, affectionately longing for you, we were well pleased to impart to you not only the gospel of God but also our own lives, because you had become dear to us. (1 Thessalonians 2:7–8)

We see the same heart reflected in Christ to all his people. He loved them all, calling them by name, gave himself for them, and loved them freely. This is how he pleads with us by his Spirit. This is how we are to entreat one another. We are to come before him with pleadings from the heart.

Pleading incorporates the affections and heart longings for the response to our prayers. From heart entreaties to heart compliance to our Savior's words creates an atmosphere most pleasant to the heart of our God (Psalm 133). "How good and how pleasant it is for brethren to dwell together in unity" and breathe this atmosphere of sacrificial love to God and one another.

So, what is it to plead?

1. It is an urgent request. Without response and action, dev-astation, horrible plight, and despairing conditions will result.
2. It is an appeal from felt helplessness. There is no other help from within or without, but my eyes are on you alone. Don't let the vulnerable, helpless, and languishing who trust and call upon you die.
3. It is a legal request for righteous judgment and conclusion. Unless you act, wrong will result, injustice will reign, chaos will engulf, and disillusionment takes over. "You will not put those who trust in you to shame and confusion. You will not. You cannot let that happen."
4. It is an affectionate appeal to take up specific responsibili-ties and legitimate duties.

My dear wife with four young children felt her desperate need for the grace of Christ to be supplied to her. She longed to be the mother she knew God wanted her to be. The weight of cleaning, laundry, cooking, training, beginning homeschooling, being a young pastor's wife, and a faithful church member was all overwhelming. She would get on her knees and hold on to the bedpost, imagining her laying hold of Christ, like the woman taking hold of his garment and not letting him go until he helped her!

As a young mother—or an older one—can you enter my wife's cries for help? "Oh my Lord Jesus, I have entrusted my soul to you. You tell me of your faithfulness to be a help in time of need. On this day and in the moments of the day, I need your grace. I will not let go until you commit to be my help today. I cannot keep my composure, my heart, or my focus on you! Please, I trust in you. I rely on your word. Oh, don't stand at a distance and let my heart struggle with whether you care. Don't leave me to myself! I fear this. You tell me you will tend your flock like a shepherd. You will gather the lambs in your arms. You will carry them in your bosom and gently lead those who are with young. I have young ones. Please, gently lead me. Be true to your word and promise. I am counting on you to be faithful to your word this day. You are too kind and gentle to let me down. I believe and trust you." I want to say she was still doing this with nine and ten children.

If you are a young mother, do you believe that if you cried out and made pleadings to the Lord Jesus like this, he would respond? Do you fear he would turn a deaf ear or stand at a distance? No, dear sister, he is full of compassion and tender of heart to all who call upon him. The soul that calls upon him with a trusting, relying belief he will not put to confusion. He tells us this and gives his word:

> In you, O LORD, I put my trust; let me never be put to shame. (Psalm 71:1)

> I cling to your testimonies, O LORD, do not put me to shame. (Psalm 119:31)

> Whoever believes in him will not be put to shame. (Romans 10:11)

Do you know what your greatest temptation would be? Do you know what your greatest folly would be? To think you have to first get things together and then come to the Lord! We all have this tendency. It is a devastating merit mentality and works-reliance foolishness, which is really self-reliance. It is natural to fallen man and our remaining sin. No, rather come to the Lord and, together with him, work on your needs as an expression of companionship. Here is your wisdom. This is your best approach to sanity in your overwhelming world. With the eye of faith, see Christ moving toward you in your need. Turn to him first, not your needs. Go to him in your undoneness.

Can you come before your Lord and say, "Beloved Spirit, help me pray. Lord Jesus, help me ask for help! Show your tender care I read about in your own words. You are a help in time of need. This is a time of need. Arise and do the right thing for me as I trust you to be faithful to your word—your word, which has made me hope in you. You made me confident you would respond in faithful ways. 'I have called upon you, for you will hear me, O God; incline your ear to me, and hear my speech' (Psalm 17:6)."

I hope the word *plead* is coming alive and taking shape for you. Don't let this be mere information for your head! Ask the Lord to weave these truths into your heart and bear fruit in your prayer life. Then look for Christ's response. Paul said, "Continue in prayer, and watch in the same with thanksgiving" (Colossians 4:2).

So if we are to be a people who plead with God, what would it actually look like and feel like? This becomes the subject of the next chapter.

When God intends great mercy for his people, the first thing he does is set them a-praying.

—Matthew Henry

6

A Definition of Pleading (Part 3)

Prayer is nothing, but the promise reversed,
or God's word formed into an argument
and retorted by faith upon God again.

—William Gurnall

Restraining prayer we cease to fight; prayer makes the
Christian's armor bright; and Satan trembles when
he sees the weakest saint upon his knees.

—William Cowper

As we come to understand the word *plead* and how the Bible uses it, we must not come short or content ourselves with mere understanding. Divine information purposes our transformation. What makes up the power of a believer's life? It is never how much we know. Power rests in the truth of God's Word becoming engrafted into our life and practice as a believer. God's truths and principles become woven into the fabric of who we are and how we live. As these influence our approach to day-to-day existence, they evidence our growth in grace and make up Christian maturity. It is the living Word living in us.

Christ tells us how important this is:

> And it happened, as He spoke these things, that a certain woman from the crowd raised her voice and said to Him, "Blessed is the womb that bore you, and the breasts which nursed you!" But he said, "More than that, blessed are those who hear the word of God and keep it!" (Luke 11:27–28)

> He answered and said unto them, my mother and my brethren are these which hear the word of God, and do it. (Luke 8:21)

It is not the knowing but the doing God looks for. It is a great blessing to hear the word of God, but it is not enough. The real blessing, the eternal blessing, is the word of God entering our souls and bearing the fruit of obedience. The power of our lives is never in how much we know. It is in what we weave into the fabric of our hearts and lives. More of God's truth, his Word, incorporated into our "living," constitutes the power of our lives.

> Let the word of Christ dwell in you and me richly! (Colossians 2:16)

So with pleading, we should ask, "What does pleading look and feel like in our experience?" To answer this, we come to what I call an experiential definition.

First, let me tell you the difference between "experiment" and "experience." An experimental faith is what I call the obedience to truth as an act of faith. Prayer itself is like breathing to human life. It is the natural expression of life. We never hope a newborn baby will get around to breathing. It is natural to life. So it is with a newborn believer. However, praying with others or leading others in prayer is another thing.

I felt awkward and inadequate when asked to pray in a group, yet I knew I was to be a praying person, so I tried not to let my "feelings" dictate my obedience. This was the obedience of my faith, willing to step out into the "experiment" of praying. It was a humbling time. At a college gathering at church, before the prayer time started, they asked me to close in prayer after others prayed. I was so nervous I prayed first!

I am grateful this was not all there was! As I went forward, seeking to develop my prayer life, there was the "experience" of actual prayer, a genuine connection with God. Through practice, habit, and exercising obedient faith, my inner man grew, matured, and developed. This is how we grow; we must take up a spiritual responsibility, struggle, fail forward, and cultivate our souls before God. Christ and the Holy Spirit work within the child of God. They work at assisting all of God's people in their praying. Even in public, as I prayed, people were no longer in my thoughts. Rather, the God with whom I was drawing near to was before my soul.

Remember, we cannot feel our way into action and obedience. However, we can take up responsibility by "experimental" faith, or the obedience of faith, and act ourselves into the "felt experience" of the blessing of God upon our willingness. Isn't this the way to approach everything God requires of us? This thought is worthy of some meditation, and perhaps it will be a help to you as you act upon it. I pray it will be so.

An experiential definition of pleading

What does this word feel like in our experience? What are the living realities of its actual use in our prayers? Obviously, the activity of pleading goes beyond mere definitions. True prayer is more than an intellectual exercise—so is pleading with God. Prayer and pleading are tangible, though spiritual, connection with God. There is personal and actual interchange between two persons. Our spirit with God, who is spirit, connects in prayer.

Focus on an accurate understanding of the words of the Bible is incredibly important. However, we are to seek the practical comprehension of what the Scriptures teach. Ask the Holy Spirit to take you by the hand of your soul (which is faith) and lead you to actual practice and living out truth in your life experience. Divine information should lead to actual transformation in the way we live and experience life. This is a vital part of walking "with" God. Not to do this is dangerous.

Not pursuing experienced truth is the issue Christ is addressing in Matthew 7:21–23:

> Not everyone who says to me, "Lord, Lord," shall enter the kingdom of heaven, but he who does the will of my Father in heaven. Many will say to me in that day, "Lord, Lord, have we not prophesied in your name, cast out demons in your name, and done many wonders in your name?" And then I will declare to them, "I never knew you; depart from me, you who practice lawlessness!"

What was missing? What did they lack? First, personal acquaintance and genuine relationship with Christ. They did not have union with Christ that included communion with him—the building of an actual mutually enjoyed relationship. Second, they were lawless. They did not bring their inner world and outer world into heart compliance with his teaching. Whether through pragmatism or self-freedom and personal boundaries, they were laws to themselves. The dictates of their preferences ruled their lives as the supreme law they obeyed. They were content to follow the determinations of their own hearts. They assumed he would be just fine with what they did. He wanted them to obey and incorporate into their minds, hearts, lives, and experiences conformity to the mind, heart, and directives of his words. They had no heart for that.

Ultimately, this subject of pleading should lead us to conformity to the person and activity of Christ himself—he who prayed with powerful cries and pleadings. The Scriptures witness this kind of praying throughout his ministry in the garden of Gethsemane and on the cross.

> Who, in the days of his flesh, when he had offered prayers and supplications, with vehement cries and tears to his Father who could save him from death and was heard because of his godly fear. (Hebrews 5:7)

Let us not forget, this is part of our "conformity to Christ."

As we understand pleading, it should bring us into a deeper, more personal experience of real acquaintance with God our Father, the ever blessed Lord Jesus, and the comforting, securing person of the Holy Spirit.

So how are we to experience pleading? There are three ways it should become known in our heart's practice of drawing near and entreating God. As we open the experience, examine your own practice and what you experience in prayer or pleading. God has given an abundance of models in Scripture. These models are for us to imitate.

> For whatever things were written before were written for our learning so we through patience and comfort of the scriptures might have hope. (Romans 15:4)

I often think of the spirituality of David and Paul. What precious examples for us to follow as they delighted in their God. Their God is our God. We are to be imitators of these God-given models. The people of God, recorded in the Bible, practiced this pleading in prayer.

> When I remember you on my bed, I meditate on you in the night watches, because you have been my help, therefore in the shadow of your wings I will rejoice. My soul follows close

behind you [there is energy in my soul to draw close to you], your right hand upholds me [to draw close to you is by your help imparted to enable me]. (Psalm 63:6–8)

1. This pleading is an investment of soul energy.

Any of us can tell the difference between our heads being in something and our whole person being into it. Right? Now read what Jeremiah says about his "pleading" with God:

Righteous are you, O Lord, when I plead with you; yet let me talk with you about your judgments. Why does the way of the wicked prosper? Why are those happy who deal so treacherously? (Jeremiah 12:1)

We can read these words and yet not get the flavor of the original. The Hebrew term Jeremiah uses, "I plead," has a primary meaning of "to strive in the sense of physical combat." Think of strain and sweat. There was energy of heart going out to the LORD as Jeremiah pled his concerns before his God. He was struggling with the events he had experienced and witnessed. He came before God with soul-draining exertion, expressing his consternation and perplexity over the events. As he did so, his soul felt like a wrung-out rag. His longing was to have a better understanding of God's ways. He entered reverent verbal wrestling with the Lord concerning God's own activities and proceedings.

We see a vivid physical picture of this activity when Jacob met the angel of the LORD in Genesis 32:24–28. All night, Jacob wrestled with the angel and would not let him go until he received a blessing—which he received and had his name changed from Jacob (deceiver, supplanter) to Israel (a prince with God, one who strives with God) because he wrestled with the angel and won the match. Jacob would not let him go until he received the blessing he desperately needed—an amazing display of how God takes weak and feeble people, strengthens them with overcoming ability, and then blesses them with an acknowledgment of victory. God enables his own people to overcome him with his own strength. This is what Jeremiah was doing as he wrestled with the Lord in prayer. As J. Edwin Hartill expressed it: "Prayer is the slender sinew that moves the muscle of omnipotence." Yet it was omnipotence gently breathed into Jacob's soul that enabled him to "overcome the Almighty."

How many times have we dads wrestled with our little ones and let them throw us to the floor and be victors of the match? We enjoy letting them show their strength. I remember arm wrestling with my little girls. After a struggle, I would throw myself over as if overwhelmed by their power. I did this in play. God does it to strengthen our faith and build our character. With our God, when we wrestle with him, he delights and builds maturity in us.

Wrestling with God exhausted Jacob. Pleading with God exhausted Jeremiah. The word shows a "verbal combat" and struggle which he had with God. He exuded energy in his openhearted struggling it out with the Lord. He was pleading for a better understanding of God's ways in his life context.

Do we see much of this anymore? Where is there spending energy in laying hold of God and expressing our perplexities to him? Would we experience more personal openings of the heart of Christ if we sought him with more energy? Are we too polite and content to "say our prayers"? As the assemblies of Christ, would we see more infusions of his power in our midst if we sought him more energetically? Does he mirror our faith and earnestness? "Be it to you according to your faith." "He did not do many mighty works there because of their unbelief." As A. W. Tozer said, "Where is the 'O God!' in our churches?"

David prayed for light to understand God's word. Jeremiah could have prayed similarly to these expressions.

> The entrance of your words gives light; it gives understanding to the simple. I opened my mouth and panted (an expression of intense longing, earnest desires, and fervent entreaties), for I

longed for your commandments. Look upon me
and be merciful to me, as your custom is toward
those who love your name. (Psalm 119:130)

Here is an earnest soul longing for God's personal help to under-
stand the Scriptures and their practical shaping of his entire person.
Has an intense "panting" ever described our longing for God's Word?
Has it led you to lay hold of God with "I so desperately need to know
this, understand, and experience this"? This expresses his pleading
prayer for God's personal tutoring and his life's conforming to the
Word of his God. Do you think we would make greater progress in
Christian maturity if we knew this "hungering and thirsting"?

This word also takes on "a legal-judicial significance, like laying
out a case in court." We noted this earlier; however, the word implies
energy in expressing the arguments—as in a lawyer at court pleading his argument before the judge and jury, which includes mental
and physical energy. In each case, it involves the investment of soul
energy: our hearts, souls, minds, and even bodies are engaged in this
praying activity.

Pleading with God is not having a chat with the Almighty, nor
is it information sharing. It is not casual dialogue with the LORD of
hosts. It is not informing God. Prayer is not a polite exchange as with
the teller at the bank when we make a transaction. It is not stating
requests and words before God and being content with having done
so. Especially, it is not an irreverent "buddy" talk or bold inappropri-
ate familiarity with the great I AM. Pleading is an energetic investment of the soul in an earnest purpose of heart to get something from
the Almighty something our soul desperately needs. Pleading arises
from our belief in God's mercies, which are tender and free, but also
firm confidence in what he promised he is able and willing to do.

Blessed are those who hunger and thirst for
righteousness, for they shall be filled. (Matthew
5:6; illustrated in Abraham, Romans 4:20–22)

From Christ, this is basic Christianity 101.

I wonder if we would experience more dynamic growth in grace, visible maturity in the fruit of the Spirit, and advance in manifesting the graces and character of our Savior if we sought to walk with God in this manner? Is this not worthy of seeking with all our hearts, all our souls, all our strength, and all our might? What if we "binged" a pleading session instead of a Netflix series? Would it develop a different richness in our walk with Christ? Is this legalism? How could we even think such a thing?

> Christianity is the total commitment of all I know of me to all I know of Jesus Christ. (William Temple)

> Were the whole realm of nature mine, that were an offering far too small; love so amazing, so divine, demands my soul, my life, my all. (Isaac Watts)

Surely we do not believe these expressions are too excessive.

Christ declared that his Father's house is to be a house of prayer! Surely we would see more spiritual health in the assemblies of our Lord if this marked our prayer meetings—that is, if we still have them. If the house of God is to be a house of prayer, why is there so little praying? Are we afraid to pray with earnestness or with an effectual fervency in the assemblies of our Savior? Could it be that we have so little of his authoritative presence because we ask not?

2. This pleading is personal contact with God.

I love this about the word *plead*. It is personal activity between us and our great, awe-inspiring, and gracious GOD.

> Then Moses pleaded with the Lord his God, and said: "Lord, why does your wrath burn hot against your people whom you have brought out

of the land of Egypt with great power and with a
mighty hand?" (Exodus 32:11)

The word Moses uses literally means "to stroke the face" of GOD!
This was to soothe and appease his anger while entreating him to do
differently from what he said. Moses literally approaches the LORD face-
to-face and engages him to change his countenance toward the people.
He strokes the face of God, the Almighty, with verbal oil calculated
to soften his visage. Do we think of prayer or pleading as face-to-face
engagement with our God? Though we do not touch the Almighty, our
triune God, with our physical being, do we touch him with our souls?

Is this radical? Or is this what our God delights in and desires
for us and from us?

Through the years, when they were young, I would wake my
kids up by rubbing their backs and then say "Come on. We got to get
the blood flowing" and rub their face. One of my children, when she
was young, struggled with moodiness. First thing in the morning, I
would meet her at the bedroom door and say, "Now, honey, you are
going out for the day. Let's make sure you have a friendly attitude
and be kind to your sisters." Then I would rub her cheeks and tickle
her to get her to smile. It was my attempt to soften the face and
attitude of one of my children. Years later, this delightful daughter
bought me a coffee mug with these words: "The Attitude Adjuster."

The passage in Exodus speaks of Moses pleading, or stroking
the face of God! The strokes Moses soothed the face of God with are
three holy arguments or pleas. They are truths from God's communication, which Moses embraced and then argued back to God.

a) Israel is your people, for whom you have done so much.
Surely you will not destroy them and undo your own work!

Oh, my gracious God, you have every reason to be angry with your people; yet you have
taken up a task. Surely you will finish what you
started. Oh Lord, finish your word and work in
your people: do not forsake the work of your

hands. Make us know you will complete the work you began.

b) What about Egypt?

What will be your reputation before them? The Egyptians will delight and triumph if you destroy Israel! They will think you are just like their false gods. Your actions will remove your own impressive demonstration as the only true and living God. They will misunderstand such action and attribute it to your inability to do what you said you would do. Oh Lord, take up the honor of your name and guard your reputation. Don't give the pagan world arguments against you and your people.

c) What about the promises made to Abraham, Isaac, and Jacob, which had received a partial fulfillment of what you have done already?

If you destroy them now, it would seem like revoking your promises! It would seem like you have withdrawn promises and gone back on your commitments. O Lord, we are not to put stumbling blocks before others. Surely, you will not do so! Lord God, this will make it difficult for people to rely on your promises and words. You will come across as whimsical and unreliable. Do you want your people to struggle with such thoughts?

To these verbal pleadings, the LORD was pleased to respond most favorably. It was as though Moses won the day and brought the Almighty into compliance with his reasoned requests! Notice Moses drew his arguments in pleading before the LORD from God's own concerns, his words, his character, and the honor of his name.

Years ago, John Trapp wrote,

> It is the ingenuity [skill and resourcefulness]
> of saints to study God's ends [ultimate purposes]
> more than their own, and drown all self-respects
> in his glory.

Moses was a master at this. Yielding all his life and "rights" was part of the quality which made Moses the meekest man on earth—by God's own estimation. There is power in Spirit-wrought meekness! No wonder it is "the meek" who inherit the earth. Moses was saying, "No, I want your name honored, respected, and exalted! I want your promises viewed as reliable."

Notice there is this personal engagement with God in which Moses contacts the face of God. This delights the heart of our heavenly Father. Our God delights when we, his people, pray this way. Our triune God wants a personal connection with us. Is this becoming clear? Is this attractive to you? Can you think of yourself as crawling up into your heavenly Father's lap, turning to his face in adoration, and then bringing your requests to him? Read Psalm 131 in the light of this question. Can you see yourself as invited to lean on your Savior's chest and unburden your heavy heart? He wants you to do this. It is the actual expression of your living faith.

3. This pleading is a confident, secure, and affectionate appeal for God's personal companionship in our sense of need.

In our poverty of soul, he is with us, bringing his infinite treasury of divine riches.

Paul sought the Lord about a personal issue he was struggling with. It was a source of pain. He called it a "thorn in the flesh."

> Concerning this thing I pleaded with the
> Lord three times that it might depart from me.
> (2 Corinthians 12:8)

"I pleaded"—literally "I called the Lord to my side." As Paul engaged in this pleading, he was calling to the Lord to come alongside him to listen as he presented an earnest, reasoned argument for his relief of pain. While the Lord did not do exactly as Paul desired, he did exceedingly and abundantly more for him. This is by Paul's own confession!

Pride is the disease of the devil infecting the soul. Here is a more deadly virus that has infected the whole human race. Our Lord would rather his people experience pain so as not to grow in likeness to our soul's enemy. Paul saw this for the mercy it was—a kind and merciful medicine from the lover of his soul: "Lest I should be exalted above measure" and "think of myself more highly than I ought to think" (2 Corinthians 12:7; Romans 12:3). Exalted views of ourselves, pride and arrogance, are dangerous maladies of heart. To the extent they live within, they reduce likeness to Christ. If you want to please the devil, admire yourself.

> Pride is the mother of all contempt of God.
> (John Calvin)

I want you to notice how Christ responded to Paul. He did not turn a deaf ear to such entreaties and pleadings from the heart of Paul. The Lord Jesus responded in a confiding closeness. He assured Paul, "You have my heart and my responsive care. You will know my provision, Paul" (vv. 9–10). "And he said, 'My grace is sufficient for you, for my strength is made perfect in weakness.' Therefore, most gladly, I will rather boast in my infirmities, so the power of Christ may rest upon me. Therefore, I take pleasure in infirmities, in reproaches, in needs, in persecutions, in distresses, for Christ's sake. For when I am weak, then I am strong." Strong in a precious, present Savior who breathes divine strength into my heart, my soul and life. Paul testified many times, "The Lord stood by me."

Paul had the same values, beliefs, and filter system as John the Baptist:

I must decrease and he must increase.

My heart and soul will have it no other way. The afflictions of this life are not worthy of being compared to the glory that awaits us.

We glorify God in our dependence. God created us to depend upon our Creator. It intensifies this dependence in our fallen state, for there is no approach to God, no remedy for our self-imposed plight unless God is the aggressor to provide a way back into his acceptable presence, which is the good news of the gospel of Christ.

The Serpent, the Prince of Darkness, whispered into our first parents' ears the freedom and pleasure of being independent from God:

Be the one who determines your own truth. Establish your own boundaries and personal determinations for what is right for you. You know God is afraid of these things. That's why he keeps things from you by his own silly little restraints upon your freedom. Do you want genuine joy and happiness? Disregard his word. Live by your own perception of what brings you pleasure. Go on, live by the clear sight of your own reasoning. Why, you are intelligent. Follow the dictates of your own heart and thoughts. You know what's best for you more than anyone else. Sure, he has his truth, but you have yours. To your own self be true.

And so they did! Here is the fountain of all human misery and sorrow.

What is the condition of man by nature? Not independence from God but alienation from God. Existing as enmity toward God, not subject to God or his commands.

> This I say, therefore, and testify in the Lord, that you should no longer walk as the rest of the Gentiles walk, in the futility of their mind, having their understanding darkened, being alienated from the life of God, because of the ignorance (not an innocent ignorance) that is in them, because of the blindness of their heart; who, being past feeling, have given themselves over to lewdness, to work all uncleanness with greediness. (Ephesians 4:17–19)

The state of man is a denied dependence on the Creator. The Gospel unites the soul to God through Christ. Now the way of happiness and inner delight is dependence upon the strength and power of his grace. How important it is for us to see the Christian life as a continuation of dependence upon God's storehouse of supplies in Christ. Our Lord told his disciples, "Without me you can do nothing" (John 15:5). The Lord Jesus loves to have his people drawing upon his purchased provisions every day of their pilgrimage in this world. It is our wisdom to do so. Like the mother hen delighting in her chicks rushing to find shelter under her wings, Christ says, "So would I gather you." As the entire land of Egypt looked to Joseph to provide their needs from his granaries, so we are to look to Christ, our Joseph, to do the same with the granaries of heaven.

Remember: a self-made man will worship his creator, and a self-righteous man will adore his savior. If you think about this, you will end up praying, as Augustine did, for God to save you from yourself and self-delusion. May we glorify God through whole-hearted dependence.

To conclude this section, here is a working definition of pleading:

Pleading is the soul drawing near to God as his affectionate and compassionate Father, in a spirit of reverent humility, gripped with a deep and urgent sense of need, expressing a blood-bought confidence and boldness, with energy of soul, forming biblical arguments to persuade God to engage his whole being in a willing compliance to our holy longings and requests. He roots this in a firm belief God is his companion. This pleading draws from the Bible the desires of God's own heart, the concerns of his own esteemed values, and forms reasons for God to act on his behalf, consistent with his own priorities.

> *The prayer that reaches heaven must be lifted up by a strong faith, earnest desires, and a direct intention to the glory of God.*
>
> —Matthew Henry

> *Cold prayers shall never have warm answers. God will suit his returns to our requests. Lifeless services shall have lifeless answers. When men are dull, God will be dumb (silent as a person who cannot speak).*
>
> —Thomas Brooks

7

Basic Truths to Prepare Us
for Pleading with God (Part 1)

*Prayer is only true when it is within
the compass of God's Word.*

—John Bunyan

In the next several chapters, we will look at examples of forming arguments from God's Word which fuel our pleading. These are valid arguments, entreaties, and pleadings God expects us to use. He scatters them throughout the Scriptures so we would find, read, and study them in order to use them. One of the great purposes of the Bible is learning to think like God thinks. This promotes our greatest comfort, wisdom, and power throughout our earthly journey.

Believers receive the Spirit of adoption (Romans 8:15–16). This is not like human adoptions. When God adopts, he gives the Spirit of adoption, working in us the spirit of being actual children in the family of God. The Holy Spirit, in the new birth, works in the children of God, a family spirit which is lovingly devoted to God as Father. The Spirit produces a delight in God and dependence on him as a father.

In a home, parents influence their children. Children pick up parental values. Things important to the parent are important to the

83

children. As God's children, we are to learn from him, align with his views of reality (which are infallible), absorb his values into the depths of our souls, and embrace his worldview. As we find the things God values and cares about, we value and care about them. We pray the Holy Spirit would ignite our affections and heighten our love for our Father and his pursuits. This is part of "imitating him as dear children" (Ephesians 5:1).

Embracing God's values and priorities was clear in the beginning content of prayer our Lord taught us:

> Our Father in heaven, hallowed be your name. Your kingdom come. Your will be done on earth as it is in heaven.

The honor of his name, the advance of his kingdom, and his will accomplished are the overarching priorities in anything we bring to him. Ask God to write this truth in your heart: God's glory and our blessedness (or true happiness) are one goal, not two. Embrace this way of thinking, and you are in harmony with each person of the Trinity. This is to have a heart for God. Christ showed us, even when life hurts, we are to put the priority of the Father's will over our own:

> Not my will, but your will be done. (Luke 22:42)

What are the basics of pleading? Drawing out arguments from Scripture which give divine authorization for our requests.

> Now this is the confidence that we have in him, that if we ask anything according to his will, he hears us. (1 John 5:14)

> If the word of the LORD is with them, let them now make intercession to the LORD of hosts. (Jeremiah 27:19)

> Nothing lies outside the reach of prayer
> except that which lies outside the will of God.
> (John Blanchard)

Promises or stated purposes, which God gives in his Word, are valid for pleading. This should embolden us to pray with confidence in the same way the saints of old did. Prayer is not wrestling with God's reluctance to bless us; it is laying hold of his willingness to do so.

> God's promises are to be our pleas in prayer.
> (Matthew Henry)

In presenting the perplexities, needs, and concerns we have, we give to the Lord his own words and expect his favorable response. God takes great delight when his people think this way, live this way, and pray this way. The same is true in pleading with God for the needs of others—even more so and chiefly as we pray for the kingdom of Christ. There are many basic truths centering on God, Christ, and the Word he gives us, which present effective arguments in our reasoning with God in humble yet forceful prayer. It is our wisdom to use these gracious tools to become mature and sweetly skillful in prayer. This is what we are learning to do in this book.

Here are four basic truths which prepare us to pray and plead aright—truths, which are ways of thinking, to help us approach prayer and pleading in a proper frame of mind and heart. Please realize these points are not just more information; they represent the way Christ would have his people think. These truths are to be our reality. They become the lens through which we look upon life, the Christian life, and the subject of prayer and pleading.

There are four truths I want to bring into focus: (1) We are not sufficient in ourselves to pray. (2) God the Holy Spirit is our sufficiency and helper for genuine prayer. I will open and explain these in this chapter. In the next chapter, we will take up. (3) Christ has given real people, just like us, to follow as examples of prayer. (4) In all honesty, how real are the demands and requirements of Christ to us personally?

1. We are not sufficient in ourselves to pray.

In approaching the Christian life and any responsibility given to us, Christ would have us live with this truth: "without me, you can do nothing" (John 15:5). Make sure we see our Lord's invitation in these words: "I am vitally connected to you like a vine to its branches. Draw from me, for you are not sufficient in yourself." Let his teaching sink deep within our hearts. Our Lord gives the Holy Spirit to be our enabler. For what? To live the Christian life and perform every duty and responsibility associated with that life. The fruit of our lives, if it is pleasing to God, is in God alone.

> Your fruit is found in me. (Hosea 14:8)

This is how God sees us and how he thinks. Do we actually think this way? Make his thoughts your thoughts.

Paul embraced this great reality in Christ. He drew from the grace of Christ. What was the result?

> I can do all things through Christ who strengthens me. (Philippians 4:13)

He matured through the years, learning from Christ, grace working in him, the Holy Spirit's influence led in practical growth, enabling him to say, "I have learned in whatever state I am to be content. I know how to be abased, and I know how to abound. Everywhere and in all things I have learned both to be full and to be hungry, both to abound and to suffer need."

All the people we so love and respect recorded in the Scriptures testify that all their abilities were not in themselves. It was God alone who strengthens and enables them to do anything as it ought to be done. Take the apostle Paul again:

> Not that we are sufficient of ourselves
> to think (or claim) of anything as being from

ourselves, but our sufficiency is from God. (2 Corinthians 3:5)

Paul knew where his sufficiency came from. The poverty and bankruptcy of his own soul demanded that he hang upon God's provision of grace to do what God commissioned him to do. As a branch, he had to draw the sap of enablement from Christ the vine.

Are we called to pray, worship, obey, and plead with God? Yes, we are. We cannot do these things without the enabling of the Spirit. I say it reverently—the Holy Spirit is the sap that flows between the Vine and the branches, giving life and fruit. Apart from the work of the Spirit, there would be no salvation, and there could be no acceptable prayer. This teaches us first, we are not to look within ourselves for the ability which, simply, is not there and second, to move us to seek the ability where it is to be found, specifically the Holy Spirit, our enabler or helper.

> And I will pray the Father, and he will give you another Helper, that he may abide with you forever—the Spirit of truth, whom the world cannot receive, because it neither sees him nor knows him; but you know him, for he dwells with you and will be in you. (John 14:16–17; 15:26)

Christ Jesus tells his disciples the Spirit "is one just like me. God, the third person of the holy Trinity. You are always in our care, therefore, always draw upon your God. He will be to you such a wise and powerful friend, a companion, as I have been. I have an eternal interest in you. The Spirit will take charge of you now on a whole new level. He will live and dwell in all my people, my disciples. He will be your source of strength, understanding, wisdom, perseverance, and joy. The Spirit will support you to do what, by nature, you cannot. He makes your doings acceptable."

In ourselves, we are weak, inconsistent, subject to a multitude of infirmities, and quite inadequate for Christian living and responsibilities. Our Lord secured a precious, friendly, and all-sufficient remedy, like himself, in the divine person of the Holy Spirit.

This is the principle that removes our boasting. It also moves us to call upon and draw our abilities from our internal divine companion. This perspective requires humility, dependence, but most importantly, a genuine relationship, a companionship, and an actual fellowship between persons. This is one practical way we are "partakers of the divine nature!"

> His divine power has given to us all things that pertain to life and godliness, through the knowledge of Him who called us by glory and virtue, by which have been given to us exceedingly great and precious promises, that through these you may be partakers of the divine nature. (2 Peter 1:3–4)

The Scriptures tutor us in our insufficiency. The first quality of his genuine people, our Savior declares, is acquaintance with the poverty of their soul.

> Blessed are the poor in spirit, for theirs is the kingdom of heaven. (Matthew 5:3)

Paul follows up on this same truth:

> For if anyone thinks himself to be something, when he is nothing, he deceives himself. (Galatians 6:3)

> For I say, through the grace given to me, to everyone who is among you, not to think of himself more highly than he ought to think, but to think soberly, as God has dealt to each one a measure of faith. (Romans 12:3)

> If anyone thinks he knows anything,
> he knows nothing yet as he ought to know.
> (1 Corinthians 8:2)

I hope we can all take this seriously. Why? There is a subtle danger of offending God. How? Without this truth rooted in our approach to all of life, we run the danger of walking down a path described by Jeremiah.

> For my people have committed two evils:
> they have forsaken me, the fountain of living
> waters, and hewn themselves cisterns—broken
> cisterns that can hold no water. (Jeremiah 2:13)

Perhaps this is more of a problem in our day than we like to think. There is all too little reliance on the work of the Holy Spirit in our lives and churches. Too many can "do the Christian life" on their own. We sing, "I'm desperate for you," then go about our lives without a sense of desperate drawing on divine resources to enable us.

Here is an example of our dependence and security based on God's working in us. What is the proper basis for our peace? How are we to be secure that peace will be our true possession and experience? Observe carefully what Isaiah tells us:

> Lord, you will establish peace for us, for you
> have also done all our works in us. (Isaiah 26:12)

Our Lord affirmed this truth in his own ministry.

> But he who does the truth comes to the
> light, that his deeds may be clearly seen, that they
> have been done in God. (John 3:21)

All the good works done by us are results of grace.

The Christian life is not what we give to God but what God gives to us. First and foremost, he gives himself to us. From this, he gives peace, wholeness, humanness at its authentic best. He makes us a refreshingly real people. God moves us along the path of conformity to Christ. He gives us the solid basis of our acceptable standing with him: the accomplishments of Christ and the works of God in us.

Let the one who boasts boast in the Lord. (1 Corinthians 1:31)

> "Let him who glories glory in this, that he understands and knows me, that I am the Lord, exercising loving-kindness, judgment, and righteousness in the earth. For in these I delight," says the Lord. (Jeremiah 9:24)

In contrast, the Bible warns us: "He who trusts in his own heart is a fool." Wisdom warned us: "To seek one's own glory is not glory" (Proverbs 25:27). It is self-deception (Proverbs 28:26).

> Trust in the Lord with all your heart, and lean not on your own understanding. (Proverbs 3:5)

David was a man after God's own heart. He was mighty and powerful when he thought as God thought and, thus, relied upon his God. Even on the battlefield, hear the way David acknowledges the source of his enabling:

> For by you I can run against a troop; by my God I can leap over a wall. (2 Samuel 22:30)

Our tendency is to say, "Hey, leap over a wall! That's a cinch. I can handle this." The LORD declares how all true God-honoring accomplishments actually come about:

> "Not by might nor by power, but by my Spirit," says the Lord of hosts. (Zechariah 4:6)

We need to make God's thoughts our thoughts.

Back in 2 Corinthians 3:5, Paul declares he had no ability in himself to think a good thought or do a good action to the pleasing of God. He looked to God for that ability. His reliance was, in reality, upon the Holy Spirit, bringing the tangible strength of God, the provision of God's grace in Jesus Christ, infusing it into his life—just like power went out of Christ to the woman who touched his garment and healed her.

Paul continues to make it clear where his ability came from:

> But by the grace of God, I am what I am,
> and His grace toward me was not in vain; but I
> labored more abundantly than they all.

True historically, but look how quick Paul was to make an important clarification:

> Yet not I, but the grace of God, which was
> with me. (1 Corinthians 15:10)

Believers, living in the truth of who they are and who their God is, attribute nothing to themselves, which belongs to God. In fact, it is dangerous to ascribe too little to the grace of God, for then we rob him of his glory. If we ascribe to our own strength, that which is the proper work of grace, then we blemish God's glory by taking too much to ourselves.

Paul tells us the right way to look at this:

> It is God who works in you both to will and
> to do for his good pleasure. (Philippians 2:13)

Your workings and God's workings are to be concurrent, confluent, interdependent necessities. Don't go about the Christian life alone or without God's companionship. You will fall on your face. Israel went up to Jericho in wholesome dependence on the Lord. God and Israel went together. What was the result? A mighty victory.

91

They went up against the small town of Ai, presumptuously, and relied on their own abilities. It was a cinch, they thought, so they went it alone—and what was the result? A devastating humiliation, disaster, and defeat.

We are to learn, whether praying, reading our Bible, or living the Christian life: we are not sufficient of ourselves. The Holy Spirit is our precious enabler. God alone is our strength. Think this way in all you do: "I cannot without God, and he will not without me." Go to him, rely upon him, and draw from his abilities: ask him for his grace and enablement. We cannot keep our hearts without his aid. Act upon these truths. Make them the lens through which you see your Christian life. He gives grace to the humble. As the burdens grow greater, he gives more grace. He gives himself to you!

I hope you see the beauty of this. It will beautify the soul with humility and strengthen our reliance on God. There is sweet security and confidence which these truths bring. God does all things well and will be successful in all he does. Above all, this communicates the intimate relationship we are to have with God through our Lord Jesus Christ. The exceeding great loveliness of each person of the holy Trinity shines into our hearts. Paul's expressions change from mere words to enjoyable, relational realities.

> The grace of the Lord Jesus Christ, and the love of God, and the communion of the Holy Spirit, be with you all. Amen. (2 Corinthians 13:14)

2. God the Holy Spirit is our sufficiency and helper for genuine prayer.

Prayer is essential to the Christian life. As Christ is the "author and finisher of our faith" (Hebrews 12:2), the indwelling Spirit is the author of acceptable prayer. The act of prayer is a manifestation of the Holy Spirit working both in us and with us.

> We could not pray at all were it not for the
> Holy Spirit. (D. Martyn Lloyd-Jones)

He does not do this without us but with us. There simply cannot be true prayer, heaven-bound prayer, without the Spirit's help.

> The spirit of prayer is the fruit and token of
> the Spirit of adoption. (John Newton)

Prayer without the help of the Holy Spirit could not possibly be "according to the will of God," nor can it be acceptable. Paul makes this clear.

> Likewise, the Spirit also helps in our weaknesses. For we do not know what we should pray for as we ought, but the Spirit himself makes intercession for us with groanings which cannot be uttered. Now he who searches the hearts knows what the mind of the Spirit is, because he makes intercession for the saints according to the will of God. (Romans 8:26–27)

a. The Spirit "helps." How? He takes on himself a part of the actual expression of true prayer. The word *help* implies putting one's shoulder under a burden. The Holy Spirit comes under the burden of acceptably communicating to God in prayer. He moves our souls up to God and assists in expressions from the heart. For the psalmist to say, "Unto you, Oh Lord, do I lift up my soul" (Psalm 25:1), the help of the Holy Spirit was there.

We take the yoke of Christ upon us to live life together (Matthew 11:29). I hope we all see it that way. The believer is to say, "Christ and I are true yoke fellows." When thrown into prison for loyalty to Christ, Samuel Rutherford said, "Christ and I are able to bear it." Our Lord, of course, bears the heaviest portion of weight. We are colaborers with him in all we do.

The same imagery and concept is true in our relationship with the Holy Spirit. This verb, *help*, speaks of support to infants too weak to support themselves. It speaks of holding up the sick, tottering person to enable them to walk. It communicates giving strength to those unequal to a task or carry their burden alone. In Psalm 89:21, the Greek translation of the Old Testament uses this word: "My arm shall strengthen him." The Spirit "strengthens" us to pray as we ought. This will be true until we reach our eternal home.

Jude speaks of this as "praying in the Holy Spirit" (v. 20)—that is "in, with, or by the Holy Spirit." We are to pray with the movings, influences, enlightenings, and grace of his presence working in us. The Spirit works appropriate affections as we pray. The Holy Spirit may bring to mind promises or passages in our praying. He will enlighten your conscience to bring confession, uncovering areas of sinful tendencies which we must bring to the Lord. He helps to know what to pray for and how we ought to pray.

Paul writes to the Ephesians:

> Praying always with all prayer and supplica-
> tion in the Spirit, and watching to this end with
> all perseverance and supplication for all saints.
> (Ephesians 6:18)

The concept of "praying in the Spirit" is not a tag-on statement. It has depth and meaning. The expression shows our dependence upon the Holy Spirit for all acceptable prayer—prayer according to the will of God.

Notice how the psalmist describes these workings:

> Lord, you have heard the desire of the hum-
> ble; you will prepare their heart; you will cause
> your ear to hear. (Psalm 10:17)

How does he prepare their heart? By stirring holy desires, strengthening their faith, collecting their thoughts, and raising their affections to things above that they may pray as they should. What does God do in response? He opens his ear to hear and to prepare for giving answers. He treasures up bright designs as he works his sovereign will, but he brings his people along with him as companions in the process.

b.   He does this because of our "weaknesses" or "infirmities."

In a practical sense, what are these infirmities? There are many—notice it is plural. There are too many to list. What do you struggle with? Wandering thoughts, dullness of mind, weakness of faith or doubt, coldness of heart, too focused on your wants or this world, preoccupied with your agendas, lack of faith, just going through the motions, ignorance, distrust, double-mindedness, etc. Sometimes we are too lazy to pray. At other times, we are proud and presumptuous. Sometimes, like the Pharisees, we just pray with ourselves.

Awareness of sin may come to the conscience, but we are too attached to take it up honestly. Matters of pride, self-reliance, presumption, turning our ear from the force of God's authority. Perhaps drifting into gossip or evil speaking marks our lives. We could go on and on. What do all these workings of the flesh do? They either stop us from praying or keep us from bringing our whole soul to the Lord in prayer. The Holy Spirit works in the soul to bring us to confession and repentance. He digs the hidden sins out.

If we tuck sin away in our hearts and make provision for it in the future, it will close the windows of heaven, and God will not hear our prayers. He says so (Isaiah 59:1–2; Psalm 66:18; Romans 13:14). The work of the Holy Spirit moves within to take away all deceit in our relationship with God (Psalm 32:1–5). He works to make us like Nathaniel as our Lord describes him: "an Israelite indeed, in whom is no guile." The Spirit works to withhold and then give the sensible

joys of the Lord as he brings us to greater heart—honesty with ourselves and our heavenly Father.

> God knows full well when times of gladness
> Shall be the needful thing for you.
> When He has tried your soul with sadness
> And from all guile has found you free,
> He comes to you all unaware
> And makes you own His loving care.

Remember, all believers deal with remaining sin. Sin's working
renders us unfit for every duty but especially prayer. What does sin
do in all of us when it gains ground? It weakens the soul and deprives
it of spiritual strength. When David harbored lust and unconfessed
sin in his heart, it broke all his bones and left him weak and crippled.
That's his way of saying he had no strength for prayer. He com-
plained he was sick, weak, wounded, faint.

> There is no soundness in me. (Psalm 38:3)

> I am feeble and sore broken. (v. 8)

> I cannot so much as look up. (Psalm 40:12)

Sin will dry up our spirit and all the strength of soul and weaken
us for every duty we have before God.

In the same way, sin darkens the soul. It acts like a thick cloud that
spreads itself over the soul and intercepts all the beams of God's love
and favor. It takes away the sense of privilege in our adoption; and if
the soul gathers up thoughts of consolation, sin quickly scatters them.

The Spirit alone can break this bondage. Through the Spirit
and the Word of God:

> My soul melts from heaviness; strengthen
> me according to your word. The entrance of your
> words gives light. (Psalm 119:28, 130)

Paul tells us the Holy Spirit alone is the strength, and he enables the believer to subdue sin and drain its strength, or death grip, on the soul (Romans 8:13).

We live in a fallen world. All creation is dysfunctional and existing contrary to its original design.

> For we know that the whole creation groans
> and labors with birth pangs together until now.
> (Romans 8:22)

As believers, we have the same groanings and longings to experience the perfection of our adoption into the family of God. We are the people of God but not yet experiencing what is ours in its full display.

> We also who have the firstfruits of the Spirit,
> even we ourselves groan within ourselves, eagerly
> waiting for the adoption, the redemption of our
> body. (Romans 8:23)

Notice how intricately interwoven the Spirit and the bride of Christ are in the expressed longing for the coming of Christ:

> And the Spirit and the bride say, "Come!"
> (Revelation 22:17)

They express their longing as one voice. This "one voice" was the experience of the Spirit and bride throughout life's journey. The saving plan of God's decree has united the Spirit and the redeemed soul in genuine prayer throughout redemptive history. Without the Spirit, there would be no bride and no voice of the bride. This passage is the "one voice" praying for the crescendo of divine redemption. The same groaning and longing for redemption's perfection and victorious completion will be a reality—to be forever with the Lord!

The Spirit moves to produce desires in us to war against the flesh or sinful outbreaks. The flesh moves in the soul to resist an effective prayer life.

> For the flesh strongly arouses forces within us against the Spirit, and the Spirit against the flesh; and these are contrary to one another, so that you do not do the things that you wish. (Galatians 5:17)

Desire to never sin again arises within, but we do sin again. Longings to love and serve the Lord without end stir in our affections, but we don't. We would abandon prayer and live lazily, but we can't. We would pray with ardor and connection without end, but we don't. Despite all this, God, the Holy Spirit, gives us life, vigor, courage, and comfort by bearing witness to and giving a sense of the privileges of our adoption.

> The Spirit bearing witness with our spirits that we are the children of God. (Romans 8:16)

Amid all this battle, within and without, with our failures and frustrated longings, the Holy Spirit helps us in our praying. He is compassionately in tune with all that is going on, and he is perfectly in tune with the will of God the Father. He moves us to pray. The Spirit gives our prayers to Christ. Christ perfects our prayers and presents them to the Father. The Father gives loving responses to our prayers through Christ, our Mediator. Christ gives the Father's loving responses to the Spirit. The Holy Spirit provides the living application to our hearts. This Trinitarian communion is a blood-bought privilege. None but God's children possess this incredible privilege.

You may say, "I never knew this! I don't know that I've had the help of the Spirit." Well, as a believer, you have, whether or not you know it. To call upon the name of the Lord, in the focus of faith in his saving work, is the work of the Spirit. Find his role in the Bible. Study his care and ministry to you personally. Ask for his help. Don't look for "feelings." Look for greater openings of heart. Look for passages of sweet assurance of God's love and acceptance. Then ask that light and warmth would enter your soul, which draws you to express gratitude. Anticipate passages of Scripture to capture your attention with comfort. These are some of the tender ways the Spirit assures us we are the children of God.

    c.   He moves us to pray according to the will of God.

God recognizes the voice of his own Spirit because the prayers that the Spirit prompts are in strict accordance with his will.

> He who searches the hearts knows what the mind of the Spirit is, because he makes intercession for the saints according to the will of God. (Romans 8:27)

> Now this is the confidence that we have in him, that if we ask anything according to his will, he hears us. (1 John 5:14)

We offer the echo of the thoughts of the Spirit to God. As one saint tells us, "I have always received what I asked for; or what I should have asked for."

Consider our Lord's words in Luke 11:11–12:

> If a son asks for bread from any father among you, will he give him a stone? Or if he asks for a fish, will he give him a serpent instead of a fish? Or if he asks for an egg, will he offer him a scorpion?

Left to ourselves, thinking we pray for bread, we ask for stones. Thinking we pray for fish, we ask for serpents. Thinking we ask for an egg, we ask for scorpions. We are prone, in our own limited thinking, to ask for what will do us harm. We pray against what will bring maturity and eternal value. We pray for what, in reality, is worldliness. The only remedy for these soul-damaging prayers is the internal residence and ministry of the Holy Spirit. Augustine, by the insightful promptings of the Holy Spirit, prayed, "O Lord, save me from that wicked man: myself." The gift of the Father and Son in the person and work of the Spirit safeguard from this danger. God secures our attraction to his divine will.

From the Holy Spirit arises, as a spring, all holy desires toward God, which are often more than words can utter. The Spirit, who searches the hearts, can perceive the mind and will of the spirit of man, the renewed mind, and advocates his cause and need to assist in the longings of his soul. The desires which he stirs in the heart of the Christian are those which are according to his will; they are such as God desires to exist. For instance, the Spirit aids in the production of contrite, humble, and repentant pleadings of sinners for mercy. Then God responds with the bestowal of the very mercy needed and prayed for. It is the same for the child of God throughout his earthly life.

This is beautifully captured in a hymn written in 1680 by Joachim Neander and translated by Catherine Winkworth in 1863. Let these two stanzas sink into your heart and mind:

> Praise to the Lord, who o'er all things so won-
>   drously reigneth,
> Shelters thee under his wings, yea, so gently
>   sustaineth!
> Hast thou not seen how thy desires e'er have been
> Granted in what he ordaineth?
> Praise to the Lord, who doth prosper thy work
>   and defend thee!
> Surely his goodness and mercy here daily attend
>   thee;
> Ponder anew what the Almighty will do,
> If with his love he befriend thee!

So the Spirit helps the child of God throughout his life. This does not mean prayers are infallible as a Christian expresses them or that they never make improper petitions or have improper desires. The acts of God's kindness brushes all that away. Any sin or guilt is accounted for in the cross of Christ. There is a general superintendence over their minds and deep longings within the soul. This is never mechanical. This teaching is one that is full of consolation to the Christian. We are poor and needy and ignorant and blind left to ourselves, but amid our feebleness, we may look to God for the aid of his Spirit and rejoice in his presence and in his power to sustain us in our sighings and to guide us in our wanderings. He woos the soul into the will of God.

As we learn more about pleading with God, please don't take fear or intimidation as a counselor. Seek to be influenced more by the promised help of God. See God saying to you, "You can do this! I will help you. I have given you an inner helper in the person of the Holy Spirit." Wisdom teaches us to ask the Spirit for help and guidance in our praying. This is a foundational principle in developing a healthy, mature, and real prayer life.

Prayer is a sincere, sensible, affectionate pouring out of the soul to God, through Christ, in the strength and assistance of the Spirit, for such things as God has promised.

—John Bunyan

8

Basic Truths to Prepare Us
for Pleading with God (Part 2)

*All the prayers in the Scripture you will find to be reasoning
with God, not a multitude of words heaped together.*

—Stephen Charnock

The Gospel writers introduce Peter. The unfolding of his character and behavior brings some obvious conclusions. Peter lived in his
head. His subjective thoughts, without objective checks, ruled him.
This produced a man who was rash, impetuous, presumptuous, and
self-confident—at least in appearance. What I mean is this: Peter had
high opinions of his opinions. His great need was for the word of
Christ to dwell in him richly as a check to his thoughts and become
the guiding light for his behavior and choices.

The more he experienced Christ's presence and the realization
of who he truly was, Peter's sins and character flaws came to light.

> When Simon Peter saw it, he fell down at
> Jesus' knees, saying, "Depart from me, for I am a
> sinful man, O Lord!" (Luke 5:8)

There is a penetrating ultimate reality in the Lord Jesus that removes human facades. All hearts become open and revealed before him. The effect of this experience was temporary as a check upon his action but impressionable in deepening Peter's attraction to Christ. Peter had "high self-esteem." The problem was he did not have true and accurate views of himself. There is a vast difference. It takes time and heart surgery to change.

In the concluding events of Christ's time on earth, Peter plays a significant role. Peter boasted, "Though everyone else betrays you, I will never do so." Our Lord cautioned and warned him. Christ revealed Peter's terrible denials. He told Peter of three separate times he would deny him along with the rooster's crow. The evil one wanted to take hold of him and sift him as wheat. However, this great Shepherd of souls told him, "Peter, I have prayed for you that your faith would not fail."

On that terrible night, Peter came to realize Christ knew him better than he knew himself. This is the beginning of the heart surgery Peter needed. A young maiden observed he was one of Jesus's disciples. The denials began. The third time Peter even cursed! Then the rooster crowed, bringing the piercing realization of his betrayal far outpacing the other disciples. Peter glanced over to the soldiers leading his Lord from the mock trial. He caught the eyes of Christ set upon him. That eye contact broke him, and he went away weeping bitterly.

It is not for us to know his cries, tears, prayers, and pleadings expressed in deep repentance. His soul, gripped by the ugliness of his boasting, contrasted with his vile behavior in the courtyard, replayed thought after thought in his reflections. There was a conclusion agonizing in his soul like an internal tormentor: gone was his acceptance! He no longer would be welcome to walk beside such a one he came to know and love.

Then there was a strange message delivered to the disciples from Mary Magdalene, Mary the mother of James, and Salome:

> Tell His disciples—and Peter—that He is
> going before you into Galilee; there you will see
> Him, as He said to you. (Mark 16:7)

Time and space do not allow to detail the steps our Lord took in the restoration and commission of Peter. Christ was at work to shape the contours of his inner man into a shepherd of souls. Peter was learning healthy self-distrust and what a supreme love for Christ is.

Did Peter make more mistakes? Yes, of course, but I'm sure not as many or as profound. Paul had to rebuke him later on when he, again, fell into the fear of man. The Scriptures let us know Peter was a praying man. In Acts 10:9, he went up to the rooftop to pray. They had flat roofs with a fence around the edge, so you could go up there in the evening's cool. While Peter was on the roof, the Lord gave him significant direction on the advancement of the Gospel to the Gentile nations.

Peter deeply realized the central place of prayer. He fell asleep in the garden the night he betrayed his Lord. Christ reproved his disciples for doing so. Perhaps he thought upon this with regret and wondered if the rest of the night would have gone differently if he had continued steadfastly in prayer. Peter warns of the roaring lion that creeps about seeing whom he can devour:

"Be serious and watchful in your prayers,"
he tells the saints. (1 Peter 4:7)

Peter learned to nurture a praying atmosphere with his wife, and he encourages the saints in the same (1 Peter 3:7). "Live with your wife according to knowledge," understand and love her, cherish and nourish her as your companion in life. Why? So it will not hinder your prayers. Peter learned how "God resists the proud but gives grace to the humble."

We can draw many encouragements out of the histories of real people, the saints, given in the Bible. We are to walk with God in loving devotion and uprightness of character. God commends this to us in the cloud of examples recorded. The Lord commanded Abraham to walk before him and be blameless (Genesis 17:1). As believers, our calling is the same. We are possessors of the same saving faith as Abraham, and we are to pursue the same walk as God commanded him. Abraham lived by faith, and he prayed by faith. That is God's will for us.

To live by faith is to pattern your heart and life according to the will of God revealed in his Word. This is to walk with God. To pray by faith is to pray with a humble confidence that God will give what you ask. The prayer of faith, however, moves us to follow up with action. We look for God's response to our prayers. If I pray, "O Lord, open my eyes to see the wondrous truths in your Word," then I take up and read the Word, looking for God to meet me and open the eyes of my understanding.

All the saints we so admire had to learn these four great truths from the previous chapter: (1) We are not sufficient in ourselves to pray. (2) God the Holy Spirit is our sufficiency and helper for genuine prayer.

In this chapter, we take up the last two great truths. Here is a wonderful, relatable way our God encourages us in the matter of prayer: he gives models and examples from real people whom he set his love upon.

3. Christ has given real people, just like us, as excellent examples of prayer.

Remember, the strongest and best argument for real prayer is a genuine heart resolved, fixed, on getting a spiritual blessing directly from God! There is simplicity in this. Our heavenly Father holds out the lives of real people we love and admire to encourage us: Joseph, Hannah, Samuel, David, Ezra, Daniel, Peter, Paul—just to name a few. They all prayed. The Holy Spirit recorded some of their prayers in the Bible for our edification, encouragement, and imitation.

Let these wonderful examples become models for us to grow toward and imitate. If we want to become good at something, find those who have developed a successful characteristic in that thing then imitate them. Follow them as they follow Christ. Good examples are God's gift and encouragement for us to do the same.

> Brothers, join in imitating me, and keep
> your eyes on those who walk according to the
> example you have in us. (Philippians 3:17)

The apostle was urgent in pressing the saints to grow and advance in the faith.

> Therefore, I urge you, imitate me. (1 Corinthians 4:16)

Paul lived looking unto Jesus, and we are wise to imitate him.

> Imitate me, just as I also imitate Christ. (1 Corinthians 11:1)

As you read these invitations and exhortations of Paul, think of his life choices and personal disciplines or priorities. He lived with unbelievable demands and challenges. His prayer life was a conduit to receive strength, wisdom, and guidance. Think also of his prayers recorded for us in our Bibles. They are excellent models. Take them, and turn them into prayer for yourself and for your fellow church members and for all the saints on the earth.

All of us grow weary and get lazy in the Christian life. This is true of our prayer lives as well.

> We desire that each one of you show the same diligence to the full assurance of hope until the end, that you do not become sluggish (or lazy), but imitate those who, through faith and patience, inherit the promises. (Hebrews 6:11–12)

James gives Elijah as an example of prayer (James 5:16–18). He does this to encourage us! In what? To pray more effectively by praying more earnestly, to pray with greater fervor as need requires just as our Lord instructed us. Notice how James tells us Elijah had a nature just like ours. He was not some "super" elite believer. He was a man of like passions, had bouts of depression, lost sight of reality, and feared the vindictive wrath of Jezebel. Elijah was a real person— just like us.

James writes: "The effective, fervent prayer of a righteous man avails much." He is saying, "Here is an example of such praying. Look at Elijah because I want you to take courage in difficult times and imitate him."

> Elijah was a man with a nature like ours, and he prayed earnestly that it would not rain; and it did not rain on the land for three years and six months. And he prayed again, and the heaven gave rain, and the earth produced its fruit. (James 5:16–18)

Elijah did this at the command of God. Don't focus on the rain! Focus on the example of Elijah and his praying. That is what James wants us to learn. The rain was circumstantial to the purposes of God in dealing with wicked Ahab and Jezebel. The praying man, Elijah, the child of God in difficult times, is the focus James wants us to have. He is our example of believing, earnest, and effective praying.

The words "prayed earnestly"—literally "he prayed in his prayer." It was a "working, effectively operating, alive, energized, and energizing" prayer. In praying, he really prayed! He put his soul into it. Elijah poured out his heart.

> Trust in him at all times, you people; pour out your heart before Him; God is a refuge for us. (Psalm 62:8)

Elijah labored like Jeremiah. He put "heart sweat, soul sweat" in his praying. He poured himself into it and out to the Lord in his praying. There was intensity, prayerful praying. Think of the definitions of pleading we looked at. This is perhaps the greatest need in the churches today. We fail to use heaven's greatest weapon as we should in the battles of our own life and times.

David speaks from his own experience and practice in Psalm 62:8. He tenderly and invitingly commands all the people of God to be familiar with such approaches to God. From this Psalm, what does David counsel all of God's people to do?

1. To confide in God: "Trust in him"; open your heart and mind to him. Be willing to open your soul and trust him. Depend upon him to perform all things for you as one who cares. Rest in his wisdom and goodness, his power and promise, his providence and grace. How often? At all times. We must have habitual confidence in God. We must live a life of dependence upon him. He admonishes us to trust in him at all times and at no time to put that confidence in ourselves or in any other. An actual confidence in God upon all occasions, trust in him in every emergency. Look for him to guide us when we are in doubt, to protect us when we are in danger, to supply us when we are in need, to strengthen us for every good word and work he calls us to.

2. To converse with God: "Pour out your heart before him." The expression seems to allude to the pouring out of the drink offerings before the Lord. When we pray as we should, it is pouring out the heart before God. We must lay our grievances before him, offer our desires to him with all humble freedom, and then entirely yield ourselves to his disposal, patiently submitting our wills to his. This is pouring out our hearts. David prayed throughout the Psalms in this manner. This is how Hannah prayed—without speaking a word. Her heart prayed this way (Adapted from Matther Henry).

Yet notice it is prayer to God as a refuge for us. There is a personal reality David had in mind. Think of a child becoming afraid, running into his parents' arms! The parent will not simply be a silent barrier to danger. The parent speaks comforting words to the child. There is communication and exchange between them. The child runs into the arms of a real person who values the relationship.

Who is to pray this way? David tells us "all you people," which simply means all the people of God. Included in "all you people" are you and me.

We may consider ourselves to be but infants in the school of Christ as to our prayer life. I know what this is like. Remember, there are others, as we have learned, who are seniors and advanced believers in this holy skill and spiritual activity. Stop and remember they were formerly as you are now. It is essential to recognize this basic truth. They were not born "super-spiritual" saints. Their growth did not happen in four or five major life experiences. Their maturity came in the small decisions, disciplines, and habits within the world no one could see but God. Growth took place in the accumulation of life's day-by-day routines. They came to know God more personally and learned to open their hearts to him without reserve. These people, our brothers and sisters in Christ, learned more and more of God's character. They studied God's promises and put their soul's trust in the God who gave them. All of us can learn to do the same.

God set Abraham as an example to us. "And not being weak in faith."

> He did not waver at the promise of God through unbelief, but was strengthened in faith, giving glory to God, and being fully convinced that what he had promised he could also perform. (Romans 4:19–21)

We should not just repeat the words of God's promises. God does not want us to put our trust in words. Our hearts are to go out to God, in faith, as the one who gave them and will perform what he said he would do.

You may consider yourself to be unfit to pray so earnestly and press your needs to God with persistence and boldness. In drawing near to the God of "all mercy," follow the beautiful guidance of Joseph Hart:

> Let not conscience make you linger, nor of fitness
> fondly dream;
> All the fitness he requires is to feel your need of
> him;

> This he gives you; this he gives you; 'Tis the
> Spirit's rising beam.

Whether you feel "immature" or "unfit," they both become arguments to plead with Christ. Take your "immaturity" and your "unfitness" to Christ.

> Now to Him who is able to keep you from
> stumbling, and to present you faultless before the
> presence of His glory with exceeding joy. (Jude
> v. 24)

"I am weak, Lord."

Christ says, "I know. It is good for you to realize it. Come to me. I am strong and will be your strength."

"But I am sinful, Lord."

Christ says, "Oh, I know all about it. When I was on the cross, my Father placed your sins on me. I loved you and gave myself for you to remove all obstacles, even every sin of yours. Don't focus on your unworthiness and make it larger than my provision for you. Where your sin abounded, my grace much more abounded. Be careful you don't minimize my accomplishments for you. Now, I want you to stop this hellish logic. You are making my blood-bought provision less adequate and powerful than your sin! Believe me and pray as I taught my disciples to pray. Now listen to me—you are not alone! I gave you the Holy Spirit to help you. Don't minimize or neglect his help. Ask for his help, and rely upon him. Though in heavenly places, I am praying at this very moment for you. Let's do this together. Say what I told you: 'my God is my helper.'"

"But I am immature and unfit."

Christ says, "I know. Do you wish to continue in that condition? Be careful those views, feelings, and arguments don't become excuses for apathy or stubbornness. Decide to strengthen your prayer life. How much do you desire to grow? Be determined to reform your ways according to my provisions as your Savior. How passionate are you to follow what I give you in my instructions? My will is that you grow and mature. Make it your will! Make my thoughts your thoughts. How much do you long to please me? I purchased you with my blood? Remember, I am praying for you right now?"

> Therefore he is also able to save to the uttermost those who come to God through him, since he always lives to make intercession for them. (Hebrews 7:25)

Again, let the words of Joseph Hart sink into your soul:

> Come, ye weary, heavy laden, bruised and broken by the fall;
> If you tarry till you're better, you will never come at all:
> Not the righteous, not the righteous—Sinners Jesus came to call.

We are to gain skill, capability, and spiritual dexterity in becoming one of heaven's campaigners and promoters. Remember, if it is a skill, then it is learnable. The only way we learn to pray is to pray. We grow and develop with repeated activity. Maturity occurs when we have our souls and spiritual senses exercised by practice (Hebrews 5:14).

I hope you will read your Bibles differently. Look there for pleadings. Our Lord scatters them throughout the Scriptures like the stars to give us light on the pathway of pleading prayer. Why does he do this? That they would become seed sown into our hearts and practice as we incorporate them in our lives. Why were the Psalms given to the people of God? The Psalms are, in themselves, a prayer book. They are an anatomy of all the parts of the soul pouring itself out to God. They teach us what we are to believe and do toward God, people, trials, fear, danger, and a host of other issues we encounter in life. The Psalms are particularly helpful in making believers aware of their needs. They also tell where to find the remedies and cures.

Take a Psalm that God has encouraged your heart by, then take it phrase by phrase, and turn it into your own prayer to God. Pour your soul out to God through the expressions given in that Psalm. God tells us to do this:

> Take words with you, and return to the Lord. Say to him, "Take away all iniquity; receive us graciously." (Hosea 14:2)

Surely you can do this, but don't do it alone. Ask the Holy Spirit to help you.

Prayer is the greatest way to bring our souls to greater confidence in God. The Psalms show us a lifestyle of authentic godliness. Increased godliness requires prayer, for prayer diminishes self-love and multiplies dependence on God. Prayer, correctly entered and used, unites God and man in will and purpose.

We can look in the Psalms to see the nature of Almighty God, his wisdom, goodness, gentleness, and mercy toward his people, his children, and us individually. We eminently see example after example of how to plead with God.

If we want to learn to pray and crave mercy and blessing from him, here are excellent exhibitions of true, hearty, and earnest prayers—effectual working prayers. Again, in the Psalms, we will find comfort in temptation, trouble, and affliction, and learn with patience to bear them by uniting our hearts to the Lord.

Chiefly, do we want to know God more intimately, know his presence, and have his sweet influences in our souls? There is no better place to plant ourselves and drink in the expressions of such longings. There is no part of the Bible more fragrant with the comforting aroma of God with his people than this book of Psalms. Therefore, it should be our delight and study, and we ought to spend more time reading and meditating in so excellent and worthy a book. Take the Psalms up as the gift of Christ to teach you how to pray and plead as he taught us.

Now, ask yourself the following question:

4. In all honesty, how real are the demands and requirements of Christ to me personally?

A boy in one of the Southern states was dabbling at sports. No passion seemed to be ignited within, calling forth commitment, dedication, and sacrifice. The concept of giving his all never registered and certainly did not apply to him. His wise mother saw a troubling outlook on life taking root. She first asked some questions about discouragement, preoccupations, and inner insecurities. None of those hindrances were there.

She said, "Son, you have a decision to make. In life, we must dread the state of limited commitment. Your approach to this sport seems like a waste of time. You think about it: either get all the way in, or get all the way out." Wise words from a wise mother.

The Lord Jesus gave his all for us and communicates a gracious, free invitation. In him is eternal life. He was and is "all the way in" for us! Are we all the way in for him? Christ declares the same need for all-out-commitment in those who want to follow him.

> Then one said to Him, "Lord, are there few who are saved?"

Our Savior did not give a direct answer to this question, for he came to guide men's consciences, not gratify people's curiosity. In his answer, he implies, "Don't ask 'How many will be saved?' You should ask, 'Shall I be one of them?' or 'What shall I do? What will become of me?'"

Our Lord says,

> Strive to enter through the narrow gate, for many, I say to you, will seek to enter and will not be able. (Luke 13:23–24)

What was their fatal and eternal flaw? He contrasts "seek" with "strive." Some would only "seek," which requires a smidgeon of concern and effort. Such people will add Christ to their lives. Maybe they will include church attendance or Bible reading. Jesus has always had more fans than followers. Other people had a heart to "strive" for something precious and desperately needed. These come with repentance and faith in Christ, whom they must have. There is an attraction in the Person of Christ for them. He is precious, beyond price. They must have him!

Listen afresh to Christ's statements concerning the doorway to being his genuine disciple:

> Whoever does not bear his cross and come after me cannot be my disciple. (Luke 14:27)

> So likewise, whoever of you does not forsake all that he has cannot be my disciple. (Luke 14:33)

Christ must be the supreme focus of devotion, loyalty, and attachment. He comes with massive supplies of mercy, love, forgivenesses, and affectionate embraces. For who? For those who see their enormous need for him as the only Savior of sinners. As Henry Drummond wisely said, "Don't touch Christianity unless you mean business. I promise you a miserable existence if you do." Christ tells his would-be disciples, "Get all the way in, or get all the way out." These are gracious words of the Savior telling them to face ultimate reality radically. Christ is warning, "Don't dabble with following me. If you are desperate, you won't contemplate the pros and cons of being my disciple." These are words of love and care.

Do we love the Lord with all our hearts, all our souls, and all our might? Do we long to? What greater question can we ask ourselves? God commands this. If we do, the following chapters on arguments in prayer will make perfect sense. The prayers are in perfect alignment with seeking God's kingdom and righteousness foremost. Though we have to think and meditate on their application to our lives, there is great value in studying the arguments in the entreaties presented. The pleadings mentioned in the following chapters are in perfect harmony with our Lord's instruction on prayer. They align with longings for our Father's "will to be done on earth as it is in heaven."

However, if we give Christ and Christianity a slice of our lives or if we make them a mere addition, there will lack a captivating interest. If we have a mindset of "allowing God" to be acknowledged yet setting limits on his demands or setting boundaries on what he can expect of us, these prayers may seem ridiculous, disconnected from our reality, and simply too much of a bother. Then the danger is having the marks of a dabbler in Christianity.

Questions to ask ourselves are these: Do I see this life as temporary and a gracious opportunity to prepare for eternity? Is my heart bent toward God being honored and glorified as much as possible in my life? Even though I fall short—miserably short—yet this is true of me. Like the needle in the compass springs back to north, so my heart comes back to this. If this is you, the following prayers and arguments will create interest in your soul. They will tap into a longing for whole-souled devotion to the one who loved you and gave his all for you.

If this describes you, simply take little steps in following these examples. Simply use arguments in prayer: "O God, you said you would do this for me. I so desire to experience your activity in my life. You said you shall put no one who calls upon you to shame. I know you will not make me an exception."

Now, to provide practical benefit and guidance in this skill of pleading, in the next several chapters, we will consider three significant areas to use in our approach to God. Remember, these are scriptural arguments other saints have used.

The first will concern pleadings focused on God himself.

The second will concentrate on pleadings for ourselves.

The third will focus on pleadings for ourselves drawn from others.

True prayer is rooted in the promises and covenants of God, in his past achievements, in his ability to do immeasurably more than all we ask or imagine.

—Bob Cotton

9

Pleadings which Relate to God (Part 1)

That which God abundantly makes the subject of his promises, God's people should abundantly make the subject of their prayers.

—Jonathan Edwards

The mightier any is in the Word, the more mighty he will be in prayer.

—William Gurnall

The aroma of freshly baked bread, hot out of the oven, with butter melting into its warmth creates an instant craving in me. I want to devour, I confess, too much. For most of my life, my wife and daughters baked the most delicious breads. I loved it.

Why bring this up? To illustrate a precious activity of the Holy Spirit. He brings the attractive aroma of God's presence into the soul, hungering and thirsting for God results. It makes the believer exclaim,

> Oh, taste and see that the Lord is good;
> blessed [or happy] is the man who trusts in him!
> (Psalm 34:8)

David expresses this another way:

> As the deer longs with pantings for the water
> brooks, so pants my soul for you, O God. My soul
> thirsts for God, for the living God. When shall I
> come and appear before God? (Psalm 42:1–2)

How does this relate to prayer and pleading? God reveals his name and character to his people. The Spirit presents this as pleasing, fitting, and appealing as the perfect solution to their need or longing. This attracts them with humble praise to a confiding rest in who he is. They come to trust his reliable character. God's people find rest, safety, delight, and comfort in God's name, character, and promises. They sense security and assurance of being cared for by his glorious competence. Their soul has come to their true home.

> Sing out the honor of His name; make his
> praise glorious. (Psalm 66:2)

The honor of his name is foundational for our comfort. It is also the basis of legitimate pleading.

We will look at this in the present chapter and take up two more in the following chapter.

The Great Honor of His Name

Our glorious God delights to thrill our souls with displays of his glory, power, and great faithfulness to all who put their trust in him.

> Who is like you, O Lord, among the gods?
> Who is like you, glorious in holiness, fearful in
> praises, doing wonders? (Exodus 15:11)

> O Lord, our Lord, how excellent is your
> name in all the earth, who have set your glory
> above the heavens! (Psalm 8:1)

The child of God embraces the Lord's own commitment to honor his name. God is jealous for the glory of his name and reputation. We are to be jealous for this as well. This becomes a foundational basis for our prayers and pleadings. You can see the comfort and security David possessed in this:

> I have gone astray like a lost sheep; seek
> your servant, for I do not forget your command-
> ments. (Psalm 119:176)

We can identify with this condition, I'm sure. David declares the Lord's faithfulness: "He restores my soul; he leads me in the paths of righteousness." Why? What is God's motivation to do so?

> For his name's sake. (Psalm 23:3)

Why is God so faithful and David so confident? God will prove himself to be all of what he said he would be! He will defend the honor of his name through being reliable in his mercy, faithfulness, and goodness. The LORD is a Shepherd to his people. He will not allow his name to be dishonored, which would happen if he failed in his promises. You can take this to the throne of grace.

Let's look at some examples of pleading with God from this vantage point.

1. The example of Moses

We looked at this passage earlier. Notice the free flow of Moses's soul:

> God declares to Moses, "Now therefore, let me alone, so my wrath may burn hot against them and I may consume them. And I will make of you a great nation." Then Moses pleaded with the LORD his God, and said: "LORD, why does your wrath burn hot against your people whom you have brought out of the land of Egypt with great power and with a mighty hand? Why should the Egyptians speak, and say, he brought them out to harm them, to kill them in the mountains, and to consume them from the face of the earth? Turn from your fierce wrath, and relent from this harm to your people. Remember Abraham, Isaac, and Israel, your servants, to whom you swore by your own self, and said to them, I will multiply your descendants as the stars of heaven; and all this land I have spoken of I give to your descendants, and they shall inherit it forever." So the LORD relented from the harm which he said he would do to his people. (Exodus 32:10–14)

It was as if Moses was pleading, reasoning, and saying, "LORD, what about your glorious name? How will your grace, your wisdom, your faithfulness, and your long-suffering appear if you do this? How can your people see these qualities if you deny my request? LORD, will this not be a great disparagement to your glory in the eyes of your enemies if you do this to your people? LORD, you forbid us to lay a stumbling block before the blind, and will you lay such an occasion of offense and stumbling in the way of blind foreigners?"

Moses was thinking and reasoning biblically. This is an amazing passage. It is as if Moses's devotion was stronger than God's devotion to the honor of his name! Now we know this is not true. However, God is showing a wonderful quality in Moses. This is part of what made Moses the meekest man on earth—by God's own evaluation and testimony! Moses was actually in harmony with the way God thinks and reasons.

Great is the power of prayer. It is able, in a manner of speaking drawn from this passage, to transform a paralyzed hand of unwillingness to bless and a determination to destroy into a hand of omnipotence to do good! (Think of the two parables—Luke 11, the indifferent neighbor, and 18, the unjust judge.) Prayer, with holy pleading for the honor of his glorious name, can turn a hand of righteous indignation into a hand of gentle guidance and provision.

It is important to clarify something here. God's relenting or turning was a change of his workings, not his will. We can learn from this—whatever our circumstances are, no matter how sad and hopeless they seem, we must plead with God! We must learn to use holy arguments in our praying, which focus on the honor of his glorious name: "Lord, what glory will it be to your name if you do not come with support, strength, and the supply of grace? It will move me or tempt me to question your promises. How will that honor you? I am trusting the very words you gave me to trust. Support me. Help me wait for you. But, O Lord, how long?"

Men, can you seek the help of the Lord this way to be enabled to lead your families with God's wisdom, grace, and tender faithfulness? Dear sisters, can you seek the grace of Christ in devoting yourselves to the high calling of motherhood and all that accompanies such critically necessary work? Oh, young people, can you seek the Lord in this way as you consider your entire future with all its unknowns? What about you, under-shepherds of Christ's flocks? Can you bring the great dishonor of God's name both in society and in the professing church of our day into your pleadings before the Lord? "O Lord, for the great honor of your name, revive your work!

Humble proud man within and without the church. Move in your churches to create more humble cravings for the sweet character of the Beatitudes! Make us such a people."

Our God never takes his hands off the reigns of providential rule. We are to be assured of this fact:

> All things work together for good to those
> who love God and are the called according to his
> purpose. (Romans 8:28–29)

So whatever we face, get our eyes off the present issue and problem. Look at your Father as first cause. Know that this is part of what we need to conform us into the likeness of Christ. This is the trying of your faith to purify it, manifest it, and mature it. Then meditate on the promises and words of Scripture as they relate to your situation. Draw out how to honor, adore, view, and believe God within your circumstances.

What is it to glorify God? To glorify God is to draw attention to the perfections of God: his wisdom, power, goodness, faithfulness, reliability, etc., in the specifics of your situation. Look at how Joseph summarizes many years of life. He is referring to his life and the lives of his brothers.

> But as for you, you meant evil against me;
> but God meant it for good, in order to bring it
> about as it is this day, to save many people alive.
> (Genesis 50:20)

Think of what he included in that brief word *it!* Every moment God was working. Did Joseph always see it? No. However, Joseph came back to this continually to set his soul, thoughts, and emotions right. We are to do the same.

C. H. Spurgeon wisely said, "It is not a brave thing to trust God: for true believers, it is a simple matter of sweet necessity." If we make prayer secondary, we make God secondary.

Every believer will declare, when looking back over their lives from heaven's untainted view, "the will of God, in every facet of my life, is truly good, acceptable, and perfect" (Romans 12:1–2). He shaped every intricate piece of the puzzle of my life to perfection. Every thread in the tapestry of who I am as a redeemed soul was flawless in design. To God alone be glory, praise, and honor. His wisdom and power are now set on display.

God focuses his great attributes upon you every second of your existence. There is no interruption. Whatever you are facing, bring the purposes of God the Father, God the Son, and God the Holy Spirit into the middle of it all. View God's enveloping care as part of the equation. Start with the large goals of the Almighty, then work your way down to the intricate details of your life, knowing it is all part of the divine plan. What are God's goals? What are his concerns?

> God moves in a mysterious way his wonders to
> perform;
> He plants His footsteps in the sea and rides upon
> the storm.
> Ye fearful saints, fresh courage take; the clouds ye
> so much dread
> Are big with mercy and shall break in blessings
> on your head.
> Judge not the Lord by feeble sense, but trust him
> for His grace;
> Behind a frowning providence he hides a smiling
> face.
> His purposes will ripen fast, unfolding every
> hour;
> The bud may have a bitter taste, but sweet will
> be the flow'r.
> Blind unbelief is sure to err and scan His work
> in vain;
> God is his own interpreter, and he will make it
> plain.
> (William Cowper)

So often we get into troubled emotions because we are believing in the Lord God almost Almighty! The greater your struggles are, get your eye of faith upon a larger God. He will give you peace. Paul tells us, "Be strong in the Lord and in the power of his might." Dread biblical amnesia, doubt, and carnal reasoning. Why? They will overcome us by the strength of the difficulties and the power of unbelief. See that for what it is. Proverbs 19:3 tells us,

> The foolishness of a man twists his way, and
> his heart frets against the Lord.

Rather, be like Abraham—"strong in faith, giving glory to God." Seek the Lord that he will honor his name in the events you pass through. Ask him to bring your whole life into alignment with what honors him. God draws near to such a soul.

2. The example of Ezekiel and the light it sheds on the prayer of Moses

Notice Ezekiel's confirmation of this legitimate point of argument in our pleading. Ezekiel is communicating the way God thinks and reasons.

Remember, our thoughts and ways are not God's thoughts and ways by nature. This will not change completely until we are with him in heaven. Here we must meditate on his Word so we may conform to his thoughts and ways.

Ezekiel quotes God recounting the event when Moses was pleading with him in Exodus:

> But they rebelled against me and would not obey me. They did not all cast away the abominations which were before their eyes, nor did they forsake the idols of Egypt. Then I said, "I will pour out my fury on them and fulfill my anger against them in the midst of the land of Egypt." But I acted for my name's sake, so it would not be

> profaned before the Gentiles among whom they
> were, in whose sight I had made myself known
> to them, to bring them out of the land of Egypt.
> (Ezekiel 20:8–9)

> Nevertheless I withdrew my hand and acted
> for my name's sake, so it would not be profaned
> in the sight of the gentiles, in whose sight I had
> brought them out. (v. 22)

Ezekiel does not mention Moses. What this passage tells us is what God told Moses he would do and what Moses pleaded for God to do was, all along, the intention of God. God ordained to show the danger rebellious Israel stood in. He also sets on display the open humble boldness of Moses in the Exodus account. Moses was pleading what God had deeply imbedded in his purposes all along! Moses was tapping into the values, motives, and beliefs of the Almighty. When Moses prayed, he was in full alignment with God's concern for the honor of his name. Do you see the power of such an alignment of heart, value, and motive in our own thinking and praying? It is our wisdom to do the same as Moses.

Let us seek to be truly wise. Think as God thinks, reason as God reasons, value maturity and becoming full-grown children of God! What will further the honor of his name in my situation? How is his glory working in these days of trouble? What attributes of God need to be displayed here in my life? It is the wisdom of saints to study God's ends and purposes more than their own and immerse all self-focus and self-concern in his glory, in his purposes. This way of living is what he has redeemed us for.

> Or do you not know that your body is the
> temple of the Holy Spirit who is in you, whom
> you have from God, and you are not your own?
> For you were bought at a price; therefore glorify
> God in your body and in your spirit, which are
> God's. (1 Corinthians 6:19–20)

Do you think you will ever go wrong thinking this way? No, this is scriptural and eternal sanity in a world gone mad in its alienation from God. Dread the state of becoming a practical atheist. Despise and refuse to be a practical agnostic. Lose sight of God, and the gravitational pull of our remaining sin will plunge us into this pit of despair. I know it to be so, for I have visited that pit; but I bless the Lord, who drew me up out of that horrible pit, planted my feet upon the rock, and put a new song in my heart. I firmly believe the humble will hear of this with gladness of heart (Psalm 40).

3. The example of Asaph, a Levite that King David assigned as worship leader in the tabernacle choir

We find this same way of pleading:

> Help us, O God of our salvation, for the
> glory of your name. (Psalm 79:9–10)

This is a powerful argument! God will do much for his own glory. It is essentially a matter of infinite concern to him:

> And deliver us, and provide atonement
> for our sins, for your name's sake! Why should
> the nations say, "Where is their God?" Render
> to them the reproach with which they have
> reproached you, O Lord.

They needed God's help, but they rooted the basis of their argument why he should involve himself and invest his divine energies to be their actual help—in the honor of his own name! Where God's name and glory are involved, these matters are of substantial weight, and we ought not to be ashamed or afraid to plead them before the Lord. There are many things of this nature in God's Word. If the Lord should deny his people, he would deny himself! God will not do such a thing. Yet God would have his people take up the matter in prayer with holy reasoning and earnest pleading.

God promised to do incredible things for the nation of Israel. However, he tells them they must ask for them to be done!

> Thus says the Lord God, "I will yet for this be inquired of by the house of Israel, to do it for them." (Ezekiel 36:37)

What might we be missing?

> You have not because you ask not. (James 4:2)

Well then, if we asked more often, what would we see of God's responsiveness? Are we too passive in the churches? Are we too passive in our own prayers?

These are examples to help pastors pray for their churches, the assemblies of Christ's people. Read the prayers of Paul for the saints. You will find the priorities of Christ's heart in them. This consumed the heart and mind of Paul, the honor of the name of Christ. He was the apostle of the heart set free. His longings centered on the people of God coming into greater acquaintance with Christ, greater maturity in Christ. This is the only course to exalt and glorify the Lord of glory and exalt his glorious name.

4. The example of Samuel

This is a recurring note of concern in the godly as they are before the LORD in times of holy pleading. We see it as Samuel speaks and then prays for the sinning people of Israel. They wanted a king like the other nations had. God specifically stated this was wrong. God was their king. Samuel reminded them:

> You said to me, "No, but a king shall reign over us," when the LORD your God was your king. (1 Samuel 12:12)

Samuel anointed Saul to be their king on this occasion because they demanded it.

Then Samuel, wanting to impress them with the wickedness of their requests and actions, asked God to do something for this purpose.

> So Samuel called to the Lord, and the Lord sent thunder and rain that day; and all the people greatly feared the Lord and Samuel. (1 Samuel 12:18)

This deeply pressed upon them the sense of their great wickedness.

> All the people said to Samuel, "Pray for your servants to the Lord your God, that we may not die; for we have added to all our sins the evil of asking a king for ourselves." (v. 19)

Observe carefully what Samuel tells the people:

> Then Samuel said to the people, "Do not fear." As if Samuel says, "Be sober but do not despair, don't cast away your confidence in God's commitment: they who go down into this pit of despair, faithlessness, and drawing back from the Lord cannot hope for God's interventions." (1 Samuel 12:20–22)

It is a way of taking away the Almighty to limit his boundless mercy and strength; despair is a high point of practical atheism. Perhaps we have all been there, but remember, even in such a place, Christ moves toward you! No matter how much you have blown it.

> There is no one like the God of Jeshurun, who rides the heavens to help you, and in his

excellency on the clouds. The eternal God is your refuge, and underneath are the everlasting arms. (Deuteronomy 33:26–27)

Samuel continues:

You have done all this wickedness; yet do not turn aside from following the LORD [as the devil, the old man slayer, would have you to do, tempting you first to presume and sin, and then to despair because you did sin], but serve the LORD with all your heart. And do not turn aside; for then you would go after empty things which cannot profit or deliver, for they are nothing. For the LORD will not forsake his people.

Why? "For his great name's sake."
Samuel charges the people:

Don't let your fear, despair, unbelief, and even your sense of deserved rejection by God to begin to rule your thoughts and actions. Whatever the devil and your own misgiving hearts may suggest to the contrary!

Don't measure God's dealings with you according to your thoughts unregulated by Scripture.

Don't reduce God to the inclinations of your ways of impatience.

Don't create a god after your imaginations!

Don't think God is going to deal with you the way you have dealt with him or even others.

Micah declares,

There is no God like our God! Who is a God like you, pardoning iniquity and passing over the transgression of the remnant of his heritage?

> He does not retain his anger forever, because he
> delights in mercy. He will again have compassion
> on us, and will subdue our iniquities. You will
> cast all our sins into the depths of the sea. You
> will give truth to Jacob and mercy to Abraham,
> which you have sworn to our fathers from days of
> old. (Micah 7:18–20)

You can see that Samuel had the same view of God as Micah did! It is the same view of God presented from Genesis to Revelation. Who is a God pardoning sins of all sorts and sizes? *Why?* Why does he pardon and delight in mercy? What is the great motive for God to not forsake us? Samuel answers this question:

> For his great name's sake, because it has
> pleased the LORD to make you his people.

He chose you for his love; and he still loves you for his choice. Go to him, therefore, again and again, and he will receive you. We should well wear two paths in our lives—the pathway to the cross of Christ and the pathway to the throne of grace for his help in time of need. Remember, it is a mercy seat, not a merit seat we approach.

Catherine was a great help to Martin Luther. Overwhelmed by anxious thoughts and fear-fostering concerns, he sat with a heavy brow and a despairing countenance in his study. Catherine came into the room dressed in black. He asked, "Catherine, did someone die?" She said, "Yes! From the looks of it, God did!"

5. The example of David

> For you are my rock and my fortress; there-
> fore, for your name's sake, lead me and guide me.
> (Psalm 31:3)

> Revive me, O Lord, for your name's sake.
> (Psalm 143:11)

Can you pray this way? Can you enter the heart and words of David?

> Revive me, O Lord, for I am no better than a walking dead and dull person. I feel so lifeless. O bring my soul out of trouble, dullness, lifelessness! I can bring my soul into trouble, but only you can bring it out. Would you do this for your name's sake? My only hope is in you and the greatness of your name, in which you have made me to trust: O LORD, do not let me down. I know I have let you down, but I have made your word and promise my hope. You are my hope, not myself.

This is not rocket science, nor is this complicated. It is straightforward and quite simple. Remember, in so many struggles and difficulties we experience in life, there are no easy answers, just simple ones. Ask the Lord for help to ask him for help.

> Glory in his holy name: let the heart of them rejoice that seek the Lord. Seek the Lord, and his strength: seek his face evermore. (Psalm 105:3–4)

Notice seek his strength and then seek his face.

The truth of our hearts is often told right here. Is the concern for the name of the LORD really and truly upon our hearts? Is this concern a value and motive in our lives?

> As for you, my son Solomon, know the God of your father, and serve him with a loyal heart and with a willing mind; for the Lord searches all hearts and understands all the intent of the thoughts. If you seek him, he will be found by you. (1 Chronicles 28:9)

Now connect this with another passage:

> For the eyes of the Lord run to and fro throughout the whole earth, to show himself strong on behalf of those whose heart is loyal to him. (2 Chronicles 16:9)

This has not stopped; it is still true today!

The heart we are describing is the heart the LORD is looking for. What will God do for the person who has such a humble pursuit and outlook? He will rejoice in such a one with love. Oh yes! But much more: "to show himself strong on behalf of those" with such a heart. Paul knew this. Consider his prayer for the saints in Ephesians 3:14–19. Notice also the confidence he has of God's responsiveness to such a people:

> Now to Him who is able to do exceedingly abundantly above all that we ask or think, according to the power that works in us, to Him be glory in the church by Christ Jesus to all generations, forever and ever. Amen. (Ephesians 3:20–21)

This becomes another expression of our sincerity and self-denial when we plead this way—not so much for ourselves but for the Lord himself and his glorious name and cause. We need his guidance, reviving, protection, encouragement, provision. Many other needs are to be pleaded. What is the chiefest concern in our hearts? "Do this for your name's sake."

His cause in the redeemed community is to be pleaded by his people.

> O LORD, though our iniquities testify against us, do it for your name's sake; for our backslidings are many, we have sinned against you. O the hope of Israel, his savior in time of trouble, why should you be like a stranger in the

land, and like a traveler who turns aside to tarry for a night? Why should you be like a man astonished, like a mighty one who cannot save? Yet you, O Lord, are in our midst, and we are called by your name; do not leave us! (Jeremiah 14:7–9)

We acknowledge, O Lord, our wickedness and the iniquity of our fathers, for we have sinned against you. Do not abhor us, for your name's sake; do not disgrace the throne of your glory. Remember, do not break your covenant with us. (vv. 20–21)

Some of the seven churches in Revelation 2–3 should have prayed like this.

It was this kind of pleading which brought in the restoration of Israel in the days of Ezra and Nehemiah.

It was the fruit of imploring and pleading with God which brought about wonders in the days of Esther, Mordecai, and defeating the treacherous wicked Haman.

It was this kind of pleading which put into the heart of Cyrus, king of Persia, to build Jerusalem. This kind of pleading made King Artaxerxes give Nehemiah everything he needed to build the walls of Jerusalem! None of these acts took place apart from the pleading of the people of God.

Do you want to see God change the hearts of leaders? Do you crave God to destroy the forces of darkness in this place? Are there cravings for Christ's presence doing mighty things in the assemblies of his people? These things will not take place without the people of God pleading! Is it a concern that heaven's record book may declare,

He did not do many mighty works there because of their unbelief? There were no people who would stir themselves up to lay hold of their God to do these wonderful things. (Matthew 13:58; Mark 6:6; 16:14)

Let us all take these truths to heart. Better yet, take them to our prayer closets. Take them to our pulpits.

In the next chapter, we will take up two other foundations for arguments to bring to God:

- "A concern for the glory of God is the ultimate motive for Christian living."
- "We should give God the same place in our hearts that he holds in the universe."

This is the proper business of the whole life, in which men should daily exercise themselves, to consider the infinite goodness, justice, power and wisdom of God, in this magnificent theater of God.

—John Calvin

10

Pleadings which Relate
to God (Part 2)

God loves us; not because we are loveable but because he is love;
not because he needs to receive but because he delights to give.

—C. S. Lewis

Moving from the honor of his name, we come to two other foundational truths which form the basis for pleading with God to be at work in our lives. These motivate us to look for God's response to our prayers. Each person in the holy Trinity is engaged as uniquely devoted to every believer. Eternal love and mercy invades the life, interrupts the course of human existence, and omnipotent (all-powerful) determination brings a dead soul to life. Then God loves his child as if he were the only child to love. Yet God loves all his people this way. Only an immense, immeasurable God could love like this.

God designs the eternal plan of redemption to give himself to us and take us to himself. We are family. In all this, as recorded in the Bible, God made promises to the believer and to the redeemed community.

> For what great nation is there that has
> God so near to it, as the Lord our God is to

134

us, for whatever reason we may call upon him?
(Deuteronomy 4:7)

Relate this truth to this passage:

> But you are a chosen generation, a royal
> priesthood, a holy nation, his own special people,
> that you may proclaim the praises of him who
> called you out of darkness into his marvelous
> light; who once were not a people but are now
> the people of God, who had not obtained mercy
> but now have obtained mercy. (1 Peter 2:9–10)

A special people—not because of who we are but because of
who and what God is in relationship with us. God tenderly determines to put his loving-kindness, mercy, grace, and hope in us. We
confess with Jacob; we are not worthy of the least of God's mercies
nor of all the truth he has revealed to us.

Let's look at the precious and special relationship we have with
God. Our purpose is to draw out foundational truths which become
the basis for our pleading with God. Here is the second:

The Relationship He Has with Us

*1. The holy Trinity, our one true God, binds himself to us for
all eternity. God has, in the covenant of grace, undertaken to
be our Savior! His covenant is his oath-sworn promise to us.*

> God smothers repenting sinners in forgiv-
> ing and redemptive love. (Al Martin)

Look again at Asaph's entreaty in Psalm 79:9:

> Help us, O God of our salvation, for the
> glory of your name; and deliver us, and provide
> atonement for our sins, for your name's sake!

The psalmist was pleading, "O God, you are called the God of our salvation. We, by your grace, do own you to be so: therefore, show that you are truly the God of our salvation by owning us and saving us! Show us, prove it to us, and make us to know beyond a doubt that this is true and not an empty title. Lord, what could be more suitable to a God of salvation than to save your people from their present plight? How can that name and title of yours be more glorified, exalted and magnified and sealed to your people's hearts than in your delivering your people? Here is a time for you to act. Our eyes and hearts are upon you alone."

What would happen in our prayer closets if we prayed this way? Better yet, what would happen in our churches if we prayed this way? In times of perplexity, bewilderment, or confusion over what is happening in your life, would it not be healthy to pray this way and seek the Lord's guiding, protecting, and providing hand?

This is pleading, which takes the relationship God has with his people—seriously—and reasons it out with the LORD in holy arguments. This kind of reasoning God delights in when he hears and sees it in his people! Isaiah 63:16 says,

> Doubtless you are our Father, though Abraham was ignorant of us, and Israel does not acknowledge us. You, O LORD, are our Father; our Redeemer from everlasting is your name.

This is as if they said, "O Lord, we have no other helper or father but you. To whom shall children seek relief and help from? From whom should they expect a speedy and timely hand of securing comfort but from their father? O LORD, we resolve to own no other for our Father but you, and can a father stand afar off from his needy children when it is in his power to relieve them and help them? How could any father stand motionless and silent when his child cries to him for help? Surely you will not behave less than a good earthly father would!"

Can you pray, "Doubtless, you are my Father, O LORD. I want to know you more intimately and confide in you more fully. Please, by your Spirit's witness and work in my soul, make me to know this.

Give help to me in my struggles. Take away my doubts, and support me in my life's responsibilities."

Does this seem too bold? Only to doubt, insecurity, and dreaded unbelief! No, the book of Hebrews commands us: "Let us come boldly before the throne of grace." We are to have a humble boldness and a contrite confidence in approaching our tenderhearted Father. It is the work of the Holy Spirit to put such reasoning into our hearts.

> And because you are sons, God has sent
> forth the Spirit of his Son into your hearts, crying
> out, "Abba, Father!" (Galatians 4:6)

This is to be characteristic of the assemblies of his people, for we are the household of God, the "called out" from this world to be his sons and daughters, the house and family of God in Jesus Christ, our elder Brother!

Does it appeal to your heart? This kind of confident belief in the words of God is what delights his heart. Can the words of your God motivate you to take him at his word? I wonder if we tend to study the Bible and learn and store up knowledge but all too passively. We are to act upon what we learn and study. The hymn asks this question: "What more can he say than to you he has said?" I hope this type of praying is becoming clear and attractive to you. May its aroma infiltrate our souls and create a hunger for it. What changes would we see in our lives if we prayed this way? What workings would we see in the churches if the people of God became more earnestly engaged in seeking their God and his responsiveness in their midst? May we reverently make God know we believe in what he says.

2. From this relationship he enters with us, God's mercy revealed in the Bible and in our lives is to create greater faith in him as merciful.

We find a further aspect of the relationship between God and his people in this: God presents his mercy to us. There is a purpose for this—to raise our faith in him. God does not mock us by calling upon us to trust in him and his offered mercies! However, we are to see "the suitableness" of the mercies we ask from God. His mercies are the very thing—the perfect thing—we need.

What do I mean? They are suitable for God to give and suitable for us to receive. Hear another prayer and entreaty of Moses:

> And now, I pray, let the power of my LORD be great, just as you have spoken, saying, "The LORD is long-suffering and abundant in mercy, forgiving iniquity and transgression; but he by no means clears the guilty, visiting the iniquity of the fathers on the children to the third and fourth generation." Pardon the iniquity of this people, I pray, according to the greatness of your mercy, just as you have forgiven this people, from Egypt even until now. (Numbers 14:17–19)

It is as though Moses prayed, "It is fitting for a sinning people to get pardon from their God as they repent. It is very suitable for a sin-pardoning God to give the pardon of their sins when they humbly seek that pardon from him! This is the only foundation upon which we look for the application of the pardon promised to us." It is as though they prayed, "The blood of the sacrifice is hope of atonement, for we look to the coming of the ultimate sacrifice. They put their trust in the ultimate provision of God, which cast the shadow back through Old Testament sacrifices—the blood shedding of Messiah, who will bear the iniquities of the whole redeemed host."

> If you, LORD, should mark iniquities, O Lord, who could stand? But there is forgiveness with you, that you may be feared (reverently worshipped). (Psalm 130:3–4)

> As if David argued, "I must not scruple about this, as though you are so strict with a poor, desolate, tempted and torn soul, grieved

and repentant, as to mark their sins with a vengeance and to condemn or confound such a one as I am. For there is forgiveness with you! With you there are forgivenesses (it is plural), many pardons I need for my many and multiplied sins; I must have hope and confidence in your multiplied mercies that you have in readiness and abundance. You cannot deny the benefit of your mercy and forgiveness to me in my case, for I cast myself upon you! O LORD, I will, and I do, conclude it as a granted case, there are forgivenesses with you. You do so that we might fear you, reverently worship you as a forgiven people who are driven to be lost in wonder, love, and praise. You, as you long for, we worship, adore, praise and love. Yet we cannot do this unless you grant mercy to us." (Adapted from John Owen's treatment on Psalm 130)

To be pleaders before the Lord, we must have such a good view of God, of his generous nature, that if he denies us mercy, he would disparage himself in our eyes, for we have better thoughts of him! This is faith in the testimony of God. This requires us to be solidly familiar with God's purpose in the covenant of grace.

What kills this praying? What destroys and strikes a death dagger into the heart of this biblical concern and pleading? Why do we hear so little pleading, entreaty, and soul sweat like this?

Slight views of our sins—this is the greatest culprit. When we get preoccupied with "man's delicate ego" and dread to make him feel guilty or bad about himself, we will diminish the hideous nature of sin. We think of sin but lightly. Low views of sin produce low views of Christ. Man's importance grows large, and God, in his holiness, grows manageable for man. However, a manageable god is not the Lord God Almighty found and revealed in the Scriptures.

Wise words from Joseph Alleine:

> Two sorts of peace are more to be dreaded than all the troubles in the world—peace with sin, and peace in sin.

Paul warns us of the deceitful nature of sin. Sin keeps us from knowing the true nature of sin. The prince of darkness loves to have it so. Every sin is God's would-be murderer. It works with subtlety and stealth, securing the conscience, dulling it, cauterizing it as it takes more ground. What is it driving at? The dethronement of God to make his professing people an offense to him, to bring them into a state where his glory departs from their midst. This is the doctrine of Balaam, Revelation 2:14. Our culture and religious climate tempts to make sin no big matter.

Ponder the words of this hymn by Thomas Kelly in 1804:

> Stricken, smitten, and afflicted see him dying on
> the tree!
> 'Tis the Christ by man rejected yes, my soul, 'tis
> he, 'tis he!
> 'Tis the long-expected Prophet David's son, yet
> David's Lord
> By his Son God now has spoken 'tis the true and
> faithful Word
> Tell me, ye who hear him groaning. Was there
> ever grief like his?
> Friends through fear his cause disowning foes
> insulting his distress
> Many hands were raised to wound him, none
> would interpose to save
> But the deepest stroke that pierced him was the
> stroke that Justice gave
> Ye who think of sin but lightly nor suppose the
> evil great

Here may view its nature rightly, here its guilt
    may estimate
Mark, the sacrifice appointed, see who bears the
    awful load
'Tis the Word, the Lord's Anointed, Son of Man
    and Son of God
Here we have a firm foundation, here the refuge
    of the lost
Christ, the Rock of our salvation, his the name of
    which we boast
Lamb of God, for sinners wounded sacrifice to
    cancel guilt!
None shall ever be confounded who on him their
    hope have built.

In the last chapter, we saw that the honor of his name is grounds for arguments in prayer and pleading. We just considered the relationship he has entered with us as fuel for prayer and pleading. Now we look at the final scriptural truth concerning God, which is to be used in prayer:

The Little Gain God Would Get in Denying Our Requests

I cried out to you, O Lord; and to the Lord I made supplication: "What profit is there in my blood, when I go down to the pit? Will the dust praise you? Will it declare your truth? Hear, O Lord, and have mercy on me; Lord, be my helper! You have turned for me my mourning into dancing; you have put off my sackcloth and clothed me with gladness, to the end that my glory may sing praise to you and not be silent. O Lord my God, I will give thanks to you forever." (Psalm 30:8–12)

Simply, Lord, if you don't answer me, what praise will you receive? How can it bring you delight and joy if my heart is heavy and in need of supporting grace?

> Return, O Lord, deliver me! Oh, save me for your mercies' sake! For in death there is no remembrance of you; in the grave, who will give you thanks? (Psalm 6:4–5)

It is like saying, "Lord, you delight when people come to you with thankful hearts. Move in our lives and in our church in ways that give life and vigor to our thanksgiving. Make us exuberant in our praises because of how you answer our prayers and supplication."

There is powerful pleading with God when the saints acknowledge what God could justly and righteously do. God could justly condemn and put us all to confusion of face. He would be just when he speaks and clear should he judge (Psalm 51). He could cast us out and cast us off. There are plenty of arguments for this in our sins. He may, with righteousness, continue to frown upon us and withdraw his Spirit's influences within us. He could, with an unblemished record, deny our request for just causes. *But what would he gain by this?*

Oh, but if he would grant us our requests for mercy and help, he would gain many praises! That's right, and that's the point stressed in our pleading! What good will it do the Lord to see his people oppressed by the enemy of their souls? Satan, the evil one, that old serpent, hates God and us. He is the eternally ugly Accuser of the brethren. Our very sins despise God. They are enmity against him and work with force in us to alienate us from God.

But what delight would it be to God to see us sighing and fainting under the sad, defiling nature of these forces? We need a real deliverer! We need a Savior! A help in time of need. God alone is such a Savior. He tells us so. We are to draw near to him and open our soul's longings for his powerful workings, leading us to victory over sin, Satan, and the world's forces or efforts to oppress us.

God is most pleased and delighted when his people plead this way. The testimony of Scripture is that this is often successful in obtaining desired mercies. It is the forerunner of the kind and powerful workings of God.

There are a multitude of other arguments to be studied to fuel pleading with God. God gave the Scriptures, so we might do this. Many arguments, besides these, form the basis of our pleading. We have seen three forms of pleas that relate to God: the honor of his name; the relationship he has with us; and the little gain he would get in denying our requests. Brethren, use these to get good things for your heart and home. Use them for the assemblies of Christ and the furtherance of his kingdom on the earth.

Perhaps these will motivate you to read your Bibles afresh and draw many other truths that will fuel your own prayer connection with your God. I hope these passages and truths encourage you to put the full weight of your soul's trust and confidence in the promises given with divine authority specifically to you as a believing soul. Take those promises and let them press you into the embrace of your Father, who will throw a robe upon you, place a ring on your finger, and take you into his arms and celebrate with you.

Jacob was a rascal in so many ways. He was an opportunist with his brother, deceived his father, and followed the carnal counsel of his mother, who trusted more in her manipulations and deceptions than the word and promise of God. However, when Jacob was right with God and brought to a healthy believing frame of soul, this is what he said:

> I am not worthy of the least of all the mercies and of all the truth which you have shown your servant. (Genesis 32:10)

We do not deserve to be valued and treated in the way of God's kindness and mercy. Thank God he does not deal with us or view us in the light of what we deserve. He deals with us as a great and tender

Savior. He deals with us in the light of what Christ, our Redeemer, deserves.

Before we leave these two chapters relating to God, you may ask, "Well, how do I connect this to my personal life? How do I use this information?" Hopefully, what we cover in the following chapters will help show how to use these truths in the battle of life.

The only thing that a man can contribute to his own redemption is the sin from which he needs to be redeemed.

—William Temple

There can be no thought of "cheap" forgiveness when we remember that our redemption cost God the life of his beloved Son.

—Geoffrey B. Wilson

11

The Disciples Were Slow to See
Reality—Christ Lived in It

Ignorance of Scripture is ignorance of Christ.

—Jerome

I am starting this chapter with an appeal to you as a reader. Please be patient. These five chapters are actually a unit. They form a bridge from what we have covered to what lies ahead. I hope to give helpful guidance in applying the basics of pleading to our day-to-day experiences. If we are to advance, mature, and develop in effectual and fervent prayer, we must face reality. Facing reality is a great incentive to earnest prayer. Facing reality is the theme of these five chapters.

In a graveyard in England, a tombstone reads,

> OUT OF SHADOWS AND IMAGININGS, INTO
> THE TRUTH.

A fitting description for this fallen world. In this life, we do not see things perfectly or fully as they are. We see through a tiny keyhole, and our perception is always partial, skewed, and clouded by our interpretations. This contributes to Solomon's expression,

"Vanity, vanity, all is vanity." Edmund Burke said, "What shadows we are, and what shadows we pursue!"

Take notice of two general realities which never change throughout our life in this world.

There are positive realities which strengthen faith, ignite courage, and instill a Christ-centered confidence. When Elisha's assistant walked outside in the early morning, he saw the Syrian army surrounding them. Panic, fear, and gripping alarm took hold of him.

"Master, what shall we do?"

Elisha calmly and tenderly said, "Do not fear, for those who are with us are more than those who are with them."

> Elisha prayed, and said, "Lord, I pray, open his eyes that he may see." Then the Lord opened the eyes of the young man, and he saw. And behold, the mountain was full of horses and chariots of fire all around Elisha. (2 Kings 6:17)

What a great lesson in faith. Living by sight produced fear. Living by faith produced calm confidence. What this man saw was there all along.

> As the mountains surround Jerusalem, so the Lord surrounds his people from this time forth and forever. (Psalm 125:2)

As followers of Christ, we are to engage in a faith-strengthening study of God's Word. We are to bring our souls to seek the Lord with all our hearts. We take the promises of God, the committed character of our Lord, confident of his abiding presence, and have confidence in his provision, protection, and leadership. Paul tells us "we walk by faith, not by sight" (2 Corinthians 5:7). This approach to life and service is what our Lord was teaching and nurturing in the disciples. Genuine engagement in prayer is the only course to enter such a life.

There are sobering realities as well. When Paul wrote of spiritual warfare and described the forces of darkness, it is a sobering reality.

The activity of Satan, demons, all the forces of darkness have been robust in the spiritual realm since the garden of Eden. Paul expects the saints to recognize this:

> Lest Satan should take advantage of us; for
> we are not ignorant of his devices. (2 Corinthians
> 2:11)

Would Paul describe our generation as "not ignorant of his devices"?

We are not to be outmaneuvered or robbed by Satan's designs, schemes, and strategies. He is the relentless adversary of our souls. The evil one and demonic forces are unrelenting and seek to work without detection. They have two primary targets: the unconverted and the church of the Lord Jesus. Embracing this reality would move us to pray without ceasing and pray with strong cries to our mighty Savior when needful. With Micah, we can declare,

> Do not rejoice over me, my enemy; when I
> fall, I will arise; when I sit in darkness, the Lord
> will be a light to me. (Micah 7:8)

The words of David will come to life as we engage with our reality:

> The Lord is my strength and my shield; my
> heart trusted in him, and I am helped; therefore,
> my heart greatly rejoices, and with my song I will
> praise him. (Psalm 28:7)

We now turn to the event in the life of Christ, which becomes the focus of five chapters.

The writers recorded it in the first three Gospels. Toward the end of his ministry, Christ focused on essential lessons the disciples needed to learn before he went back to his Father. We find it in Matthew 17:14–21; Mark 9:14–28; and Luke 9:37–42. Within the month, they would crucify our Lord. It would help if you paused and read the passages. Then we will look at the event from the vantage point of Christ's heart and soul.

There are five realities woven into this narrative. Our Lord saw these in their raw and vivid existence, open and naked before his soul's gaze. These are realities we live with. They are part of the narrative of our lives. It would be our wisdom and safety to recognize them. If we did, it would have a powerful influence in the way we engaged our faith and prayed. It would give birth to effectual praying. Let's take them up one at a time.

1. The reality of religious externalism and delusion

The Lord Jesus had been on the Mount of Transfiguration with Peter, James, and John (Mark 9:2–13). On that mountain, Moses and Elijah met with Christ. In a moment, the three disciples witnessed the transfigured Christ. He emanated the splendor of God from his person. It was the brilliance of his second coming glory. Though destined for humiliation on the cross, he permitted a glimpse of his victorious sin-and-death-conquering grandeur. His brilliant whiteness is his Deity and the glory of his eternal Person. Here is the Victor who will destroy the works of the devil. Here is the Ultimate Judge: all humanity will appear before him. The Father's voice declares approval of his beloved Son with the exhortation: "listen to him." The disciples saw One who is "the radiance of God's glory and the exact expression of His nature" (Hebrews 1:3). Here is the ultimate reality on display.

We do not see displays of his glory as these three disciples, yet we are to grow in beholding the glory of his person in our inward perceptions of Christ.

> And we all, with unveiled face, beholding the glory of the Lord, are being transformed into the same image from one degree of glory to another. For this comes from the Lord who is the Spirit. (2 Corinthians 3:18)

148

Our growth in grace is growth in internal perceptions of the majesty, power, and glory of Christ. In a moment, our Lord sovereignly transfigured himself, showing his true glory and perfection. Our perfect transfiguration culminates in heaven.

In stark contrast to this mountaintop experience, a chaotic scene confronts our Lord (Mark 9:14–29). He comes upon a scene of human misery, disciples' failure, and spiritual warfare. At the base of the mountain, nine feeble disciples could not cast a demon out of a man's tormented son. This is the only record of a public failure of the disciples. It is important to remember this: Their failure shook this dad with a gripping despair and threat of no hope for his son, not even in Christ. Our Lord saw it all deep within his soul. The crowd viewed Christ as a sensational wonder worker and came running.

> And when he came to the disciples, he saw a great multitude around them, and scribes disputing with them. Immediately, when they saw him, all the people were greatly amazed, and running to him, greeted him. And he asked the scribes, "What are you discussing with them?" (Mark 9:14–16)

The scribes were disputing heatedly with the disciples. Their failure to cast the demon out, along with the Master's absence, gave them opportunity and fuel to argue Christ's claims as false. This was the continual focus of the scribes and Pharisees during the ministry of our Lord.

The first reality to notice, for us, is that we live in a world filled with false religions and human-centered worldviews. The forces of darkness filled the philosophies of the world with lies and partial truths. Even the "Christian religion" has varying degrees of purity, commitment to Scripture, and an acquaintance with spiritual "life." There are false Christianities, mixtures of Christian truth and Pagan beliefs. The popular "progressive Christianity" of our day denies the essentials of the Christian faith. They view the Bible as inadequate to handle the issues of our time. The actual issue is not that complex.

The scribes represented a religious world hostile to what God cherished, prized, and looked for. What is that? "Heart religion," or "true religion" of the redeemed soul. In their religious blindness, they were enemies to God's work in the human heart! They were determined to justify themselves and find fault with Christ throughout his ministry. Why? Our Lord saw through their false presentations, their religious facades. Christ revealed the corrupt motives they lived by. They were worldlings in heart and soul.

The scribes and Pharisees were quite content with their religious system of externalism. When the Lord Jesus began teaching and preaching, he exposed the hollowness of the world they created. Outwardly white and clean, they were so impressive. Inwardly dead, heartless, and alienated from God, they were abhorrent to God. Devotion to ego, pride, and arrogance describes their internal values. They had to be in control of their world. Their self-absorption blinded them to reality as God saw it. They had high self-esteem and treated others as beneath them—the pedestal pit view of worldly values. Others were in the pit of unacceptability, and they were on the pedestal of earning God's smile of approval. They actually believed themselves to be "God's favorites." They would tell God this and belittle others at the same time.

> The Pharisee stood and prayed thus with himself, "God, I thank you I am not like other men—extortioners, unjust, adulterers, or even as this tax collector." (Luke 18:11)

They defined others by their failures, sins, or status. They had high opinions of themselves, contrary to God's commands.

Our Lord will expose them as not being the "seed of the woman," the true children of God as in Genesis 3:15. Though they were the physical seed of Abraham according to the flesh, they were not Abraham's spiritual seed according to the faith of Abraham. Therefore, they were the seed of the serpent! Think of that. The devil's children, not God's (John 8:37–59).

The scribes and Pharisees lived in their own world of self-admiration, busy schedules, routine engagements, and commitments to religious devotion but were far from reality. They had an antagonistic relationship with reality and lived in religious delusions. Heart religion was not on their radar. This is a dangerous condition anywhere it shows up, and God is not an idle spectator.

This was the same problem in Israel's history. Through Isaiah, God quotes the people in words, describing what they were saying "in reality." They were told to trust in the LORD and bring their hearts to him, not to Egypt, to deliver from Assyria. When people put their trust in the wrong place, they are called "a refuge of lies" (Isaiah 28:16–19). God says,

> So will I choose their delusions and bring
> their fears on them; because when I called, no
> one answered. When I spoke, they did not hear;
> but they did evil before my eyes and chose that in
> which I do not delight. (Isaiah 64:4)

What did God not delight in? What evil did they do? They engaged in heartless religious activity—drawing near to God with the mouth while the heart is far from him.

> Inasmuch as these people draw near with
> their mouths and honor me with their lips, but
> have removed their hearts far from me, and their
> fear toward me is taught by the commandment
> of men. (Isaiah 29:13)

Isaiah addressed this throughout his ministry. This has always been a problem. It is a widespread problem in our day.

Our Lord Jesus represented God's great delight and attraction to heart religion, the true religion of the soul. James describes this as "pure and undefiled" religion (James 1:26–27). The Gospel actually pulverizes human pride and brings souls to value the mercy and kindness of God to the unworthy.

> For thus says the High and Lofty One who inhabits eternity, whose name is Holy: "I dwell in the high and holy place, with him who has a contrite and humble spirit, to revive the spirit of the humble, and to revive the heart of the contrite ones." (Isaiah 57:15)

Notice the Lord's use of the word *with*. He wants to be with such people. The true and living God tells us who attracts his attention and affection, drawing him to be "with" them.

> On this one will I look: on him who is poor and of a contrite spirit, and who trembles at my word. (Isaiah 66:2)

We live in a society that views feelings of unworthiness as contrary to one's true awesomeness. God views honesty with your unworthiness as the doorway to exuberant praise for his great mercies, kindness, and tender love. It is the pathway to rich "with-ness" with God. The one who is forgiven much loves much. The one who is forgiven little loves little. Honestly, is there anyone who could ever claim to be forgiven "little"? Only a self-deceived person would think like that. Our Lord asked this of a Pharisee, a person who would not face reality. If this Pharisee saw things as they really were, he would be on the ground before the Lord Jesus just like the woman (Luke 7:47).

This is not just Old Testament stuff. James (1:26–27) was telling the saints,

> When God's mercies enter the soul and the magnitude of his immense kindness and love swallow up our sinful ugliness, nailing it to the cross, we become merciful to others. Blessed are the merciful for they have received the great

mercy of the Almighty. This mercy and kindness will extend to the most easily overlooked and needy ones of society. The widows and orphans in their afflictions.

Read what Paul tells us:

> We are the circumcision, who worship God in the Spirit, rejoice in Christ Jesus, and have no confidence in the flesh. (Philippians 3:2–3)

"Circumcision" speaks of the new birth where God takes out our natural heart of stone and implants a pulsating heart of life and respond-ability to truth. Reality shifts our placement of confidence in ourselves to our triune God brought to our heart and soul through Christ.

> God resists the proud, but gives grace to the humble. Therefore humble yourselves under the mighty hand of God, that He may exalt you in due time.

Paul was honest and real in his self-evaluation. Listen to him facing the reality of his remaining sin in Romans 7:24:

> Oh wretched man that I am! Who will deliver me from this body of death?

This is the doorway that leads him to proclaim,

> I thank God—through Jesus Christ our Lord! (7:25)

This is the same teaching of Christ in the first four Beatitudes:

> Blessed are the poor in spirit, for theirs is the kingdom of heaven. Blessed are those who

mourn, for they shall be comforted. Blessed are the meek, for they shall inherit the earth. Blessed are those who hunger and thirst for righteousness, for they shall be filled. (Matthew 5:3–6)

Before Jesus mentions what his genuine disciples and authentic people do, he describes what they are as new creations through the Spirit's birth. His people embrace realities concerning themselves the vast majority avoid:

My soul is poverty stricken. Nothing can I bring to merit or use to bargain with God. My sins, oh Lord, I grieve over and lay before you. My Lord, save me from myself, may my whole being yield to your will. I hunger and thirst for you to cover all my sins with your perfect acceptability. Oh, Lord Jesus, may Almighty God see me in you!

These represent foundational views of ourselves, which help us depend on Christ and draw from him. These are the truths that make prayer real and, at times, move us to plead with God. The scribes knew nothing of this precious perspective. The fact is, they despised it. Our world will despise this as well. All too much of professing Christianity despises it. The scribes were heartless and expressed great hatred to the author of heart religion, which is the only saving religion and only doorway to union and communion with the Godhead.

This is how Christ thinks, and this is what he taught and what he prizes.

Not everyone who says to me, "Lord, Lord," shall enter the kingdom of heaven, but he who does the will of my Father in heaven. Many will say to me in that day, "Lord, Lord, have we not prophesied in your name, cast out demons in your name, and done many wonders in your name?" And then I will declare to them, "I never knew you; depart from me, you who practice lawlessness!" (Matthew 7:21–23)

In the day of judgment, surprise will seize these people! Confusion, shock, and astonishment will grip them. "Impressed" was not in the response of Christ concerning all they did. Disconnected from reality, they busied themselves with religious activity. They impressed themselves with their accomplishments. Why are they rejected and cast away? Obviously, they saw things differently than Christ did. Their motives and values differed from his, and they never pursued honest, openhearted consultation with him. They did not learn to see through his eyes. Christ lived in the reality of it all. They would not face these realities; rather, a "refuge of lies" was their comfort.

They did not possess two essential items:

1. They knew nothing of personal love and growing acquaintance with Christ. "Knowing" the Savior had no beginning and certainly did not expand or deepen through the years. They did not have an actual knowledge of him or themselves, which brought a reciprocal joy and delight into a "real" relationship. In reality, there was no "relationship" with Christ. There was no "beholding the glory of the Lord" which had a transforming effect on their persons. There was no deepening experience from perceiving greater riches and desirable qualities in him. They had a relationship with their own thoughts. Peter tells us to "make our calling and election sure." They had no heart for this. Paul did not include these in his benediction: "Grace be with all those who love our Lord Jesus Christ in sincerity."

2. They did not have a life of loving devotion to Christ's teachings. The Bible was not the "living Word" which brought soul nourishment to them. They did not have a loving determination to receive imparted strength to do as

he taught. Clinging to him in prayer was absent. They were not part of his family:

My mother and my brethren are these which hear the word of God, and do it. (Luke 8:21)

Blessed are those who hear the word of God and keep it! (Luke 11:28)

They lived presumptuously. Union and abiding in Christ were absent. There was no fear of God with a dread of being a law to themselves or following the dictates of their own hearts. All they had was busy religious activity built upon the sands of presumption and following what they perceived as "best for them."

So in the Gospel narrative, our Lord came upon the scene and saw the scheming scribes and their effort to undermine his compassionate mission. They represented false religion and its attack upon true religion. They were taking advantage of his absence and the failure of the disciples. These nine were still raw and young in their faith. Upon their failure, the scribes argued Christ's claims were false. They were mocking the disciples. These malicious cavaliers, seeking to confound them, insinuated doubts and discredited their Lord and teacher before the crowds, puzzling them with arguments and questions skillfully calculated to unhinge their loyalty to Christ and generate suspicion toward his teachings and claims. They did this before the crowds, hoping to gain back followers. The disciples were no match for the scribes; they needed intervention. The Lord Jesus saw all this for what it was. Their Master appears with his skill to confound the religious hypocrites and shut their mouths by his wondrous teachings and deeds.

What false religion ultimately attacks—and still does—is a tender conscience intent on embracing the word, commands, and example of Christ. This counterfeit Christianity, this Christless

Christianity, is Christian in name only. It is nominal and described this way:

> You have a name that you are alive, but you
> are dead. (Revelation 3:1)

What dreadful words! Who would ever disregard such a pronouncement? Only a people hiding from reality.

Here is a reality we face. When a person becomes alive to God, pursues a passionate love for Christ, he will take up his cross and follow Christ with commitment and zeal. Heartless Christianity views these as extreme, overzealous, excessive, legalistic, and disturbers of the "business as usual" crowd. This is part of the reality we live in. This group will not embrace pleading with God. Religious externalism and false teachings abound in our day.

Three things fight against us: (1) The world and I include worldly Christianity, (2) the flesh, or our remaining and sometimes raging sin, and (3) the devil. They all exercise a gravitational pull away from such a heart engagement. They work a subtle influence toward contentment with external involvement in the things of God. If we are honest and being real, we all face and experience this temptation. The true believer cannot live in it for long.

What is the only avenue of escape? How do we "deal" with this reality?

1. Plead with God that you would not ignore or deny it. Face the danger of it together with your God.
2. Ask the Lord Jesus and the Holy Spirit to nurture a commitment to passionate love for each person of the Godhead. Ask that your heart would love and crave an accurate knowledge of his word. Study, memorize, and meditate in the Scriptures, relying on the illuminating aid of the Holy Spirit. The entrance of God's word gives light. Pray the Spirit would bless you with the quickening light and warmth of the Word of God (Psalm 119:105, 130, 154, 159).

3. As long as you are in this world, study these four subjects: the Word of God, the person of Christ, your own heart, and the devices of Satan.

4. In all your praying, really pray. Plead with God for "true religion of the heart" described in your Bible. With disciplined, affectionate, and principled living (which we get only by prayer), have your soul set on a life of companionship with your loving heavenly Father, your ever-blessed Lord Jesus, and your tender, sweet, and engaged Helper, the Holy Spirit. They will love and keep you. Crave their attention and companionship. They will give it. Christ promised they will (John 14:21, 23, 26–27; 15:9–19). Go to them and plead, "Oh, my gracious God, I so desire and long for this communion with you to be my reality."

5. Prize the Lord Jesus, embrace him as your lifelong companion. Do not let him go until he blesses you with such a personal "knowing" him and communing with him. Tell him this is the "reality" you crave. Christ promised this to you. Desire these great blessings greatly. Put energy in pursuing them. Ask him to take you by the hand of your soul (which is faith extended to him) and bring you into the enjoyment. Prize them for the treasure they are.

Johann Franck wrote these words, which were translated by Catherine Winkworth. I hope they describe your view of Christ.

> Jesus, priceless treasure, fount of purest pleasure,
>   truest friend to me:
> Ah, how long in anguish shall my spirit languish,
>   yearning, Lord, for thee?
> Thine I am, O spotless Lamb! I will suffer naught
>   to hide thee, naught I ask beside thee.
> In thine arms I rest me; foes who would molest
>   me cannot reach me here.
> Though the earth be shaking, ev'ry heart be
>   quaking, Jesus calms my fear.

> Lightings flash and thunders crash; yet, though
> sin and hell assail me, Jesus will not fail me.

Jude wrote to genuine believers. His concern was the infiltration of false professors into the assembly of Christ. He warned them of those who depart from genuine saving faith in the Gospel, revealing they did not weave it into the fabric of their souls. He teaches the "doctrine of creeps." "These having crept in unawares." "False" professors in the church are an actual concern. They knew nothing of heart work. This is his counsel to the saints.

> But you, beloved, building yourselves up on
> your most holy faith, praying in the Holy Spirit,
> keep yourselves in the love of God, looking for
> the mercy of our Lord Jesus Christ unto eternal
> life. (Jude 20–21)

Notice Jude's stress on "heart work." Keep your feet firmly planted on the truth and solid teaching of the Scriptures. Know what they teach, and stay in what they teach. Pray in the Spirit's strength and wisdom: he moves our hearts and directs our petitions. Abide in and breathe the atmosphere of the love of God. Set your affections on Christ above until he takes you to himself. Live in these realities. All this are heart-work and heart-focused concerns.

This is "keeping your heart with all diligence." Know that out of your core, your inner man, flow the issues of life (Proverbs 4:23). Keep watch on the treasure that fills your heart.

> A good man out of the good treasure of his
> heart brings forth good things, and an evil man
> out of the evil treasure brings forth evil things.
> (Matthew 12:35)

There will always be a free flow of thought in us. We cannot stop thinking. This free flow reflects what is important or most on our heart. We can command and regulate our thoughts. Paul says,

"Think on these things" (Philippians 4:8). The treasure of our hearts is to be soul-nourishing streams of thought—things like scriptural truths which speak to our inward and outward life, spiritual graces which give evidence of growth in grace and likeness to Christ; genuine experiences of communion with God, your openheartedness with him, and God's responsiveness through the years of your journey; the comforts brought to your soul by the Spirit's work—these make up healthy heart treasure. As you fill your heart with treasure, you will also lay up treasure in heaven.

Some of your greatest enemies will be the competitors for your time and heart treasure. What are some of these? Our smart phones, TVs, media, movies, programs, sports, entertainments, poor use of time, and we can go on and on. Be brave: make your own list. Bring them to Christ. Ask the Holy Spirit to enliven your conscience. Tell them that the relationship you have with them is more important than these temporary time consumers. Let these things be useful tools, but prize Christ more.

Do not feel you have to understand all the counterfeit teachings in order to avoid them. When training bank employees, they train them to detect genuine currency. Know the real so well you will detect counterfeit currency when it appears. It is the same with us and the Christian life. Embrace the invitation and privilege of knowing truth. Your Lord Jesus says to you,

I am the way, the truth, and the life. (John 14:6)

Build an intimate acquaintance with him, and you possess the right way, the solid absolute truth, and genuine life which is eternal.

If people say, "Look for your truth within. Tap into your divine, and be true to yourself," the Holy Spirit will aid you to see such words as an invitation to look away from Christ and his Word. These are modern-day delusions and become a refuge of lies. It is encouragement to follow your own deceptive inclinations. God says people who do that will ultimately regret it (Isaiah

50:10–11). The Bible is full of warning not to follow the dictates of your heart.

> He who trusts in his own heart is a fool, but whoever walks wisely will be delivered. (Proverbs 28:26)

> For whoever desires to save his life will lose it, but whoever loses his life for my sake will save it. (Luke 9:24)

> There is a way that seems right to a man, but its end is the way of death. (Proverbs 16:25)

Be true to God. He will be true to you. That's reality!

> Those who honor me I will honor. (1 Samuel 2:30)

All this comes back to the development of a real and open prayer life—prayer, which has the value of the relationship at its core. Focus on genuine connection with God through our Lord Jesus Christ. "Draw near to him, and he will draw near to you." This is his promise. Let him know your longing for his nearness. There is no other way. He will not let you down.

Here is the heart of heart religion. What motivates a soul to draw near to Christ? Peter tells us, "Therefore, to you who believe, he is precious" (1 Peter 2:7). We delight in being with one who is precious to us. We love him! Why? "Because he first loved us" (1 John 4:19). Yes, but that is just the beginning. More and more, we find attraction to Christ through discovery of the wealth and beauty of his person, and our love deepens. His preciousness expands. The Spirit generates our faith in Christ, engendered by love! "Faith working through love" (Galatians 5:6). Paul concludes his letter to the Ephesians with this sweet word:

> Grace be with all those who love our Lord Jesus Christ in sincerity. (Ephesians 6:24)

The Holy Spirit brings the very heart and thought of Christ to us with personal relevance. He makes our inner person conscious of the eternal Son, Christ Jesus our Lord, drawing near with comforting assurance of his personal care, protection, and guidance.

> Fear not, for I am with you; be not dismayed, for I am your God. I will strengthen you, yes, I will help you, and I will uphold you with my righteous right hand. (Isaiah 41:10)

> Fear not, I have redeemed you; I have called you by your name; you are mine. When you pass through the waters, I will be with you; and through the rivers, they shall not overflow you. When you walk through the fire, you shall not be burned, nor shall the flame scorch you. For I am the Lord your God, the Holy One of Israel, your Savior. (Isaiah 43:1–3)

I love his use of "with." Don't you? Notice the number of times our glorious God and Savior says "you." Here is the LORD, our Shepherd, giving personal expression of his whole being committed to "you" as his beloved sheep. The Lord knows each one of his sheep by name! He knows your name. Doesn't this cause your heart to expand with humble affection for him who "loved you and gave himself for you?" (Galatians 2:20).

Now, in the next chapters, we will look at demonic activity, human misery, the compassions of our Savior, and the disciples' failure. Our Lord is a skilled physician of souls and a gracious guide for the afflicted as well as the failing.

> How bravely does he speak! How he presumes to drive down all before him! But so soon as Faithful talks of heart-work, like the moon that's past the full, into the wane he goes: and so will all but he that heart-work knows. (John Bunyan's

Pilgrim's Progress, Christian's summary of the discourse he and Faithful had with Talkative)

*"If you will not worship God seven days a week, you
do not worship him on one day a week."
"The whole course of life is upset by failure
to put God where he belongs."
What comes into our mind when we think about
God is the most important thing about us.*

—A. W. Tozer

12

If God Be for Us, Who Can Be Against Us?

Satan promises the best, but pays with the worst; he promises honor and pays with disgrace; he promises pleasure and pays with pain; he promises profit and pays with loss; he promises life and pays with death.

—Thomas Brooks

We were visiting my uncle Robert in the mountains of Northern California. My brother and I were playing in the forest with three cousins. As a seven-year-old, all that registered was fun and play. We needed a rope. I ran into a shed. In the corner, on the dirt floor, I noticed a rope. As I reached down to grab it, I heard an alarming sound—a rattle! Yes, it was a rattlesnake, curled up and ready to strike.

The shock of danger shot through me, then the thrill of excitement. I yelled for the others, and they came running. "Stay away!" everyone yelled. One cousin told my uncle, and he came with his rifle. Uncle Robert put an end to the snake's life. With an axe, he removed its head and dangerous fangs. This was the excitement for the next hour. Then we went back to finding a rope and our mindless play.

164

Similarly, we get caught up with daily life and lose sight of dangers that lurk in the shadows. Our lives pick up a rhythm we call the Christian life. Without thought, we drift into routines of reading our Bibles, prayer, and church attendance which includes sermons, singing, and fellowship. Then we get on with our lives. We become quite good at it.

Along with this, we have our ever-present phones, computers, and TVs. We enjoy sports, projects, and other delights. Of course, we have work, responsibilities, and life demands. We have our positive assumptions about our spiritual health. Easily we slip into a blur of life, moving along its weekly path. Senseless, we become unaware of the insidious, wily, and treacherous influences within our world. There are "rattlesnakes" hidden in dark corners. Our innocent patterns camouflage the workings of the "world, the flesh, and the devil." Patterns, rhythms, and autopilot living, unconsciously adopted, perform a soothing, tranquilizing power over conscience. Whispers of "all is well" soothe the soul.

Subtle detractors, diluters, and even defilers of walking with God creep in undetected! Passion for Christ and his kingdom becomes placid, tepid, composed, mild, and assumed. Our praying gets done—kind of. We acknowledge the Savior, but the heart-melting sensibility of Christ drawing near is absent! We drift toward "cruise control" Christian living. Wily and subtle energy vampires drain the vigor of an engaged and intentional "walk with God." Imperceptibly, "sleep-walking with God" emerges, lulled into an unconscious detachment from spiritual warfare.

Unseen enemies cunning, scheming, and secretly using "innocent" things in life to work their menacing effect, Christian liberty becomes the catch-all for doing "our own thing"—especially those things on the edge. Subtly we become devoted to comfort, ease, happiness, entertainment, prosperity, needs, family, and success. We talk our Christianese. Choices for things just under the radar of conscience gain ground. The covert effect is to quiet conscience. Conscience slightly stirs, but the "still small voice of alarm" grows quieter. Enemies to our soul's well-being paves the pathway to ineffective Christian living. How? By what means? Sin's modest proposals. They gain and secure the ground of a compromised life.

We fail to distinguish between "wisdom that comes from above" and that which is "earthly, sensual, and demonic" (James 3:13–16). What are the indicators of the earthly, sensual, and demonic? "Bitter envy and self-seeking in our hearts." In contrast to a Christ-centered passion for life, we slowly descend to a life centered on what we want.

A poem by Alexander Pope (1688–1744) captures this subtle work exceptionally well. He uses an older word, *mien*, which means "demeanor, appearance, or the countenance."

> Vice is a monster of so frightful mien
> As to be hated needs but to be seen;
> Yet seen too oft, familiar with her face,
> We first endure, then pity, then embrace.

In this chapter, we see our Lord confronting an unseen non-physical demon. This demon had a powerful enslaving influence over a man's son. The cruel character of demons comes before us in a vivid, tortuous display. These foul fiends are ruthless and focused on causing all the pain and misery possible. They have no pity.

The last chapter focused on the reality of religious externalism and delusion. Such false religion, heartless shells of devotion, is one assault of demonic hatred for humanity. We move on to the second reality of Mark 9:14–21.

2. The reality of demonic conflict: the forces of darkness are real and vicious.

There is a kingdom of evil which stands in opposition to the kingdom of Christ. It is a kingdom of wickedness and darkness. This is reality. However, it is not a simple good vs. evil situation. The reality is a glorious and majestic God created heaven and earth, filled with goodness and every provision to satisfy and bring happiness. Sadly, through pride and a delusional independence from God, some angels rebelled and fell from their original place of glorious and holy purpose. One-third of the angelic host became apostate and bent on hellish purposes to defy God. This led to the fall of humanity into a state of spiritual death in sin. The human race now lives against God's benevolent rule. These foul fiends breathed their noxious breath of death in human souls made in the image of their enemy.

Notice these passages from Mark 9:17–21:

> Teacher, I brought you my son, who has a mute spirit. And wherever it seizes him, it throws him down; he foams at the mouth, gnashes his teeth, and becomes rigid. So I spoke to your disciples that they should cast it out, but they could not.

These harmful and self-destructive actions arose from the demon's merciless brutality. Obviously, they will inflict all the pain they can get away with—even to the point of taking a person's life.

> When [the demon] saw [Christ], immediately the spirit convulsed him, and he fell on the ground and wallowed, foaming at the mouth. So he asked his father, "How long has this been happening to him?" And he said, "From childhood. And often he has thrown him both into the fire and into the water to destroy him."

The nature and purpose of demons comes before us: destruction, mutilation, and cruel torture of defenseless children. This has been so throughout history. Demons promoted the sacrifice of children.

> They even sacrificed their sons and their daughters to demons, and shed innocent blood, the blood of their sons and daughters, whom they sacrificed to the idols of Canaan; and the land was polluted with blood. (Psalm 106:37–38)

It may tempt us to think this was in days long ago. Nothing of this nature could take place in our modern societies. Oh, that the Holy Spirit would grant us a needed and sobering reality check.

In our day, sons and daughters are being sacrificed to the demon idols of pleasure without accompanying responsibilities. Personal self-centeredness and meism require the removal of inconvenient obligations. If the pain and screams of the unborn happen in the womb's silence, it is easier on the conscience and conceals cruelty in dark places. This is the plight of over sixty million sons and daughters over the last fifty years in America alone. Worldwide, the number is horribly larger.

The increase in lawlessness worldwide is giving rise to a surge of demonic activity. Satanic strategies shock those who value human life. The dragon and his fallen angels cause wickedness and unthinkable cruelty in both powerful and criminal realms. The inconceivable horrors of human trafficking are real and happening at this very moment. This trafficking involves sons and daughters and is taking place all around us and throughout the world. They annually enslave two million children for sex, work, or organ harvesting. This abhorrent plight is a living hell for real people who see no way out. Evil forces create wicked business plans that trap others for use and financial gain.

In recent years, the modern madness of pseudo-science puts itself in the position of mini-gods, engaging in re-creation! Innocent children are being taught ideas they cannot understand or process. Especially is this true of real-life consequences which follow. In this context, children are being victimized and their childhood is being destroyed by gender transitioning. No one can change anyone's sex. God made them male and female. Pseudo-science will not change the DNA nor divinely created chromosomes formed in the womb after conception. Drug and surgical procedures leave mutilating scars on these children. Many, before their frontal lobe matures, the center for connecting the dots of life, are misguided in choices which radically alter the trajectory of their lives. Sterilization results, taking away their hopes of happiness. Evil forces are at work promoting demon involvement in this detestable madness.

Demons put wind in the sails of any ideology that promotes atheism, genocide, the dismantling of the natural family, or destruction of human life. I include Marxist socialism and communism as devices of the evil one. They need three absolutes to regulate society: 1) the removal of religion and belief in God; 2) elimination of private property, including private opinions; 3) the dismantling of the natural family. Marriage eradicated and parental roles set aside as the state is the owner and sole developer of future generations. The authorities of this world despise Christ and seek to cast off the authority of God. Psalm 2 is an international reality.

What do we do with all this? How are we to respond?

- Indifference is offensive to God. God gave Ezekiel a vision and command. Go through the city and place a mark on those who sigh and cry over the abominations. They are my genuine people. Everyone else will perish in their indifference. Ezekiel 9. David, as a man after God's own heart testifies: "Indignation has taken hold of me because of the wicked who forsake your law." (Psalm 119:53). The Psalmist describes another proper response in verse 136: "Rivers of water run down from my eyes, because men do not keep your law."

- Feelings of overwhelm, defeatism, or paralyzation is a form of practical atheism. Daniel Webster tells us: "All that is required for evil to triumph is for good people to do nothing." No, it is with us as it was with Joshua. "Have I not commanded you? Be strong and of good courage; do not be afraid, nor be dismayed, for the Lord your God is with you wherever you go." (Joshua 1:9) It is true that the whole world lies under the sway of the evil one. (1 John 5:19). That's reality. However, we are to embrace the promises of our great and triune God. "You are of God, little children, and have overcome them, because He who is in you is greater than he who is in the world." (1 John 4:4).

- Efforts to stop or change these horrible atrocities in our own strength is an offensive folly on our part. "Trust in the

LORD with all your heart and lean not to your own under-standing." Proverbs 3:5. We can repeat the foolishness of the Israelites going up against Ai with their presumptuous adequacy for the battle.

- Our greatest wisdom and safety is to draw near to our Lord Jesus. To cry out to him. For demons recognize him and cannot but obey his authority.

We see the demons' obvious recognition of our Lord, their ulti-mate and unavoidable judge. On another occasion, Christ cast out demons. They communicated with him:

> They cried out, saying, "What have we to do with you, Jesus, you Son of God? Have you come here to torment us before the time?" (Matthew 8:29)

They knew the one who stood before them though clothed in our humanity. Our Savior is the Lord God omnipotent who reigns and will judge all in the last day. Jeremiah identifies the eternal Son in these words:

> The Lord is the true God; he is the living God and the everlasting King. At his wrath the earth will tremble, and the nations will not be able to endure his indignation. (Jeremiah 10:10)

The authority of Christ is without dispute.

> He rebuked the unclean spirit, saying to it, "Deaf and dumb spirit, I command you, come out of him and enter him no more!" Then the spirit cried out, convulsed him greatly, and came out of him. And he became as one dead, so that many said, "He is dead." But Jesus took him by the hand and lifted him up, and he arose. (Mark 9:25–26)

Notice when Christ speaks, there is no alternative or escape. Though scorned and detested by them, they must obey his word. His authority is without question as King of kings and Lord of lords. Demons knew this. James tells us,

> Even the demons believe—and tremble! (James 2:19)

So what about Satan and demons? We must avoid extremes! We are not to approach this topic with undue curiosity, speculation, or superstition, nor are we to think it a nonreality. Satan and the demonic host would delight in either approach. Both are unhealthy and unbiblical.

Our Lord defeated Satan and all demonic forces. God's sovereign rule includes thwarting their designs and making all they do "work together for the good of God's people" (Romans 8:28–39). Our union with Christ secures and includes our victory over them. There is, however, a spiritual warfare we are involved in. There is no discharge from this war until the discharge from this life. The battlefield is primarily our thoughts.

> For though we walk in the flesh, we do not war according to the flesh. For the weapons of our warfare are not carnal [physical] but mighty in God for pulling down strongholds, casting down arguments and every high thing that exalts itself against the knowledge of God, bringing every thought into captivity to the obedience of Christ. (2 Corinthians 10:3–5)

Paul also tells us,

> Lest Satan should take advantage of us; for we are not ignorant of his devices. (2 Corinthians 1:11)

The term *devices* speaks of "mental strategies."

Christ tells us what he does to the kingdom of darkness, to the actual realm of Satan and demons.

Look at Mark 3:22–27. In this passage, Christ speaks a parable. They accused our Lord of casting out demons by the power of Satan! They used the name Beelzebub for Satan.

> So he called them to himself and said to them in parables: "How can Satan cast out Satan? If a kingdom is divided against itself, that kingdom cannot stand. And if a house is divided against itself, that house cannot stand. And if Satan has risen up against himself, and is divided, he cannot stand, but has an end. No one can enter a strong man's house and plunder his goods, unless he first binds the strong man. And then he will plunder his house."

What does he mean? Our Lord is proclaiming his incredible power over Satan and demons to save his people! Here is what our Lord is teaching. Satan is the strong man of his kingdom and the house of death. This is the kingdom of darkness enslaving the souls of fallen humanity. Satan's house is this fallen world, alienated from God. His goods, his plunder, are the souls of the human race, dead in trespasses and sins, imprisoned by the devil and held firmly in his diabolical chains. Satan, demons, devils, enemies of God have a death grip upon humanity.

What does our Lord do? He binds the evil one and robs him of precious souls! Christ plunders Satan's prison chambers of confinement for those given to our Savior to redeem. He loves them and comes for them. With authority, our Lord enters the very house of the devil, binds him, and renders him helpless. No power or authority can contest the Lord of glory. He throws out every demon standing in his way. Then Christ takes hold of his precious ones, once the bull's-eye of God's wrath, now to experience the bull's-eye of his eternal love, gathers them in his saving arms, and takes them to himself. Christ says to them, "I have loved you with an everlasting love. Therefore, the time has come to call you to myself. You are mine, and now you are to know I am yours. I have redeemed you with my blood and everlasting affection. We will be together for all eternity. We are family!"

What is the foundation for this victorious work? Christ himself is the Gospel! Through his death, burial, and resurrection, he triumphed over the devil.

> Inasmuch then as the children have partaken of flesh and blood, he himself likewise shared in the same, that through death he might destroy him who had the power of death, that is, the devil. (Hebrews 2:14)

As our Immanuel, the eternal Son entered humanity fully clothed with our flesh and blood. He entered our cursedness, taking that condition upon himself to deliver us. It took God with us in our plight to bring us out of danger and tuck us into the bosom of God! The Lord Jesus satisfied divine justice in his death on our behalf. Christ took our sins upon himself and paid the price. He clothes us with his righteousness and acceptability before God. The Father is well pleased with Christ and with us in Christ Jesus. The Father sent him—now the Father embraces us. Now the Gospel is the power of God to salvation to everyone who believes.

I love the way Hosea declares this as he quotes the Lord:

> You shall know no God but me; for there is no savior besides me. I will ransom them from the power of the grave; I will redeem them from death. "O Death, I will be your plagues! O Grave, I will be your destruction! Pity is hidden from my eyes." (Hosea 13:4b, 14)

Do you feel the intensity of our Lord Jesus? That demon afflicting the boy departed when the Son of God gave command! Saving, redeeming, delivering us was the laser focus of omnipotent, earth-shaking, death-gate-shattering power! When it comes to confronting his and our enemies, what language and terms are uttered!

> "Who can stand before his indignation?
> And who can endure the fierceness of his anger?
> His fury is poured out like fire, and the rocks
> are thrown down by him." Our Lord says to his
> enemies, "I will dig your grave, for you are vile."
> (Nahum 1:6, 14b)

The Lord Jesus is a jealous God for his people's safety.

Isaiah foretold this activity of the Lord Jesus. Christ quotes this passage at the beginning of his ministry because it referred to himself. This passage was living in the heart of our Savior in the face of the five realities we are addressing. It is very important you remember this.

> The Spirit of the Lord God is upon me,
> because the Lord has anointed me to preach good
> tidings to the poor; he has sent me to heal the
> brokenhearted, to proclaim liberty to the cap-
> tives, and the opening of the prison to those who
> are bound; to proclaim the acceptable year of the
> Lord, and the day of vengeance of our God; to
> comfort all who mourn, to console those who
> mourn in Zion, to give them beauty for ashes,
> the oil of joy for mourning, the garment of praise
> for the spirit of heaviness; that they may be called
> trees of righteousness, the planting of the Lord,
> that he may be glorified. (Isaiah 61:1–3)

Look at how Paul describes the ongoing work of God and Christ, saving souls from Satan's captivity.

> It is the God who commanded light to shine
> out of darkness, who has shone in our hearts to

give the light of the knowledge of the glory of
God in the face of Jesus Christ. (2 Corinthians
4:6)

Our Lord Jesus is victor.

God has delivered us from the power of
darkness and conveyed us into the kingdom of
the Son of His love. (Colossians 1:13)

Notice the word *conveyed*. He transplanted us into a whole new
place to live—from a perishing existence to the imperishable inheritance of God and joint heirs with Christ, our glorious and beloved
Elder Brother in the family of God.

Charles Wesley captured this with precious expressions in the
hymn "And Can It Be?"

Long my imprisoned spirit lay fast bound in sin
and nature's night;
Thine eye diffused a quickening ray, I woke, the
dungeon flamed with light;
My chains fell off, my heart was free, I rose, went
forth, and followed thee.

I must touch upon one more passage our Savior gave us. Our
Lord spoke of building his church in Matthew 16:18. We are talking
about his beloved bride! He tells us the "gates of Hades [death]
shall not prevail against it." The "gates" represent the imprisoning
power of death; spiritual death and enslavement cannot keep and
hold the church of the living God from being built. Physical death
cannot keep souls from arriving in the country of their appointed
citizenship.

You have come to Mount Zion and to the
city of the living God, the heavenly Jerusalem, to
an innumerable company of angels, to the gen-

eral assembly and church of the firstborn who are
registered in heaven, to God the Judge of all, to
the spirits of just men made perfect, to Jesus the
Mediator of the new covenant, and to the blood
of sprinkling. (Hebrews 12:22–24)

Note that we are "registered in heaven." Paul says our citizenship is in heaven, from which we also eagerly wait for the Savior,
the Lord Jesus Christ (Philippians 3:20). The believer triumphs over
death and Satan in Christ. Now "to live is Christ, and to die is gain"
(Philippians 1:21).

The gates of Hades will resist, fight, repel, and counterattack.
Our Lord says, "They shall not prevail. I will prevail and be the
Victor. I will break through the gates and take what is eternally mine.
I will assemble all who make up my bride."

In Scottish history, there were the "killing times." Horrible as
it was, religious externalism hated those who held greater loyalty to
a known Christ than to mere forms of religion authored by man.
Demonic instrumentality joins such hellish pursuits. They would
hunt down and kill those who would not comply. This is how the
people of Christ described it: "They did but chase us up to heaven."
For a believer, physical death is a funeral event for crosses, corruptions, remaining sin, sorrows, pain, and tears. It is entrance into eternal joy, to be forever with the Lord. Paul writes, "To depart and be
with Christ is far better."

These considerations should breathe boldness and confidence
in us. We are in the bosom of our Savior. We are called to spiritual
warfare. Their doom is sure. Christ Jesus defeated the foes of the
Almighty and our enemies as well.

The God of peace will crush Satan under
your feet shortly. The grace of our Lord Jesus
Christ be with you. (Romans 16:20)

Do you see how this should show up in your affectionate praise to your beloved God? The prayer of praise and thanksgiving should be unending, and it will be for all eternity!

> And they sang a new song, saying: "You are worthy to take the scroll, and to open its seals; for you were slain, and have redeemed us to God by your blood out of every tribe and tongue and people and nation, and have made us kings and priests to our God; and we shall reign on the earth." Then I looked, and I heard the voice of many angels around the throne, the living creatures, and the elders; and the number of them was ten thousand times ten thousand, and thousands of thousands, saying with a loud voice: "Worthy is the Lamb who was slain to receive power and riches and wisdom, and strength and honor and glory and blessing!" (Revelation 5:9–12)

> I heard, as it were, the voice of a great multitude, as the sound of many waters and as the sound of mighty thunderings, saying, "Alleluia! For the Lord God Omnipotent reigns!" (Revelation 19:6)

Our majestic Jesus rescued each individual in that glorious and vast host of redeemed souls. Each one he broke through the gates of Hades, taking them as brands for the burning, and made them trophies of his love and grace. What tender omnipotence! What earth-shaking authority and power—all so sweetly and gently applied to each one, precious in his sight, affectionately embraced in his heart, rescued by his kind-hearted might.

Christ would have us make demonic enemies part of our personal awareness. However, keep in your heart the victory you have in Jesus Christ.

Why keep these realities with us? Because Satan and demons hate the church.

Remember the words of the apostle Paul:

> God has not given us a spirit of fear, but of power and of love and of a sound mind. (2 Timothy 1:7)

You find your power in Christ.

> Be strong in the Lord and in the power of his might. Put on the whole armor of God that you may be able to stand against the wiles of the devil. For we do not wrestle against flesh and blood, but against principalities, against powers, against the rulers of the darkness of this age, against spiritual hosts of wickedness in the heavenly places. (Ephesians 6:10–13)

> Take the shield of faith with which you will be able to quench all the fiery darts of the wicked one. (v. 16)

Our wisdom is to stay close to Christ like the branch engrafted into the vine. Give yourself to love the Lord Jesus and, through him, your heavenly Father and blessed Holy Spirit. Love the brethren. Be sober-minded. How? Engraft the Word of God into your thinking.

Once again, we see something vitally important. For any of these truths to be real and effectual in us, we must handle and experience them in companionship with our God. Prayer is to be real, brethren. Prayer is to be the most vital part of the warfare.

> Praying always with all prayer and supplication in the Spirit, being watchful to this end with all perseverance and supplication for all the saints. (Ephesians 6:18)

"Each piece put on with prayer." No part of the Christian armor is to be handled on our own!

Prayer makes us companions with God in the use of each piece. Ultimately, Christ himself is the armor of the believer!

> Remembering without ceasing your work of faith, labor of love, and patience of hope in our Lord Jesus Christ in the sight of our God and Father. (1 Thessalonians 1:3)

> But let us who are of the day be sober, putting on the breastplate of faith and love, and as a helmet the hope of salvation. (1 Thessalonians 5:8)

David found the Lord to be true to him when he cried out to God.

> In the day when I cried out, you answered me, and made me bold with strength in my soul. (Psalm 138:3)

This has always been a most personal reality with the people of God.

> Blessed is the man whose strength is in you. (Psalm 84:5)

Do you see how vital prayer is? Do you clearly see there will be times in your life simple praying will not be sufficient? You, personally, must incorporate strong cries and earnest pleadings to obtain the strength of Christ in your soul. You and me—we are not sufficient of ourselves to fight this battle. Learn to cry to the Strong for strength. He will give it.

> The God of my strength, in whom I will trust; my shield and the horn of my salvation, my

stronghold and my refuge; my Savior, you save
me from violence. (2 Samuel 22:3)

The spiritual warfare we engage in includes something very precious. The reality of the Christian's armor is this: God, through Christ, gives himself to us. Read the way David expresses this in Psalm 18:

For by you I can run against a troop, by my
God I can leap over a wall. As for God, his way
is perfect; the word of the Lord is proven; he is a
shield to all who trust in Him. (vv. 29–30)

Not only do we get the sense David can't do anything without the companionship of God, we also see God and David are cowarriors! It is through the Lord's provision of himself that secures the victory. Brethren, nothing has changed! It is this way for us! We have a clearer knowledge of each person within the holy Trinity. However, this is only brought to experience through a growing, maturing prayer life—a life of intimacy with the Godhead.

Read David again:

It is God who arms me with strength, and
makes my way perfect. He makes my feet like the
feet of deer, and sets me on my high places. He
teaches my hands to make war, so that my arms
can bend a bow of bronze. (vv. 32–34)

You have also given me the shield of your
salvation; your right hand has held me up, your
gentleness has made me great. (v. 35)

All this talk of war, battles, fighting the enemy, yet when David turns to address the style of the LORD's investment of personal grace, enablement, and power into David, what does he highlight? The gentleness of omnipotence, the tender compassion of the Almighty to undertake for the weak and needy.

What are the dominate assaults of the evil one and demons? There are four major categories of temptations. Here are our points of vulnerability and where they will strike. I can only mention these briefly:

1. To draw you into sin

We know "the whole world lies under the sway of the evil one" (1 John 5:19).

> For all that is in the world—the lust of the flesh, the lust of the eyes, and the pride of life—is not of the Father but is of the world. (1 John 2:16)

Drawing, alluring, and fixating on the pleasure, joys, and benefits of flesh pleasing, exciting a thrill of covetous preoccupations "to have," stirring up discontentment, even murmurings, against your lot in life, defending ego, promoting one's superiority, measuring oneself with others' inferiorities, being impressed with oneself and wanting others to notice it—demonic forces, the devils, will put wind in these sails to push you along a path contrary to the life and person of Christ.

As Thomas Brooks states, "Satan presents the bait and hides the hook." The evil one is a skilled salesman. He will always promise more than sin can deliver. His promises are a mirage. He is a liar and a deceiver. Such deception is necessary because a rational person will not desire evil as evil. He or she needs to be convinced that it is good or beneficial in some way. Therefore, in every act of sin, people, by compliance with Satan, are said to deceive themselves.

> Each one is tempted when he is drawn away by his own desires and enticed. Then, when desire has conceived, it gives birth to sin; and sin, when it is full-grown, brings forth death. (James 1:14–15)

Satan loves to help a person paint his vices in virtue's colors. We disguise greed as good stewardship, pride as excellence or mere acknowledgment of good; excesses was just having a good time. A similar approach argues that it is harmless to enter a situation where temptation is likely. Finally, Satan may encourage intemperate excess in the enjoyment of lawful things, perhaps suggestions of the littleness of the thing, possibly the privacy of the matter—"no one will know"—even "well, just a little, and then I will stop." There are innumerable ways to deface the believer, thwart the Gospel testimony, and disgrace the name of Christ—which is what they drive at.

Here is what devils aim for: taking a person captive to do their will, not God's will. Paul writes to Timothy as a pastor:

> A servant of the Lord must not quarrel but be gentle to all, able to teach, patient, in humility correcting those who are in opposition, if God perhaps will grant them repentance, so that they may know the truth, and that they may come to their senses and escape the snare of the devil, having been taken captive by him to do his will. (2 Timothy 2:24–26)

The best help for people is the gentle, teaching, with patience and humility, truth of God's Word, addressing the error of thought or behavior but relying on God to do the work in the heart. We cannot change hearts. We can teach the ear, but Christ must teach and change the heart.

2. To divert you from your spiritual duties

Such as spiritual disciplines, participation in Christian community, service to others, obedience to God's commands, or any other Christian obligation or responsibility. If Satan succeeds in this, he removes our spiritual weapons and cuts off provision for our soul's health. If successful, this saves him the labor of his temptations. He robs God of honor, which these duties would have given. This way, the attack strikes at both the Christian and God himself.

Paul tells us what our heart set and mindset should be:

> Therefore, my beloved brethren, be stead-
> fast, immovable, always abounding in the work
> of the Lord, knowing that your labor is not in
> vain in the Lord. (1 Corinthians 15:58)

This is God's will for every child of God.

> We give thanks to God always for you all,
> making mention of you in our prayers, remem-
> bering without ceasing your work of faith, labor
> of love, and patience of hope in our Lord Jesus
> Christ in the sight of our God and Father. (1
> Thessalonians 1:2–3)

Let us remind one another that the forces of darkness move to make us act and live like "earth dwellers" not citizens of heaven!

Satan and his minions will present the way of the Lord as ardu-ous, sour, devoid of happiness, impractical, killjoy, and out of touch with reality. Our God declares through his experienced saints,

> Blessed [happy, the one's above all others on
> earth to be envied] is the man who walks not in
> the counsel of the ungodly, nor stands in the path
> of sinners, nor sits in the seat of the scornful; but
> his delight is in the law of the Lord, and in his
> law he meditates day and night. (Psalm 1:1–2)

3. To dilute the pure doctrine of the church

Error dilutes truth, promotes divisions, and impedes spiritual progress.

> Satan himself transforms himself into an
> angel of light. (2 Corinthians 11:14)

> Some will depart from the faith, giving heed
> to deceiving spirits and doctrines of demons.
> (1 Timothy 4:1)

> For the time will come when they will not
> endure sound doctrine, but according to their
> own desires, because they have itching ears, they
> will heap up for themselves teachers. (2 Timothy
> 4:3)

"Sound doctrine" is like sound health! Sound doctrine or sound teaching promotes spiritual health. The forces of darkness promote spiritual disease, plagues, sickness, and death! We are told some churches descend to be "a synagogue of Satan" (Revelation 2:9; 3:9).

Left to ourselves, we are no match for all the devices and strategies of the devil. We are not sufficient in ourselves.

> Do this, knowing the time, that now it is
> high time to awake out of sleep; for now, our sal-
> vation is nearer than when we first believed. The
> night is far spent, the day is at hand. Therefore,
> let us cast off the works of darkness, and let us
> put on the armor of light. Let us walk properly,
> as in the day, not in revelry and drunkenness, not
> in lewdness and lust, not in strife and envy. But
> put on the Lord Jesus Christ, and make no pro-
> vision for the flesh, to fulfill its lusts. (Romans
> 13:11–14)

> We should no longer be children, tossed
> to and fro and carried about with every wind of
> doctrine, by the trickery of men, in the cunning
> craftiness of deceitful plotting. (Ephesians 4:14)

> Contend earnestly for the faith which was
> once for all delivered to the saints. (Jude 3)

> Beloved, building yourselves up on your
> most holy faith, praying in the Holy Spirit. (Jude
> 20)

When Satan and the demonic host moved the church to cast off confessions of faith, sound teaching, and doctrine, it promoted joy in hell and celebrations in the kingdom of darkness.

4. To blur your ability to discern your spiritual state

Satan always contradicts God. Satan pronounces damnation where God pronounces grace and favor. Satan pronounces grace and favor where God condemns. Satan promotes boldness and carelessness to enter compromises and sin. Then he slays the soul with guilt. Satan moves in with thoughts and arguments of God's unwillingness to receive a repentant soul! We see him as the accuser of the brethren, doing this very work, in Zechariah 3:1–4. This is how malicious Satan and our gracious, merciful, and kind God deal with precious souls. Then he showed me Joshua, the high priest standing before the Angel of the Lord, and Satan, standing at his right hand to oppose him. And the Lord said to Satan, "The Lord rebuke you, Satan! The Lord who has chosen Jerusalem rebuke you! Is this not a brand plucked from the fire?" Now Joshua was clothed with filthy garments, and was standing before the Angel. Then He answered and spoke to those who stood before Him, saying, "Take away the filthy garments from him." And to him He said, "See, I have removed your iniquity from you, and I will clothe you with rich robes." Our beloved Lord Jesus is doing the same for each one of his people. 1 John 1:9, 2:1–2

Take each one of these before the throne of grace, and ask wisdom from your Father. Ask him to give skill and victory in each area. You will find him and his help if you seek him with the whole heart. Go to Christ as the Shepherd of your soul to watch over you and lead you out of danger. Remember, our Lord taught us to pray:

> Lead us not into temptation, but deliver us
> from the evil one. (Matthew 6:13)

> Call to me, and I will answer you, and show
> you great and mighty things, which you do not
> know. (Jeremiah 33:3)

> The Lord searches all hearts and under-
> stands all the intent of the thoughts. If you seek
> him, he will be found by you. (1 Chronicles 28:9)

Conclusion: Christ's words to Peter

> And the Lord said, "Simon, Simon! Indeed,
> Satan has asked for you, that he may sift you as
> wheat. But I have prayed for you, that your faith
> should not fail; and when you have returned to
> me, strengthen your brethren." (Luke 22:31–32)

Our Lord Jesus just washed the disciples' feet. What an embar-
rassing contrast to what takes place next. The disciples are arguing
who will be the greatest! How ugly and unbecoming is the worldly
hope of being the greatest. How unlike Christ, who took upon him
the form of a servant and humbled himself to the death of the cross!
This is the context of our Lord's communication to the disciples and
specifically to Peter:

> And the Lord said, "Simon, Simon! Indeed,
> Satan has asked for you, that he may sift you as
> wheat."

It is as though Christ was speaking in clear and blunt terms:
"Oh, my disciples, you are in a slumber concerning the realities taking place at this very moment. Satan is seeking to destroy you all by
his temptations."

"Satan has asked." Note this: as with Job, Satan must ask permission to attack the believer! You might ask why the Lord would
give permission. It will be as with Shadrach, Meshach, and Abed-
Nego being thrown into the fiery furnace. Christ kept them, but the

afflicting fires burned the ropes that bound them. The same is true of the disciples and Peter. They were wheat, but all too much chaff clung to them. Therefore, our Lord employs the effort of the evil one to separate and clean up the wheat.

"Peter, I have given permission for Satan to take you into hand! Your chaff has to be dealt with. He must sift it off. As with my servant Job, only the dross will be consumed. My gold will be refined. Peter, you are never out of my heart and hand."

"Now Peter, hear my words: 'I have prayed for you that your faith will not fail.'"

"Peter, I will bring you out of this. You will return to me in sorrowful repentance. In the whole ordeal, you will learn vital lessons from which you will strengthen your brethren."

Paul said this:

> Blessed be the God and Father of our Lord Jesus Christ, the Father of mercies and God of all comfort, who comforts us in all our tribulation that we may be able to comfort those who are in any trouble, with the comfort with which we ourselves are comforted by God. (2 Corinthians 1:3–4)

Peter will do this. He will also write two letters, which incorporate many of the lessons he is about to learn.

Peter, upheld and kept through the intercessory prayer of Christ, learned to pray honestly, humbly, and fervently by the tutoring of the indwelling Holy Spirit. Read his obedient follow-through with Christ's personal instruction:

> In this you greatly rejoice, though now for a little while, if need be, you have been grieved by various trials, that the genuineness of your faith, being much more precious than gold that perishes, though it is tested by fire, may be found to praise, honor, and glory at the revelation of Jesus

Christ, whom having not seen you love. Though now you do not see Him, yet believing, you rejoice with joy inexpressible and full of glory, receiving the end of your faith—the salvation of your souls. (1 Peter 1:6–9)

> Be clothed with humility, for "God resists the proud, but gives grace to the humble." Therefore humble yourselves under the mighty hand of God, that he may exalt you in due time, casting all your care upon him, for He cares for you. Be sober, be vigilant; because your adversary the devil walks about like a roaring lion, seeking whom he may devour. Resist him, steadfast in the faith, knowing that the same sufferings are experienced by your brotherhood in the world. But may the God of all grace, who called us to his eternal glory by Christ Jesus, after you have suffered a while, perfect, establish, strengthen, and settle you. (1 Peter 5:6–10)

On the way to eternal happiness, we must expect to be assaulted and sifted by Satan. If he cannot destroy, he will try to disgrace or distress us. Nothing more certainly predicts a fall in a professed follower of Christ than self-confidence. We heighten the danger with disregard for warnings and peril.

> Therefore, let him who thinks he stands take heed lest he fall. (1 Corinthians 10:12)

Pride, through the Lord's faithfulness, precedes a fall. Our Lord warned:

> Watch and pray, lest you enter into temptation. The spirit indeed is willing, but the flesh is weak. (Matthew 26:41)

Unless we watch and pray, our soul's enemies may draw us into those sins we resolved against! Left to ourselves, we will fall, but the power of God and the prayer of Christ keep us (1 Peter 5:6–10). Peter learned:

Satan is only God's master fencer (swords-man) to teach us to use our weapons (Samuel Rutherford)

Till we sin, Satan is a parasite; but when once we are in the devil's hands, he turns tyrant. (Thomas Manton)

"Rise, My Soul to Watch and Pray"

Spiritual warfare has been a reality for the believing soul since the fall of humanity. Spiritual conflict with the forces of darkness is the subject of these two precious hymns. Their value is in the truths, drawn from our Bibles, and presented in a beautiful melodious fashion. They portray the scriptural truths as God intended them to be understood and experienced in a believer's life.

(The sobering reality of spiritual warfare)
Written by Johann Burchard Freystein (1671–1718)
Translated into English by Catherine Winkworth (1827–1878)

Rise, my soul, to watch and pray, from thy sleep awaken;
Be not by the evil day Unawares o'ertaken.
For the foe, well we know, oft his harvest reapeth while the Christian sleepeth.
Watch against the devil's snares Lest asleep he find thee;
For indeed no pains he spares to deceive and blind thee.
Satan's prey Oft are they Who secure are sleeping and no watch are keeping
Watch! Let not the wicked world with its power defeat thee.
Watch lest with her pomp unfurled She betray and cheat thee.
Watch and see Lest there be Faithless friends to charm thee, who but seek to harm thee.
Watch against thyself, my soul, lest with grace thou trifle;
Let not self thy thoughts control nor God's mercy stifle.
Pride and sin Lurk within All thy hopes to scatter; heed not when they flatter.
But while watching, also pray to the Lord unceasing.
He will free thee, be thy stay, Strength and faith increasing.
O Lord, bless in distress and let nothing swerve me from the will to serve thee.

"A Mighty Fortress Is Our God"

(Assured victory through our mighty Lord)
Written by Martin Luther (1483–1546)
Translated by Frederick H. Hedge (1805–1890)

A mighty fortress is our God, a bulwark never failing:
Our helper He, amid the flood of mortal ills prevailing.
For still our ancient foe Doth seek to work his woe;
His craft and power are great, and armed with cruel hate,
On earth is not his equal.
Did we in our own strength confide, our striving would be losing;
Were not the right Man on our side, the Man of God's own choosing.
Dost ask who that may be? Christ Jesus, it is he;
Lord Sabaoth is his name, from age to age the same, [Lord of hosts]
And He must win the battle.
And though this world, with devils filled, should threaten to undo us,
We will not fear, for God hath willed His truth to triumph through us.
The Prince of Darkness grim—we tremble not for him;
His rage we can endure, for lo! His doom is sure—
One little word shall fell him.
That word above all earthly powers—no thanks to them—abideth;
The Spirit and the gifts are ours through him who with us sideth.
Let goods and kindred go, this mortal life also:
The body they may kill: God's truth abideth still,
His kingdom is for ever.

13

Human Sin and Misery Meet Christ

Sin keeps us from knowing the true nature of sin.

If sin was not such a pleasure, it would not be such a problem.

—John Blanchard

Our Lord returned from the glory of transfiguration to the reality of demon possession, human sin, false religion's antagonism, parental anguish, and a pitilessly tortured boy.

This event pictures the certainty that Jesus enters his glory only through confrontation with demonic activity, the sinfulness of man, and the suffering these two bring upon the world.

> The Son of Man has come to seek and to
> save that which was lost.

He pursues his saving mission of love and compassion in enemy territory, filled with hostility to himself (Luke 19:10).

> For even the Son of Man did not come to be
> served, but to serve, and to give his life a ransom
> for many. (Mark 10:45)

Knowing this would cost him his life as a substitute sin bearer for his people, he set his entire being to do the will of his Father. He embraced his mission with energetic delight and bore human sorrow, sin, and misery in the greatest act of compassionate love known to humanity and the angelic host. In doing this, he rendered the greatest service for humanity's greatest and most desperate need.

Adam had a world made for him. Look what he did with it. None of us would have done better. He filled the world with spiritual death, physical death, sin, pain, misery, and delusions.

Not knowing the consequences of his choice, he turned the world over to Satan when he embraced the counsel of the deceiver. God's benevolent authority became suspect then doubted and, finally, brushed off. What was the enormous consequence? Not only the fall of humanity into spiritual death and eternal separation from God; humanity's loyalty shifted. Now Adam's posterity, the world of people, embraces another god by default. Perfected deception leads people to think self is served. Reality is the evil one is served! Now the devil, the serpent, holds sway over this world's system.

Satan, the great liar, deceiver, and murderer of humanity, is the god this world owns (John 8:42–47).

> If our gospel is veiled [or hidden], it is veiled to
> those who are perishing, whose minds the god of this
> age has blinded, who do not believe, lest the light of
> the gospel of the glory of Christ, who is the image of
> God, should shine on them. (2 Corinthians 4:3–4)

Notice the word *of*. It is the genitive of possession "the god possessed, owned, and embraced by humanity." Though unconscious, this is the reality for all outside of Christ. This is the diabolical skill of Satan's craftiness brought to a hellish perfection (Ephesians 2:1–3; 4:18–19; Romans 1:21; 1 John 5:19).

This world is not good enough for our Lord Jesus. The Father will make him a new heaven and a new earth wherein dwells righteousness. In that place, he puts his redeemed "sons and daughters" to rule, reign, and serve for the glory of God and the eternal praise of Christ. The only thing preserving this present world is the purpose of God in drawing his purchased sheep to Christ. When the last one is in, this world is done.

> When this passing world is done,
> When has sunk yon glaring sun,
> When we stand with Christ in glory,
> Looking o'er life's finished story,
> Then, Lord shall I fully know,
> Not till then, how much I owe.
> (Robert Murray McCheyne, 1837)

Our Lord had the five realities of Mark 9:14–21 as an ever present experience within his human sensibilities. Being fully and truly human, his affections were affected. The first reality—external religion, with all its delusions, bringing eternal ruin to souls. The second reality—the activity and presence of demonic cruelty and hellish efforts to destroy the image of God and prevent true heart religion. Both stirred the holy anger of our Lord. Scripturally, you cannot separate these. In a diabolical sense, they complement each other for sinister ends. Now we come to the third reality.

3. The reality of human sin and misery

Have you noticed the blame game of Adam and Eve still permeates humanity? "If there is a God, why is there so much evil in the world?" You will never hear: "Wow, with all the evil in the world, what did we people do to mess things up so bad?" That's the actual story. The reality is people sinned, and the unavoidable result is human misery and evil in the world.

We will (a) first consider sin and what it is. Because its nature is to avoid the true and living God, it leads into two blinding delusions: (1) false philosophies of life and (2) false religion. Then we (b) will consider the consequent misery which flows from these worldviews. It is this misery our Lord witnessed in his day.

(a) First, consider sin and what it is. Sin is the greatest insanity injected into humanity.

> Sin has the devil for its father, shame for its companion, and death for its wages. (Thomas Watson)

John Bunyan describes sin most vividly:

> Sin is the dare of God's justice, the rape of his mercy, the jeer of his patience, the slight of his power, and the contempt of his love.

The apostle John tells us,

> Everyone who makes a practice of sinning also practices lawlessness; sin is lawlessness. (1 John 3:4 ESV)

Sin is enmity against God. It is hatred for him telling us what to do! Sin is avoidance of God's authority telling us how to live. Sin is resentment for God's restraining us from what we want. It is the soul's insane pursuit of a delusional independence from God. It is the soul saying, "I will break his bands in pieces and cast away his cords from me" (Romans 8:5–8; Psalm 2:1–3; 10–12). People express this with varying degrees of intensity—from simple avoidance to aggressive defiance.

There can never be a complete erasure of moral awareness and sense of answerability to God. Even an atheist needs God to say they don't believe in him! Everyone has a theology. The important issue: is it a good or a bad theology? We cannot function without God consciousness, whether it comes with a loud or soft voice. It is impossible because God inscribed it on humanity's consciousness in creation.

We cannot delete the image of God. We disfigure, disgrace, blemish, and distort it but never remove it.

Suppression of this reality is the greatest and truest "opiate of the masses." Paul tells us every human being knows three things in Romans 1–3: (1) All people know God is that he exists as Creator of all. (2) They know they are in trouble with God. (3) They know they will ultimately meet God and it won't go well.

> It is appointed for men to die once, but
> after this, the judgment. (Hebrews 9:27)

Everyone made in the image of God has a responsibility for explaining or justifying the way they lived before the face of God. It is unavoidable. The masses suppress this knowledge to help forget God and get on with life as they see best.

How does humanity cope with this "unforgettable, nonerasable reality of God"? On a large scale, indifference is perhaps the most common coping method. However, a more serious, sinister, and devastating course emerges in human history. This is the foundation for false philosophies of life and false religion.

1. This is the foundation for false philosophies of life.

Philosophers have tried to plumb the depths of humanity and the world to find the answers to life. Why are we here? What is our purpose? Where are we going? What happens after death? The vast majority are determined to leave God and the wisdom of Scripture out of it. This is the result:

> Professing themselves to be wise, they
> became fools. (Romans 1:21)

In reality, it has to be so:

> They have rejected the word of the Lord, so
> what wisdom is in them? (Jeremiah 8:9)

196

When you understand what they are saying, you end up with this: they have high opinions of their opinions. Whether in the Greek or Roman world, it will always be the same. Though the preaching of the cross appears as foolishness (1 Corinthians 1), he who sits in the heavens will laugh at their perilous folly (Psalm 2; 1 Corinthians 1:18–25).

How will they deal with the reality of sin? Deny its existence and help people blame something or someone else for the wrong they do. This philosophy of folly continues in our day. I'm not jumping off into the dizzy depths of philosophical theories. Just a brief history lesson would help because of its profound influence on our day.

The writings of Nietzsche (1844–1900) and Freud (1856–1939) before WWI were seen as a bit crazy, farfetched, out of touch, and fanciful. Their books did not sell well. Nietzsche and Freud believed we live in a nonrational universe. Reason was an enemy to human happiness and freedom. With a nasty attitude, they fervently believed that religion, especially the Christian religion, was the great enemy of humanity and oppressor of human health. Remove Christianity, and people would be guilt-free and true to themselves. They would be free to be truly human. Christianity was the enemy of personal authenticity.

At the time of their writings, the prevailing view of the universe was that it was rational, logical, and the foundation for reason. Then World War I happened. Europe expected the war to last about six weeks. It shocked the entire world when it lasted four years, 1914–1918. World War I, known as the Great War, witnessed twenty million deaths and twenty-one million wounded. No one ever heard of such horror! The entire world felt traumatized and reeling with questions: "How can humanity inflict such brutality and atrocities upon their fellow man?" This war changed the face of modern society and philosophical thought. "Truly, we must live in an irrational universe! None of this makes sense." They then viewed the writings of Nietzsche and Freud as prophetic. The reading world thought these men were on to something and were sources of important insight about life as it really is. Their books flew off shelves, purchased and devoured as bestsellers.

Absorbing their philosophy produced the "roaring twenties," with the belief, "Let us eat, drink, and be merry, for tomorrow we die." Life has no other meaning but what you make of it in the present, and the present must have personal happiness as one's truest priority. You only have one time to live. Be true to your authentic self and its impulses, desires, and longings. They soaked these writings up like a sponge in the academies of higher learning. Though Freud's theories proved false, his influence remained. Add to this the influence of Charles Darwin and the "godless" origin of man. This gave great relief to the conscience. Accountability to God was nonsense! In reality, they removed the foundation of ultimate authority. No longer was there absolute truth, certainty, or morals. The concept of "sin" was a religious tool to manipulate people. Humanity is free for their morality to dictate their philosophy.

After decades of soaking and marinating in these and other writers who followed, institutions of higher learning swelled with arrogant hatred for the Bible and the Christian religion. Socialistic indoctrination undermined the value of the family and Christian religion. By the sixties, a whole new philosophy and worldview emerged. New beliefs infused themselves into every area of society slowly showing up in music, art, movies, curriculum, politics, marriages, families, and the youth. It would influence how people approach life in every sphere. The philosophies, toxic and poisonous, spread their detrimental bias into colleges, high schools, and in our day elementary schools.

Just focusing on the family and education—they presented Christianity and the Bible as damaging to children and oppressive to their development. Schools moved toward making matters of God and religion marginalized. Religion is a choice, unimportant in places that really matter. Child care gurus, held as experts, like Benjamin Spock, B. F. Skinner, Sigmund Freud, and others of the same philosophical bent had much to say about what was wrong and what was right. The Bible and Christianity are wrong and damaging to the child. They, of course, were experts. They teach the educated and correct view of child development. In a nutshell, the child is not responsible for his behavior. Do not say no to your child; it will damage their psyche. Vulnerable young couples drank in their influence with desires to do parenting right. What have been the results over the next several decades?

The powers of darkness, demonic influences, brought about a society alienated from biblical ethics, desensitized to accountability with God, loosened morals, destruction of the natural family, distortion of personhood, antagonism to genuine authority, feeling resentful at what produces guilt or may create a conscience-stricken state. One's feelings are of superior importance. Preoccupation with "navel gazing" self-absorption and illusive seeking for the (undefined) authentic "self" removes the ability to think objectively. God's institutions are too afflictive to human happiness. Facts are a boring bother. Logic is the prison of a privileged group used to oppress others. You can go on and on with this insanity.

Here you have the colaboring of demonic forces and human sin to cast off the restraints of God consciousness. What about sin and evil? "No problem—we don't believe in them." The consequences are blindness to the eternity souls are slipping into. It is a harvest time for the serpent.

A few glaring problems emerge: (1) There are no answers to human guilt. (2) The loss of human dignity. (3) With no absolute truth, everyone is free to do what is right in their own eyes. (4) Moral confusion results, everyone is right, and no one is wrong. There is nothing wrong with alley-cat morality. No one is to correct another as it might make them feel bad. Anyone pointing out the obvious is an enemy to society. (5) The families splintered, torn apart, children and teens alienated from parents, parents desperate to make ends meet, busy running around to way too many events, effective child training mocked and cast off, and a generation emerges with the emotional struggles of abandonment, confusion, shallow thinking, and vulnerability! (6) It all eradicates common sense to a high degree. (7) This condition defies solutions especially the Gospel of the grace of God in the accomplishments of Christ.

All this mess is a triumphant accomplishment for the devil. Demonic ingenuity and human instruments of Satan colabor to create the perfect storm of hard-heartedness and cold indifference.

Truth hits the soul like water running off the duck's back producing a society of wayside soil!

What are we to do? Remember:

> The weapons of our warfare are not carnal [of the flesh] but mighty in God for pulling down strongholds, casting down arguments and every high thing that exalts itself against the knowledge of God, bringing every thought into captivity to the obedience of Christ. (2 Corinthians 10:4–5)

We need the outpouring of the Holy Spirit more than anything else! How is the battle won?

> "Not by might nor by power, but by my Spirit," says the Lord of hosts. (Zechariah 4:6)

Remember our Lord's teaching on prayer.

> Shall God not avenge his own elect, who cry out day and night to him, though he bears long with them? I tell you that he will avenge them speedily. Nevertheless, when the Son of Man comes, will he really find faith on the earth? (Luke 18:7–8)

The people who "believe" will be intensely engaged in praying. Praying, as described, "cry out day and night to him." The church does not have a "societal problem." The problem is not socialism, atheism, materialism, or secularism. It is a matter of believing God's Word and praying as our Lord taught his disciples to pray. We need the Holy Spirit for this. Beloved, we have the promise of God for the Holy Spirit!

> How much more will your heavenly Father give the Holy Spirit to those who ask him? (Luke 11:13)

Our words are powerless! However, not the Word of God.

> "Is not my word like a fire?" says the Lord,
> "and like a hammer that breaks the rock into
> pieces?" (Jeremiah 23:29)

> So shall my word be that goes forth from
> my mouth; it shall not return to me void, but it
> shall accomplish what I please, and it shall pros-
> per in the thing for which I sent it. (Isaiah 55:11)

Oh, brethren, is this not a clarion call for effectual, fervent prayer? We desperately need God to come down and make us the light and salt we are called to be. We need God to bring influence upon society's conscience. The enemy of souls has come into society like a flood of godless indifference. The things of Christ and the Father appear to have no attraction or power! We can talk to the ear, but Christ alone can talk to the heart. He speaks as one having authority. "His sheep will hear his voice!" Like Paul, we must endure these things for the elect's sake that they might be saved. The Gospel will be successful. We must "not be ashamed of it, for it is the power of God unto salvation to everyone who believes" (John 10:3; 2 Timothy 2:10; Romans 1:16).

> So shall they fear the name of the Lord from
> the west, and his glory from the rising of the sun.
> When the enemy shall come in like a flood, the
> Spirit of the Lord shall lift up a standard against
> him. (Isaiah 59:19)

We follow Christ through his Word and our prayer companionship with him. Who is on the Lord's side? Let it be demonstrated in the prayer closet! Are we part of Christ's standard? Let us follow hard after him in earnest and fervent prayer. He is our Commander, the Lord of hosts. Follow hard after him in prayer.

The evil one is having a "heyday," and we are called to battle in prayer. We are no match in and of ourselves. We desperately need to be "strong in the Lord and in the power of his might." Our primary weapon of successful battle strategy is "all prayer"—the effectual fervent prayer of a people who really know their God. Two primary strategies of the evil one are (1) reducing the awareness of sin as God sees it and (2) reducing the sense of urgency for Christ's interventions as our king in spiritual warfare.

Sin is a reality—the same reality our Lord witnessed, the same reality of sin he experienced imputed to him on the cross. Why is there so little prayer in the churches? We seem too desensitized to two things: (1) sin and (2) the great need for Christ's awe-inspiring presence.

> Because lawlessness will abound, the love of many will grow cold. (Matthew 24:12)

Brethren, to have the fear of the LORD, we must genuinely love him. The child of God understands this.

> Then those who feared the Lord spoke to one another, and the Lord listened and heard them; so a book of remembrance was written before him for those who fear the Lord and who meditate on His name. (Malachi 3:16)

> The people who know their God shall be strong and carry out great exploits. (Daniel 11:32)

The exploits mentioned is loyalty to the covenant—loyalty to God's expectations of a people who profess to be his people. These are difficult, trying, and desperate times we live in. Let us be a people who, through the strength of the Holy Spirit, rise to the need of the hour. Let us be a truly praying people.

In Christ Jesus, we shall be "more than conquerors through him that loved you." Our extreme need for his interventions shall be the very season of his effectual involvements. "Be strong then in the Lord and in the power of his might." We shall put our feet upon the head of the serpent. (Ephesians 6:10; Romans 16:20).

How does humanity cope with this "unforgettable, nonerasable reality of God?"

1. This is the foundation for false philosophies of life.
2. This is the foundation for false religion, externalism, and religious delusions.

> The devil shapes himself to the fashions of all men. (William Jenkyn)

False and external religion, rooted in a "works mindset," allows people to feel good about themselves. God is happy, so they deceive themselves to think, and they still get to live the life they want. Deceptive forces of darkness will assist human bents toward superficiality, sentimentality, sensationalism, hypocritical spirituality, and superstitious devotion. Remember, "The devil is usually good-looking" (John Blanchard). The Lord has seen all this before.

> The prophets prophesy falsely, and the priests rule by their own power; and my people love to have it so. But what will you do in the end? (Jeremiah 5:31)

What do all these avoid? What is obviously lacking? An actual knowledge of Christ that is enjoyed, the love and pursuit in prayer of genuine communion, a communion leading to worship of the Father, Son, and Holy Spirit—such worship which leads to affectionate pleas for help in conformity to the image of Christ, who is so precious and lovely to the soul—tangible efforts to walk in his ways and commands, an affection set on things above where one's beloved Lord Jesus dwells.

Sin captures souls in false religion along with profuse demonic efforts to keep out disturbers of a death-grip false peace. False teachers say, "Peace, peace, when there is no peace" (Jeremiah 6:14). The true and living God is efficiently and effectively forgotten.

> You thought I was altogether like you; but I
> will rebuke you. (Psalm 50:21)

This is what our Lord came to:

> He was in the world, and the world was
> made through him, and the world did not know
> him. He came to his own, and his own did not
> receive him. (John 1:10–11)

Why? The Lord of glory, the Messiah who saves, has come! He alone solves all humanity's problems and every individual need. What keeps them from loving and coming to Christ?

> This is the condemnation, that the light has
> come into the world, and men loved darkness
> rather than light, because their deeds were evil.
> (John 3:19)

There are sins of commission—doing what God forbids. A sin of commission involves the willful act of doing something that violates God's commands in Scripture such as lying, stealing, dishonoring parents, sexual sins, hateful thoughts, murder, coveting, using God's name irreverently, etc. The Lord walked through this world and witnessed every category of disobedience to God's expressed will. Our pure and holy Lord Jesus experienced the sewage of human rebellion against God's moral restraints. It was there at the foot of the Mount of Transfiguration. Our Savior knew and saw all this.

There are sins of omission—not doing what God commands. The neglects of heart devotion to the Lord expressed itself everywhere he went, not bringing to the Lord what he values.

> Woe to you Pharisees! For you tithe mint and rue and all manner of herbs, and pass by justice and the love of God. (Luke 11:42)

> The devil is most devilish when respectable. (Elizabeth Barrett Browning)

> "My house shall be called a house of prayer," but you have made it a "den of thieves." (Matthew 21:13)

The prophet Joel would cry out, "Rend your heart and not your garment." Samuel declared, "Man looks on the outward appearance. God looks upon the heart." Our Lord was an observer of every heart, for he knew what was in man. He is the one who knows your thought before you express it. It was so with the scribes, the crowds, the disciples, and this father.

By the simple expressions of the moral law of God, we know two important realities: (1) What God sees as the sincere expressions of our love for him and others. (2) What sin is as defined by God. Law is love's eyes, and without it, love is blind.

Because of this, a major design of the evil one has been to move the Christian church to cast off the law of God. Even though established in the person of Christ and written on the tablet of the believer's affections, it is still, to a large extent, ignored or viewed as obsolete. With that, Satan has removed the sense of sin. Many reduce the Word of God to divine suggestions. There is now belief in "a benign benevolent being existing to make us feel good about ourselves and be happy in life"—like a mutual admiration society. "God admires me, I admire me, and I admire God for it."

> Satan does far more harm as an angel of light than as a roaring lion. (Vance Havner)

It would be healthy if we recognized this truth: "God sees more sin in us in the best of our days than we see in the worst of our days." Some may say, "Oh, that's so negative, depressing, and offensive to one's self-esteem." It actually is the pathway to greater love for Christ, who is my sin bearer and Advocate. This perspective deepens and sweetens love for Christ. "He who is forgiven much loves much." No believer is "forgiven little." This is motivating to live a life indebted to Christ. He purchased my life, my eternal life, now "I will no longer live for myself, but for him who died and rose again" (2 Corinthians 5:15).

So we see people deal with the nonerasable awareness of God and, consequently, guilt from sin in two large ways: (1) false philosophies of life and (2) false religion. Sadly, sin is the cause of human misery. If people ignore the cause, they cut themselves off from the only true remedy. With this, they secure misery's entrenchment, and it spreads like a virus far worse than any COVID infection humanity has ever known. They drug themselves to numbness with the "opiate of the masses"—suppression of reality.

> (b) Second, consider the misery our Lord witnessed. The actual pain, anguish, and misery people endure are what he carried on his heart. He still does (Hebrews 2:14–18; 4:14–16).

> In all their affliction, he was afflicted. (Isaiah 63:9)

He continually expressed compassion for the multitudes. He showed the power of his care to specific people. Their individual condition drew his intentional consideration and application of relieving remedies.

A father's urgent need for help interrupted the question Christ asked the scribes:

> Teacher, I brought you my son, who has a mute spirit. And wherever it seizes him, it throws him down; he foams at the mouth, gnashes his teeth, and becomes rigid. So I spoke to Your disciples, that they should cast it out, but they could not. (Mark 9:17–18)

A lonely father struggled desperately for both the life of his son, the existence of his faith, and the recovery of a healthy home life. Hearing Christ was nearby, with desperation and hope, he left home with his son. Finding Christ was not present, he approached his disciples with hope of help. Their failure brought renewed despair, erosion of hope, and pangs of anguish and heartache.

The Lord Jesus, as a Savior and healer of souls, was never indifferent to anyone. Everything this father related to Christ, Christ knew, and the relating of it all came fresh upon his soul. More than this, he knows all the specifics of every afflicted person! It was not just the physical maladies; it was torments the heart felt in those afflictions. Read carefully these words in John 5:5–8:

> Now a certain man was there who had an infirmity thirty-eight years. When Jesus saw him lying there, and knew that he already had been in that condition a long time, He said to him, "Do you want to be made well?" The sick man answered him, "Sir, I have no man to put me into the pool when the water is stirred up; but while I am coming, another steps down before me." Jesus said to him, "Rise, take up your bed and walk."

"Oh, soul, you don't need water or help in the pool—you just need me!"

We could never adequately represent the inner world of Christ. Our hearts are too small. Christ had a personal acquaintance with that man's agony, depression, helplessness, and the years of disappointment. Jesus saw a man who regularly had "hope deferred" and the soul despair that followed. Jesus knew the entire inside story of this man, not just his sick and disabled condition. It is the same with everything you face!

The woman at the well, a Samaritan, did not remain a stranger to his awareness (John 4). Feelings of being used, a failure in marriage, compromised standards, social stigma, looks of scorn—none of which escaped his understanding. Did he see her sins? Yes, every one—none escaped his knowledge. Each turn of the conversation, he drew her out, and he drew near to uncover the miserable guilt within. The lies she lived in were no deterrent to his redeeming love. Some may say, "What, are you saying he loved her in her sinning?" Yes! He loved her, not her sinning. Christ came to bring whole-life healing. He came to save her from her sins and all the misery, pain, shame, guilt, and lonely-soul moments. She perceived his amazing perception! Much more, she realized his safety, care, uncondemning extension of hope to her.

When she ran back into town, something like these words were ringing in her soul: "Hallelujah, what a Savior! Come, everyone, meet Messiah! I have communicated with him, and he brought healing to my heart, my soul, and my life. He changed me! What a wonderful Savior. You have got to meet him. You have got to talk with him. Come. He is so easy to talk to. He knows all about you."

The Lord Jesus, the eternal Son of God, has this intimate acquaintance with every suffering soul. No one escapes his awareness and gaze. He is not an indifferent bystander. Our greatest folly is to ignore him or be indifferent to him. Our greatest wisdom is to call upon him, convinced this is his heart. Call upon him, and tuck your soul into his caring, capable, compassionate arms.

The perfection of Christ, in his care for the humanity he took upon himself, is that he bore the sorrows, misery, and pain of it all. All of it was a living reality moving in his soul. When Christ came down from the mount and the crowd was around his disciples, the realness of it all he experienced. The despairing father, with years of sleepless nights agonizing over his son—his only son—tears shed, social alienation, embarrassments, loneliness, and moments of despair. Years passed in this condition did not escape his knowledge. Hope awakened then dashed to death. The tortured son could not speak, unable to hear the words of parental love, care, cries, sympathy or express his own anguish. Locked in a world of aloneness and frightening pain, Christ was well aware of it. Then the confused disciples, their vulnerability being attacked by religious heartless faultfinders—those disciples saw the dad with his son lose hope before their eyes. They knew their failure let Christ down. Add to all this the demon's hatred for the image of God brings untold misery to the boy in Christ's very presence. He saw it all! These were realities he dealt with.

May this reality move you to open your heart to Christ in prayer. Tell him all about your concerns, sins, problems, perplexities, struggles. Open your heart, and pour all out to him who cares for you. Do this, knowing he already knows about them. He desires you not to face them alone. Rather, he invites you to join him in facing everything. There is more! He represents the Father and blessed indwelling Holy Spirit with the same disposition. They are with you in all you face and have to deal with. Don't go it alone! Call upon them to help you develop a real prayer life, a real companionship.

If you seem dull or he seems distant, call upon him with greater earnestness. These are great treasures purchased for you. Desire them greatly, and let your God know you genuinely value them. Don't let him go until he blesses you. If the dullness remains, go for a walk, do something with vigor, and then come back to him to say,

> My soul follows close behind you; your right hand upholds me. (Psalm 63:8)

Make this your resolve:

> It is good for me to draw near to God; I have put my trust in the Lord God, that I may declare all your works. (Psalm 73:28)

Why is the psalmist so openhearted and convinced this is the course in life for him? He tells us:

> Whom have I in heaven but you? And there is none upon earth that I desire besides you. My flesh and my heart fail; but God is the strength of my heart and my portion forever. (Psalm 73:25–26)

Pray these words into your own soul.

It is difficult talking about human pain and misery. We all experience it. However, if it moves us closer to Christ, it does more good than harm. Christ would have each of his suffering followers to be assured that one day he

> Will wipe away every tear from their eyes; there shall be no more death, nor sorrow, nor crying. There shall be no more pain, for the former things have passed away. (Revelation 21:4)

Our beloved Savior affectionately anticipates the complete removal of pain, sorrow, and misery from us all.

We turn now to consider Christ and his perfection as our caring, loving, competent Savior.

> *As an angel of light, the devil is utterly self-effacing,*
> *so that you would never think to charge him*
> *with the sudden trouble that has emerged.*

—R. T. Kendall

> *The whole of Satan's kingdom is subject*
> *to the authority of Christ.*

—John Calvin

14

Christ's Compassionate
Skill and Tender Care

To forsake Christ for the world is to leave a treasure for a trifle;
it is to leave eternity for a moment, and reality for a shadow.

—William Jenkyn

A few centuries ago, there was an older man whose hard heart the
Lord broke and drew to himself with saving mercy. He desired to join
the local church. When they were asking him questions about his
beliefs, some were too zealous, asking about his theological understanding. He bowed his head and simply said, "I am a sinner, that
is all. Christ is my all in all." This simple statement is a wonderful
summary of every genuine follower of Christ.

Pause for a moment and read these two questions meditatively
and answer them with sincere engagement of heart and thought: (1)
What would you say is your heavenly Father's greatest desire for you?
(2) In addition, what would your heavenly Father have as your primary focus and passionate pursuit in life? How you answer these
questions is incredibly revealing of your soul's health.

Here is the answer: it is to know Christ! To know him more and
more intimately, personally, increasingly, expansively, and relationally. He is to be your closest companion and confidant in life. The

Father would have you captivated by the loveliness, beauty, authority, sufficiency, and perfection of Christ's character. The Father would have you love Christ with all your heart and soul for the rest of your earthly existence. He would have you see the Son of God as more valuable than anything in this world. Christ is the Father's gift and solution for every need you have. Paul tells us,

> For me to live is Christ! (Philippians 1:27)

> God shall supply all your need according to
> His riches in glory by Christ Jesus (4:19)

Follow this scriptural logic closely. First, all Christ has done and still does for us flows from his love, grace, compassion, and power. Second, these flow out of his eternal relationship with his Father and from the eternal decree concerning Christ and us. Third—and this is important for all of us to understand—all these precious relational treasures flow from his Father's charge to him concerning us.

Here is what I mean. The Father eternally says to the Son, "Here are souls loved from all eternity. Love them, and give yourself for them and to them. Pay the debt of divine justice they cannot pay. Remove every obstacle so they may know me as their Father and that they are my sons and daughters. As they come into existence in the world, at the appointed time, call them to yourself as the Author and Completer of their faith. Shepherd them through life. Carry them and their every need upon your heart. Advocate for them in all their sins and failures so they will know complete acceptance based upon your merit, not theirs. At the end of their earthly lives, bring them home to heaven to be with us forever."

Here is how Christ expressed this in prayer to his Father just before his betrayal and death:

> I have manifested your name to the men
> whom you have given me out of the world. They
> were yours, you gave them to me, and they have
> kept your word. Now they have known that all

things which you have given me are from you. For I have given to them the words which you have given me; and they have received them, and have known surely that I came forth from you; and they have believed that you sent me. (John 17:6–8)

I pray for them. I do not pray for the world but for those whom you have given me, for they are yours. And all mine are yours, and yours are mine, and I am glorified in them. Holy Father, keep through your name those whom you have given me, that they may be one as we are. (John 17:9–11)

As believers, we are in the tender heart and capable hands of the Father and the Son. The Father gave us to Christ as his stewardship to carry us through life, meet our needs, and bring us to heaven. Christ does this as our Prophet, Priest, and King. He is our Mediator, Advocate, and Shepherd to secure us to the Father. The Holy Spirit secures the application of all this to us and in us. This is our eternal reality both now and forever. You may remember our Lord captures this relationship with the Father in his teaching concerning prayer:

He who did not spare his own Son, but delivered him up for us all, how shall he not with him also freely give us all things? (Romans 8:32)

Our heavenly Father wants you and me to experience Christ's protective love and caring heart. We are to grow in secure acquaintance with his heart of compassion. Christ is our Mr. Greatheart, to use John Bunyan's term for a true pastor. Christ is the LORD of all creation! Yet he is ours in the tenderest relationship! He wants every one of his sheep, whom he knows by name, to say, "He loved *me* and gave himself for *me*"! He paid *my* debt and takes *me* to his heart and affectionate embrace! All this, not for a moment but for all eternity. We will live forever in Immanuel's land (Galatians 2:20).

Ann Ross Cousins composed a hymn drawing glorious truths about Christ from the sweet pastoral letters of Samuel Rutherford. Here are two stanzas:

> Oh! Christ He is the fountain, the deep sweet well of Love! The streams on earth I've tasted, more deep I'll drink above: there, to an ocean fullness, his mercy doth expand, and glory—glory dwelleth in Immanuel's land.
>
> Oh! I am my Beloved's, and my Beloved's mine! He brings a poor vile sinner into his "house of wine": I stand upon his merit, I know no other stand, not e'en where glory dwelleth In Immanuel's land.

Paul continued throughout his life, lost in wonder, love, and praise concerning the incredible privilege given to him:

> To me, who am less than the least of all the saints, this grace was given, that I should preach among the Gentiles the unsearchable riches of Christ. (Ephesians 3:8)

Is there a desire to actually earnestly pray in your praying? Get better acquainted with the wondrous person of your Savior. The best aid to prayer is personal acquaintance, deepening intimacy, companionship, and a holy familiar conversing with Christ. Growing awareness of the perfection of his character and safety and ease of approach motivates you to open your heart to him. You will say with Peter, "O Lord, though I come so short, you know I love you!" Peter tells all genuine followers and lovers of Christ what Christ means to them:

> To those who believe he is precious! (1 Peter 2:7)

Often consider what attracts your heart to Christ. In, from, and by Christ are all our spiritual and eternal life, light, power, growth, consolation, and joy in this life. In him we have everlasting salvation and joy unspeakable, full of glory, in and with him when this passing world is done.

Our Lord Jesus brings us into the closest understanding, alliance, and friendship with God, the firmest union in him, and the most holy communion with the eternal Trinity that our finite natures are capable of. He takes us by the hand of our soul, which is faith, and leads us into the eternal enjoyment of each person of the Godhead. Because of all this, I say the chief design of our entire lives is to acquaint ourselves with him, to trust in him and to him all the concerns of our hearts, to love and honor him with all our souls, that we give ourselves to this whole-life endeavor affectionate conformity to his person in all those qualities of goodness and holiness we see in him. These pursuits embody the soul, life, power, beauty, and strength of the Christian life. Without this, whatever outward ornaments we may put upon a "profession of faith," it is but a useless, lifeless carcass. Knowing Christ is the sum and substance of genuine Christianity! It is "real" life (John 17:3). It alone is "the real thing." Drawn from John Owen's *The Person and Work of Christ*.

This is the one who came down from the mount! Here is the one, dressed in our humanity, who came upon the realities of false religion, demonic activity, and human sin with its accompanying misery. Now we take up the fourth reality. I hope to take us into the heart and soul of our Savior. Why? That we may know him and, from this increasing knowledge, advance in our prayer life.

4. The reality of our Savior's compassion and skillful competence

One of the grand purposes of the Gospel accounts is for us to experience the Lord Jesus and how he lived, walked, talked, thought, and treated those who came to him and trusted him. This has a wonderful purpose. By the Spirit's ministry, it is so we may have vivid displays of how our Savior walks with us and responds to us on our present earthly journey.

He is the same yesterday, today, and forever!
(Hebrews 13:8)

We become like those we walk with!

He who walks with wise men shall be wise.
(Proverbs 13:20)

We become like those we keep company with and enjoy having conversations.

He who says he abides in him ought himself
also to walk just as he walked. (1 John 2:6)

Only by walking with Christ will we mature in walking like Christ. Love to him is the motivating spring for this pursuit. Love to Christ, being found in him, is what makes us lovely to God!

In this narrative, we have two prominent exhibitions of our Lord's full heart of tender care and compassion.

a.   The outburst of our Lord's aching heart

It may surprise us to read the first passion-filled bursting of Christ's heart:

O faithless and perverse generation, how
long shall I be with you? How long shall I bear
with you? Bring him here to me. (Matthew
17:17)

What created this outburst? He saw what was before him: the sad combination of human need, aggressive enemies, pathetic helplessness, and crippling unbelief. In this situation, as soon as the dad said of his disciples, "they could not," Christ's compassionate heart broke out. They could not what? Help a despairing father with the horrible plight of his son. They could not help a boy trapped from his childhood in a world of darkness, agony, misery, and pain beyond imagination, locked up, confined by a foul fiendish being, one of the eternal enemies of God, the hounding of religious externalist, looking for vulnerable opportunities to pounce upon his reputation and discount his mission of compassion—his mission which was the only genuine hope for any of humanity!

Follow closely this train of thought revealing what our Lord was witnessing and experiencing within his perfect human soul coming from a fresh taste of the glory he had with the Father before the world began. He comes upon the ruinous labors of false religion to lead souls astray and secure their eternal damnation. They dogged his heals to undermine his compassionate mission of mercy. Our Lord has exposure to the stench of a foul fiend with his demonic pleasure in destroying a home, a dad's delight, and a young boy's youth. Here was a melancholy display of the devil's evil work set before the Savior's face. The Lord Jesus is walking amid the consequences attached to the fall and the fallenness of humanity. His eyes witness human depravity, sickness, disease—all the ugliness of sin's twisting, perverting, and demolition of the image of God. His humanity felt the devastating condition of the humanity he came to rescue. When you add to this the culminating words "your disciples could not help," it overwhelmed the pure soul of our Savior's compassionate affections.

These realities, crushing in upon the Lord Jesus with his pure and caring affections for people, drew out the exasperation and anguish of his soul.

> O faithless and perverse generation, how long shall I be with you? How long shall I bear with you? Bring him here to me. (Matthew 17:17)

Our Savior was an actual human being capable of righteous indignation. As with the disrespectful dishonor shown to his Father's house when he cleansed the temple, he showed holy indignation to the soul-destroying practices of the scribes and Pharisees. All with sinless perfection and holy affections, his soul gave expression to his soul's anguish at the foot of the mount.

We will take up the disciples' failures and our Lord's communication to them in the next chapter. It includes our failures as well and how our Savior responds to us. Our need here is to enter the heart of Christ as best we can.

Christ was the only human on earth to have perfect faith, belief, and trust in God! None of us can relate to that. However, that reality intensifies our Lord's response to all he saw. There are many little streams flowing into the river of gushing emotion revealed in our Savior's cry. The ravages of unbelief permeate all before him. He witnessed precious souls, twisted out of the way of truth, sincerity, and transparent honesty.

> The heart is deceitful and desperately wicked. (Jeremiah 17:9)

He saw and felt this deeply.

He expected his disciples to have sufficient faith to do what he commissioned and commanded them to do. No matter how hard it seemed to them, they were to be faithful to their calling. When it was difficult, they were to pour out their hearts in believing prayer to God. They were to grow more earnest in prayer until they received what they needed to cast out the demon. There was no other option. He told them to represent him in healing the sick, raising the dead, cleansing lepers, and casting out demons (Matthew 10:1, 8). He taught them how to pray, yet there was a painful slowness in them to grasp this and bring it into their reality. (We all can relate to this!) Now this man's agony increased, and the plight of his son seemed more hopeless. Here was a sheep on the precipice of a great gulf of despair. All these realities took hold of the soul of our Savior with powerful, gripping force. Never is our Lord a mere bystander and observer of human misery or pain—nor is he to yours.

The Lord Jesus lived with his own spirit, affected by the eternal realities of all individuals. His pure and undefiled soul felt the kingdom of darkness, greedy to sweep as many as possible into eternal ruin. In that expression "Oh, faithless generation," is the cry, "Why? Why will you die? Why will you choose eternal death?"

His pure soul had no delight in the death of the wicked.

> "As I live," says the Lord God, "I have no pleasure in the death of the wicked; but that the wicked turn from his way and live: turn you, turn you from your evil ways; for why will you die." (Ezekiel 33:11)

He will say the same thing in one month, in his last few days, as he looked upon Jerusalem.

> O Jerusalem, Jerusalem, the one who kills the prophets and stones, those who are sent to her! How often I wanted to gather your children together, as a hen gathers her chicks under her wings, but you were not willing! (Matthew 23:37)

Oh, what melancholy, sad, and mournful words! "You were not willing!"

The reality of corruption permeating humanity, twisting itself out of the moral uprightness he had made them, came before his soul's view in vivid color. This penetrated and tortured the affections he had for them.

> Truly, this only I have found: that God made man upright, but they have sought out many schemes. (Ecclesiastes 7:29)

The word *schemes* means "devious ways to destroy, twist and pervert, bringing destruction to that uprightness." Man's schemings bring about humanity's miseries. Humanity corrupting itself, marinating in alienation from God, morally warped and defaced humanity from his original glory. Our Lord saw this afresh in its raw reality. "Perverse" and "unbelieving" imply that failing to believe stems from moral failure to acknowledge and recognize the truth. Unbelief is not from lack of evidence; it arises from willful neglect and distortion of evidence (Romans 1).

Then we have these words: "How long?" He filled these words with anguish, not anger. "Till when?" The scene presented meager hope of people moving in a heavenly direction. The appearance was dreary and discouraging when he longed to do them eternal good. "How long shall I suffer you? How long shall I bear with you? Oh, how long will you continue in such a state as to try and tax, to the utmost, the patience of my heart set on your good? How long shall I agonize for your external, internal, and especially your eternal good and you turn a deaf ear?"

Excruciating pain of soul is what our Savior displays in this volcanic explosion of real human emotion. His affections for the indifferent ignited affectionate appeals to turn from their insanity.

> Seek me while I may be found. Call upon me while I am near! I am the only Savior given to humanity, and I am here standing in your midst! Come to me! Call upon me! I am the one who will have mercy on you. I am the one who will abundantly pardon! (Isaiah 55:6–7)

He lived with this reality. He lived with another reality: in one month, they would nail him to the cross.

b. The outflow of our Lord's compassionate care skillfully applied

Notice the incredible self-government of the Lord Jesus. He turns his attention to the father and son with focused affection, genuine care, and compassion. "Bring him to me." It is in the plural.

"All of you, whatever it takes to subdue him in his thrashing, pick him up, foaming mouth and all, and bring him to me." The demon did not want this. There is indignation in the heart of our Lord toward the evil spirit. There is immense compassion for the father and boy. Resident in our Savior's soul lived incredible tenderheartedness toward the afflictions of humanity as the offspring of man's own rebellion against God. He is a sinful man's only hope. "Bring him to me" for I am the remedy for evil's destructive work, sin's devastating plagues, and all human agony and misery flowing from human self-destruction. I have a heart and skill to heal this afflicting malady. "I am here for such a moment as this."

Notice how our Lord addresses the dad. With incredible poise of heart, he turns with focused gentleness to engage this caring, grief-torn father. It is with great care, sensitivity, and intentionality that he speaks. He was skilled in speaking a word in season to every weary soul. (Isaiah 11:1–5; 50:4–6: these passages describe the inner life of our Lord.)

> So He asked his father, "'How long has this
> been happening to him?"

He did not need this information. There is, however, something beautiful and tender in Christ's transactions with this father. In asking this, he wisely draws him away from the cliff of despair and hopelessness, helps settle his emotions, and engages his soul's faith. This dad had come to the location thinking Christ was there. He experienced major letdown. Christ commissioned the disciples to cast out demons, so he went to them. They could not do it! Despair and doubt were gaining a grip on this man's soul, and his inner world was growing heavy with a felt darkness. Our Lord knew this. This man needed his train of thought to be interrupted and his emotions to cool so he could focus on the person and words of Christ.

He begins with the question: "How long has your son suffered?" This invites him to tell the story of long sorrow—nights of interrupted sleep, social isolation because of the volatility of his boy, embarrassment and withdrawal from public places. Who could count the many dark moments of desperate praying for help and solutions this dad experienced? All he experienced were possibilities vanishing. All hope continued disappearing over the horizons of daily life.

Christ helps him unburden his heart. A burden shared with Christ eases some of the painful weight. Also, speaking refreshes the feeling of pain and desperate necessity for remedy. Felt need often gives birth to faith. He remembers and relates afresh his son's cruel sufferings. Christ is actually helping him align his thoughts and emotions to exercise faith. This is the way of our Lord in soul work. He does the same with us.

> Whoever is wise will observe these things, and they will understand the loving-kindness of the Lord. (Psalm 107:43)

> And he said, "From childhood. And often he has thrown him both into the fire and into the water to destroy him."

With this fresh replay of terror-filled experiences, the dad erupts with intense pleading for help! It is all so real to him—again!

> But if you can do anything, have compassion on us and help us.

The Lord Jesus knew what was in this man and, with tenderness, perfect knowledge, and perfect love, deals with this heart full of desperate sorrow. Here is one more little token of Christ's gentle way of healing. With his profound wisdom and tenderness, he helped this father to know his need afresh, and vividly feel his helpless misery. Gently he draws this father to lay hold of the only refuge from sorrow and pain.

When the father pleads with Christ for help, you can feel the dad's agony and desperation. However, the father speaks as though the Savior's ability was questionable. He just experienced the inability and failure of his disciples. Christ did not take the father's expression "if you can do anything" as an offense. Our Lord is not picking at words. Christ draws the father back from a panic-filled threat to hope being dashed again. He is settling the soul and directing his faith aright. It was essential he had accurate views of who stood before him, how capable he was, and where the limiting problem lived. The Lord Jesus makes it clear there are no—absolutely no—limitations on what he can do. If this man fully knew who was before him, he would say,

> Ah, Lord God! Behold, you have made the heavens and the earth by your great power and outstretched arm. There is nothing too hard for you. (Jeremiah 32:17)

All limitations rest in the soul of individuals. Keep that in mind as we move along through the narrative. Keep it in mind through life as well.

The Greek has this emphasis: "Jesus said to him, 'If you can? No, all things are possible to him who believes.'" Christ repeats the man's statement, "If you can?" as if he said to this desperate dad, "Oh, do not look upon me with doubt as to imply: If I can?" This expresses the sadness of surprise in the Lord Jesus. Our Lord repeats the half-believing, half-despairing words of the father in a tone of sadness, "If you can? Ah, don't speak this way, for I came to heal and do wonderful works of compassion in the skillful application of my power and tender care. Do not read the failings of my imperfect disciples as representing my abilities."

Our Lord puts emphasis on the limitless power of God. "That is not and never is the place of inability, spoiled dreams, or shattered hope for help in time of need!"

"Embrace this truth: 'If you—you, my dear heart-torn father—if you can believe, all things are possible to him who believes.'"

This was the problem of the previous failure—not only by the father but also by the disciples.

"Immediately the father of the child cried out and said with tears, 'Lord, I believe; help my unbelief!'"

Brethren, we see the power of imperfect faith in these words. We see the wisdom of bringing our imperfect faith to Christ as this father does. This father's eager, fear-stricken cry makes the most of his little faith and, to ensure the benefit, adds a prayer for an increase of faith. Tucked in this statement is a pleading prayer: "O Lord, touch, heal, and mend my unbelief with your physician's skill." Brethren, there is sweet wisdom in felt helplessness to take our experience of "it isn't all of what it should be" to Christ. When we get out of touch with our need, we get out of touch with the true spirit of prayer. Christ is always gentle and caring. He comes with compassionate understanding and soothing touches of mending assistance for our incompleteness. He knows that nothing is fully as it ought to be with us in this life.

> It does not yet appear what we shall be.
> (1 John 3:2)

That is why we have the Spirit as our internal intercessor and Christ above as our heavenly intercessor (Romans 8:26–27; 1 John 2:1–2).

The father's love was obvious and takes the best course: "help me even if unbelief is mixed with my belief."

"I can't go another moment with my son in this condition. Oh, please, don't let me be the hindrance to his cure!"

This man was facing reality. It is wisdom for the saints to bring their incompleteness and imperfections to their kind and tender-hearted God. Why? Because of his tender loving care for his trusting people—"warts and all." Sometimes our feelings are heretical! They are inconsistent with truth. In other words, they are not reflective of our Savior's heart nor accurate representations of his truth. Christ will never draw back and think, "Wow, I didn't know what I was getting into when I saved you!" To say this sounds foolish, but we sometimes feel this way. It is wrong and denigrates the love and compassion of our Savor.

Take special notice of Nehemiah's prayer:

> O Lord, I pray, please let your ear be atten-
> tive to the prayer of your servant, and to the
> prayer of your servants who desire to fear your
> name. (Nehemiah 1:11)

"Lord, we have not behaved as a people should who fully and wonderfully fear your name, but we want to!" This dad was express-ing something of the same sentiment.

Beloved, felt helplessness is not a bad thing! Felt imperfect devotion, service, and prayer are not bad! It is real. It is facing reality. Wisdom leads us to take it all to Christ. It is often the pathway to great displays of our Lord's care. "Blessed are the poor in spirit." Most likely, if the disciples had prayed like this father prayed, the demon would be gone!

We should all realize that our Lord sees our reality far clearer than we do. Once again, this heightens our need to study his Word, trust him in his leadership, and pursue a transparent companionship approach to life with Christ. Walking with God daily is the only appropriate way to live.

> When Jesus saw that the people came run-
> ning together, he rebuked the unclean spirit, say-
> ing to it, "Deaf and dumb spirit, I command you,
> come out of him and enter him no more!" Then
> the spirit cried out, convulsed him greatly, and
> came out of him. And he became as one dead,
> so that many said, "He is dead." But Jesus took
> him by the hand and lifted him up, and he arose.
> (Mark 9:25–27)

Our Lord never put on a show to give people sensational expe-riences. This evil spirit showed great disdain for our Lord, yet there is no disputing of our Savior's authoritative command. The final touch of our Lord's compassion is taking the boy by the hand and lifting him up. Graphic displays of Christ's personal kindness are set before us. Expect the same treatment toward you. He loves to give it.

Beloved brother or sister, for you to have read this far, you must be genuinely desirous of developing your prayer life. This is what I have found. The greatest help for me to pray is considering passages like this and seeking the Holy Spirit's help to behold my great Lord Jesus. Seek to learn more about his loving heart, knowing he is the same right now. Meditate much on the character and qualities of your Savior. Get to know his kind and loving heart. Like this father, he will draw you out to pray:

> Jesus, I am resting—resting in the joy of what thou art; I am finding out the greatness of thy loving heart. Thou hast bid me gaze upon you, and your beauty fills my soul, for by your transforming power, thou hast made me whole.
>
> Oh, how great your loving kindness, Vaster, broader than the sea! Oh, how marvelous your goodness, lavished all on me! Yes, I rest in you, Beloved, know what wealth of grace is Thine, know your certainty of promise and have made it mine.

Consider these few concluding exhortations:

1. Think much of the vital role your love for Christ has in your relationship with him and your heavenly Father.

Love to Christ enlivens and breathes life into all your obedience and makes it acceptable. Love to his person is the foundation of all that God will receive as lovely and genuinely acceptable from us.

> If anyone loves me, he will keep my word; and my Father will love him, and we will come to him and make our home with him. (John 14:23–24)

Notice how he separates love from obedience. Why? Love for him becomes fruitful in obedience. He does not accept just any obedience to his commands or his words. The only obedience that is acceptable is what proceeds from love to his person. This should be a matter that moves us to prayer.

Here is what I mean: the best looking, "closest to perfection," obedience and religious activity we may accomplish, if it does not flow from a heart of love to Christ, is ugly and abominable to God! He rejects it as foul and unclean in his sight. Nothing is acceptable that does not flow from love to Christ. Grateful love produces loving obedience and service.

However, the most pathetic, failing, imperfect activity any effort to obey and follow the words and commands of Christ out of love for him are precious, valuable, prized and most lovely to your heavenly Father. Christ and your heavenly Father will always have their eye upon your heart in all devotional service to them. Man can get so impressed with outward performance; God looks upon the heart.

This consideration can be motivational in our prayer life. We will need to cry out to the Holy Spirit to move us to greater, deeper, and richer experiences of his love. Why? To move us to greater love for him. We love him because he first loved us. The more we experience and study his love, the greater our love becomes.

2. No professed love to Christ that is unfruitful in obedience is true or acceptable love.

> He who does not love me does not keep my
> words; and the word which you hear is not mine
> but the Father's who sent me. (John 14:24)

It will always be the case—by our fruits, the condition of our hearts shows itself. "But I'm sincere!" Show your sincerity by your diligence to obey and follow his words and commands. It has always been this way. The love of God was the life and substance of all obedience. "You shall love the Lord your God with all your heart, with all your soul, your mind, and strength." This was the summation of the law's requirement. The fruits of love are obedience to what he commands.

What happens when the church casts off the moral law of God, the commands of Christ, and a passionate pursuit of obedience to Christ?

> Because lawlessness will abound, the love of
> many will grow cold. (Matthew 24:12)

Love to Christ grows cold, love to self grows warm, and we draw focus on externals.

Consider how serious a matter this is from the testimony of Scripture:

> If anyone does not love the Lord Jesus Christ,
> let him be accursed. (1 Corinthians 16:22)

We are not to take this lightly.

> Grace be with all those who love our Lord
> Jesus Christ in sincerity. (Ephesians 6:24)

There is such a thing as an insincere profession of love to Christ. What is the evidence that sincere love to his person lives in the soul? A life of obedience from a heart of love to him.

We need to give this serious thought. We need to be fervent in prayer concerning this matter.

3. How do we have more love in our hearts?

> The Holy Spirit who was given to us
> has poured the love of God out in our hearts.
> (Romans 5:5)

Ask the Father to give the Holy Spirit's influence to inflame greater love to Christ in your soul. Meditate on the love of Christ.

Look for the displays of it in the Gospel accounts. Pray over every line of Paul's prayer in Ephesians 3:14–19. Ask the Holy Spirit to break up the fallow ground and hard soil of your heart and nurture a tender affection for the person of your Savior. Think much of his great love for you. Ask him to make you feel the great debt of love you rightly owe him (2 Corinthians 5:14–15).

We really should be fervent in prayer concerning this matter. Demonstrate how much you treasure and value love to Christ by your diligence in prayer. Desire great things greatly.

4. Pray for the church.

How much does the church display likeness to Christ in his works of compassion? How do we treat one another through struggles and failings? Can we see Christ there?

> Assuredly, I say to you, inasmuch as you did
> it to one of the least of these my brethren, you
> did it to me. (Matthew 25:40)

5. Keep looking to Jesus as clothed with your humanity.

> *We do not have a High Priest who cannot sympathize with our weaknesses, but was in all points tempted as we are, yet without sin. Let us therefore come boldly to the throne of grace that we may obtain mercy and find grace to help in time of need (Hebrews 4:15–16)*

A proper view of our Savior's fellow feeling with us is a great motivator to pray. We will give ourselves to strong pleadings for his help in time of need. We are to come to the mercy seat and throne of grace with all our weaknesses, infirmities, struggles with unbelief, sins, and failures. Why? Because we have such a High Priest who is skillful and compassionate to render the best help in perfect application of his gentle, healing touch. You will receive the same treatment from Christ as the father of the demon-possessed son did. He is the same tenderhearted Savior for you. Ask him to draw your heart into a richer life of prayer.

Samuel Rutherford said of Christ, "Since he looked upon me, my heart is not my own. He has run away to heaven with it."

15

If Christ Commands It,
"I Can't" Is Never an Option

God likes to see his people shut up to this,
that there is no hope but in prayer. Herein lies
the church's power against the world.

—Andrew Bonar

Christianity can seem very confusing. The good news is Christ paid the debt we could not pay. He died the death we dare not die. He provides acceptance we do not deserve. So simple a child can understand. However, then he calls us to a life we cannot live. Our entire approach to life changes. Contrary to popular opinion and worldly logic, to be great in the kingdom of heaven is to be a servant of all. Like John the Baptist, we are to decrease, and Christ is to increase.

There are two graces which solve the mystery and make a clear path before us: love and faith—supreme love for Christ and through him for the Father and Spirit. The Spirit implants a love for the word and commands of Christ. The Spirit birthed us into the family of God and love to the people of God as the choicest ones on earth. Faith, authored and sustained by Christ and the Spirit, embraces the Bible as the testimony of God. To faith, the Bible is the ultimate word. It is the all-sufficient rule and guide for one's entire life. Love generates a life force in our faith.

Faith working through love. (Galatians 5:6)

Citizenship in heaven brings a unique language and value system. Like the love of God that enters our hearts, "it is not of this world," so its residence in our hearts makes us "not of this world." God makes us a "peculiar people." We are in this world as "strangers, pilgrims, and sojourners." Our Lord told us,

What is highly esteemed among men is an abomination in the sight of God. (Luke 16:15)

This applies to the Christian life and the Christian church. Our beliefs, values, and motives change. Our allegiance now is to Christ and his rule in our lives.

The disciples had been with Christ for just over three years. They witnessed him as the possessor of all supernatural powers. His authority in word and deed testified to his identity. Peter gave expression to the reality:

You are the Christ the Son of the Living God. (Matthew 16:16)

The disciples were reliant on the physical presence of Christ. To a degree, it crippled their growth. They had to learn to live by faith upon the divine surety of Christ's words. They were to be faithful to their calling and duty given to them by Christ especially in his absence.

These disciples were painfully conscious of their failure with the demon-possessed boy, most likely numb from the attacks of the scribes, embarrassed by failure before the crowds, grieved for the dad and boy, relieved by Christ's appearance and success; in private they come to Christ. Our Lord had told them many times not to doubt but believe. When they come to him, the lesson and answer will be the same.

> When he had come into the house, his disciples asked him privately, "Why could we not cast it out?" So Jesus said to them, "Because of your unbelief; for assuredly, I say to you, if you have faith as a mustard seed, you will say to this mountain, Move from here to there, and it will move; and nothing will be impossible for you." (Matthew 17:20)

Mark adds:

> So He said to them, "This kind can come out by nothing but prayer and fasting." (Mark 9:28–29)

In our Lord's answer, there are two issues we need to understand. Our Lord pinpoints the cause of the disciples' failure and gives a monumental challenge to the disciples.

A. The Failure of the Disciples

When Christ said, "O faithless," they knew he included them, so they ask, "Why did we fail?" To the point our Lord answers bluntly, "Because of your unbelief." In the Greek, it is "littleness of faith." However, he will speak of having "faith the size of a grain of mustard seed," which is exceedingly small. So the problem is not the size of faith but the "quality" of faith.

He is telling them, "In your activity, there was very little actual faith involved. Diluted and polluted faith will never accomplish what I have called you to do. You tried to do this with 'shoddy faith!'" You were "two-souled" and "double-minded" in your approach.

In the things of God, it will always be an imperative for us:

> Ask in faith, with no doubting, for he who
> doubts is like a wave of the sea driven and tossed
> by the wind. For let not that man suppose that he
> will receive anything from the Lord; he is a dou-
> ble-minded man, unstable in all his ways. (James
> 1:6–8)

What were the ingredients in this diluted and polluted faith, which was actually "shoddy" faith?

1. Shallow impressions of Christ's teachings

They were slow of heart to embrace Christ's teaching and example as absolute truth.

> Faith comes by hearing, and hearing by the
> word of God. (Romans 10:17)

As with John, later they will realize, with blazing clarity, "The Word became flesh and dwelt among us" (John 1:14). There was failure to meditate and pray over the example and teachings of Christ. If they would have been like the "blessed man" of Psalm 1:1–3, they would have been more firmly planted like a tree in fruit-bearing belief and obedience to Christ's commands.

Our Lord would often give exhortations for them to give focused energy of thought and prayer over his teaching and example. "Let these words sink down into your ears." Our Lord wanted them to ruminate on his teachings, not merely receive shallow impressions of what he said. They were to give effort to weave them into the inner fiber of their beliefs, values, and motivations. Christ's teachings were to become the lens through which they saw life and interpreted life.

He brought to their attention the need for effort to understand. Christ already instructed them to ask their Father for the illuminating ministry of the Spirit (Luke 9:44).

> Do you not yet understand? (Matthew 15:17)

Defilement comes from within, not from outside. "Do you not yet understand?" The spreading leaven of the Pharisees' way of life is toxic. "How is it you do not understand?" (Matthew 16:9, 11). I multiplied the bread and fish to feed a multitude. I will undertake and provide for you in your every need.

On the storm-tossed sea, our Lord gave them vivid lessons concerning his identity:

> "Why are you fearful, O you of little faith?"
> Then he arose and rebuked the winds and the sea,
> and there was a great calm. So the men marveled,
> saying, "Who can this be, that even the winds
> and the sea obey Him?" (Matthew 8:26–27)

Meditation on the testimony of Scripture would answer the question "Who can this be?"

> By awesome deeds in righteousness you will
> answer us, O God of our salvation, you who are
> the confidence of all the ends of the earth, and of
> the far-off seas; who established the mountains by
> his strength, being clothed with power; you who
> still the noise of the seas, the noise of their waves,
> and the tumult of the peoples. (Psalm 65:5–7)

Or take a passage like this:

> God is greatly to be feared in the assembly of
> the saints, and to be held in reverence by all those

around him. O Lord God of hosts, who is mighty like you, O Lord? Your faithfulness also surrounds you. You rule the raging of the sea; when its waves rise, you still them. (Psalm 89:7–9)

This is the one in the boat with them.

A further testimony would include the Son of God's activity before the storm began.

For he commands and raises the stormy wind, which lifts up the waves of the sea. (Psalm 107:25)

Christ was the one who gave command for the storm, wind, and waves! Therefore,

He calms the storm, so that its waves are still. Then they are glad because they are quiet; so he guides them to their desired haven. (Psalm 107:29–30)

"Who can this be?" The Lord God of hosts, the Lord of glory—that's who he was, is, and always will be for his people.

Are we any different? One has described Christianity in America as being three thousand miles wide and a half inch deep! Beware of just looking in the Bible for a shot of inspiration. Dig in to get to know your God. Study what he wants you to know concerning the great issues of life revealed for us in the Bible. Meditate on who he wants you to be and then how he wants you to live. Consider how you think, not just how you feel. Think deeply then feel deeply as you become more knowledgeable in the Scriptures.

2. Losing sight of the identity of the Savior

Christ was the Lord of glory, the fullness of the Godhead bodily, walking among them and instructing them. When Christ commissioned them, they were to carry in their soul's loyal, confident faith in Christ as possessing all authority and power—supernatural power flowing from his divine authority. This power was their enabling to do what he commanded.

So, in virtue of their fellowship with his life, the commands and mission he gave them were to be the vehicles of his power—not theirs. We are never the measure of what we can do. Their Lord commissioned and enabled them to do what he commanded to be done. Our Lord expected this:

> When he had called his twelve disciples to
> him, he gave them power over unclean spirits, to
> cast them out, and to heal all kinds of sickness
> and all kinds of disease.

Plainly he commissioned them to "heal the sick, cleanse the lepers, raise the dead, cast out demons" (Matthew 10:1, 8).

They would perform in direct proportion to the depth and energy of faith in him! They were to remember their activity had to do with Christ foremost and themselves second. Brethren, this is the only way to live the Christian life!

> For me to live is Christ. (Galatians 2:20)

We dilute and pollute the spring of our motivations and values with anything less. The results will be shoddy.

We will see more of this in the challenge given to the disciples, but I want to underscore the force of Christ's emphasis. He is saying, "If you have only the smallest grain of genuine faith, you will accomplish things of an extraordinary and seemingly impossible nature." Why? Because genuine faith is resting in who he is and what he has promised. This faith requires focus on your only source of strength and to move to an active belief that has an energy of the soul in it all.

It is as if Christ addresses his people: "My people, get out of your head, out of your self-centered concerns, out of your own resources. Get your souls embedded in me and my capabilities and what I have called you to do. Where I commission and command, I provide the enabling to fulfill and do."

Brethren, the fuel for our soul's enabling to do what our God calls us to do is in Christ alone, but know this: we are to live, pursue, and do what requires us to be desperate to get that enabling. That enabling comes through believing prayer. Desperate, clinging, dependent pleading are our course for breakthrough.

3. Preoccupied with worldly values and carnal concerns

Christ calls his people out of the world then, by the Spirit, works to get the world out of his people. After Christ talks with the disciples in this passage, they depart through Galilee. He tells them of his betrayal, then death, and that he will rise the third day. They did not understand what he was talking about. Then they came to Capernaum, and what really concerned them comes up:

Who would be the greatest? (Matthew 18:1)

They have walked with Christ for over three years. They have listened to his teachings and witnessed the wonders of his power. Christ has had to reprove them many times for their lack of faith and understanding of his instruction. He will be crucified in a few weeks. What is hot on their minds? Who is superior!

John had seen someone doing the works of God. However, these people were not walking with them. Because he did not know them, he looked at them as "competitors." In his own carnal reasoning, he reproved them, thinking his Lord would be proud of him. Not so! Our Lord corrects their faulty zeal and ignorance. He warns them of offenses and salt losing its savor. He tells them to have salt in themselves and to have peace with one another. Salt preserves from the rot of worldly values and thinking. Peace is the atmosphere of the kingdom of God.

Then they go to Judea. He teaches on marriage and divorce, blesses the children, and counsels the rich young ruler. Then he speaks of the power of God and all things being possible with God.

At this point, he speaks of his death and resurrection again—and what is on their minds?

He told them, "Whatever you ask in my name shall be given to you." Look what they did with that promise. They even got their mom to ask Christ a question on their behalf!

> Then the mother of Zebedee's sons came to him with her sons, kneeling down and asking something from him. And he said to her, "What do you wish?" She said to him, "Grant that these two sons of mine may sit, one on your right hand and the other on the left, in your kingdom." But Jesus answered and said, "You do not know what you ask." (Matthew 20:20–22)

The other disciples were angry. Our Lord tells them something very important. "My kingdom functions on principles of love, service, and caring more for others than oneself. You are still bringing the beliefs, values, and motives of the world into following me. The very concepts you struggle with are not in my heart. They are an abomination to my soul. Those things do not belong in my kingdom.

> For the kingdom of God is righteousness and peace and joy in the Holy Spirit. (Romans 14:17)

It is the same with us:

> You ask and do not receive, because you ask amiss, that you may spend it on your pleasures. (James 4:3)

All too often, you hear some variation of this confessed struggle in the community of the saints: "I thought the Lord was going to put me on the fast track to success!"

Be cautious of these beliefs and expectations. Why?

> Do you not know that friendship with the world is enmity with God? Whoever therefore wants to be a friend of the world makes himself an enemy of God. (James 4:4)

We should fear the Lord and dread bringing the beliefs, values, and motives of the world into our hearts and into the church of our Lord Jesus.

Shallow impressions of Christ's teachings, losing sight of the identity of our Savior, preoccupation with worldly values and carnal concerns are not neutral issues. These actually dilute and pollute the energy of faith within Christ's people. However, these are still plagues in the church of our day. These are real, and they are plantings of the evil one to create decay in our lives and churches. The "trinity" of pathetic failings opens the door for the unholy "trinity" of the "world, the flesh, and the devil." The result is Christ's own resistance and the Spirit of Christ being grieved or quenched. Read afresh the letters to the seven churches. They reveal actual issues Christ has against the assembly of "professed" saints.

Spend some time meditating on the words of James 4:6–12. The only remedy to shallow impressions of Christ's teachings, our losing sight of the identity of our Savior, and preoccupation with worldly values and carnal concerns is earnest pleading to our God for his healing the plagues of our heart. Prayer is always the action side of faith. We desperately need this.

B. The challenge to the disciples

> I say to you, if you have faith as a mustard seed, you will say to this mountain, "Move from here to there," and it will move; and nothing will be impossible for you. (Matthew 17:20)

You may think this is just a promise. It is not. There are promises which are actually demanding challenges. What do I mean? Here is the difference:

1. There are promises which carry no demands on us. They give no challenge. "I will never leave you nor forsake you" (Hebrews 13:5). What a wonderful and precious promise. He will unconditionally fulfill this promise. There are no demands placed on us for this to be fulfilled. God roots its fulfillment in the integrity of his person and character. Again, "I will come again and receive you to myself; that where I am, there you may be as well" (John 14:3). A wonderful promise. Notice, however, it carries no demands on us. There is no activity we are called to and nothing we have to do to assure it will happen.

2. Then there are promises which are demanding. We must do something for the promise to be fulfilled. These are challenges to exercise faith and take soul-engaging action. God gave them to stimulate us, to rouse us and get us on our feet. We have to do something.

    Oh, taste and see that the Lord is good; blessed is the man who trusts in Him! (Psalm 34:8)

    We are to "taste," to exercise thought, prayer, contemplate biblical truth, and engage our souls in drawing near to God. To trust is an activity of soul, focused thought, and energetic belief.

    Believe on the Lord Jesus Christ and you will be saved. (Acts 16:31)

    We must believe in him, exercise faith in his saving works. These require engagement, activity, and faith.

"Nothing will be impossible for you." This is both a promise and a challenge. It requires—it demands—something of us. We must attempt something that seems impossible. Christ expects his people and his church to press toward what seems infeasible to them.

> Call to me, and I will answer you, and show
> you great and mighty things, which you do not
> know. (Jeremiah 33:3)

When the church matures and becomes engrossed with the love of Christ, there will be an energizing force welling up within. And then what happens?

> Now to him who is able to do exceedingly
> abundantly above all that we ask or think, accord-
> ing to the power that works in us, to him be glory
> in the church by Christ Jesus to all generations,
> forever and ever. Amen.

Little love to Christ creates little attempts for Christ!

"This is a trumpet call to Christian energy." It is this personal expectation of Christ's enablement which led William Carey to express his powerful call to the people of God. "Expect great things from God; attempt great things for God." Love to Christ moves a heart to want to please him and stretch oneself to honor, serve, and bring all under his sweet rule.

We need clarity concerning our Lord's words:

1. What the words do not mean

What exactly did our Lord mean as he spoke these words: "Nothing will be impossible." There is a restriction implied.

a. Does he mean "nothing that the human mind can conceive will be impossible"? With gas prices as they are, if I believe, I can rise from the ground and just float down to the store. Well, doesn't the

Bible say, "Nothing shall be impossible?" Of course, that would be an absurdity. The Bible is never absurd or foolish.

b. Does our Lord mean if we have enough faith, there would be nothing—absolutely nothing—that would be impossible to us? If we have faith of a sufficient degree and intensity, then nothing would be impossible for us.

There are many Christians which believe this! There are those who will tell you that is exactly what our Lord is saying. "God will do whatever you need him to do if you have enough faith. If you have enough faith, God will heal your child with defects from birth. If you have enough faith, your spouse with cancer will be healed." My younger brother passed away from pancreatic failure leading to multiple organ failure. My mother and I watched him pass away on the operating table. My mother later died of ALS. Is it true if I had enough faith, she would have been healed? Was it my fault these loved ones died because of my lack of faith?

Brethren, there can be, in reality, cruelty spoken to others in their great distresses with a misuse of these words from our Savior. A mother I knew with a disabled child from birth had a careless individual tell her it is her fault the child is not healed. "You have a lack of faith. You are not believing enough to get the healing." It was difficult enough to cope with the child's constant care, and now to bear a load of guilt like this! So many guilty questions arose in her mother's heart: "Is it because I lack faith? Is my child suffering because of failures in me? If I believed enough, would I see a miraculous healing of my child?"

What an irresponsible and false, even cruel thing to say! Too many peddle this teaching in our day. The health, wealth, and prosperity gospel is a cruel sham. It is a ghastly perversion of Scripture. What a terrible burden that puts on God's dear people—a burden he never would place upon them.

More than that, what a twisted view of God. It makes God a cruel, malicious, heartless tyrant, looking down on his struggling children and saying, "Nice try, splendid effort, but you haven't exercised enough faith. Sorry, no miracle today. Go back, get your thoughts together, and try again later." What a horrible misrepresentation of our gracious God. It is a false god, not the God of the Scriptures.

2. *What do these words mean?*

"Say to this mountain move from here." This was an old Hebrew proverb for people facing great difficulties. The same is true of the saying "if you have faith the size of a mustard seed." Our Lord's words were understood as common expressions of the day. A little saint may enjoy a great promise.

Our Lord used this saying in the days of Zerubbabel, when he was commissioned to rebuild the temple:

> This is the word of the Lord to Zerubbabel:
> "Not by might nor by power, but by my Spirit,"
> says the Lord of hosts. "Who are you, O great
> mountain? Before Zerubbabel, you shall become
> a plain! And he shall bring forth the capstone
> with shouts of "Grace, grace to it!" (Zechariah
> 4:6–7)

This was a great and challenging work—to build the temple of the Lord in what became enemy territory. Humanly speaking, it was impossible. However, it came about by God's great enabling—not human might or power but by the Spirit of the living God. Zerubbabel, commissioned by God, empowered by the living God, built the temple. Just like Paul said, the real enablement in his life was grace. Grace is not just the capstone of the temple; it is the capstone of the church which Christ is building.

The context is doing the will of God, which, by human estimation, is difficult or impossible. Doing the work which God has entrusted to us is demanding and humanly impossible. The failure of the nine disciples to drive the demon out of this boy was difficult. They could not do it, yet they had his command and commission to do it! Here is Christ's commission to them:

> And when he had called his twelve disciples
> to him, he gave them power over unclean spirits,

to cast them out, and to heal all kinds of sickness and all kinds of disease. (Matthew 10:1)

As you go, preach, saying, "The kingdom of heaven is at hand." Heal the sick, cleanse the lepers, and raise the dead, cast out demons. (Matthew 10:7–8)

They had experienced success before.

This was the disciple's duty and commission. Christ gave authority and enablement to fulfill that commission. Where God guides, he provides. When the Levities were commanded to take the ark of the covenant and step into the waters of the Jordan River at flood stage, it was their duty to obey and take the step. He gave the disciples a special authoritative commission to represent the compassionate mission of Christ. Christ put his reputation in their care.

This was part of signaling to the Israelites that the Messiah has come. These disciples had an unusual supernatural endowment to fulfill this calling specifically entrusted to them.

In that day, the deaf shall hear the words of the book, and the eyes of the blind shall see out of obscurity and out of darkness. (Isaiah 29:18)

Say to those who are fearful-hearted, "Be strong, and do not fear! Behold, your God will come... He will come and save you." Then the eyes of the blind shall be opened, and the ears of the deaf shall be unstopped. Then the lame shall leap like a deer, and the tongue of the dumb sing. (Isaiah 35:4–6; 61:1–3)

Their failure is highlighted as blameworthy because of the endowment and commission assigned to them by Christ. Their failures misrepresented Christ and his fulfilling of prophecy concerning himself. This is why our Lord's expression "faithless" applied to the disciples as well. They did not do what Christ commanded them to do. Christ had assured them he would enable them. This is the context:

"Nothing I have commanded you to do shall be impossible for you. All that is your God-given task or responsibility shall be possible for you to do. Nothing for which you have a promise of my enabling grace shall be impossible." Therefore, when they failed to cast the demon out, this was the problem. It was with the disciples and the state of their hearts, thoughts, and faith. They were not acting because of Christ's promise and love for him. Distracted with other matters, their belief dwindled into weakness.

Here is a concern for the church: today Christians are not facing mountains. The church is not approaching some great need for mountains to be removed. It is all just a flat plain of comfort and ease.

What mountain are you facing? What mountains in our hearts, home, personality, work, or society do we face? Where are your impossibilities? Christ expected his people to face impossibilities. We will take this matter up in chapter 17 and draw upon the pleadings we are to use which God gave us. He gave promises to strengthen us in overcoming impossibilities we face. Why is there so little prayer in our day? Why so little bringing of God's promises to him in humble desperation to see their fulfillment? No mountains are being faced!

Inscribe these truths in your heart, and fasten them in your memory. You have mountains. The church has great mountains before her. Whether or not we are facing them, they are there. We have great and threatening mountains facing the Christian church. If God gives himself to us in promises, we must give ourselves to him in earnest prayer to the God of the promises and faith-filled obedience.

God's providence will fulfill all his promises.

—John Blanchard

16

The Motivational Force in Developing
an Effectual Prayer Life

*Could we, with ink the ocean fill, and were the skies of
parchment made; were every stalk on earth a quill, and
every man a scribe by trade: to write the love of God
above would drain the ocean dry, nor could the scroll
contain the whole though stretched from sky to sky.*

—Possibly a paraphrase of Jewish
poetry written in AD 1050

The news report imprinted a picture in my memory that has lasted
to this day. On January 13, 1982, an Air Florida jet crashed into
the 14th Street Bridge and plunged into the ice-covered Potomac
River. Bystanders jumped to rescue any they could. Lenny Skutnik,
a federal employee, dove into the water from the bridge to rescue the
first person he could reach, a flight attendant. To enter the icy waters
again would be certain death. It was a dramatic scene of desperate
rescue efforts. Only four passengers and one crew member survived.
Seventy-eight people perished that day.

The picture embedded in my memory is Lenny on the shore
with the woman clinging to him out of gratitude for saving her life.

I experienced grief for the horrible loss of life. However, immediately, profound gratitude welled up in my heart for the incredible rescue Christ accomplished for me—not in icy waters, but taking to himself the fierce wrath of God, which I deserved. I pictured myself clinging to him with affectionate gratitude for his saving mercy and sacrifice on my behalf. He plunged himself into the role of substitutionary sin bearer in my place, receiving the just retribution I should eternally bear for my sins. He satisfied divine justice, which in all eternity I never could.

With this picture of clinging grateful love in mind, take to heart the words of Psalm 91:14–16:

> Because he has set his love upon me, therefore I will deliver him; I will set him on high, because he has known my name. He shall call upon me, and I will answer him; I will be with him in trouble; I will deliver him and honor him. With long life I will satisfy him and show him my salvation.

In the first thirteen verses, there are two speakers. One, in the second person, states the blessings of dwelling, abiding, and connecting with the Most High's personal provisions. The other, in the first person, states his commitment to make the Almighty his refuge, fortress, and focused personal trust. Then the Almighty steps in as speaker in these last three verses of the Psalm. The Lord of Hosts makes promises in his own person. There is a vital connection between the Most High and a specific type of believer.

God is speaking to someone who is unrevealed about a relationship he has with a believing soul. He describes this person with three simple statements of heart behavior toward God, which God clearly identifies. These behaviors draw the Most High toward him with steadfast loyalty, loving-kindness, and divine determination to be his companion and help in life and in time of need. Everything in this Psalm communicates relational integrity.

There are two items to notice before we look at the three heart behaviors:

1. The Most High speaks of this individual in the third person. Why? So anyone fitting this description would know it included them! God has great and precious promises to such a person as he describes. These are actual qualities which God recognizes, and the Most High looks for them.

    > The eyes of the Lord run back and forth
    > throughout the whole earth, to show himself
    > strong on behalf of those whose heart is loyal to
    > him. (2 Chronicles 16:9)

    Such a heart is both the result of the Spirit's work and a powerful attraction to God, drawing the care of the Almighty. Reflect for a moment on this question: "How does God think and talk about me?" If you have these three behaviors of heart, you are the person God is speaking about. As you find yourself described here, this is how the Lord God Almighty talks about you, thinks about you, and affectionately responds to you.

2. God is talking to someone about this believer. Who is it? We are not told. Could God the Son be speaking to God the Father and God the Holy Spirit? As in creation, "Let us make man in our image." Could it be the angelic host whom he commands to watch over and protect his people?

    > For he shall give his angels charge over you,
    > to keep you in all your ways. (v. 11)

In the same way, when God spoke to the two angels about Abraham when he sent them to destroy Sodom, when the Lord said,

> Shall I hide from Abraham what I am doing,
> since Abraham shall surely become a great and

mighty nation, and all the nations of the earth
shall be blessed in him? (Genesis 18:17–18)

Even though we cannot discern who the Most High is speaking
with, it does not hinder our profiting from what he says about the
trusting believer.

Three qualities which draw the heart of God to any individual:

1. A love that clings to the Lord with an affectionate purpose of heart

The expression "set his love upon me" means "clings to me with
love." Love glues the soul to the Lord. It is grateful, clinging love for
the Lord himself and the great love wherewith God has loved and
given himself to this person. God has said, "This soul is mine. I own
him as so." This soul responds, "This God is mine. I own him as so."
It is the beginning of a mutual loving relationship.

In the words "set his love upon me," beautiful as it is, the original suggests even more. It implies the binding or knitting oneself
to him. Think of the firm, warm, and affectionate embrace of fresh,
real, soul-nourishing love found, the embrace that says, "I will never
let you go." Love is the true cement by which we are bound to God.
The word itself takes in a wider area than the concept of love. It is
not my love only that I am to fasten upon God but my entire self
that I bind to him. God delights in us when we cling to him in this
whole-souled affectionate way.

What set Joshua and Caleb aside from the other spies going into
the land of Canaan? What preserved their lives and brought them to
the Promised Land many years later? Moses tells us:

But you who held fast to the Lord your God
are alive today. (Deuteronomy 4:4)

What made them "hold fast to the Lord their God"? They
loved the Lord with all their hearts, all their souls, and with all their
strength. That love created a clinging dependence upon God. Their

love glued them to the Lord with strength of heart faith. The driving force of faith grew strong through love for their great God.

Faith working through love. (Galatians 5:6)

Yes, we are justified by faith alone. That faith comes from an act of the Holy Spirit implanting an attraction to the person of Christ. The attraction arises from the heart of stone being replaced with a heart of pulsating respondability to the overtures of saving kindness and mercy revealed in Christ Jesus. He becomes desirable! We view him as the perfect answer to the guilt and need within. This love will always be the distinguishing trait of genuine believers and the producer of heart religion. It is a great help to us when we see the vital, life-giving connection between love and faith. It infuses a beauty and life force in our relating to God.

Barnabas encouraged the disciples in Antioch to remain faithful to the Lord with a steadfast purpose of the heart.

With purpose of heart, they were to cleave to the Lord. (Acts 11:23)

With a fixed resolution in the grace and strength of Christ, they would hold to his person. Cling to the Lord; glue yourself to the Lord with adoring, grateful affections springing from your core, your heart.

It is not a white-knuckled force of will. Why is this emphasis so important? It is important because faith in Christ brings us into an actual relationship with the Almighty. The essential atmosphere in that relationship is love—reciprocal love. If it is not love, it will drift toward external determination drained of relational sweetness.

We saw in chapter 14 the compassion of Christ is part of the reality we experience and are to meditate upon. There is an attracting power, a drawing magnet upon the metal of our soul in Christ's compassionate heart. To experience the compassionate nature of his person draws us into his heart. What do we find there? A heart of love. A heart gentle, humble, and approachable.

That heart of love is an eternal ocean of inexhaustible fullness. This leads us to a life of never-ending acquaintance, advancement, a growing in knowing and enjoying the incomprehensible love of Christ. This is a central and vital necessity to the Christian religion (Ephesians 3:8, 14–21).

This ocean, in our experience, grows deeper and wider in its immensity. How? By Christ taking us by the hand and leading us to behold the love of the Father who sent his Son on this mission of loving rescue. We experience the love of the Spirit, shedding abroad in our hearts the love of God in ways undeniable and experienced, and creating a motivating influence to crave an actual relationship with the one we love. This leads us to a life of worship, devotion, clinging love, and relational communion.

Think how central and vitally important this is. A personal love for the Lord is the motivating power to break through all barriers to pray and lay hold of the Lord, to wrestle with God for blessings. It is this atmosphere of prayer that enables us to lay hold of the strength to live the life we cannot live on our own. As our love grows, we will delight ourselves in the Lord. His ways, his commands, his words, his demands, even his cross are lovely and bring sweetness into the soul!

Why is prayer less and less a marked characteristic of Christianity in our day? Why is wrestling with God so little heard of? The only accurate answer is diminishing love for God. Declining love produces the ugly fruit of prayerlessness. A dwindling affection for Christ, and through him for the Father and Holy Spirit among the professing church, closes the eyes of the church to departing glory. It is the unseen Ichabod syndrome. He can leave us to our busy activities and religious routines. There is far too much head devotion and intellectual contentment in the churches. Vance Havner said, "Never before has there been so many degrees in the church, yet so little temperature." Little temperature speaks of lukewarm conditions. This sets the stage for shallow, formal, predictable prayers which lack the "O God" found in the Psalms.

When Christ restored Peter to himself, what did he focus on? The answer: the quality of love in his heart! There are two Greek words used for love in this dialogue. Christ asks three penetrating questions concerning Peter's love for his person (John 21:15–17):

> "Simon, son of John, do you love me [with supreme love] more than these?" He said to him, "Yes, Lord; you know that I love you [as a friend loves a friend]. ("He said to him, 'Feed my lambs.'")
>
> "Simon, son of John, do you love me [with supreme love]?" He said to him, "Yes, Lord; you know that I love you [as a friend loves a friend]. ("He said to him, 'Tend my sheep.'")
>
> "Simon, son of John, do you love me [our Lord uses the word Peter had been using—as a friend loves a friend]?" Peter, pierced in heart and grieved because he said to him the third time, "Do you love me [as a friend loves a friend]?" and he said to him, "Lord, you know everything; you know that I love you [as a friend loves a friend]. ("Jesus said to him, 'Feed my sheep.'")

The last bursting of Peter's heart is as if he was saying, "In the light of how I have behaved, how can I say I love you supremely? Lord, I'm so ashamed of myself and repent for the way I have boasted and fallen so low. But, Lord, please, don't doubt the very least of love in my soul for you. Don't doubt the very essence of love in my heart. Lord, you know all things. You know that I do love you and want to grow to have greater strength of love for you. O Lord, I am clinging to you with what pitiful love I have and long for it to be more!"

Here is Peter, after he boasted, sinned, and failed miserably, expressing an honest view of himself. Consider how Christ connects with him and restores him. Why take special notice of this? Because you will receive the same treatment from your gracious and loving Savior. In our failings, sins, and mess-ups, he is a Wonderful Counselor. As the Good Shepherd, he restores his sheep to the paths of righteousness. Why? For his great name's sake. Christ loves his people even in their failings. The same one speaking to Peter had said to sinning Israel,

> Return, you backsliding children, and I will
> heal your backslidings. (Jeremiah 3:22)

As we do so, he receives, restores, and embraces us graciously with his love and affection.

Satan and the forces of darkness seek to destroy us. Satan had asked for Peter, but it was not to do him good. Our Lord masterfully uses it to purify, strengthen, and mature Peter. Remember, your Lord is doing the same with you.

There is a precious scene in John Bunyan's *Pilgrim's Progress*. The Interpreter (the Holy Spirit who illumines our understanding) takes Christian into a room. There is a little fire at the base of a wall, and the devil is throwing water on it, trying to put the fire out. The fire is the life of a child of God living by faith in Christ. As much water as he puts upon the fire, the fire will not go out! Why is this? How can it be? What does it mean? The Interpreter takes him behind the wall, and what does he see? There is Christ throwing the oil of his grace upon the fire, which will not allow it to go out! The Lord was doing this with Peter. He will do this for all his sheep. Now let us go on with the conversation between Christ and Peter.

Our Lord was saying to Peter, "Peter, remember I told you what you would do and that you would fail miserably when Satan sifted you like wheat. Remember, I also told you I would pray for you that your faith would not fail. We are here together because of my intercession for you. What you are experiencing right now is the fruit of my affection and prayer. Peter, I carried you in prayer because you are in my heart. You needed to know the insufficiency of your own boasting and self-confidence. You were self-determined to not forsake me. Your self-confidence and self-reliance bring your demise and fall.

"Peter, you must learn the spring and strength of your love for me does not live in you. It is not your resolve, grit, and self-determination. You cannot 'will' yourself into loving me more! It is in my love for you, which is supreme love you nurture love back to me. You will love me as you ought as you draw from the spring of my pure love for you. In my love, you will find the strength for loving, clinging gratitude. Drawing from me, you will love me more and more as you ought to love me. It is in pursuing that love that you show the chief qualification I require in caring for my sheep. Peter, you will love me supremely."

Let us remember the words of our Savior to the church at Ephesus:

> I have this against you, that you have abandoned the love you had at first. Remember, therefore, from where you have fallen; repent, and do the works you did at first. If not, I will come to you and remove your lampstand from its place, unless you repent. (Revelation 2:4–5)

The erosion of clinging love for Christ is a descent. It is a fall. Diminishing, dwindling, subsiding love, which had created a clinging gratitude for Christ, is moving toward the lukewarm professing of love for Christ. Tepid love produces tepid prayers. The first step in falling away from Christ is drifting away from that clinging, grateful love to him that moves the soul. What is the course to take? Repent. Go back to your first love. Convert to Christ all over again! Therefore, Jude exhorts the believers to "keep yourselves in the love of God" (Jude 21).

This is the first quality which draws the heart of God to any individual or church. When this quality is not there, it turns the heart of God away. As this love diminishes, Christ becomes nauseous. Part of the removal of the lampstand is the disappearance of the authoritative and affectionate presence and voice of Christ in the soul and church.

We come to the next quality, which draws the heart of God to any individual and church.

2. A knowledge of God, which is the child of love

Love, attaching the soul to the Most High, gives birth to personal knowledge of God. This is hunger to know God's name. His name reflects his person, nature, and character.

God speaks of himself and this person in the Psalm as having a history together. The Most High clearly states that "this person set his love upon me and further desired, in his heart, personal acquaintance with me. He pursued that acquaintance and gained a personal knowledge of my name, my character, and my devotional commitment to all who so love me and desire to know me. Out of love for me, he sought me with all his heart and found me."

How can a finite person comprehend the infinite God? He cannot! To ever think he can is gross, sinful ignorance at best. This knowledge of God is a bottomless ocean. It is to gaze upon the boundless sky. This knowledge of God is an invitation to step into the incomprehensible, inexhaustible expanse that has no limit—just like the incomprehensible love of Christ. The center of God is everywhere, and the circumference of God is nowhere. The best response is to make haste to bow and worship him as he makes himself known to us.

God knows our name. Now he invites us to begin an endless journey of knowing his name. Here is an eternal education capable of ravishing the soul with unending surprise, wonder, and thrill. It fills the soul with wonder, love, and praise that will never grow dull or old. There is a continual life-giving, rejuvenating quality in the knowledge of God—knowing God gives, sustains, and expands life. Knowing God gives joy unspeakable and full or glory. This entire pursuit of knowing God in his self-revelation is to experience life and that more abundantly.

There is progression in these qualities. The setting of love upon God created a soul thirst for personal acquaintance with God. This is the heartbeat of experiential Christianity. The knowledge of God's name is familiarity with his self-revelation or the manifestation of his nature and character. It is getting to know who he actually is as a person. Remember, God is a person. The word *know* is the same word

John uses to show the deep sense of intimacy. It is a great deal more than mere intellectual acquaintance with facts of divine revelation about God. Those biblical facts are vitally important. However, it is mutual self-disclosure between two persons which those facts should produce. That is why the marriage relationship is often used to illustrate the concept of developing a "deep-down togetherness." We are to have this "deep-down togetherness" with the Most High.

He is a person and not a system of truth. We are never to love theology more than we love God. We are not to love study, even of the Bible, more than we love meeting with God and learning more of who he is, which gives birth to communion. Our responsiveness to who he is will show itself in our prayer life. There should be times of earnest pleading with God to draw near and not be at a distance. There also should be times of humble exultant worship as he fills our minds and hearts with maturing views of his glorious and majestic Godness!

> Who is like you, O Lord, among the gods?
> Who is like you, glorious in holiness, fearful in
> praises, doing wonders? (Exodus 15:11)

How do you know people? Only by familiar acquaintance with them. You spend time in communication and enjoying life together. When you have summered and wintered with someone, lived with them, and developed a familiar acquaintance with them, you get to know who they really are. This is the meaning of "he has known my name." He glued himself to me in love, and he has pursued a personal, expanding, enriching, deepening knowledge of who I am. I am desirable to him.

Here is a vital question: Does God sense he is desirable to me? Do I have an attraction in my heart for the person of Christ? Would the Father say that I long to know him more intimately? Is the Holy Spirit affectionately appreciated and a person of value to be known in my life? (2 Corinthians 13:14).

When you look into the names of God, you will find again and again a combining of his essence and nature as the eternal God with what he is to and for his people. We cannot take up a study of the names of God here. This knowledge will include the head for study, meditation, and understanding. It will include the heart for affectionate worship and responsiveness to who he is, and it will include the spirit for whole-souled devotion in a relationship between the Most High and me.

The point of the passage is that God says, "This person has set his love upon me and has known me. He has become acquainted with me and is very familiar with me in fellowship and communion. The more he learns of me, my character, trustworthiness, holiness, and my all-sufficiency, the more he relies upon me in his life. He calls upon me. His prayers are the reaching out of his heart and soul in genuine connection with me and draws from me as the God he knows."

Our longing should be that God would say this about each one of us. The only knowledge which is born of love creates personal familiarity with God. This is the only knowledge worth calling knowledge at all in the Christian life. As we bind ourselves to God with mind and heart and will and life with love, as true "yoke fellows" in life, we cleave to one another in the deepening joy of personal self-disclosure. Christ Jesus says to us, "I have purchased this relationship for you. Now draw from my love, grace, and example to advance and mature in this deepening relational knowledge. This knowledge will feed, guide, and expand your love for the Godhead. This loving knowledge will be your soul satisfaction. It will be your refuge, security, and the greatest safety in life."

It is out of the loving-kindness of the Lord that he is describing the qualities which attract him. Yes, they are the fruit of the Spirit's work in the soul. Yes, Christ is the author of them as he brings into existence "new creations" in himself. He makes us a new humanity destined for the new heavens and new earth. We are born into a relationship with the Almighty, the Lord God, the Lord Most High, who is ours. He graciously tells us the vital "realness" of what that relationship looks like. What are we to do? Be colaborers with the Godhead in your own growth in Christian maturity.

So we see it is a love that clings to the Lord with an affectionate purpose of the heart. It is an intimate knowledge of God, which is birthed by love. Now the third quality:

3. Turning to him in prayer as the only genuine help in time of need

> He shall call upon me, and I will answer him; I will be with him in trouble; I will deliver him and honor him.

God loves the practical religion of the heart. It is what he purposed to produce in the work of redemption. All three persons of the holy Trinity are involved in its production. Notice, included in the qualities which attract the heart of the Most High, is prayer. It is the capstone and fruit of the first two qualities. It is like the three legs of a stool. If one is missing, it falls over and is of no use.

When a baby is born, it is a sign of life that he breathes. It is evidence of life. The same is true with newborn believers: two vital signs of life are hunger for God's Word and prayer. Prayer is the breathing of the newborn soul. Peter writes,

> As newborn babes, desire the pure milk of the word, that you may grow thereby. (1 Peter 2:2)

When Saul of Tarsus underwent the recreative birth into the apostle Paul, he became a new creation in Christ, and something vital changed. As a Pharisee, he said many prayers. He uttered many words, which he thought were prayers. Now, however, the Lord declares something new was happening in him. He sent Ananias to remove the scales from his eyes and baptize him. Ananias was afraid of the famous persecutor of Christians. Here is the argument Christ gave him to encourage him to go.

> Arise and go to the street called Straight and inquire at the house of Judas for one called Saul of Tarsus, for behold, he is praying. (Acts 9:11)

This was a whole new experience for him. These are the first utterances to God, which God would call "real prayer." It is evidence of the new birth.

Why does God prize and highly value practical heart religion? Because it leads to true communication with him in prayer. Here is one who clings to the Lord with an affectionate purpose of heart and craves knowing God more intimately, which comes to life by love. Love must connect with the one loved. This soul loves God, knows God, and calls upon God in a living, breathing prayer life as the fruit of an actual relationship. If a person does not pray, that person does not have a relationship with God.

Catch how the Almighty, in this Psalm, describes the relationship as being in life together. This person calls upon God as a companion to him. "I will be with him in trouble," the Most High states. It is to be there when he calls for help. That is true. It is true because he will never leave nor forsake him. He is his helper (Hebrews 12:5–6).

> Fear not, for I have redeemed you; I have called you by your name; you are mine. When you pass through the waters, I will be with you; and through the rivers, they shall not overflow you. When you walk through the fire, you shall not be burned, nor shall the flame scorch you. For I am the Lord your God, the Holy One of Israel, your Savior. (Isaiah 43:1–3)

Paul, an example to us all, could say, "The Lord stood with me and strengthened me" (2 Timothy 4:17).

> The following night the Lord stood by him and said, "Be of good cheer, Paul." (Acts 23:11)

These are the treasured ways of the Lord to such as set their heart on him and have known him with grateful praise and thanksgiving.

Prayer is evidence the first two qualities are a present reality. As well, prayer will be reflective of the quality of these qualities! It will move us to earnest prayer and even pleading with the Lord when God's sensible presence is not there.

> Search me, O God, and see if there is something you must resist within me. Help me live with a conscience void of offence with you and man.

Remember, in this life, and because of our remaining sin, we need the ebb and flow of life. We will grow dull, and we will experience the reviving of life in our hearts.

Prayer will increase during difficult times. There will be seasons of strong crying out to the Lord if we pray like the people prayed, which are recorded in the Bible for our example and encouragement.

This chapter concludes as an introduction to the next, where we take up the practical impact of what we studied from chapter 11 through 15.

God gives not only generously but genuinely, not only with an open hand but with a full heart. God is never less than generous, even when we are less than grateful.

—John Blanchard

17

Unite Your Needs with the Name, Character, and Promises of God

The titles of God are virtually promises.

—David Clarkson

God's name, as he set it out in the word, is both a glorious name, full of majesty; and also a gracious name, full of mercy.

—William Gouge

The apostle Paul was a person just like us. Christ made him strong through grace infused in his soul by the Holy Spirit. That same grace is available to all Christ's people. He was a chosen vessel to bring us a major portion of the New Testament. Besides this, Christ appointed him as an example and an encouragement for us in our growth as believers. Paul was, as we are, a branch in the vine, which is Christ himself. He grew and became fruitful to the glory of God the Father and the good of Christ's church.

Reading through the Acts of the apostles, it is staggering to read Paul's experiences. We only have a sampling. There were many others, yet we have the testimony of his triumphant passage through them all. As an example, take the time of imprisonment at Philippi.

Paul and Silas, after being beaten with rods, had many stripes laid upon them then put in prison with their feet in the stocks. We read this:

> At midnight Paul and Silas were praying and singing hymns to God, and the prisoners were listening to them. (Acts 16:25)

Through their sufferings and labors, they planted a church in Philippi.

Ten years later, imprisoned in Rome toward the end of his ministry, Paul wrote a letter to the saints at Philippi. He tells them of his growth in the Christian life. A flip of the switch does not attain maturity. There is a process. This process will never be "here are the five steps to maturity."

The process will include a cultivated relationship with God, learning humble honesty with yourself and God, the living word of God, the grace of God, and time. Maturity will never be how much we know. It will be a companionship process between God and our souls—the Spirit's colaboring with us to incorporate God's Word into our lives, producing a shaping influence on our inner beliefs, values, motives, and worldview. This creates a way of life that is found defined in the Bible as "a disciple of Christ." A disciplined learner, follower, and lover of God—this alone is the pathway to maturity in Christ Jesus.

Paul tells the saints, "I have learned in whatever state I am to be content." There was a time in Paul's life contentment did not come easy. He prayed over the issue. How long the learning process took until he made significant progress, we are not told. However, Christ's school of character building includes the process described above. Paul's testimony here is of maturity and growth in his life regarding contentment. Every one of us should be able to say, "I have learned this and that in the school of Christ." It will be part of walking with God.

A. Seeing Paul As a Pattern for Our Own Growth in the Christian Life

What was the process of Paul's growth? Much like the "thorn in the flesh," Paul would take his sins, character needs, and felt deficiencies before the Lord. He would align his struggles with the reliable character of his gracious God, the honor the Lord would receive through his growth, and the trustworthiness of promises given in the Scriptures. God says, "He will call upon me, and I will answer him." Then, according to the loving response of the Lord, grace strengthened Paul to live and do according to the will and purpose of God. Paul could say, "I have learned to be content." He testified to his growth in this grace.

God never moves without purpose and plan. Assuredly, our Lord is always accomplishing more than we realize. Love motivates the soul to say, "Whatever my God ordains is right." Submission to the Lord's will is always the wisest path to take. The thorn and contentment are just two examples where Paul faced a mountain of difficulties stretching him beyond his natural abilities. Paul learned to draw on the grace of Christ. The thorn remained for wise reasons. However, he attained contentment as a Christian virtue and command of God.

> Godliness with contentment is great gain.
> (1 Timothy 6:6)

Here is his testimony for both the thorn and the needed contentment.

> I can do all things through him who
> strengthens me. (Philippians 4:13)

Paul found it to be true. Christ's grace is sufficient! Nothing shall be impossible for him to do the will of God. If God calls us to do and obey, he will strengthen and enable us to do and obey through the grace which is in Christ Jesus.

What did Paul do? He united his needs to the character, name, and promises of God. From his own example, he tells the saints at Philippi,

> My God shall supply all your needs according to his riches in glory by Christ Jesus. (Philippians 4:19)

This was a living reality for him, and he assures the saints it will be the same for all Christ's people.

The expression "all your needs" is emphatic—every need you have, spiritual and temporal, not, however, every wish. The word *riches* means "his abundant fullness; his possessing all things; his inexhaustible ability to supply every need." It is the same as the psalmist:

> In my distress, I called upon the Lord and cried out to my God; he heard my voice from his temple, and my cry came before him, even to his ears. (Psalm 18:6)

The Lord assures all his people,

> Call upon me in the day of trouble; I will deliver you, and you shall glorify me. (Psalm 50:15)

This is what Paul did. This is to be "the way of the saints throughout their earthly pilgrimage to glory."

There is a treasury of divine supply for every need we have. Christ is our heavenly dispenser, like Joseph from the storehouses in Egypt. Our Lord provides for us throughout our journey on earth by supplies of his grace to do and live as he taught. All our growth and ability nurtured in our lives is the product of the operations of the Holy Spirit applying the grace of Christ. It is the same concept of the vine and branches. We will always find his grace is sufficient. However, he ordains Christian living to stretch us beyond our abilities.

B. The Christian Life Is Both a Gift of Mercy and Flesh-Withering Demands in an Atmosphere of Relationship with Christ

The Christian life is a heroic calling, requiring an energy beyond our own small store. To live the God-centered life means making the quest for spiritual and moral holiness the glorious business of life. Christlikeness is our Father's purpose and our aim.

1. This is the purpose of the promise "nothing shall be impossible for you."

In this pursuit, Christ expects us to face challenges which seem impossible! Our determination to advance and grow as believers will bring us face-to-face with a mountain of difficulties and impossibilities. Our Lord tells us "nothing shall be impossible for you." Paul echoes Christ's words with "I can do all things through Christ." The "nothing" Christ speaks of is the "all things" Paul refers to. He takes the teaching of Christ and brings it into genuine Christian living. In the same way, we are to follow Christ and Paul in our Christian living.

Here are some important questions to ask ourselves: How important are these words of Christ's promise and Paul's affirming testimony to you? Is there a sense we reserve them for emergencies and extreme situations? Do they speak of a promise you must know the power of regularly? Do they offer a fountain of living water from which you must drink? Is there a needed strength promised which you need and must have?

Being a follower of Christ and walking with God is demanding. That is why Christ spoke of cross bearing, loving him more than ourselves, and counting the cost of being his disciple. A major danger in our day, and we all face this, is to reduce what Christ requires to what we can manage. That is the pathway to loss of saltiness! As well, it produces a tepid Christianity which lacks the needed heat. It will require we get out of our heads, on to our knees, and crave a practical hands-on approach to living what we read in the Bible. We sweetly express our devotion to Christ in these words: "Let others after earth aspire; Christ is the treasure I desire." Do these words echo your soul's priority?

2. "I can do all things through Christ who strengthens me." Who is this promise given to?

(a)   Here is someone who would not appreciate this promise.

Think of a person who just finished eating a big Thanksgiving meal. He goes into the living room to sit by a nice warm fire in his cozy, soft chair. As he sinks in, he is so grateful for the wonderful meal and feels his eyes closing and about to drift off to sleep.

Now, suppose his wife comes in and says, "Honey, I was reading this from the Bible: 'Nothing shall be impossible for you!' Isn't that a great promise?" Without opening his eyes, he says, "Oh, yes, that is a wonderful promise. Now I'm about to do something that is very possible. I'm going to take a nice nap."

There is something striking about American Christianity represented in this brief story. We have too many full, drowsy, comfortable professing believers in our day. They enjoy a full spiritual meal in their regular Sunday routine. They receive great truth in messages, books, podcasts, even family devotions. Wonderful knowledge builds them up in the faith, and they feel so "satisfied," relaxed, at peace, and comforted. They enjoy a wonderful rhythm of Christian living. They hear this promise and maybe wonder if it only applied to the apostles or possibly is useful but does not move them to lay hold of its truth. Why?

> A satisfied soul loathes the honeycomb,
> but to a hungry soul, every bitter thing is sweet.
> (Proverbs 27:7)

When our Lord said, "Without me, you can do nothing" (John 15:5), he was speaking about the life we would be living. Is Christ's view of the Christian life different from ours?

(b) Here is who this promise will be as a glass of refreshing water.

Someone who is contemplating the impossible, someone who faces what seems to them an utter impossibility—what would that be? Christ gave this promise to someone who is saying, "I know I must do this, but I can't. It's impossible. I have tried, and every time I fail. It is too overwhelming for me?"

When I was in Bible college, I met a couple who attended as well. They lived next door to us. We were talking with them by the fence. The wife introduced herself by saying, "I'm Irish, redheaded, and I have a temper. God made me this way, and I'm not changing."

Two thoughts came to me. The first was *I don't want to get on her wrong side.* The second was *what if Christ wanted her to have his mind in her and put to death carnal anger and being quick-tempered?*

Now, don't you think if she came under conviction and wanted to grow more in grace, Christlikeness, and the fruit of the Spirit, to do so would be like facing a mountain of impossibilities? Yes, it would! When Paul, confronted with his need for contentment, did it first seem an impossible challenge to subdue his impatience? Was it a matter of prayer and earnest effort to subdue his thoughts and bring them to the obedience of Christ? I'm sure there were challenges he faced. Did the promise of Christ's enablement encourage his soul? Of course, it did. That promise gave him the hope of victory over it.

This promise is for you and me as we take up Christ's commands. What things should we think of? Enduring hardships patiently and cheerfully. Forgiving others when it seems impossible to stop thinking about the offense. Lead my family in worship. Honor the Lord on his day for more than just a few hours. When a mother faces the challenges of childbearing, household management, and maintaining her devotions, along with keeping her heart, she needs Christ's words of promise. My wife has been there. What about giving an answer to someone for the reason of the hope we have in Christ? What about overcoming temptation and resisting the devil? How are we to live the description of love in 1 Corinthians 13? We could go on and on, but I intend to take up other challenges in the following chapters on the pleadings we are to use concerning ourselves.

God has provided supplies of grace and help. What is the condition most to be dreaded? The condition that says, "I am doing well. We have so much. There is no sense of need" (Revelation 3:15–19).

We are to study the Scriptures to learn what God expects of us. What are the specifics of Christ's commands? What does he want us to be and do as his people? It appears many are attempting too little. Where are our mountains that must move? Embracing the Christian life, as recorded in the Scriptures, will require us to get to the supplies of grace and lay hold of the help promised. Just the development of a healthy prayer life demands we get the grace from Christ to do so!

C. My Personal Testimony

I grew up without a father. My mom did the best she could, but she entered life's large world ill prepared herself. For me, there was no real understanding of what a husband or father was to be. In studying family and marriage, my heart was so heavy with how unprepared I was for life.

My wife was going through the same struggle of heart. Donna's mother battled with mental illness and was in and out of clinics from my wife's earliest years. When Donna turned ten years old, her mother was committed by the state into a mental institution until she turned seventeen. There was the absence of mothering and nurture in the home my wife lived in. Her oldest sister was a sweet influence, but she was a child herself. Now, as Donna became a mother with an entire world of responsibilities, demands, she faced a role those years did not equip her for.

We came from what is popularly called dysfunctional homes. The reality, they were sin-soaked homes where sinners lived. Both our parents did not realize their responsibilities to prepare or equip us for life. Life was more a challenge to survive back in our youth. I asked her to forgive me for entering marriage before I was practically and more adequately prepared! We cried and prayed together. Our determination was to get help from God, who cared more for us than anyone else. We felt desperate to get to him and receive from him the supplies of his care.

"Oh, God, where do I begin?" was the cry of my heart.

This is what I did in response. First, I saw in the Bible the role of God as a Father to help and be a Father to the fatherless. These passages were precious to me at the time of my conversion. Now they became an urgent need to know their real-life application to my real-life experience. I was a fatherless person who had become a father! I needed his fatherly care, influence, and tangible engagement with me. Passages were promises, fully consistent with his name, nature, and character.

The helpless commits himself to you; you are the helper of the fatherless. (Psalm 10:14)

A father of the fatherless, a defender of widows, is God in his holy habitation. (Psalm 68:5)

Therefore, I would go to passages like these and many others. Then I would take them up in prayer and lay them out to the Lord. "Oh, God, my Father, you speak so compassionately of your care and commitment to the fatherless. You know how my dad would have nothing to do with me. I have never known the love and care of a father. Your words give hope to me. I need you to care for me as a father is to care for his children. Take me up and help me. Teach me as your child. I believe you when you say, 'I will be a father of the fatherless and help them.' You are the only one I can go to. I have never known this experience. I ask you to give me the experience of your Fatherly care, influence, and investment."

Again and again, I would take God's promises to him and tell him, "Oh, Father, I need your care, love, and help. I will not let you go until you help me. You said you would do this. Be faithful to your promise so I don't lose heart. Teach me what my father should have taught me to be prepared for life. I'm seeking refuge in your care and provisions in the middle of a life of demands. I know you see it all. Draw near to me." He did!

The second thing I did was to study the Scriptures and godly books on what a man was to be as well as a husband and a father. As I studied, I focused on these topics: What does a wholesome man, husband, father, worker look like? What describes the integrity of their maturity? I wrote the descriptions on three-by-five cards. Then I prayed over them, line by line, concept by concept. I brought what I was learning to each person of the Godhead, asking them to help me.

As I learned more, I would adjust the definitions. I poured my soul out to God with a confession of faults and failings, pleading with the Father to take me as his child and give me the attention and instruction a good father would give his son to prepare him for life. I did the same with the Lord Jesus, the Shepherd of my soul and my Elder Brother: "O Lord Jesus, lead me into the pastures of nurture to grow into what I need to be. For your name's sake, bring me to the paths of righteousness in these areas. I need you to take me by the hand and lead me in life with your instruction." I would take the passages describing him in these roles and pray over every line and present them to him as what I put my hope in as a description of what he would do for me.

"Oh, Father, make me into a man of integrity and help me mature into what I must be. You are my Father, and I need the fatherly attention you promised." Again, I would take the passages and present them to him as what I needed him to do for me.

I entreated the Spirit to be my personal tutor, to illuminate my understanding, and to help me grow in these areas. "Oh, beloved Spirit, you give illumination into the Scriptures for your people. Help me understand. I feel so in the dark." Searching the Scriptures, I would find descriptions and promises that would encourage me. Then I would present them to the Holy Spirit in the same way I did to the Father and the Son. Remember this: God binds himself to us through his promises. I believed this. We are to believe this.

I felt like my head was beating against a brick wall. It seemed like I faced a mountain of impossibility. For the first year, I felt no actual progress. However, minor changes were taking place. Sometimes God does not let us see growth so we will continue to seek him. Over time, perceived growth was sprouting. Slow, agonizing progress took shape. God heard my cries and encouraged my heart.

Honestly, my experience was like what I read in Isaiah 50:10:

> Who among you fears the Lord? Who obeys
> the voice of his Servant? Who walks in darkness
> and has no light? Let him trust in the name of the
> Lord and rely upon his God.

The next verse warns of the danger of trying to produce our own light. No, we are to get the light from God through his Word. Verse 10 tells us to trust in the name of the Lord. His name puts on display the essence of his character and immense abilities in love focused and graciously given to us, his people. These come to us with a personal invitation to place our trust and faith in him.

Then we are to "rely" or "stay upon our God." Make the steadfast gaze of our souls to be fixed on him. Place the full weight of your soul's reliance on him, his word, his personal promises. This alone preserved the people in the wilderness.

> You who held fast to the Lord your God are
> alive today, every one of you. (Deuteronomy 4:4)

This is how Barnabas, returning to the saints at Antioch, "encouraged them all that with purpose of heart they should continue with the Lord," or "cleave" to the Lord.

Another way to say this is unite your needs to God's great power that works within you as his child. In the obedience of faith, unite your struggles, whatever they are, with God's holy character and precious promises. He commits himself to be your enabler. He gives strength to the strengthless, to be and do all he commands you to be and do. Think of these passages:

> Now to Him who is able to do exceedingly
> abundantly above all that we ask or think, according to the power that works in us. (Ephesians 3:20)

Think of that expression, "in us." Do you see the personal application of divine power at work in every member of Christ's church? He infuses grace and strength into the depths of your soul. He does this in a most precious and personal way to you individually!

Then take this other passage in Philippians 2:13:

> For it is God who works in you both to will
> and to do for his good pleasure.

This speaks of the spring of thought, the enablement of will, and the actual fruit of action tenderly at work in you. It is the hand of infinite omnipotence, gently holding the finite and feeble hand of your soul. What is the hand of your soul? Your faith in him. What is being done? His working and your working are concurrent, confluent, interdependent workings. It is the companionship of God and the soul of a believer making progress in the Christian life.

Beloved, you also will increase in faith, grow in grace, and witness the responsive kindness of your God as you seek him in developing your prayer life.

> Therefore, the Lord will wait, that he may
> be gracious to you; and therefore he will be
> exalted, that he may have mercy on you. For the
> Lord is a God of justice; blessed are all those who
> wait for him. (Isaiah 30:18)

That expression "a God of justice" is not to be intimidating. Don't put a frown upon the brow of your God! It isn't there! He is simply underscoring the faithful integrity of your God. He is a God of righteousness and will fulfill his word to those who wait upon him.

> I sought the Lord, and he heard me, and
> delivered me from all my fears. They looked to
> him and were radiant, and their faces were not
> ashamed. (Psalm 34:4–5)

In the day of my trouble I will call upon
you, for you will answer me. (Psalm 86:7)

God will respond to you. He commits himself to this. His desire is for all his children to believe this and hang upon the promise of it to them. Have the same confidence in your God as you find in these passages.

What does all this mean? How are these truths to affect our daily lives? Does this have an intimidating feel to it? Is there a sense of "heavenly truths" just a bit out of reach for you in the dailiness of life?

Don't give in to that kind of thinking. Rather, contemplate what your needs are. Whether in life, character, insight, wisdom, provision, and growth, you make your list—whatever they are! Then go to the Scripture and find passages which either address the matter or show God's character and promise to be there for you to rely upon. Draw near to him in personal and intimate confiding.

In the day of my trouble I will call upon
you, for you will answer me. (Psalm 86:7)

I will praise you, for you have answered me,
and have become my salvation. (Psalm 118:21)

Call to me, and I will answer you, and show
you great and mighty things, which you do not
know. (Jeremiah 33:3)

Hear the heart and clear statements of
promise your God gives you. He is your God
"who cannot lie." (Titus 1:2)

John Newton wrote many other hymns besides "Amazing Grace"! Take these words into your heart, and meditate upon them. Then take them to Christ in praise and prayer.

> Come, my soul, thy suit prepare: Jesus loves to answer prayer; he himself has bid thee pray, therefore will not say thee nay.

> Thou art coming to a King, large petitions with thee bring; for his grace and power are such, none can ever ask too much. (a hymn by John Newton, 1779)

> *That prayer is most likely to pierce heaven,*
> *which first pierces one's own heart.*

—Thomas Watson

18

Pleadings That Relate to Ourselves (Part 1)

What more powerful consideration can be thought on to make us true to God, than the faithfulness and truth of God to us?

—William Gurnall

God places enormous value on every single individual. He has a deeper awareness of the mess the fall created than any person of humanity. The fall has shattered all harmony between man and God. The fall into spiritual death separates people from people. It also creates division within our own personhood. It left broken vessels who find separation within themselves. Humanity is a mess!

But God, who is rich in mercy, broke into the wreckage of humanity with grace and love (Titus 3:1–7). Divine omnipotence, the immense power of God, shattered the death grip of sin, Satan, and spiritual death to save souls. Our personal condition was imprisoned, held captive by the prince of darkness, held by the fetters no man could break. But God, who commanded light to shine out of darkness, shone in our hearts to give the light of the knowledge of the glory of God in the face of Jesus Christ. His eye diffused a quickening ray of Gospel light.

In that moment, our chains fell off, and he set our hearts free to embrace Christ as our hope and Savior. The Great Victor reached into the wreckage of humanity to pluck a precious soul from an unavoidable and eternal destruction. With the whispers of love, he declares, "You are mine. I have loved you for all eternity. I am here to be with you through life and then take you to be with me forever."

As believers, we already are the children of God. However, it does not yet appear what we shall be. In this condition, God meets us with promises and guaranteed provisions of grace, help, and companionship. God is fully aware of our remaining sin, our failures, our strayings, and falls. We experience God's incredible, tender understanding heart toward us in our imperfections.

Your struggles and difficulties are real, no matter what they are, and God sees it all for what it is. Temptation pulls at our hearts and minds and lingers at our feet to lead us astray. We may become trapped in the cul-de-sac of our inner world, trying to find answers. God does not promise us a life free from problems, hardships, and eventual death. In reading Hebrews 11, it shows there are no general promises of safety for God's children outside of being kept by God in his family. Throughout the Bible, the Spirit weaves a broad tapestry to show how our complex reality becomes challenging, difficult, and how unfair much of life is.

Remember the five realities Christ faced at the base of the Mount of Transfiguration? They are the same realities we face throughout life. The reality of false religion. It woos us to live on the surface, be friends with the world, and find contentment in an undemanding profession of faith. Demonic activity works with the subtlety of a serpent, but looks for opportunities to spring aggressively, like a lion upon his prey. Sin and misery surround us. They have their own dwelling within us, bringing varying degrees of their menacing presence. Failure in the lives of Christ's followers is an ever present reality. However, ruling overall, and riding victoriously onward with perfect wisdom, power, purpose and plan, is Christ. He never relents, relaxes, or allows interruptions to his compassionate care and skill.

Now may the God of peace who brought up our Lord Jesus from the dead, that great Shepherd of the sheep, through the blood of the everlasting covenant, make you complete in every good work to do His will, working in you what is well pleasing in his sight, through Jesus Christ, to whom be glory forever and ever. Amen. Hebrews 13:20–21.

Our Savior gives us a guidebook filled with promises, principles, directions, and guarantees. All these come with his personal signature: "These, I promise you, are valid and real. You are to receive them as the gift of my affections, purchased for you when I bore the agony of divine wrath that was yours to bear. You are safe, for I have given you my personal righteousness and beloved acceptance before the Almighty. He receives you as myself and sees you in me."

From these promises, principles, and guarantees are a treasury for prayer and pleading. We can say, "Lord, I put the full trust of my soul in your Word." These should melt our hearts and draw our affections for communion, prayer, and even pleading with each person of the Trinity.

Opening this topic could easily be like wading in the ocean; it is so full of arguments to lay out before God. There is so much and so many it is hard to narrow down and limit what fills our relationship with God in the light of who we are in this condition. In this section, we are especially emphasizing arguing the cases and complexities of our souls in the context of how God relates to us in the relationship he brought us into. What are the biblical arguments to use in our pleading with God relating to ourselves?

Take to heart these three passages. Ask the Holy Spirit to enlighten and illuminate your understanding. We stand on the shore of a great ocean. Let's put our feet in.

For what great nation is there that has God so near to it, as the Lord our God is to us, for whatever reason we may call upon him? (Deuteronomy 4:7)

The Lord is near to all who call upon him, to all who call upon him in truth. (Psalm 145:18)

> You are a chosen generation, a royal priest-
> hood, a holy nation, his own special people, that
> you may proclaim the praises of him who called
> you out of darkness into his marvelous light; who
> once were not a people but are now the people of
> God, who had not obtained mercy but now have
> obtained mercy. (1 Peter 2:9–10)

Now we are the nation that has the Lord our God even nearer to us for whatever reason we may call upon him! We have the ear and heart of God.

The Spirit and the Word are ours to teach us and help us draw near to God with seasonable, strong, and gracious arguments and prevailing pleadings. Remember, the best plea is a sincere heart, intent on getting a spiritual blessing from him, who is the fountain of every blessing (James 1:17). God is no stranger we come to! He is no stranger to our realities. He is our Father in heaven. He does not look for fault in our words; he delights to hear our hearts.

We will address three areas, each to be taken up in its own chapter.

First, we underscore the relationship God brings us into, show-ing the pleadings we can draw from it. This present chapter will focus here.

Second, we consider pleadings which have to do with the dependence and neediness of our condition. This will be the focus of the next chapter.

Third, we consider pleadings which have to do with the good, the excellence, and the benefits from grace working in us. I will unpack this in the third chapter of this section. Let the trophies of God's grace shine. We are the trophies.

A. The Relationship God Has Brought Us Into

Why do I want to underscore and highlight the blood-bought relationship, the affectionate Father-child relationship God brought us into? As we understand this gracious relationship, our fears and reluctance to open our hearts will dissipate.

Perfect love casts out fear. (1 John 4:18)

The Holy Spirit who was given to us has poured the love of God into our hearts. (Romans 5:5)

The more we understand how God embraces and envelopes us in tender mercies, we will have more of that humble confidence to open our hearts, confide in our God, and bring our needs to him.

Trust in him at all times, you people; pour out your heart before him; God is a refuge for us. (Psalm 62:8)

God is the strength of my heart and my portion forever. It is good for me to draw near to God; I have put my trust in the Lord God, that I may declare all your works. (Psalm 73:26, 28)

1. We have the relationship of being born into his family.

The Holy Spirit conceives us in the new birth (John 3:5), and we are born of the will of God. This is the clear message of John 1:12–13:

Who were born, not of blood, nor of the will of the flesh, nor of the will of man, but of God.

Clearly God purposed for us to be in his household as family members. To accomplish this, God the Spirit has placed us into Christ, plunged or baptized us into him, being made a complete new creation.

A different illustration of the same truth is found in the concept of the vine. The Father takes us off Adam's dead wild grapevine, with its sour, bitter, and putrid fruit that cannot be eaten or enjoyed. Then he, as the husbandman, engrafts us into Christ, his eternal Son, the true vine. He makes us fruitful, tends to us, and prunes us in wisdom and love so the fruit of our lives will be more abundant, sweet, and enjoyable. This precious illustration is found in John 15. When you take that upper room discourse found in chapters 14 through 16 and our Lord's prayer in chapter 17, you find the consistent imagery of family oneness, inclusion, care, support, love, and mutual delight.

Now we are a new humanity. We no longer have a connection to Adam as the head of our fallen race. Christ is our new head, the head of a new race of redeemed people.

> Therefore, if anyone is in Christ, he is a new
> creation; old things have passed away, behold, all
> things have become new. (2 Corinthians 5:17)

Now we possess God as our Father, bearing his image and family likeness!

> Therefore be imitators of God as dear chil-
> dren. And walk in love, as Christ also has loved
> us and given himself for us. (Ephesians 5:1–2)

"O Lord Jesus, you have loved me and bought me with your precious blood. Make my heart and life a devoted vessel to sing and show your praise. Help me grow as a newborn babe through the stages of spiritual development. Make me into your likeness and an imitator of the loving heart of my heavenly Father. Beloved Spirit, nourish my soul in the rich nutrients of the Scriptures and the grace that flows from Christ who is precious to my soul."

2. We have the relationship of being justified and righteous in God's presence.

We now, upon the merits of Christ's sufferings, intercessions, and advocacy, have all our sins freely forgiven! God washes our original sin in the appointed Lamb's blood. All actual sin, with all the guilt and punishment that belongs to those sins, has been accounted for in the death of Christ upon the cross. God imputed our sins to Christ as he went under the wrath of God for them. We have a full pardon with free forgiveness. All the righteousness of Christ is freely and fully imputed to us, and therefore, God is so reconciled to us that we are approved as righteous in his sight! God views us in his Son. This is the Great Exchange.

> For he made him who knew no sin to be sin for us, that we might become the righteousness of God in him. (2 Corinthians 5:21)

Paul can speak of us in Romans 3:24:

> Being justified freely by his grace through the redemption that is in Christ Jesus.

> You were bought at a price; therefore glorify God in your body and in your spirit, which are God's. (1 Corinthians 6:20)

"O Lord, my God, let my life show forth loving gratitude, and may I no longer view myself or my life as my own but entirely yours."

3. We have the relationship of being Christ's, and we stand with him.

Christ frees us from Satan's bondage. Christ is our Elder Brother, and now we are fellow heirs of his heavenly kingdom. In that kingdom, we are a kingdom of priests to offer spiritual sacrifices to God by Jesus Christ. We are "heirs of God and joint heirs with Christ" (Romans 8:17).

God now spares us as a man spares his own son that loves, obeys, and is devoted to him. How does a father treat a son who loves his dad, seeks to please his dad, and is devoted to his dad, yet he messes up? That dad will be full of compassion, understanding, gentle in restoring his son, and caring to assist in learning vital lessons from such a "mess-up":

> "They shall be mine," says the LORD of hosts, "on the day I make them my jewels. And I will spare them as a man spares his own son who serves him." (Malachi 3:17)

This great truth forms a wonderful foundation for our affectionate pleading with God as our caring Father.

All these three points are great doctrinally sound truths. These are biblically and theologically profound realities, but none of these are to be mere information for the library shelves of our minds! Each are rich with relational living and vitally authentic communication. They all speak of an incredible living relationship. I realize our spiritual sight is foggy, blurry, and at times obscure. However, it is crystal clear on God's part. His view of us is never obscured. His desire is for us to lay hold of this by faith.

B. What Does This Mean in Our Prayer and Pleading?

1. As a Father, God does not take notice of every fault but bears with our infirmities.

> And the LORD passed before him and pro-
> claimed, the LORD, the LORD God, merciful and
> gracious, long-suffering, and abounding in good-
> ness and truth, keeping mercy for thousands,
> forgiving iniquity and transgression and sin.
> (Exodus 34:6–7)

In this passage, God expounds the attributes found in his names. God gives Moses not so much a vision of his power and majesty, but of his love, of how he relates to his people. The real glory of God is his character, his nature, especially toward his sons and daughters. His names are indicators of his nature, reminders of what we can expect him to do as we live by faith and trust in his provisions for us in Christ.

This reality is to be aligned with our needs, our struggles, our temptations, and our failings. We come to him as one who cares for us and will help us. So take whatever you are struggling with, and bring it to your Father in an atmosphere of his mercy, graciousness, long-suffering, and abounding goodness.

A loving father will not cast off his child and throw him out the door in his sickness, nor will he go into a rage over every trifling mistake or failure or even sin. You know in your own conscience that God does not act this way toward you—not that he is compromising nor that you are getting away with anything. He is sparing you in his patience, long-suffering, and anticipation of being gracious to you.

Take this precious old hymn:

> Father like he tends and spares us; well our
> feeble frame he knows. In his hands he gently
> bears us, rescues us from all our foes. Praise him,
> praise him, widely as His mercy goes.

There is a dangerous neglect of practical Christianity practiced in the church. The lack of this made the scribes and Pharisees even more repulsive to Christ. They had a devotion to God which was devoid of love for God and man! Where is humility practiced and experienced within the churches based on confident certainty about God's conduct toward his children? As children of God, we ought to know how tenderly he treats us. Then we are to imitate God as dear children in our treatment of one another.

> Be kind to one another, tenderhearted, for-
> giving one another, even as God in Christ forgave
> you. (Ephesians 4:32)

> Finally, all of you be of one mind, having
> compassion for one another; love as brothers, be
> tenderhearted, and be courteous. (1 Peter 3:8)

It was said of the early church, even by their persecutors, "Behold, how they loved one another!" This became a powerful visible display of the Gospel echoing from their lives.

> By this all will know that you are my disci-
> ples, if you have love for one another. (John 13:35)

People are individuals going through life with all its challenges, and we ought to possess a broader understanding of the difficulties of life in a fallen world? Remember, we only see through a keyhole into another's life.

> Above all things have fervent love for one another, for "love will cover a multitude of sins." (1 Peter 4:8)

> We are bound to thank God always for you, brethren, as it is fitting, because your faith grows exceedingly, and the love of every one of you all abounds toward each other. (2 Thessalonians 1:3)

> Now we exhort you, brethren, warn those who are unruly, comfort the fainthearted, uphold the weak, be patient with all. See that no one renders evil for evil to anyone, but always pursue what is good both for yourselves and for all. (1 Thessalonians 5:14–15)

In these passages, we find the family atmosphere of the household of God. It is a climate of an ungrieved Holy Spirit. We are to jealously guard such a divinely prized context of life together as his sons and daughters.

"Oh, my gracious God, help me trust in your character and expression of tender understanding. Help me not be ruled by my fears, but Lord, melt my heart in loving gratitude to imitate you in your loving and kind ways. Take away my self-righteousness, pride, and self-serving tendencies. Make me more like yourself. Oh, beloved Spirit, assist me to live in love and the fruit of your workmanship in my soul."

Bring whatever you struggle with to your Father, your Savior, and your comforting companion, the Holy Spirit. Confide in each one with whatever troubles your heart. You can do this with full conviction and belief your God wants you to do this.

2. As a Father, he does not make our punishments when he chastens us—as great as we deserve.

> He has not dealt with us according to our sins, nor punished us according to our iniquities. (Psalm 103:10)

Why? On what basis is he so understanding, merciful, and kind to us? Because "as far as the east is from the west, so far has he removed our transgressions from us" (v. 12). Because "as a father pities his children, so the LORD pities those who fear him" (v. 13). What is it in his thoughts and heart that causes him to deal with so much kindness and mercy, even tender mercies? Well, it is because "he knows our frame; he remembers that we are dust" (v. 14).

Listen to the prayer of Ezra:

> After all that has come upon us for our evil deeds and for our great guilt, since you our God have punished us less than our iniquities deserve, and have given us such deliverance as this. (Ezra 9:13)

This should bear witness to our conscience. This is the true story in our relationship with our heavenly Father. What Ezra said, every one of us can say.

In this light, open your heart to him with all the foulness you find within. Take your failures and shoddy way of living, or handling things, and seek his forgiving hand upon you. When you sin, plead with God that he would make you easy to correct.

In life's events, as you sense God's fatherly corrections, take Micah's advice:

> Wisdom shall see your name: "Hear the rod! Who has appointed it?" (Micah 6:9)

Your God, as your loving Father, appoints the rod of correction in life. It will always have lessons to learn. "Hear the rod," but make sure you see his loving hand at the other end of the rod of correction. Settle it in your heart. He corrects the children he loves (Hebrews 12:5–11).

John Winthrop asked God to "so break his stubborn will, as a broken colt, that a child could easily back him into the harness." Plead with God that you would hear the still small voice of conscience. Ask him to help you hide his Word in your heart so you might not sin against him (Psalm 119:9–11).

3. As a Father, he only chastens us moderately when he sees we will not be corrected by any other means.

Take to heart the way of God in covenant commitment to his believing child.

> I will be his Father, and he shall be my son.
> If he commits iniquity, I will chasten him with
> the rod of men and with the blows of the sons of
> men. But my mercy shall not depart from him, as
> I took it from Saul, whom I removed from before
> you. (2 Samuel 7:14–15)

God will be faithful. He will also be tender and clothe all his actions with mercy.

Habakkuk knew Israel had sinned terribly against the Lord, yet, knowing the character and commitment of the Lord, he could pray, "In wrath remember mercy" (Habakkuk 3:2). David could pour out his heart in the same way:

> O LORD, do not rebuke me in your anger,
> nor chasten me in your hot displeasure. Have
> mercy on me, O LORD for I am weak; O LORD,
> heal me, for my bones are troubled. (Psalm 6:1–2)

The Bible reveals the nature of God and his indisposition to come to acts where wrath and anger must be exhibited. In Isaiah 28:21, Isaiah speaks of the incredible hardness of heart and utter rebellion of the Israelites, which showed the majority were not the people of God from the heart. This forced the LORD to take up extreme measures. What I want you to notice is how God relates to such forced activity.

> For the Lord will rise up as at Mount Perazim, he will be angry as in the Valley of Gibeon—that he may do his work, his awesome [that is, his awe-inspiring strange] work, and bring to pass his act, his unusual act [that is, his strange, foreign, alien act].

The words give us this understanding: when God must bring his wrath and anger, he does not feel in his element! I say this reverently: God behaves in his justice and will glorify his righteousness, defend his glory, but wrath and anger are not the atmosphere he feels at home in. It is foreign and alien to him. God wants us to know this about him! Why? Because the atmosphere of the holy Trinity is perfect love, peace, delight, joy, and every pleasant experience. When God must display anger, wrath, and hot displeasure, he does not feel at home in it!

> But when we are judged, we are chastened by the Lord, that we may not be condemned with the world. (1 Corinthians 11:32)

God will take stern measures to secure his people if he must. However, we are to be assured God has our best and eternal interest at heart!

King David came to a vulnerable state of prosperity. If adversity has slain its thousands, prosperity has slain its tens of thousands.

> Satan stood up against Israel, and moved David to number Israel. (1 Chronicles 21:1)

It was an act of pride on David's part. "God was displeased with this thing; therefore, he struck Israel. So David said to God, 'I have sinned greatly, because I have done this thing; but now, I pray, take away the iniquity of your servant, for I have done very foolishly.'"

The prophet Gad was sent by the LORD to David, saying, "I offer you three things; choose one of them for yourself, that I may do it to you."

> So Gad came to David and said to him, "Thus says the Lord: Choose for yourself, either three years of famine, or three months to be defeated by your foes with the sword of your enemies overtaking you, or else for three days the sword of the Lord—the plague in the land, with the angel of the Lord destroying through-out all the territory of Israel." Now consider what answer I should take back to him who sent me. (vv. 7–12)

David knew man's tendency to act with incredible cruelty. Christ warned his disciples of religious people who would pursue them to death, believing they did God service. With men are terrible deeds of inhumanity to man—even within the professing church! All too often people are devoid of empathy, compassion, and gentle regard for others. But with God, there is the greatest hope of mercy. Notice carefully David's response:

> David said to Gad, "I am in great distress. Please let me fall into the hand of the Lord, for his mercies are very great; but do not let me fall into the hand of man." (v. 13).

What should we do with this amazing point of the Father's moderate chastening? Take everything you know God is or would be displeased with and go before him. In prayer, confess it as it truly is. Do not misrepresent it. Declare it in its full ugliness, then plead the promises and displays of his character in the passages above. Cultivate a radical honesty with God, then ask him to assist you by his Spirit in radical repentance and the changing of your ways to be conformed to his ways. This is the pathway of peace. This is to gladden the heart of God.

4. As a Father, he graciously accepts our endeavors toward obedience even though they are filled with imperfections.

Take this to heart and then take this before the throne of grace. Note carefully our Father will even prefer the willingness of our heart before the worthiness of our works or actions.

> For if there is first a willing mind, it is accepted according to what one has, and not according to what he does not have. (2 Corinthians 8:12)

This is worth your meditation. It should bring us to marvel at God's tender and gracious priorities. Our wisdom is to have the same priorities.

In the light of this, what would you not want to open up and bring to him? Here is your God, and he is worth confiding in. Take all your shortcomings to him. This should free us to confess all to him. When we have difficulties and hardships, even the by-product of our sins and failings, take them to your God in prayer because of Christ's effectual work as our Great High Priest, as sin bearer and intercessor, our Father graciously delights in our willing service and obedience though filled with imperfections.

As you keenly feel your imperfections, sins, failures, and infirmities, consider this truth: you will never realize nor see them as much as your God does. However, it is in these moments we are to act upon the precious provisions your Father has made for you for such a time. What are those provisions? Christ ever lives to make intercession for you in the middle of them all. He is your Great High Priest who has paid the punishment each one of your imperfections, sins, failures, and infirmities deserve. He is a High Priest touched to the core of his being with a fellow feeling with you in every one of them. He tenderly commands you to come with unfettered boldness to the throne of grace to receive mercy and find grace to help you in such times of need. This is not all! The Holy Spirit has been given to you by your Father to help you with your infirmities—both in over-coming them and in bringing them to God in prayer.

5. As a Father, he turns the curses which we deserve into crosses and fatherlike corrections.

He takes and makes all things, all calamities in this life, even our very sins, and makes all to work together for our good. We should know this! Why? Because he tells us so:

> And we know that all things work together for good to those who love God, to those who are the called according to his purpose. (Romans 8:28)

> If they break my statutes and do not keep my commandments, then I will punish their transgression with the rod, and their iniquity with stripes. Nevertheless, my loving-kindness I will not utterly take from him, nor allow my faithfulness to fail. (Psalm 89:31–33)

Look at how grace in the soul of a believer brings a gracious response to God's correcting afflictions in life.

> Before I was afflicted I went astray, but now I keep your word. (Psalm 119:67)

He bowed with humble gratitude for the fatherly afflictions which brought correction and pulled him out of his folly. The child of God is to see goodness in the Father's corrective steps.

> It is good for me that I have been afflicted, that I may learn your statutes. (v. 71)

Paul saw compassion, wisdom, and protective care in Christ's response to his painful needs.

> And lest I should be exalted above measure by the abundance of the revelations, a thorn in the flesh was given me, a messenger of Satan to buffet me, lest I be exalted above measure. (2 Corinthians 12:7)

> And the Lord said, "Simon, Simon! Indeed, Satan has asked for you, that he may sift you as wheat. But I have prayed for you that your faith should not fail; and when you have returned to me, strengthen your brethren." (Luke 22:31–32)

Peter, fiery trials must purify your faith. I will uphold you through it all and you will come out better. Like my child and servant Job humbly declared,

> But he knows the way that I take; when he has tested me, I shall come forth as gold. (Job 23:10)

6. God the Father gives us the Holy Spirit in loving response to our needs, desires, struggles, and felt failures.

This has been mentioned in chapter 7 and in point 4 above. My desire is that we see and sense how our heavenly Father has completely provided for our every need. We are in the loving, tender, and incredibly merciful grip of his gracious provisions:

> And I will pray the Father, and he will give you another helper, that he may abide with you forever. (John 14:16)

See also Luke 11:13; Ephesians 5:18. He is our helper, our aid in the Christian life. In every step of Christian living, the Holy Spirit is our companion and sufficiency. God provides himself. He gives himself to us! Oh, precious brother and sister, the sweet and rich reality of Christianity is the companionship we have with God. Each person of the holy Trinity loves us and provides everything we need. They do so in a most personal way. With full awareness of our every failure, sin, struggle, and infirmity, they want us to put the full weight of our dependence upon them and their personal provision to meet our every need. All this is in the context of a relationally rich fellowship.

Fellowship has been described as "two fellows in a ship." Think of God and you in the vessel of your life navigating the ocean voyage of life. He has secured your safety and final arrival in that eternal haven of heaven.

The Holy Spirit opens our eyes to the beauties of the Christian faith. Internal changes within the soul produce a sight of the loveliness of Christ. The personal work and assistance of the Holy Spirit flows from his loving devotion to you. The Holy Spirit sanctifies you by degrees throughout your soul and life so you may more and more die to sin and live to righteousness as a way of life.

Romans 8:26: He helps you express and exhibit spiritual life. He inwardly works with unutterable groans, longings, cravings to move you to pray—even plead with God concerning your felt needs and spiritual longings.

God secures you by the indwelling Holy Spirit. He seals you as the Spirit of promise and is the guarantee of your inheritance until you come to the actual possession of all you are redeemed for. This is your relationship with God. You should be impressed with this to the point of acting upon it in the way you live. Especially, this reality should affect the way you pray.

The Holy Spirit encourages you to come with boldness and confidence into the presence of God:

> Let us, therefore, come boldly to the throne
> of grace, so we may obtain mercy and find grace
> to help in time of need. (Hebrews 4:16)

> In whom we have boldness and access with
> confidence through faith in him. (Ephesians
> 3:12)

He assists you to come with assurance of his fatherly care and acceptance. This is secured through your faithful, merciful, always-caring mediator, Christ Jesus. However, the Holy Spirit brings all of this to life in your soul by his personal ministry and service.

> He will glorify me, for he will take of what
> is mine and declare it to you. All things that
> the Father has are mine. Therefore, I said that
> he will take of mine and declare it to you. (John
> 16:14–15)

The Holy Spirit moves you without fear to say to God, "Father."

> And because you are sons, God has sent
> forth the Spirit of his Son into your hearts, crying
> out, "Abba, Father!" (Galatians 4:6)

The "Abba" is expressive of a child climbing into the lap and snuggling close to a father in a complete atmosphere of secure, warm affection. Do you know your Father desires you to experience this? (Romans 8:15–16). The Holy Spirit works in you an actual, real, experienced relationship with God as his child.

The Holy Spirit pours into your heart the gift of sanctified prayer—movings, stirrings, promptings to open your heart to God and call upon him. The Holy Spirit persuades you that God hears you and your prayers with acceptance for Christ your mediator's sake.

> For the kingdom of God is not eating and
> drinking, but righteousness and peace and joy in
> the Holy Spirit. (Romans 14:17)

Oh, may you and I see the encouragements and actual practical help God has supplied through the person of the Holy Spirit for us. All this should sweetly embolden us in humble childlike confidence to commune and plead with God concerning all our needs.

I say this as a brother in Christ in the journey of life with you. We must confront the inner reluctance to open our hearts to God. Every one of us should have a sense of unworthiness because we are unworthy. However, they are not arguments against approaching God; they are arguments to come to him through Christ! Combat these feelings and thoughts with scriptural argument. God is merciful, and the fact that you need his mercy is an argument to plead! The basis of your pleading is his nature and stated kindness along with his promises of merciful acceptance.

From this relationship, what are the pleadings that relate to yourself that God expects you to use in your seeking him with all your heart? Every need you have, every failing you experience, every sin committed, every sense of coming short, and every encounter of overwhelm—your God wants to hear you bring these to him. God has given you arguments throughout the Scriptures to plead and spread before him along with these needs. This is the course of intimacy and honesty with God.

I want to make pleading with God a manageable reality in your own prayer life. Please don't be intimidated by these concepts, and don't conclude that this is for some spiritual elite group. No, these are the sincere expressions of a real soul's intent on drawing close to God and getting tangible responses and provisions from the God who really cares for his people as individuals.

You must desire this. You must discipline yourself in this. The Holy Spirit will assist you in silencing your fears, insecurities, and subtle unbelief or distrust. You must decisively apply yourself to this kind of praying because this is not for the idle, the selfish, the presumptuous or the slothful. This is for the believing soul. It is for those who view God as their exceeding great joy. It is for the Father's sons and daughters.

This relationship is yours. Pursue it with purpose of heart. Write down some of the ways you can plead with God, open a verse of Scripture, and take them with you to prayer. Make your list, and continue adding to that list all the ways you need to take this relationship to heart and act upon it in believing prayer. Practice makes better. It is by reason of use we have our senses exercised in spiritual disciplines. The real treasure in this pursuit is having the triune God as the companion of your heart.

The only grounds of God's love is his love. The grounds of God's love is only and wholly in himself. There is no love nor loveliness in us that should cause a beam of his love to shine upon us.

—Thomas Brooks

God is ever giving to his children, yet he has not the less. His riches are imparted, not impaired.

—Thomas Watson

19

Pleadings That Relate to
Ourselves (Part 2)

Man's faith will fail him sometimes, but
God's faithfulness never fails him.

—William Greenhill

I had many talks with children in our home during our foster care years. These chats centered on how little we are in control of what happens in life. "At times we must go through experiences that feel like a current in the river of life, taking us where we would never choose to go." Then two subjects would freely open: (1) The problem of human disobedience to God. Life in a fallen world produces hardships. Sadly, the very one who knows how best to produce true happiness has been unloved and spurned. (2) The comfort of knowing God personally through Jesus Christ. He brings the wisdom, power, kindness, and compassion of God to convert the most painful events in life to bring about what is good, most acceptable, and perfect for us. God, in Jesus Christ, is safe to trust!

Job had this experience. James tells us to think of the "patience" or "perseverance" of Job as we pass through difficult times. Because of our limited understanding, life holds many mysteries, and God does not give all the answers.

> The secret things belong to the Lord our
> God, but those things which are revealed belong
> to us and to our children forever, that we may do
> all the words of this law. (Deuteronomy 29:29)

We may not trace out what God is doing, yet we can trust him in what he is doing. Press toward a heart which affectionately embraces what we know God would have us do. To trust and obey from the heart is the path to peace. A chief activity God wants us to engage in is to bring all our perplexities and struggles to him.

The book of Job communicates realities that stare us in the face.

> Man is born to trouble, as the sparks fly
> upward. (Job 5:7)

I love the down-to-earth practical savvy used here:

> Man, who is born of woman, is of a few
> days and full of trouble. (Job 14:1)

It is wise to get a firm grip on the obvious. These hardships and troubles may be light and ordinary or excruciating and extreme as with Job. The book of Job is not God's typical work, and we ought to be grateful. The book incorporates vital principles on how to navigate hardships successfully wherever we are on the sliding scale of "difficult" as the "workmanship" of Christ.

> Then Job arose, tore his robe, and shaved his
> head; and he fell to the ground and worshiped.
> And he said: "Naked I came from my mother's
> womb, and naked shall I return there. The Lord
> gave, and the Lord has taken away; blessed be the
> name of the Lord." (Job 1:20–21)

> Though he slay me, yet will I trust him.
> (Job 13:15)

> He knows the way that I take; when he has
> tested me, I shall come forth as gold. (Job 23:10)

To prepare for the material that follows, we need to have the right perspective on our condition as God sees it. The sin which remains in the believer creates a complex set of challenges, problems, and potential spiritual impairments, even wreckage, in our souls and lives.

Our Savior possesses an infallible, exhaustive, and perfect understanding of us and everything we face in life. Nothing eclipses or shadows this from his view.

> There is no creature hidden from his sight,
> but all things are naked and open to the eyes of
> him to whom we must give account. (Hebrews
> 4:13; Psalm 139)

He knows us better than we know ourselves. It would foster humility and trust if we would remember this.

We have a responsibility to keep a close watch on our inner world of thought and emotion, bringing them into obedience to Christ. Solomon describes this as "keeping our hearts with all diligence." Our Lord tells us, "Take heed to yourselves" (Luke 17:3). Pay close attention to your inner world of thought, belief, and motive, which influences your choices and behavior. "The issues of life" are the outcome of what is going on inside.

Sin reigns in the unbeliever. Sin lives in and sometimes rages within the believer. It is the devil's ally in our soul. Satan had nothing in Christ with which to connect, influence, or manipulate. Our Savior was holy, undefiled, and separate from sinners. He is in a human category all his own. This is so with him, yet he is a friend of sinners. It is not so with us. Our remaining sin will always exercise an influence upon us. Our sin has an affinity with "the world, the flesh, and the devil!" We are told,

> The heart is deceitful above all things, and
> desperately wicked. (Jeremiah 17:9)

The next verse tells us God alone knows our heart perfectly—both the surface things in our thoughts and feelings at the moment and the deeper issues of hidden values and motives that we may not even discern. He knows us better than we know ourselves.

Why do I bring this up? Because wrong motives could corrupt what follows. Our remaining sin makes our hearts an idol factory. Sin creates a "disinformation center" in our souls. We are prone to "self-deception." We actually see life through the keyhole of our limited awareness and understanding. None of us sees life in its full reality. That's why we must rely on God and his testimony of truth and reality in the holy Scriptures. He tells it like it is with a greater fullness than we are aware. Often our excuses in life are merely the skin of a reason stuffed with a lie! This is a gruesome reality, and it is safest to acknowledge.

Now, on a sweeter note. As believers, the supreme motive in all we do is love for God. We are to love him with all our hearts, all our souls, all our minds, and all our strength. Thomas Manton said, "The design of the Scripture is to teach us the holy art of loving God." The greatest aid to prayer is love. The best help to prayer is a growing personal intimacy with Christ. We give birth to our spiritual skill in prayer out of intimate and expanding acquaintance with Christ.

We often stifle our maturity by a contentment in our present level of ignorance. In thinking we know, we know nothing as we ought to know it (1 Corinthians 8:2). Is it attractive to you to pray in this manner? "Lord Jesus, I plead with you to help me know you. Help me go on asking to know you better. Do not let me stay in the shallows. Nurture the roots of my soul, sink them deeply in the good soil of your Word. Make me a strong tree of righteousness, the planting of your own hand. Help me move from the seed of the Word in my new birth to desire the pure milk of your Word. Ah, Lord, don't let me be content there. Help me enjoy the solid meat of Scripture and move on to maturity. In all this, draw me near your heart, and help me know you more intimately, more thoroughly, and through you to know my heavenly Father and blessed Holy Spirit in the same growing fashion of personal acquaintance." Is that the "yes and amen" of your soul? Do you see these longings as evidence of health in the heart? That is exactly what they are.

With the eyes of your soul looking unto Jesus, fix your attention on his great heart of compassion, and let this draw you into his heart of love. In that place, take up the realities of false religion's dangerous allurements to you with its superficiality. Tell him of the sin and misery you experience. Cry out to him for help against the demonic warfare you face. Confess and confide the failings experienced in your life as he carries you in his heart. Christ prays for you. In fact, he is doing so right now (Hebrews 7:25).

Having considered the relationship God has with us, we move on to this next basis for our pleading that has reference to ourselves.

The Dependence and Neediness of our Condition

a. We are his creation, the work of his hand.

The Scriptures make it the foundation for prayer and pleading that we are God's creation. This is true both as people brought forth to inhabit the earth and especially as saints in the new creation in Christ Jesus. We are the workmanship of his hand, and so we plead for his gracious attention and help. Job made this reality into an argument before the Lord.

> Your hands have made me and fashioned me, an intricate unity; yet you would destroy me. Remember, I pray, that you have made me like clay. And will you turn me into dust again? (Job 10:8–9)

As if he said, "You have taken so much trouble and care to make me, and now will you mar me by afflictions and testings which cause the clay to crack?" This is a legitimate way of pleading with God. God knows we have actual flesh and blood and not disembodied spirits!

The redeemed community is to plead this way: "Surely you are our Father. You brought us into being. We are the clay. You are the potter that formed us and brought us into existence." That's what we have here in Isaiah 64:8–9:

> But now, O LORD, you are our Father; we are the clay, and you, our potter; and we are the work of your hand. Do not be furious, O LORD, nor remember iniquity forever; indeed, please look—we all are your people!

It is as if they argue, "We may displease our fathers for a moment, but they recover and come back to love and care for us! Nor do they correct their children beyond what they need to correct their ways. We are your people! You brought us forth, you are our Father, and we are your children! Oh, we need to know the assurance of your love and commitment."

David used this in his own pleading as he stressed his creaturehood before God.

> Your hands have made me and fashioned me; give me understanding, that I may learn your commandments. (Psalm 119:73)

God himself makes it an argument to himself why he will bear and carry his people in his arms.

> Even to your old age, I am he, and even to gray hairs I will carry you! I have made, and I will bear; even I will carry, and will deliver you. (Isaiah 46:4)

This is a prevailing reason with God to be kind, tender, and gentle. Isaiah 57:16 says,

> For I will not contend forever, nor will I always be angry; for the spirit would fail before me, and the souls which I have made.

Our tender Father and gracious Savior are fully aware of our breaking points.

God wants this argument to be a help for those who feel they are weak in faith. Think of this: God wants us to think this through and rise above our fears or anxious thoughts.

> Thus says the Lord, who created you, O Jacob, and he who formed you, O Israel: "Fear not, for I have redeemed you; I have called you by your name; you are mine. When you pass through the waters, I will be with you; and through the rivers, they shall not overflow you. When you walk through the fire, you shall not be burned, nor shall the flame scorch you." (Isaiah 43:1–2)

It may tempt you to say, "Who thinks like this?" Your God does. He also wants you to think like he thinks! Yes, his thoughts and ways are above ours. So he says, "Come up to my thoughts and ways. It is the path to health and growth and peace. If you would do so, you would experience more of my companionship with you."

> How can two walk together unless they are agreed? (Amos 3:3)

b. We are frail in our nature and makeup.

Job pleads for the speedy manifestations of God's pardoning and reconciling grace to him.

> Why then do you not pardon my transgression, and take away my iniquity? For now, I will lie down in the dust, and you will seek me diligently, but I will no longer be. (Job 7:21)

His expressions are as if he said, "Lord, if you intend to renew the former beams of favor and pardoning mercy (and I am persuaded you are), you do not need to defer too long, lest it comes too late, for I won't last long in this weak and frail state. I will soon return to my dust!" I hope you see the tender way Job opens his heart to God. It is all so very real. Be encouraged to do the same.

David used this type of pleading:

> Hear my prayer, O LORD, and give ear to my cry; do not be silent at my tears; for I am a stranger with you, a sojourner, as all my fathers were. Remove your gaze from me, that I may regain strength, before I go away and am no more. (Psalm 39:12–13)

David is giving arguments in prayer to remove the heaviness of the LORD's rebuke!

> When with rebukes you correct man for iniquity, you make his beauty melt away like a moth; surely every man is vapor. (v. 11)

So David prays with increasing intensity. His prayer, his cry, and his tears are full of pleading, arguing his frail nature. The Lord's affliction lay hard and heavy upon him. "Lord, if you continue this course of your rebuking gaze, my strength will vaporize, and I will be no more."

Job pleads,

> Will you frighten a leaf driven to and fro?
> Will you pursue dry stubble? (Job 13:35)

His expressions are as if he would plead, "What credit is it to so great a majesty as yours to show your power against a poor leaf? Or to run after a poor leaf, which every puff of wind will whisk here and there? Is it an honor for a man to pound a poor little leaf into nothing, which can't even make a resistance?" It is true Job went too far in some of his statements. The accusations describe God as a bully, which he is not. I'm simply bringing out the openness of heart and the argument flowing from the soul of Job in extreme pain.

Capture the relationship David and Job have with God. They speak freely of their finite frailty as an argument for God's tender mercies, compassion, and understanding. God, indeed, knows our frame and knows we have physical, emotional, and mental limits.

> He will not test, press, and try us beyond
> what we are able. (1 Corinthians 10:13)

When a working man or a laboring mother feel weary to the bone, God provides this as a basis for you to speak in vivid terms to him and express how you feel. This gives a way of pleading your need for his help. Our Lord expects us to be real with him, acknowledging how we need answers when our hearts are heavy and strength is spent.

Notice Abraham's encounter with the Lord and the argument he brings. Abraham pleads for God's ear and God's patience in hearing him. Why? Because he is "but dust and ashes." Who talks like this? Well, to be honest, the sweet and precious saints in Scripture who were very close to God. They talk that way and are a better example for us to follow than many in our modern times. Look at Genesis 18:27:

> Then Abraham answered and said, "Indeed
> now, I who am but dust and ashes have taken it
> upon myself to speak to the Lord."

This was when he interceded for Sodom—actually he was asking God to spare Lot, his nephew. However, try to enter the heart and mind of Abraham and how he approached his God. James tells us he is the "friend of God"! So, how does the friend of God talk to God?

The expression "dust and ashes" was not some contrived statement but the free flow of his orientation and sincere view of himself before the majesty of God. This communicates a wholesome view of things and a fitting approach to God's majestic presence—even by a "friend of God." "Dust" expresses his lowly origin and position arising from his creation. "Ashes" convey the reality of what he truly believed he deserved apart from God's grace and mercy. This man, the father of the faithful and example of faith for the New Testament believer (Romans 4) gave an unforced and natural utterance of his heart. It was the way he thought. "O Lord, I am of humble origin, from the dust of the earth. I have nothing in me to merit your positive answer. I come to receive mercy and get a gracious hearing from you. If you would be pleased to hear, I will not trouble you long. I confess my weakness and frailty. Don't let me become discouraged with a denial of my requests." Oh, brethren, let's learn from our father Abraham. Paul and James tell us to learn and imitate him. Abraham speaks with humble boldness and sweet confidence.

God has given us ways to present arguments to him. He says to us, "Here, say it this way as you ask me to show you mercy." See for yourself in Psalm 103:13–14:

> As a father pities his children, so the LORD
> pities those who fear him. For he knows our
> frame; he remembers we are dust.

Brethren, this prevails with the Lord not to lay it on his poor and fragile people too hard! Now think of this: God uses this argument to himself. The saints use it to place their requests before the Lord. This argument is to be used by us as we earnestly seek the Lord for personal needs and requests. It pleases the Lord, and that should be motive enough.

Can we abuse these pleadings? Yes. However, the humble soul will take them up in their genuine intent. The heart of pulverized pride will see the wisdom and fitting argument they contain and put them into practice with energy of heart. Practice makes better. It also leads to more mature and scripturally based praying.

c. We are to plead our miseries before the Lord.

Whatever you face in life, remember this: your extremities are God's opportunities to hear and help you. It seems we rob ourselves from sweet experiences with God arising from our busyness, short and shallow prayers, and surface Bible reading. Listen to David:

> Turn yourself to me, and have mercy on me. (Why? "For I am desolate and afflicted.") (Psalm 25:16)

> Answer me speedily, O LORD. (Why? "My spirit fails! Do not hide your face from me, lest I be like those who go down into the pit.") (Psalm 143:7)

It's like David says, "I have but a little spirit left, O LORD, to breathe after you and speak to you. Let me not spend my breath in vain! LORD, my soul is dying away. Answer, Lord, before I faint away. Lord, a gracious answer would bring life to me again. Nothing else but that will recover me. Therefore, hear me speedily, a poor dying, sinking, fainting spirit. O LORD, I entreat you." No wonder David was a man after God's own heart! It pleased, thrilled, and delighted the Lord to hear David pray to him! Your God will delight in you seeking him in this fashion.

Hear David again, and notice how he lays out his argument to the LORD:

> Save me, O GOD! For the waters have come
> up to my neck. I sink in deep mire, where there is
> no standing; I have come into deep waters, where
> the floods overflow me. (Psalm 69:1–2)

This plea is saying, "Lord, I am ready to drown. If ever you would save a poor perishing servant of yours, save me now! My troubles and temptations are too deep for me. I am ready to sink and, therefore, Lord, reach forth your gracious hand and hold up my head above the water. Otherwise, I'm gone."

Another ground for pleading arises from extremely difficult circumstances going on and on. As they continue, they create intense anguish. We are to bring this as an added argument for presenting our plea before the Lord.

> LORD, why do you cast off my soul? Why do
> you hide your face from me? I have been afflicted
> and ready to die from my youth; I suffer your
> terrors; I am distraught. (Psalm 88:14–15)

Now Heman, the author of this Psalm, is a peculiar example of extreme affliction and felt desertions from God. Think of Job. It is a Psalm that does not record an answer, relief, nor does it end in praise for deliverance. Some interpreters have thought he suffered from depression. I don't. I think it represents the steadfastness of a soul when answers are excessively long in coming. For whatever wise purpose God has, his ways are always right. We need a Psalm like this. Thank God there is only one!

Remember, God has a purpose in what he records in the Bible. He is teaching us how to plead with him by telling us how he thinks especially if we are in affliction. We are to form reasonable arguments before God to show us mercy in our affliction based on how he thinks. For example,

> I have held my peace a long time, I have been still and restrained myself. I will bring the blind by a way they did not know; I will lead them in paths they have not known. I will make darkness light before them, and crooked places straight. These things I will do for them, and not forsake them. (Isaiah 42:14–16)

There are times God allows us to experience confusing seasons when life makes little sense. What do we do? First, we can trust what he is doing even when we don't understand! Second, take a passage like this and have a quiet talk with the Almighty. He has set his love upon you. He assures you he is in control, so prize him and commune with him. "All things," even the present thing you experience, "work together for good to those who love God and are the called according to his purpose." His ultimate purpose is to make you like Christ, so say to him, "O Lord, you are faithful, and even this is part of what I need to conform me to the image of your Son. I love and trust you."

I hope you are seeing: pleading is openhearted, honest, personal addressing of God in a way of experiencing life as it really is. Pleading is taking communications from God about his character, name, works, and promises to use them as gracious arguments, persuading him to respond to us and meet our pressing needs. There is no impersonal stance within the Godhead! Take God to be your companion in life. Demonstrate your value of him as in life with you. Beware of unreality or fanciful thinking. We are to enter life fully engaged and responsive to life as it actually is; resolve to know an active and responsive involvement from God.

d. We plead our helplessness.

David expresses helplessness in Psalm 22:11:

> Be not far from me, for trouble is near; for
> there is none to help.

Read Jehoshaphat in 2 Chronicles 20:12:

> O our God, will you not judge them? For
> we have no power against this great multitude
> that is coming against us; nor do we know what
> to do, but our eyes are upon you.

He is saying, "Either you must help, O LORD, or else your enemies, which are our enemies, will prevail!"

Hear David again in Psalm 60:11:

> Give us help from trouble, for the help of
> man is useless.

We can identify with this statement! When people are helpless
and (what seems to them to be) in a perishing condition, it must not
keep them from God, but they must take this as an argument and an
actual plea to present before the Lord. In fact, they must base their
requests for mercy upon the reality of their helplessness!

Now, in these experiences, God is often at work to uproot carnal self-reliance and self-righteousness. Our wisdom is to humble
ourselves before the Lord, cooperate with him, yield all rights, and
embrace genuine meekness before him. Yes, it is hard for us to live
like this. It is hard to press on with this reality of utter dependence
on God. Why? What are the deep-down issues? Our pride fights and
desires to be in control.

Whatever becomes a spiritual oppressor in our lives, it is always
our wisdom to make our recourse drawing near to the Lord. We
are not to resort to our wit, wisdom, or skill. God's counsel is "lean

not to your own understanding, in all your ways acknowledge him." Instead of white-knuckle determination to be your deliverer, enter a companionship with the Lord to prevail in your life with needed security and help. Make the Lord your recourse and trust.

> They will cry to the LORD because of the oppressors, and he will send them a savior and a Mighty One, and he will deliver them. (Isaiah 19:20)

It is a covenantal engagement of Christ to do for us what no other helper can do. Solomon said it:

> For he will deliver the needy when he cries, the poor also, and him who has no helper. (Psalm 72:12)

We run to others too quickly.

God himself urges his people to come to him with this plea in their hearts and mouths. The LORD speaks to a people who were so helpless they didn't even know what to say! God, however, helps the helpless.

> O Israel, return to the LORD your God, for you have stumbled because of your iniquity; take words with you, and return to the LORD. Say to him, "Take away all iniquity; receive us graciously, for we will offer the sacrifices of our lips. Assyria shall not save us, we will not ride on horses, nor will we say anymore to the work of our hands, 'you are our gods.' For in you the fatherless find mercy.'" (Hosea 14:1–3)

Oh, do you see the depths and the riches of God's kindness and compassion in these ways of your caring Lord?

The fatherless represent the most helpless people on earth, the forlorn orphan that is left defenseless and helpless in the wide world and cries out to God. "Lord, I am in abject circumstances. Oh, make me an object of your pity!" Listen to the heart of your God in Jeremiah 30:17:

> "For I will restore health to you and heal you of your wounds," says the LORD, "because they called you an outcast saying: 'this is Zion; no one seeks her.'"

Have you experienced feeling reduced to a "nobody"? No one cares about you or seeks you as a desirable person to know? Have you brought yourself to such places of helplessness, the author of your own miseries? God says, "Then I will come, and I will be your help!"

God is the God of the fatherless. He delights in that title. God also delights when his people utter a felt sense of their helpless reality. However, and this is important for us to realize, God works to reduce us so we will feel our emptiness. The worst condition we can be in is to be too full of ourselves! We find God chooses the "weak things of the world to put to shame the things which are mighty" (1 Corinthians 1:27). Why is this?

> That no flesh should glory in his presence.
> (1 Corinthians 1:29)

Jesus Christ said, "I will not leave you like orphans!" Outwardly, you may think you are, but I want you to trust me, rely on my word, and walk by faith. Do not walk by sight. Rather, put your whole soul's reliance upon my faithful word. Brethren, God will always regard the cry of the destitute!

> But you have seen, for you observe trouble and grief, to repay it by your hand. The helpless commits himself to you; you are the helper of the fatherless. (Psalm 10:14)

Behold, God is my helper; the Lord is with
those who uphold my life. (Psalm 54:4)

He will have compassion and come to their aid when he sees
that their power is gone—but often not till then. Beloved, do you
see the wisdom of keeping your eyes off second causes and riveted on
God as the first cause? Do you see the wisdom of not being wise in
your own eyes? Do you see the wisdom of tucking yourself under the
shadow of the Almighty with childlike meekness?

Pride leads us to folly. Our self-interests bring us into God's
resistance. Our self-seeking, face-saving motives stir up spiritual
plagues in our souls. The disease is significant when we don't see it or
don't want to. Often other people see it before we do. Our condition
is far healthier when we cry out, "But, oh, my sin is great! My need
is great!"

e. We are to plead the greatness of our sins not to keep us from mercy but to prevail for it!

Read these passages slowly, and meditate on what is being
argued before God:

For your name's sake, O LORD, pardon my
iniquity, for it is great. (Psalm 25:11)

I said, "LORD, be merciful to me; heal my
soul, for I have sinned against you." (Psalm 41:4)

O LORD, though our iniquities testify
against us, do it for your name's sake; for our
backslidings are many, we have sinned against
you. (Jeremiah 14:7)

Listen carefully to these pleadings before the Lord. They should
be a great encouragement to anyone who trembles at God's Word
and struggles with the greatness of their sins.

This is a strong and powerful form of honest pleading, when sincerely urged by a humble and contrite individual. It glorifies God as one that is abundant in goodness, rich in mercy, and one with whom are forgivenesses (this is not a misspelling; it is plural) and plenteous redemption. With the Lord are "forgivenesses" in the plural.

> There is forgivenesses with you, that you may be feared. (Psalm 130:4)

This honors Christ as infinite in mercy and triumphant as a savior of sinners, even saving sinners to the uttermost. Write this truth in your heart: an honest view of the enormous ugliness of your sins leads to enormous gratitude for Christ. Our Lord told us one forgiven much loves much! Now, honestly, can anyone say God forgives me my little cluster of sins? Such a thought speaks more of self-delusion. If you desire to have large and great views of Christ, let him show you how deeply indebted to him you really are!

Solomon identified a healthy state of soul in 1 Kings 8:38–40:

> Whatever prayer, whatever supplication is made by anyone, or by all your people Israel, when each one knows the plague of his own heart, and spreads out his hands toward this temple; then hear in heaven your dwelling place, and forgive, and act, and give to everyone according to all his ways, whose heart you know (for you alone know the hearts of all the sons of men), that they may fear you all the days that they live.

It is so healthy when we "know the plague of our own hearts!" There are dangerous and soul-damning influences in our day which fight against such healthy God-blessed concepts. I trust they will not deceive you.

You may say, "But this is so negative!" No, it is so necessary! "What? Would you have me to despair because of my sins?" Well, I would have you despair of finding goodness or reliance in yourself or to have a better opinion of yourself than God has. I would have you come to a genuine perspective of finding your all in all in Christ.

God invites us to heart honesty that leads to humility, the fear of the LORD, and draws near to him with what he delights in. What are the conditions of the heart he takes greatest delight in? A broken and contrite heart—the sacrifices of praise flowing from a soul affected by the enormous mercy he has received (Psalm 51:17).

I wanted to conclude this chapter with two lines of thought for you to meditate on:

1. Do you struggle with repeating sins?

Have you thought the Lord will grow impatient with you or that you are just a hypocrite by falling into the same area of defeat? Are you prone to conclude yourself a "dog returning to its vomit"? (2 Peter 2:22).

Think on Peter's question to Christ in Matthew 18:21:

> Peter came to him and said, "Lord, how often shall my brother sin against me, and I forgive him? Up to seven times?"

Peter was really stretching himself in generous, loving patience toward a sinning fellowman! At least he thought so.

Think carefully on our Lord's response:

> Jesus said to him, "I do not say to you, up to seven times, but up to seventy times seven." (Matthew 18:22)

Four hundred and ninety times! I don't think he intended us to keep count. Love doesn't do that (1 Corinthians 13:4–8; 1 Peter 4:8). Now, will God do less than he tells us to do? In Christ, no matter how high a number of sins pile up, they will never overwhelm the power of his love, his blood, and his advocating intercession for us! Will God require of us what he is not willing to do? No! He condemned the scribes and Pharisees for putting tremendous burdens on others, which they were not willing to apply their little finger to. God will not engage in such hypocrisy.

Think of this in another way. Did Christ say seventy times seven because that is more in the category of what he has had to do with us? Beware of thoughts which produce harsh and unkind views of God. Meditate on this passage:

> Who is a God like you, pardoning iniquity and passing over the transgression of the remnant of His heritage? He does not retain his anger forever, because he delights in mercy (better—steadfast love). (Micah 7:18)

The word for "steadfast love" here and in verse 20 is the familiar Hebrew term *hesed*. We often find it translated "loving-kindness." It refers to God's utter commitment to the covenant relationship that he sovereignly instituted and that persists despite the waywardness of his covenant people. He delights to display his resolute and effective commitment by securing pardon and acceptance for them—no matter the cost or difficulty involved (footnote in the Geneva and Reformation study Bible).

Could we abuse this? Yes, and it has been abused. However, grace will be "with all those who love our Lord Jesus Christ in sincerity" (Ephesians 6:24). God has many ways to bring his people to sincere love to Christ. Is this the direction your affections are bent? No matter how much you seem to fail, he is more incredibly forgiving and kind than you think. Are the longings of your soul to be genuine in your love to Christ even though you fail so often and so much? Isaiah tells us, "Let him return to the LORD, and he will have mercy on him; and to our God, for he will abundantly pardon." Why? How can this be? God answers those questions:

> "For my thoughts are not your thoughts, nor are your ways my ways," says the LORD. "For as the heavens are higher than the earth, so are

my ways higher than your ways, and my thoughts
than your thoughts." (Isaiah 55:7–9)

Our thoughts and ways are not the measure of God's great mercy.

2. What opens the door of our hearts to experience fresh influences of grace and movings of soul to open the floodgates of affection in prayer, supplications, and true pleadings?

The answer: a fresh look upon him whom we have pierced with our own sins!

> And I will pour on the house of David and
> on the inhabitants of Jerusalem the Spirit of
> grace and supplication; then they will look on me
> whom they pierced. (Zechariah 12:10)

To realize, my sins demanded the driving of the nails. My iniquities required the piercing of his side and heart. It was my transgressions, imputed upon his sinless soul, which drew down the unbearable wrath of God. I crucified him!

Honestly, I think we give too little time to the Lord's Supper. It offers a season for soul-melting views of Christ's great sacrifice on our behalf. We are to be in sweet, intimate contemplations on how our very spiritual life draws its nourishment from his giving of himself for us. Look piercingly on the scene of your sins piercing him with the wrath you should receive. If we connect to the reality of that, it will open the door of our hearts and affections afresh. We will pray with a fresh sense of grace upon our souls.

Not until we have become humble and teachable, standing in awe of God's holiness and sovereignty...acknowledging our own littleness, distrusting our own thoughts, and willing to have our minds turned upside down, can divine wisdom become ours.

—J. I. Packer

20

❧

Pleadings That Relate to Ourselves (Part 3)

You are those worthies "of whom the world
is not worthy." (Hebrews 11:38)

You are the princes "that prevail with God."
(Genesis 32:28)

You are those "excellent ones" in whom is all
Christ's delight. (Psalm 16:3)

You are his glory. You are his picked, culled,
prime instruments which he will make use of to
carry on his best and greatest work against his
worst and greatest enemies. (Thomas Brooks)

We come to the third group of scriptural truth concerning ourselves,
which we may use in our pleading with God.

The Goodness and Beauty of Grace Shining in Us

Let's begin with the conclusion of what God, through grace, is
doing in our lives now. His present focus includes the crowning glory

of redemption's purpose. What is that glorious purpose? To fashion and beautify a bride for the heavenly marriage! Her revealing takes place at the marriage supper of the Lamb.

The apostle John describes the scene:

> I heard, as it were, the voice of a great multitude, as the sound of many waters and as the sound of mighty thunderings, saying, "Alleluia! For the Lord God Omnipotent reigns! Let us be glad and rejoice and give him glory, for the marriage of the Lamb has come, and his wife has made herself ready." And to her it was granted to be arrayed in fine linen, clean and bright, for the fine linen is the righteous acts of the saints. (Revelation 19:6–8)

Who is this bride? The church of the Lord Jesus Christ, the called out from the world and washed in the very blood of the Lamb. He loved her and bought her with his own precious blood. Who makes up the church triumphant? Those whom the Father set his love upon from all eternity, brought to life by the Spirit's birthing and sealing, securing them as members of his household. These came to experience redeeming love. Then, full of amazement, they humbly proclaimed, "My beloved Lord Jesus, you loved me and gave yourself for me!" Welling up in the hearts of all these who are in Christ Jesus flow these affectionate and sincere sentiments: "Oh, my God, I adore you! I love you. May I live for you all the days of my life. My glorious God, your Son has captured my heart. I plead with you to make me like him, holy and undefiled, all glorious within and perfect in all gracious living. Oh, that you would make me like the beloved Lord Jesus who has loved me and whom I love."

In this heavenly scene, the bride's heart is overflowing with amazed wonder, love, and praise for the lover of her soul filled with humble gratitude words cannot fully express. All sorrows and ugliness behind her, now forever the recipient of eternal love, joy, ravishing delights, to be forever with her beloved Lord and experiencing the longing of her heart—she is now with him and like him forevermore!

Look closely at John's description of the bride, the Lamb's wife. She "has made herself ready. To her it was granted to be arrayed in fine linen, clean and bright, for the fine linen is the righteous acts of the saints." The righteous acts or deeds of the saints! Does that surprise you? What are these?

Every individual making up the bride of Christ, washed in the blood of the Lamb, possesses two righteousnesses! What do I mean? Well, they are essentially one as they come from the Lord Jesus Christ. What are they? Imputed and imparted righteousness.

First, the pure righteousness of Christ imputed to them secured their personal standing before the holiness, justice, and righteousness of God. They have complete and perfect acceptance, just like the Son of God, for they are in Christ Jesus. Here is the basis for the divine cherishing and nurturing love they receive from the Godhead.

Second, this cherishing and nurturing brings a sweet and powerful influence through the conduit of grace. This is the means of providing the imparted righteousness of Christ, which is growth in Christlikeness. Nurturing grace works in her daily life the practical righteousness of Christ. They grow and mature in their walk with Christ to walk like Christ. Full perfection of imparted righteousness becomes complete in heaven. This is where the two righteousnesses meet. At the point of Revelation 19, she is with him and, like him, righteous in her standing and person.

What are the "righteous deeds" done on earth which make up the bright linen of the bride?

1. They came from the heart of the redeemed flowing from grateful amazement over the love of Christ.

These come from loving God: the Father, Son, and Holy Spirit. The loving-kindness of God and the displays of incredible mercy affected their souls and motivated them to become imitators of God as dear children.

The Holy Spirit works in these souls, attraction to the beauty, desirableness, and loveliness of Christ, and a longing to be like him. Coming to saving faith in Christ implants a bent of heart to be godly and behave differently. The grace of God that brought salvation to them taught them and nurtured in them holy inclinations and desires of the heart.

> Teaching us that, denying ungodliness and worldly lusts, we should live soberly, righteously, and godly, in this present world; looking for that blessed hope, and the glorious appearing of the great God and our Savior Jesus Christ; who gave himself for us, that he might redeem us from all iniquity, and purify unto himself a peculiar people, zealous of good works. (Titus 2:11–14)

2. As new creations in Christ Jesus, God appointed them to good works.

Engrafted into the vine, they were branches bringing forth fruit to the glory of the Father. This fruit elevates their character and makes the believer's life attractive. Others see their good works and glorify God (Matthew 5:16). These are Spirit-born souls who manifested the fruit of the Spirit. The acts of kindness, demonstrations of sacrificial love, or living by faith, flowed freely from their new hearts. When Christ says, "You did this to me," they will say, "I don't remember that" (Matthew 25:40). It came naturally from who they were as new creations.

> Those who have believed in God should be careful to maintain good works. (Titus 3:8)

> We are His workmanship, created in Christ Jesus for good works, which God prepared beforehand that we should walk in them. (Ephesians 2:10)

3. They result from the sovereign decree of God.

"To her it was granted" (v. 8). The gift of the Godhead is that each glorious person is involved with us in developing the beauty of the bride. We see that our graces, our growth in grace, and these beautifying "acts" are a precious indicator of companionship with God in the practical progress of our lives. What do I mean? We have seen this before.

> Work out your own salvation with fear and trembling; for it is God who works in you both to will and to do for his good pleasure. (Philippians 2:12–13)

The acts of beautifying grace result from God's working and our working. They are concurrent, confluent, interdependent necessities. God and we are developing our beauty. It is a companionship with the Almighty!

Think of it this way: right now we—God and us—are imperfectly weaving the fine linen of the bride! On that day of the marriage, the fine linen will be perfectly clean and bright—perfection of our beauty!

The Scriptures exhort Christians to give glory to God, show proof of the power of the Gospel of grace and true devotion to God by their good works and holy lives. These flow from humble, amazed gratitude for undeserved mercy, grace, and salvation.

What's the point of all this? We are now to be praying and pleading for God's enabling power to cultivate the "acts" of beautifying our souls! How? By growing in grace and likeness to our Lord and Savior Jesus Christ. Pray and plead that we may adorn the doctrine of God our Savior in all things (Titus 2:10).

> "They shall be mine," says the Lord of hosts, "in the day [the last day of redemption's completion] when I make up my treasured possession." (Malachi 3:16–17)

On that day the Lord their God will save
them, as the flock of his people; for like the jewels
of a crown, they shall shine on his land. For how
great is its goodness and how great is its beauty.
(Zechariah 9:16–17)

Sometimes we hear how important it is to be in tune with our culture so we can identify with people around us and them with us. I understand the practicality and importance of "not being so heavenly minded that we are no earthly good." However, we also run the danger of "being so earthly minded we are no heavenly good." I believe the second concern is more the issue of our day.

I would often tell my children, "You are becoming today what you will be for the rest of your life. Give thought to the kind of person you want to be." As believers in the Lord Jesus, our outlook on the life we live now ought to be a pursuit of companionship with our gracious God to mature toward what we will be throughout eternity (Ephesians 4:13; 1 John 3:2).

Foremost, we ought to seek the influence of heaven's culture. There should be conformity to the culture found in the Scriptures. How about being influenced by the culture of Paul's heart of devotion and David's spirit of living and praising the God of his salvation? Those longings are to be affectionately and earnestly longed for! This is the subject of this chapter, and here is how to do it:

1. We are to plead God's own stirring us up to pray for such mercies.

There is something wonderful and spiritually rich when a petitioner can plead with God this way: "Oh, my gracious God, you have stirred me up to pray for the mercies you promise! Lord, I am not coming to your blessed and holy court uninvited! You have appointed a place of hearing, and I have come through the door of your grace at your bidding, or else I would never have come! Your Spirit moved me, your promise encouraged me; therefore, O LORD, upon your Word, I humbly expect the fruit of my coming at your invitation!"

> Lord, you command me with your promise
> to come boldly to the throne of grace, that I may
> obtain mercy and find grace to help in time of
> need. (Hebrews 4:16)

"Here I am, Lord, with an expectant heart to receive from your heart and hand the meeting of the needs I have to be more like Your Son, to have his mind and exhibit his grace in my life. Is this not what you desire for me? O, my gracious God, I do hunger and thirst for this. Continue to make me hunger and thirst, but also grant, according to your promise, that I shall be filled! Grant me what I long for, Lord." This is a very comforting and effective form of pleading. What if we filled our homes and churches with such movings of heart and soul? We even have a throne of grace to get the help to possess such homes and churches! Ah! We have not because we ask not! This is one of the greatest plagues in the church—its prayerlessness!

This is how David pleads:

> Now, O LORD God, the word which you
> have spoken concerning your servant and con-
> cerning his house, establish it forever and do as
> you have said. (2 Samuel 7:25)

> For you, O LORD of hosts, God of Israel,
> have revealed this to your servant, saying, "I will
> build you a house." Therefore, your servant has
> found it in his heart to pray this prayer to you.
> (v. 27)

As the Lord spoke graciously to David and gave him many promises to trust in, David made it a point of pleading the mercies God made him to hope in. We are wise and growing in the skill of pleading with God when we do the same. Don't we have many great and precious promises (2 Peter 1:2–11)? Don't leave them on the shelves of sixty-six books. Take them down, pull them out, and bring them with you to your gracious King.

All of us should be concerned not to drift into a "devotional" pattern, which does not breathe and echo the devotional quality of the Scriptures and modeled by the gracious people of God recorded there.

> Hear, O Lord, when I cry with my voice!
> Have mercy also upon me, and answer me. When
> you said, "Seek my face," my heart said to you,
> "Your face, Lord, will I seek." Do not hide your
> face from me; do not turn your servant away in
> anger; you have been my help; do not leave me nor
> forsake me, O God of my salvation. (Psalm 27:7–9)

See how David makes use of God's invitation to seek his face? He makes it an argument for God's answering him.

As we read the communications of God's kindheartedness, mercies, and willingness to do us good, remember, they are not empty words! They are written and communicated as God's "living word" with the intent of stirring up an attraction in us for them and to move us to pray for them to be living in our own souls.

> Return, you backsliding children, and I will
> heal your backslidings. Indeed we do come to you,
> for you are the Lord our God. (Jeremiah 3:22)

Catch the heart harmony conveyed in these words. Oh, brethren, may our God stir us up to seek such heart harmony as we read the Scriptures.

God stirs up and strengthens us to seek him when he intends to be found by us!

> Lord, you have heard the desire of the
> humble; you will prepare their heart; you will
> cause your ear to hear. (Psalm 10:17)

God works to put the humble into a praying frame and, in this way, prepares them to be the recipients of those very things they need and long for! Dear one, mark it down—where God gives a praying heart, he will show a pitying heart to them. If he prepares the heart, he will also bend his ear—just like when we bid our children ask us for this or that, we mean to give it to them! It is the same with our God. This was Christ's own point in his teaching us to pray.

Oh, I hope we can get a sweet view of the heart of God!

It shall come to pass that before they call, I will answer; and while they are still speaking, I will hear. (Isaiah 65:24)

Do you see the picture of the Prodigal Son's father seeing his son coming down the road? The father ran to him, interrupted his confession of sin and unworthiness with embraces and kisses! What a picture of the mercy-indulging heart of God to his people!

For your Father knows the things you have need of before you ask him. (Matthew 6:8)

For the Father himself loves you. (John 16:27)

Do you see the heart harmony between Isaiah, Christ, and the Gospel writers? This is our true God and a reflection of his heart. It is the same yesterday, today, and tomorrow. Why? Because he changes not.

Look at a few more passages which communicate these wonderful realities.

And I will pour on the house of David and on the inhabitants of Jerusalem the Spirit of grace and supplication; then they will look on me whom they pierced. Yes, they will mourn for him as one mourns for his only son, and grieve

for him as one grieves for a firstborn. (Zechariah
12:10)

Why does he do this? Because he intends to work in and for
them with rich goodness and bring upon them gracious blessings and
kind mercies.

And you will seek me and find me, when
you search for me with all your heart. (Jeremiah
29:13)

To do this requires more than saying some prayers. In our praying, we are to really pray and plead for things desired.

God makes it an argument to himself that if he says to any,
inwardly as well as outwardly, "Seek my face," that he speaks this in
righteousness and truth—he will not frustrate their prayers and bid
them seek his face in vain!

I have not spoken in secret, in a dark place
of the earth; I did not say to the seed of Jacob,
"Seek me in vain"; I, the LORD, speak righteousness, I declare things that are right. (Isaiah 45:19)

I'll not lead you out on a limb of trust in me only to leave you
in peril or danger.

Even our Lord Jesus gives us many examples. When Christ
called the blind man to him to tell him his grievance, it was truly and
properly said to him by those people who spoke to him, "be of good
cheer. Rise, he is calling you" (Mark 10:46–52). When Christ said to
any person, "What would you have me to do for you?" What a heart
full of grace, kindness, and power. No one asked in vain! Does our
God call us to himself? Does our God bid us ask him to fulfill his
own word to us? Oh, brethren, "Be of good cheer!"

2. We may plead the work of the Lord's implanting hope in us to receive what he has promised.

This is both lawful and desirable to plead before God. It shows that we have truly and reverently taken God at his Word. We all know the inward frustrations with a politician who raises hopes in a people only to fail them! God is no politician! It is something unfit for anyone to cause a petitioner's expectations of receiving good to be raised—only to fail him. Our God is no failing ruler.

Asa knew this; therefore, he pleads with God accordingly in his prayer for help:

> And Asa cried out to the LORD his God, and said, "LORD, it is nothing for you to help, whether with many or with those who have no power; help us, O LORD our God, for we rest on you, and in your name we go against this multitude. O LORD, you are our God; do not let man prevail against you!" (2 Chronicles 14:11)

An army of Ethiopians, one million strong, were coming against Asa and Judah. That army perished when God came to answer Asa's prayer.

> Teach me good judgment and knowledge, for I believe your commandments. (Psalm 119:66)

David well used God's commandments. He drew sweet promises out of them. He would have read and meditated upon this passage from Deuteronomy 4:5–6:

> Surely I have taught you statutes and judgements, just as the LORD my God commanded me, that you should act according to them. Therefore, be careful to observe them; for this

is your wisdom and your understanding in the sight of the peoples who will hear all these statutes, and say, "Surely this great nation is a wise and understanding people."

Any of us can pray like this:

O my God, I trust in you; let me not be ashamed; let not my enemies triumph over me. (Psalm 25:2)

Lead me, O Lord, in your righteousness because of my enemies; make your way straight before my face. (Psalm 5:8)

Let integrity and uprightness preserve me, for I wait for you. (Psalm 25:21)

Cause me to hear your loving-kindness in the morning, for in you do I trust; cause me to know the way in which I should walk, for I lift up my soul to you. (Psalm 143:8)

All these passages reveal the expectations of faith that were raised by the Lord in the soul of his trusting child. For the Lord to lead him and make God's way straight before his face is to make him fruitful in righteousness. For the Lord's loving-kindness to be made recognizable to him is to infuse encouragement in the heart and prize a genuine companionship with the Lord.

Do you see how this is a great argument with people? Think of a mother or a dad. "Does my child depend upon me, and have I given my word to do this for him? Does my child, who I made to trust in me, now come to me for what I promised? Does my child come according to my encouragement for him to do so? Does he come with a legitimate expectation of what I promised him? Well then, I cannot—I must not fail him!" I ask you, is man more upright than

God? Is man more concerned about keeping his word than God is? To take the words of Christ,

> If we, being evil by fallen nature, know how
> to keep our word to our children who depend on
> us not to fail them, how much more will our God
> not fail us who depend on him?

Do you see the argument? Is man more upright than God? Is man more concerned about keeping his word than God is?

The people of God are told to have confidence in what God has said and promised.

> You will keep him in perfect peace, whose
> mind is stayed on you, because he trusts in you.
> Trust in the LORD forever, for in YAH, the LORD
> is everlasting strength. (Isaiah 26:3–4)

God says to himself, "Because this one trusts in me, I will not fail him."

> The helpless commits himself to you; you
> are the helper of the fatherless. (Psalm 10:14)

Our God is a helper, not a deceiver! He cannot lie.

> In Jesus, combine all the riches of grace.
> What glory and grandeur I see in his face;
> Jehovah's eternal and co-equal Son,
> Took all our transgressions and made them his
> own.
> Ye children of Zion, now dry up your tears;
> For you, the Redeemer in glory appears;
> Now he lives, now he reigns, now he dwells in
> the sky,
> To answer the needy whenever they cry."

Afflicted believer, thy cause he'll maintain;
Though rough be thy way, he'll revive thee again;
In dark dispensations of his kindness he'll prove
And teach thee to prize his immutable love.
What though thy corruptions are many and
  strong,
Thy gracious redeemer will help thee along;
His promise assures thee, when troubles assail,
Though Hell should oppose thee, thy faith can-
  not fail.
(H. Fowler, #1033, *Gadsby's Hymns*)

3. We may (in all humility) plead our heartbreakings and weepings.

Now there are tears of frustration and tears of a despairing unbelief. These have no faith in them; rather, they are the complaints of one whose will has been crossed. There are tears of one sincerely longing for the nearness of his God and the supplies of his promised grace or some mercy. We should ask the Holy Spirit to help us make such distinctions.

> My soul breaks with longing for your judg-
> ments at all times. (Psalm 119:20)

The desire is God's involvement in setting things right.

We can plead these heartbreakings, longings, and even tears especially when we sense a lack of the mercies we crave. We may plead our pantings and faintings (you get these expressions from the Psalms) after these desired mercies.

> Hear my prayer, O LORD, and give ear to
> my cry; do not be silent at my tears; for I am a
> stranger with you, a sojourner, as all my fathers
> were. (Psalm 39:12)

See how his ardent desires in prayer grew by degrees? Also, did you notice the "with you" he mentions? It is companionship with the Almighty. It availed much! (James 5:16) Perhaps we would see more of God's workings in our midst if there were more sincere tears and breakings of heart for such workings. Let the Lord see that we are in good earnest, and then we may have what we need. Take this to your heart, to your home, and to your church.

David, who based all his pleadings strictly and only upon the free mercy and grace of the Lord, says,

> Have mercy upon me, O God, according to your loving-kindness; according to the multitude of your tender mercies, blot out my transgressions. (Psalm 51:1)

Yet he pleads the brokenness of his heart!

> The sacrifices of God are a broken spirit, a broken and a contrite heart—these, O God, you will not despise. (v. 17)

Often we provoke God to take harsher measures because we stand too stout in our whining and determinations to carve out our own lot in life. Oh, if we would but break! Yet remember, we can have a stage performance that is an act of attempted manipulation. God sees the genuineness of a truly broken heart. We feel that Spirit-wrought brokenness with meekness, gentleness, tenderness, and affection! These workings draw the soul in to the embrace of God.

It is a moving argument with a compassionate parent when his child craves this or that needful thing from him—with tears! I say it is a moving argument not to deny his child what they needed and what they crave! So God may say, "My grace is sufficient for you. I will bring my strength to complete display in the presence of your weakness. Be assured that I am not and will not be indifferent to your pain, longings, and sense of need for my help."

Brethren, without a doubt, so it is with the LORD toward his own children. God shows his tender heart toward his erring child Ephraim when Ephraim smites upon his thigh, is ashamed, and even confounded because he bore the iniquity of his youth. This affected the heart of God! We can see this in his reply:

> Surely, after my turning, I repented; and after I was instructed, I struck myself on the thigh; I was ashamed, yes, even humiliated, because I bore the reproach of my youth. (Jeremiah 31:19–21)

Now hear the LORD's response:

> "Is Ephraim my dear son? Is he a pleasant child? For though I spoke against him, I earnestly remember him still; therefore, my heart yearns for him; I will surely have mercy on him," says the LORD.

You may have blown it, even blown it big time! If you turn to the Lord like this, you will experience the Lord's response like this.

Look how Isaiah is told by the LORD to go to weeping Hezekiah and tell him his voice and prayers have been heard. Isaiah 38:5 says,

> "Go tell Hezekiah," thus says the LORD, the God of David your father: "I have heard your prayer, I have seen your tears."

As if he had said to Isaiah, "Go run to this dear child of mine. Tell him not to weep so painfully. Tell him he shall have his request."

> Depart from me, all you workers of iniquity; for the LORD has heard the voice of my weeping. (Psalm 6:8)

David's prayer itself spoke, but his tears also speak aloud in God's ears and prevailed!

4. We may plead the integrity of our hearts and ways in God's service (in all holy humility)

As we place our faith in Christ, as all our justification, we may yet plead the integrity of our hearts and ways in the service of our God!

> Then Hezekiah turned his face toward the wall, and prayed to the LORD, and said, "Remember now, O LORD, I pray, how I have walked before you in truth and with a loyal heart and have done what is good in your sight." And Hezekiah wept bitterly. (Isaiah 38:2–3)

> O God, you have taught me from my youth; and to this day, I declare your wondrous works. Now also when I am old and gray headed, O God, do not forsake me, until I declare your strength to this generation, your power to everyone who is to come. (Psalm 71:17–18)

> With my whole heart I have sought you; oh, let me not wander from your commandments! (Psalm 119:10)

The Lord himself makes this a motive to himself to show mercy to his people.

> For he said, "Surely they are my people, children who will not lie." So he became their savior. (Isaiah 63:8)

> Go and cry in the hearing of Jerusalem, saying, "Thus says the LORD: I remember you, the kindness of your youth, the love of your betrothal, when you went after me in the wilderness, in a land not sown." (Jeremiah 2:1)

Now we must use this plea more sparingly, in a self-denying way, and only with our faith in Christ's righteousness as made ours by free grace! It is a humble expression of what God has done in you. We bring the work of his hands, and we present what he has done in us and for us.

We may make the same plea before the Lord about the behavior of our integrity with men. When we have walked uprightly before men, yet they cast reproach, slander upon us, or even enter some injurious dealings with us, we may turn this into an appeal before God. This is what it looks like:

> O LORD, you know; remember me and visit me, and take vengeance for me on my persecutors. In your enduring patience, do not take me away. Know that for your sake I have suffered rebuke.

> The LORD shall judge the peoples; judge me, O LORD, according to my righteousness, and according to my integrity within me. (Psalm 7:8)

5. We may plead our sufferings.

Especially those that are endured for God and his cause. This is part of what Paul meant by "the fellowship of his sufferings." We may plead as well other sufferings.

> Now therefore, our God, the great, the mighty, and awesome God, who keeps covenant and mercy: do not let all the trouble seem small

before you that has come upon us, our kings and
our princes, our priests and our prophets, our
fathers and on all your people, from the days
of the kings of Assyria until this day. However,
you are just in all that has befallen us; for you
have dealt faithfully, but we have done wickedly.
(Nehemiah 9:32–33)

Make us glad according to the days in which
you have afflicted us, the years in which we have
seen evil. (Psalm 90:15)

But especially plead those which are undergone for the LORD's
sake.

Yet for your sake we are killed all day long;
we are accounted as sheep for the slaughter.
Awake! Why do you sleep, O Lord? Arise! Do not
cast us off forever. (Psalm 44:22–23)

Paul suffered incredible things, yet he received even more
incredible consolations. The Lord never turned a deaf ear to him.

For as the sufferings of Christ abound in us,
so our consolation also abounds through Christ.
(2 Corinthians 1:5)

6. We may plead our former experiences of mercy.

"Look down from heaven, and see from your habitation, holy
and glorious. Where are your zeal and your strength, the yearning of
your heart and your mercies toward me? Are they restrained?" Which
is as if he said,

Lord, you have been a compassionate God.
I have had experience in various conditions and

cases of your hearty mercies; how is it now? Why is it you have cut off and shut them up now? (Isaiah 63:15)

O God, you have taught me from my youth; and to this day, I declare your wondrous works. Now also when I am old and gray headed, O God, do not forsake me. (Psalm 71:17–18)

From the end of the earth I will cry to you, when my heart is overwhelmed; lead me to the rock that is higher than I. For you have been a shelter for me, a strong tower from the enemy. (Psalm 61:2–3)

This is an argument and encouragement for us not to forget his mercies, and all the benefits our God bestows upon us. (Psalm 103)

7. We may plead the good we would get and the usefulness we would be if he answers us.

God put this very plea in the mouths of his covenant community.

Take words with you, and return to the LORD. Say to him, "Take away all iniquity; receive us graciously." (Hosea 14:2)

Why? What will be the profit of it? "For we will offer the sacrifices of our lips."

Assyria shall not save us, we will not ride on horses, nor will we say anymore to the work of our hands, "You are our gods." For in you the fatherless find mercy. (v. 3)

EFFECTUAL PRAYER NOURISHED IN THE HEART BY CHRIST

This is saying that God's benefits shall not be wasted upon an unthankful people. They, as recipients of God's mercies, would present to him a sacrifice that will please him better than an ox or bull.

> Therefore by him let us continually offer
> the sacrifice of praise to God, that is, the fruit
> of our lips, giving thanks to his name. (Hebrews
> 13:15)

They would put away their two great sins of idolatry and creature confidence from them! In summation: if God would have mercy, he would also receive glory and honor and loyalty from a grateful people.

Do you at times feel so left without direction in your life? Do you long for God to give you real understanding as to how you should live and proceed in your life context? Depending on your motivation and sincere heart's longing, this need becomes wholesome pleading before God.

> Teach me, O LORD, the way of your statutes, and I shall keep it to the end. Give me understanding, and I shall keep your law; indeed, I shall observe it with my whole heart. (Psalm 119:33–34)

If God were to deal with you in mercy, what good would it do? Not that we bargain with God but that we should have definite reasons for the mercies we long for—reasons that go beyond the mere need for immediate forgiveness. What will you do with the mercies? What impact will it have on you in the future?

> Restore to me the joy of your salvation, and
> uphold me by your generous Spirit. Then I will
> teach transgressors your ways, and sinners shall
> be converted to you. (Psalm 51:12–13)

As the people of God may plead the good which they may do, so also they may plead that if God answered their prayer, they would receive so much good, inward quickening, encouragement, and enlargement of heart! Their souls would thrive if God answers.

> Oh, satisfy us early with your mercy. (Why should he do that? "That we may rejoice and be glad all our days.") (Psalm 90:14)

"Surely, Lord, there is no honor for you from a gloomy, depressed, defeated people! Would you not be glad in the gladness and rejoicings of your people? Oh, satisfy us early with your mercy then!"

I sincerely hope you see your God and Savior are more large-hearted, understanding, and available to you than you or I can imagine. They surround us with compassion and provision. They have "given to us exceeding great and precious promises" (2 Peter 1:4). Through neglect, we are poor in a wrong and needless way. We have the riches of God's mercies, and he wants us to avail ourselves of those riches.

> *When I stand before the throne, dressed in beauty not my own,*
> *When I see thee as thou art, love thee with unsinning heart,*
> *then, Lord shall I fully know, not till then, how much I owe.*

> *When the praise of heaven I hear, loud as thunders to the ear,*
> *loud as many waters' noise, sweet as harp's melodious voice, then*
> *Lord shall I fully know, not till then, how much I owe.*

> *Chosen not for good in me, wakened up from wrath to flee,*
> *hidden in the Savior's side, by the Spirit sanctified, teach me,*
> *Lord, on earth to show, by my love, how much I owe.*

—Robert Murray McCheyne, 1837

21

⊶❦❧⊷

The Pleadings We Use for
Ourselves Drawn from Others

*What various hindrances we meet in coming to
the mercy-seat; yet who, that knows the worth
of prayer, but wishes to be often there?*

—William Cowper

We considered our Lord's gracious treatment of Peter earlier. He told
him of his coming testings and failures, when Satan would sift him
like wheat. The chaff had to go. Peter was true wheat and needed a
sanctifying, humbling experience to bind him to Christ as the source
of his wisdom and strength. The Lord Jesus told Peter of his restoration. What a kind word and thoughtful communication from
Peter's Savior. Then he mentions an indispensable responsibility:

> When you have returned to me, strengthen
> your brethren. (Luke 22:32)

These were words of hope and commission to take up a vital
role to which Peter was called.

Christ does not want any of his people to think of themselves in
isolation from the brethren. We are the sheep of Christ's pasture. He

shepherds us. Sheep flock together. We are not mountain goats off on our own. Besides, goats do not have a happy ending.

Did you know the saints above, in the glorious presence of Christ and of God, never stop thinking of us?

> God having provided something better for us, that they should not be made perfect apart from us. (Hebrews 11:40)

They eagerly look for the consummation of redemption's work. They longingly wait for all the chosen race to be brought to saving union with Christ and then united with them.

God has taken us into his family, and he loves us all in his own dear Son. We stand in solidarity with the household of God. We are fellow members and possess fellow feelings with all the saints. The same humanity is common to us all. No one of us is an island to himself. We are in vital connection with one another as the body of Christ. Our identity includes being living stones built together as one holy temple. We are a holy nation, and our citizenship is in heaven.

God's gift of the Scriptures provides many benefits too many to mention here. However, one great advantage is the recording of life experiences from fellow believers.

> For whatever things were written before were written for our learning, that we through the patience and comfort of the Scriptures might have hope. (Romans 15:4)

The Scriptures record the people of God in a vast array of circumstances much like our vast array of circumstances. Those believers give expression to God's Word, dwelling in them and guiding them. Out of their verbal and living witness, we find edifying wisdom, instruction, and admonition for our enrichment, wisdom, and hope. Though they have gone on to the assembly of "just men made perfect," they speak to us "in all wisdom, teaching and admonishing" us. Sometimes this is "in psalms and hymns and spiritual songs" so we, with them, are "singing with grace in our hearts to the Lord" together.

The more we become acquainted with the saints in both Old and New Testaments, we find legitimate arguments to plead before the Lord. These are ways of pleading, holy reasonings, and arguments which God takes great delight in, drawn from their lives.

Here are a few ways to consider the saints and use arguments from them and their experiences for our pleading with God.

1. We are to plead the experiences of the saints for the same mercies they received.

We are to plead that we would receive the same treatment they received in the same situations we find ourselves in.

> No temptation has overtaken you except such as is common to man; but God is faithful, who will not allow you to be tempted beyond what you are able, but with the temptation will also make the way of escape, that you may be able to bear it. (1 Corinthians 10:13)

The word *temptation* is a neutral word. It does not carry a positive or negative meaning. It means "testing, trying, or proving." Our response to the testing will make it a positive or trying event that provokes to sinful actions. As the saints of old were "tested," we see positive and negative responses. We read of their victories, triumphs, and failings, sins, or defeats. We should not stand in judgment; rather, fear God, know our own hearts, and use both in pleading prayer as a people "of like passions." This would be more in harmony with God's purposes.

There are testings which are common to man universally, whether believers or unbelievers. However, there are testings which are unique to the saints.

> Humble yourselves, therefore, under the mighty hand of God so that at the proper time he

343

may exalt you, casting all your anxieties on him, because he cares for you. Be sober-minded; be watchful. Your adversary, the devil, prowls around like a roaring lion, seeking someone to devour. Resist him, firm in your faith, knowing that the same kinds of suffering are being experienced by your brotherhood throughout the world. And after you have suffered a little while, the God of all grace, who has called you to his eternal glory in Christ, will himself restore, confirm, strengthen, and establish you. To him be the dominion forever and ever. Amen. (1 Peter 5:6–11)

These are wise words from a tested Peter. Do you see how Peter is drawing from his own actual experiences and now is seeking to "strengthen" his brethren?

The Holy Spirit wrote the historical books of the Bible and real-life circumstances of the epistles to encourage the saints in this way! A few examples to illustrate the point will help.

a.   The psalmist. Read carefully this prayer from the psalmist.

Look upon me and be merciful to me, as your custom is toward those who love your name. (Psalm 119:132)

He is asking God to treat him with mercy, just like he treated others of his people with mercy! "Lord, do not change your ways. Do to me as you have always done to others in my case who have trusted your name! Let me not be the first oddity!" (Of course, the Lord will not do so, yet your entreaty ought to express your faith.)

b.   Paul.

At my first defense, no one stood with me, but all forsook me. May it not be charged against them.

> But the Lord stood with me and strengthened me,
> so that the message might be preached fully through
> me, and that all the Gentiles might hear. Also, I
> was delivered out of the mouth of the lion. And
> the Lord will deliver me from every evil work and
> preserve me for His heavenly kingdom. To Him be
> glory forever and ever. Amen! (2 Timothy 4:16–18)

Can you read these words and pick out ways God kindly expressed companionship with Paul and was there to help him? Can you take these before your Lord and ask him to do the same for you? "Lord, as it is your way with your people, you were there for Paul! O Lord, be there for me as your custom is. You showed yourself faithful to Paul, reliable for him. Lord, I see it so clearly in Paul's own testimony. Oh, my gracious Savior and Shepherd, let me make the same testimony of your reliability. I long to speak of your faithfulness as you show up for me. Is this not your way with your people? Do you not delight in thrilling your people's hearts and build up their faith in these ways? Oh, my beloved Lord, I love you. Thrill my heart, build up my faith by hearing and answering me. My gracious God, show up for me as you have done for others."

There is something so simple, so childlike, in this form of laying hold of your God. More than this—God loves it! It is attractive to him. Do you want to be attractive to God in a way that draws him close and moves him to act on your behalf? Here is the way—walk in it.

> c. David. Read the words of David. He gives testimony to
> waiting patiently upon God and then God's responsive-
> ness. David was not in a physical pit! But it felt like it.
> Have you ever felt like you were in a pit, needing God to
> pull you out? I have!

> > I waited patiently for the Lord; and he
> > inclined to me, and heard my cry. He also
> > brought me up out of a horrible pit, out of the
> > miry clay, and set my feet upon a rock, and estab-
> > lished my steps. He has put a new song in my

mouth—praise to our God; many will see it and
fear, and will trust in the Lord. Blessed is that
man who makes the Lord his trust, and does
not respect the proud, nor such as turn aside to
lies. Many, O Lord my God, are Your wonderful
works which you have done; and Your thoughts
toward us cannot be recounted to You in order; if
I would declare and speak of them, they are more
than can be numbered. (Psalm 40:1–5)

Brethren, I have gone over this Psalm many times, praying over
every line and personalizing it before the Lord. With humble gratitude, I can testify that the Lord heard me and put that fresh praise in
my mouth. He will do so with you. It is his custom to do so.

d. Ruth. The LORD tenderly led Ruth along a pathway leading
to blessings. She did not know what would happen to her. She was
a Gentile, from the land of Canaan, from a nation which was an
enemy to Israel. However, her devotion to Naomi—and more so to
Naomi's God—is famous. It is also incredibly precious and sweet.

Entreat me not to leave you, or to turn back
from following you; for wherever you go, I will
go; and wherever you lodge, I will lodge; your
people shall be my people, and your God, my
God. (Ruth 1:16)

In a short while, her reputation became well known. Boaz recognized it:

The LORD repay your work, and a full
reward be given you by the LORD God of Israel,
under whose wings you have come for refuge.
(Ruth 2:12)

You may say, "Oh, but there were purposes in Ruth's life that
were far more important than my life." You would never have con-

vinced Ruth of that before the unfolding of God's gracious plan. She never made her choice based on the end result! No, she sincerely devoted herself to the LORD whom she came to trust and love. She did not see how the Lord was treasuring up bright designs for her as he worked his sovereign will. You don't see what God is doing now either. However, just like Ruth, you are to trust and love the Lord and tuck yourself under his wings as you go to him for refuge.

Pray that you would take the steps of faith, humility, obedience, love, and trust, which she did, and your God, just like her God, who is the same God, will bring about the bright designs he has for you. They are bright! In fact, they are good, most acceptable, and perfect! (Romans 12:2). This is your God's custom with his children.

e. Joseph. Here was a young man who dreamed of a bright future. What did he experience? The seeming shattering and dashing of dreams. For twenty-one years, he lived with "hope deferred." He experienced the treachery, cruelty, and unfaithfulness of his fellow man. However, in companionship with the God in whom he put his trust, his heart did not grow bitter, nor brittle, but better.

The bent of his soul was to love, fear, and seek not to offend his beloved God. In whatever condition he was in, he learned to be content and to seek ways of usefulness, service, and being profitable to his God. Here is his testimony:

> In all things he obeyed his masters according to the flesh, not with eyeservice, as men-pleasers, but in sincerity of heart, fearing God. And whatever he did, he did it heartily, as to the Lord and not to men, knowing that from the Lord he would receive the reward of the inheritance. (Colossians 3:22–25)

Can you pray and plead with God to be such a person? We should, since God commands us to be.

Every intricate detail of Joseph's life, cradled in the heart of the Lord in whom he trusted, worked together for good. This pleased Joseph. Trace out all the details of Joseph's life, and he summed them up beautifully. Speaking to his brothers, who did not have the same maturity or the faith nurtured within Joseph's soul, he says,

> But as for you, you meant evil against me;
> but God meant it for good, in order to bring it
> about as it is this day, to save many people alive.
> (Genesis 50:20)

It may tempt you to say, "Oh, but that was Joseph! God obviously had big plans for him. I'm no Joseph." Well, none of us are Joseph. All of us are who God shaped and made us to be for purposes beyond our ability to comprehend. What if Joseph, David, Ruth, and Paul looked you in the eyes and said, "Now wait just a minute. You are to know something very important. Listen to your God—just like we learned to listen to our God. 'We know that all things work together for good to you who love God, to you as one who is called according to his purpose.'"

Dear ones, I trust you might read your Bibles differently. These are just a few examples. We could go on and bring out other recorded testimonies of God's kindness, love, faithfulness, and purposefulness. However, I believe the Lord wants you to experience the thrill of discovery.

Read the lives of the saints which God gives you in the Scriptures. Their God is your God. Look at the customary way he treats his beloved people. Draw out arguments to place before the heart and mind of your triune God. As is fitting, take up precious truths of God's own ways and press them to your Father's loving heart, to Christ and the fullness of his grace and truth, to the Holy Spirit who inspired the written Word for you. Ask them to be your companion in life—God and you pursuing your own growth in grace and in developing a maturing prayer life which incorporates times of pleading. Demonstrate you truly desire great things greatly.

Take notice of the maturity of many of their prayers: "Every true prayer is a variation on the theme 'Thy will be done.'"

> Prayer is not a convenient device for impos-
> ing our will upon God, or bending his will to

ours, but the prescribed way of subordinating our will to his. (John R. W. Stott)

To pray effectively, we must want what God wants—that, and that only is to pray in the will of God. (A. W. Tozer)

It is in prayer—real prayer—we mature in the tender working of the Spirit in the inner depths of our souls, a harmonizing of our will with the divine will. The pathway to this is to take the truths of God's Word with us in prayer as we pour out our requests before him.

2. We are to plead against other saints' discouragements and for their encouragements in our prayer lives.

So many truths of Scripture drives a nail through our self-centered selfishness—right to the cross of Christ.

Never tell me of a humble heart where I see a stubborn knee. (Thomas Adams)

James tells us all too often we have not because we ask amiss. We often get caught up with asking to consume from God what feeds our lusts or selfish desires. It is strange that in our praying, we seldom ask for a change of character but always a change in circumstances. Nothing is discussed more and practiced less than prayer.

Christ came to save us from a self-centered life. Does it ever cross your mind that an argument for answered prayer includes the good it would be for others? We are to bring our concerns and needs before the throne of grace, yet I fear we can be all too self-absorbed.

No man can pray scripturally who prays selfishly. (John Blanchard)

Within the first two years of my Christian life, I heard this simple prayer: "Lord, let me live from day to day in such a self-forgetful way that even when I kneel to pray, my prayers will be for others. Others, Lord, yes, others. Let this my motto be. Lord, let me live for others that I might live like thee."

There is a line of biblical truth which helps us in two ways: (1) It gives us powerful arguments to present to God for answered prayer. (2) It feeds into our souls a sincere and humble longing for the good of our fellow saints, our brethren. Honestly, this can be a powerful incentive to pour our hearts out to the Lord. It is a form of biblical logic that weighs well on the Lord's heart.

What we read in the Psalms gives us a glimpse into what a "heart after God" looks like. I fear we read over these passages and don't take notice of precious details. Perhaps we are too self-focused even when we read our Bibles. We all do it, but stop and notice David's great concern:

> Let not those who wait for you, O Lord GOD of hosts, be ashamed because of me; let not those who seek you be confounded because of me, O God of Israel. (Psalm 69:6)

It is as if he were saying, "Lord, I'm out on a limb trusting in you. Unless you come through, I fear others will be discouraged!"

Consider how David makes the impact of God's response to him on others, the dominant force of his pleading to the Lord.

> But I am poor and sorrowful; let your salvation, O God, set me up on high. (Psalm 69:29–32)

Why should the Lord do this? "I will praise the name of God with a song and will magnify him with thanksgiving. This also shall please the LORD better than an ox or bull, which has horns and hooves. The humble shall see this and be glad, and you who seek God, your hearts shall live." Oh, when they see this, their hearts will really live. "Oh, my gracious and merciful Lord, when you answer my prayers, the humble will be glad, and your reviving strength will enliven your people."

"If you hear me and answer me, others will be encouraged, or if you do not answer me, they will be ashamed or confused! Lord God, don't put a stumbling block before others by not answering my prayer. Rather, place a stepping stone for others to step up to loftier heights of praise and encouragements. Lord, through this, bring your people to greater confidence to put their whole soul's trust in you."

These are not just precious sentiments. They are powerful arguments that win the day with God.

3. The subtle and malicious desires of our and God's enemies are to be pleaded before the Lord.

The forces of darkness are stirring up human instruments and powerful ideologies to destroy the Christian religion in the Western world. God's enemies are mounting a vicious attack which has been in the works. Yes, it has been so since the fall. There have been the ebbs and flows of demonic aggressions throughout history. The greatest weaponry the church has wielded has been "all prayer." However, "nothing whatever can atone for the neglect of praying" (E. M. Bounds).

> Other duties become pressing and absorb-
> ing and crowd out prayer. "Choked to death"
> would be the coroner's verdict in many cases of
> dead praying. (E. M. Bounds)

Prayer is, perhaps, the weakest link in the Christian chain of defense in our day. The church will not win the day with intellectual arguments. The enemy is indifferent, for absolute truth does not exist in the enemy's worldview. Political power plays are equivalent to trusting in the "arm of the flesh" and argues the heart departing from the Lord as its refuge and strength.

We will display the actual evidence of our power and strength in our prayer meetings. Like I said, we are in great danger. We have our busyness, routines, demanding schedules, overload with counseling, our teaching, teaching, and more teaching; but if we were to take the temperature of our prayers, where is the fervency, the determination to lay hold of our God? Don't display your "I'm desperate for you" with mere sentimental singing. Demonstrate life, connection with God, and desperation in effectual fervent praying!

Unless there are indications of God's reviving power in the church, a "perfect storm" is brewing. The enemy is gaining strategic ground and positioning. If the church does not begin to fervently and seriously return to prayer, the Lord is not pleased. He knows how to get us to pray in desperation—by placing his people in desperate situations! However, these can be mere words falling on deaf ears. Read the seven letters of Revelation 2–3, and see how serious Christ is with the state of the churches. He knows how to do something about the varying degrees of spiritual sickness and malady.

"O Lord, spiritual lowlife existence is seen in our prayerlessness! Our God, we get all distracted with our self-importance, busyness, preoccupations, miseries, snags, fears, difficulties, temptations, and stumblings. These are what our enemies wait for! If we struggle, they rejoice. If we stumble, they use it to excuse their own sins. Sometimes they plot evil just so we would look helpless and without help. They stand ready to reproach us for these things. Therefore, come and take up our case. Our greatest need is to return to you. Cause our souls to be moved out of our present state of poor praying habits. Stir us up to love and fear you more. Revive your people to be a praying people, oh, God! At least start with me!"

Our sins are like a wall between us and God which prevents him from hearing our prayers. What about the sin of weak, tepid praying or even prayerlessness itself? (Isaiah 59:1–2).

Brethren, the appointed way to get doctrine and truth out of our heads and into our hearts and lives is through prayer! Our faith will lie idle and even dead without prayer. The great test of all our faith lies in prayer. At best, it is poor praying which is only words. The best prayers are often more groans than words.

> Prayer requires more of the heart than of the tongue. (Adam Clarke)

Listen to the counsel of C. H. Spurgeon on this matter:

> Do not reckon you have prayed until you have pleaded, for pleading is the very marrow of prayer.

> He who prays without fervency does not pray at all.

> I know of no better thermometer to your spiritual temperature than this—the measure of the intensity of your prayer.

> Let your fleece lie on the threshing floor of supplication till it is wet with the dew of heaven.

> Only that prayer which comes from our heart can get to God's heart.

> The habit of prayer is good, but the spirit of prayer is better.

Knowledge is essential. Sound doctrine is critically important. It is health to the church and argues for the church's role as pillar and ground of the truth. However, it is not expert knowledge that argues a church's power. You see that in the church at Ephesus, Revelation 2:1–7. With fine-tuned precession, they detected false teachers, yet their love was cold! Their prayers were not filled with the warmth of affection to the Lord. The church's power is found at the throne of grace. That's where mercy is received and grace—divine enablement—is found! In prayer alone we become "strong in the Lord and in the power of his might!" The church at the throne of grace is the greatest need of our day. No one can really pray except those who, with a sincere heart, love, fear, and worship him.

Open your heart to the words of this Psalm:

> My tears have been my food day and night,
> while they continually say to me, "Where is your
> God?" (Psalm 42:3)

May God prevent this experience from being a "strange thing" to us. Prayer that costs nothing is worth nothing; it is simply a by-product of a cheap Christianity. How would you describe David's prayer in this Psalm? David had conviction:

> I will offer to the LORD nothing which cost
> me nothing! (1 Chronicles 21:24)

There is no doubt as to the engagement of his soul, his affections, and his faith riveted in his God. God has given a rich treasury of promise and truth in the Scriptures. Prayer digs those treasures out, which faith sees.

Hear the cry of the prophet Joel:

> Let the priests, who minister to the LORD,
> weep between the porch and the altar; let them
> say, "Spare your people, O LORD, and do not give
> your heritage to reproach, that the nations should
> rule over them." Why should they say among the
> peoples, "Where is their God?" (Joel 2:17)

Hear afresh the prayers of other saints who were in tune with reality. We can plead this as they have:

> Lead me, O LORD, in your righteousness
> because of my enemies; make your way straight
> before my face. (Psalm 5:8)

"Lord I need clarity from your Word on how to conduct myself. Don't give the enemy ammunition to mock you or ridicule me."

> For I said, "Hear me, lest they rejoice over me, lest when my foot slips, they exalt themselves against me." (Psalm 38:16)

"Truly, Lord, they lie in wait to see my failings. Don't give it to them."

> And now, Lord, what do I wait for? My hope is in you. Deliver me from all my transgressions; do not make me the reproach of the foolish. (Psalm 39:7–8)

"Ah, Lord God, the fool says in his heart there is no God. Don't let them find arguments in my failings."

These saints want God to have a "hands-on" relationship with them. They felt the need for God's presence and preservation of Spirit-enabled spirituality. Cravings for God to hear and respond when they called saturated the utterances of their hearts.

God will do something concerning the state of prayerlessness all too characteristic in our day. God is not indifferent to our situation. Either to our weak or little praying or to the potential use of the rod to correct a church that will not pray as it ought. If the silver has too much dross, it must be put into the boiling pot—just like Peter needed sifting.

The next section of this book takes up this question: Why is it so important for us to plead with God?

O Holy Spirit, give me yourself without measure, as an unimpaired fountain, as inexhaustible riches. I bewail my coldness, poverty, emptiness, imperfect vision, languid service, prayerless prayers, and praiseless praises. Suffer me not to grieve or resist thee.

—The Valley of Vision by Arthur Bennett

22

Why Pleading Is So Important (Part 1) Promotes Spiritual Health

Prayer is weakness leaning on omnipotence.

—W. S. Bowden

Why is pleading so important? The answer is short and simple. Our reality complicates it as we will see.

1. Our supreme responsibility in life is to love the LORD our God with all our heart, all our soul, all our mind, and all our strength. This is the first and greatest commandment given to us. It is also our supreme and greatest joy.

    I will go to the altar of God, to God my exceeding joy. (Psalm 43:4)

    It is good for me to draw near to God; I have put my trust in the Lord God. (Psalm 73:28)

    Oh, love the Lord, all you his saints! (Psalm 31:23)

2. We live in a fallen world with an environment hostile to this. Our remaining sin has an affinity with forces of evil that work against us. They defy our loving God this way. The world, the flesh, and the devil hate God and oppose our affectionate devotion to him. The battle lines are obvious. Our enemies are sinister, subtle, malicious, and unrelenting all our days on earth. An enemy lives within us in the force of our remaining sin, the devil's ally. Our remaining sin disinclines us toward God, prayer, the Bible, and true-hearted worship. It pulls us away from the only one who can help us. The result is we do not love the LORD as we ought, as we want. Our struggle to get to our beloved Lord will demand powerful energy from the soul. It will require pleading for God's help.

We desperately need God's help. As I stated, while the answer is short and simple, loving God this way is more complex than we often realize. We are complex. Our remaining sin throws a "monkey wrench" into the mix. Life brings a never-ending array of challenges, trials, and testings on a vast spectrum of complication and entanglement. To keep our hearts and love God supremely, with our eyes fixed, looking unto Jesus, the author and completer of our faith, is hard! We will need to cry out to the strong for strength to do so. It is a precious pathway, but our abilities come short of this labor of love. There are many times in a day we urgently need the Lord as a present help to love him as we ought.

> Prayer is not some mystic reasoning after the unknown; it is response to the God who speaks in Scripture, the God who personally acts in the lives of his people. (Iain Murray)

In the next few chapters, we will take up the theme "Why pleading with God is so vitally important!" We will touch on the first in this chapter.

Pleading with God Is Essential for Spiritual Health

Why do I say it is essential for your spiritual health? It is healthy to live in reality. Pleading with God gives evidence certain essential realities are alive in your soul.

What are these realities? I will touch on two. Seeing God in everything and pleading prevents spiritual sickness.

a. Seeing God in everything.

Whatever you do, begin with God. (Matthew Henry)

"Walk before me and be blameless." God spoke these words to Abraham in Genesis 17:1. We are to follow in the footsteps of our father Abraham as evidence we are of the same faith as Abraham. Our Lord said,

If you are [spiritual] children of Abraham,
you would do the works of Abraham. (John 8:39)

To set your heart on this, as a way of life, is the epitome of spiritual health. This is intimacy, companionship, union, and communion with the Most High. Such a life is desiring the LORD with integrity, affection, devotion, a sought-after togetherness that is prized and friendship at the deepest level. While never perfect in this life, healthy spirituality rebounds to this again and again.

There are two great motives springing up from our inner being to live this way:

1. It expresses supreme love to God in the soul.

Such love is worked in our hearts by the Holy Spirit, and it influences us. "The love of God is efficacious (powerful). To know him is immediately to love him."

The commencement of godliness is the love
of God. No man will actually obey God, but he

who loves him. Our life will not be regulated aright till the love of God fills all our senses. (John Calvin)

What is the motivation to walk with God this way? It is to love him. What is it to love him? What does this love to God look like? It allows no substitute to eclipse God within our souls. John pleads with the saints, "My little children, keep yourselves from idols." The word *idol* means substitutes (1 John 5:21). To state this another way, "It is to have no other gods (idols or substitutes) before him." This is the first commandment. What is required in the first commandment? I love this answer to the question:

> The duties required in the first commandment are the knowing and acknowledging of God to be the only true God, and our God; and to worship and glorify him accordingly, by thinking, meditating, remembering, highly esteeming, honoring, adoring, choosing, loving, desiring, fearing him, believing him, trusting, hoping, delighting, rejoicing in him, being zealous for him, calling upon him, giving all praise and thanks, and yielding all obedience and submission to him, with the whole man, being careful in all things to please him, and sorrowful when in anything he is offended, and walking humbly with him. (Question 104 of the *Westminster Larger Catechism*)

When I first read this, my heart experienced joy and gratitude for its clarity and faithful representation of responsible love to God expressed in Scripture. Here is a lifetime of worthy meditation and sweet pursuit. This puts loving God in the most practical of terms. Does your heart echo a longing to love God this way? Don't you truly believe it is so incredibly healthy to love him like this?

Now sin is not loving and living like this. I ask you, in the light of such clear statements, how grateful should we be for the death of Christ on our behalf? He paid the price for every failure to love the Lord as he desires and commands. From this, how much do we need God's help and grace to live in this affectionate and loving way? We need his grace and Spirit to teach and nurture us to live godly in this present evil age. We have Christ inviting us to the throne of grace and mercy seat. Why? To receive mercy for every failing and to find grace to help us live this way.

Here is reality: We are called and commanded to love God as described above. It includes affectionate devotion to each Person in the holy Trinity in this manner. What glorious duty. Only sin, the world, and the evil one would present it as a chore!

Do we render to God what is due to him? The reality is no, we don't, but a healthy heart longs to. We can say with the apostle Paul,

> The thing that I want to do, I do not! The
> thing I don't want to do, I do! (Romans 7:19)

When we honestly face how far short we come, there is everything right in joining the cry of Paul:

> O wretched man that I am! Who will deliver
> me from this body of death? I thank God—
> through Jesus Christ our Lord!

We live out our days with internal contrarieties. "So then, with the mind I myself serve the law of God but with the flesh the law of sin." What enables and even emboldens us to press on?

> There is therefore now no condemnation to
> those who are in Christ Jesus, who do not walk
> according to the flesh, but according to the Spirit.
> (Romans 7:24–8:1)

Think of the greatness of the Father's provision for all our short-comings in the mediation of his Son, our beloved Savior.

> Here is love vast as the ocean, loving-kindness as the flood, when the Prince of Life, our ransom, shed for us his precious blood. Who his love will not remember? Who can cease to sing his praise? He can never be forgotten throughout heaven's eternal days! (Originally in Welsh, written by William Rees)

To deepen our love and appreciation for the Father's provision, think of this expression:

> If God is for us, who can be against us? He who did not spare his own Son, but delivered him up for us all, how shall he not with him also freely give us all things? (Romans 8:31–32)

Absolutely everything in our lives works for us and serves our eternal benefit! Correctly understood, this should inflame our love all the more.

At this point, I need to give an explanation of a term: "first cause."

I have used this expression earlier in the book. I believe many may not know what it means. Understanding this will help us to adore, praise, and glorify our majestic and awesome God. He is beyond our comprehension and his wisdom is infinite. A few passages will help to highlight its meaning.

Joseph's life was an amazing display of God's loving faithfulness and promise keeping. It also demonstrates the trying of Joseph's faith and rebounding belief in God's loving purposes. After the death of Jacob, Joseph sums up the history of his brothers, himself, and his God. Notice carefully what he says.

> But as for you, you meant evil against me; but God meant it for good, in order to bring it

about as it is this day, to save many people alive.
(Genesis 50:20)

God was first cause in all that transpired through the years. Second causes included his brother's activities and choice. They acted freely, uncoerced, and according to the unforced flow of their natures, thoughts, emotions, and choices at every moment and event. This is the free working of second causes.

We have God as first cause directing every detail to accomplish a wonderful purpose. Never were God's purposes threatened, thwarted, or hindered. The purposes of the Lord brought about the perfections of his wise and eternal decree. In all existence, there can be no power greater than God. If there were forces in the universe greater than God, it would make God to be the LORD God almost almighty. That would be a gross misrepresentation of God, even the portrayal of a false god.

It is also expressed as "decree" in the singular, for there is no progression of thought with God, for that would imply he is not omniscient (all-knowing). We speak of "second causes" plural because this term includes everything—whatever comes to pass in the vastness of things, elements, people, choices, and actions. Remember, we are finite; God is the infinite, incomprehensible one who inhabits eternity, whose name is holy. His perfections will never fit into our little minds. It is wisest, safest, and always most appropriate to make haste and bow in genuine worship before him.

Another important passage highlights this concept of first and second causes—the crucifixion of our Lord Jesus. On the Day of Pentecost, Peter preached to a great multitude. Notice how he portrays the events of Christ's crucifixion:

> Him, being delivered by the determined purpose and foreknowledge of God, you have taken by lawless hands, have crucified, and put to death; whom God raised up. (Acts 2:23)

God was obviously first cause in the accomplishment of the death, burial, and resurrection of Christ. Nothing would stop or thwart the provision of salvation through Christ's substitutionary death. However, who could number the multitude of free-flowing, uncoerced thoughts, attitudes, motives, and ugly deeds by Jews and Gentiles leading up to and in the cruel death of Christ? These were all second causes.

Because God is first cause, Romans 8:28 is a secure reality, never threatened or in danger of not being a soft pillow for the heart of God's child. "And we know"—we are assured of the fact—"that all things work together for good to those who love God, to those who are called according to his purpose."

Many passages could be cited which demonstrate the tiny details which are included in God's decree. Basically, it is "whatsoever comes to pass." Only heaven's perspective will reflect the perfections of our God and his infallible wisdom in his overruling providence. This is the glorious omnipotent, omniscient One we adore.

These truths should bolster and strengthen our confidence in God, his promises, and his reliability. This should inflame our love for him, which, in turn, becomes the strength of our pleading in prayer.

God expects his people to plead with him in prayer as evidence they set him before them as their supreme love. From this, they see him in everything and view him as first cause and ruler over all things for their good (Romans 8:28–32; Genesis 50:20).

This is what Joseph did. Think of the torments of heart he experienced! Thrown into a pit with no pity from his brothers, he pled with them with tears and anguish. They were heartless and indifferent. They sold him into slavery to a caravan heading for Egypt. As far as they knew, he was gone forever!

As a slave, the traders sold Joseph, and he was placed in Potiphar's house. Eventually, he was falsely accused and thrown into prison. Oh, how he was tested! Yet he did good to others with a caring heart even in prison. What was the result? On a human level, after doing good, asking for help, he was forgotten! In all this insanity, unfairness, and injustice, what gave sanity to his soul? How many people would have lost their minds and concluded God doesn't care for me? What gave Joseph levelheadedness, rationality, and good sense? What infused buoyancy within his heart?

He set the Lord always before him. He did not want to sin against his God in all these trying events and circumstances. Why? Because he loved the LORD and did not want to offend him. He wanted to please the God of his supreme affection. God was purging his soul of the youthful pride which defiled his heart. Joseph testified to his brothers, "You meant all you did for evil, but God overruled and meant all for good." Joseph knew the incredible love and kindness of God. Joseph displays a soul in spiritual health. Grace was at work, and God was his companion.

God sums up Joseph's life this way:

> He sent a man before them—Joseph—who was sold as a slave. They hurt his feet with fetters, he was laid in irons. Until the time that his word came to pass, the word of the Lord tested him. The king sent and released him, the ruler of the people let him go free. He made him lord of his house, and ruler of all his possessions, to bind his princes at his pleasure, and teach his elders wisdom. (Psalm 105:17–22)

Did Joseph do this perfectly? No, no one does. If we desire it, we will plead with God for greater maturity to live this way. Did Joseph plead with people? Yes—his brothers, Potiphar, and the butler—but he pleaded with God more than anyone else.

Not to see God this way is evidence something is wrong in our perspective or approach to life. A lack of love makes us suspicious of God. Job went through unimaginable torments of life and heart, yet he says, "Though he slay me, yet will I trust him." What creates that? Love to God! As believers, we are no "atheists," but how often do we slip into "practical atheism" by losing sight of God and his wise eternal purposes? When we do, it is a sickness of soul and breeder of disease, which leads to no good thing. Seeing God in everything expresses supreme love to God, which is health and life giving.

One other evidence of spiritual health:

2. It expresses preeminent trust in God.

Why do I say seeing God in everything and everywhere is a healthy outlook on life? God commands it and requires it from us. God only commands what is for our good! There are practical reasons.

> Trust in the LORD with all your heart, and lean not to your own understanding; in all your ways acknowledge him, and he shall direct your paths. (Proverbs 3:5–6)

Notice it is in all our ways!

> We know that all things work together for good to those who love God, to those who are the called according to his purpose. (Romans 8:28)

When we lose sight of God or when we limit the word *all*, we give our hearts to anxiety, fear, and bring emotional distress upon ourselves. It breeds spiritual sickness.

If we do not see life this way, our perspective is skewed, and it becomes a forerunner to conflicts with God. This failure to see things as God does leads us to not see God in all things. It shows a lack, even in small ways, of walking with God in the scriptural way of life. People and events grow large, and God grows distant and small. By the time we wonder where God is with all we are facing, we lost sight of him long before. There has already been a shift. God is no longer viewed as the center of our universe. We become the center, problems become the center, or people become the center. That is most unhealthy.

All of us need the exercise of pleading with God to retrieve us from this pathway. Every one of us takes steps down that path. How do we get back? By getting back to having the Lord always before us. Getting out of the way is easy. Getting back is often difficult. Demonstrate how important it is to you to have your God always before you by your earnest prayer for the Lord's help. He will give it! But we will need to seek it with all our hearts and with all our souls, with all our minds and, yes, with all our strength. Think of "strength" as energy, earnest, persistence. It is desiring great things greatly.

God expects his people individually and corporately to use holy pleading in their praying. Why? When they don't, God sees it as a sinful defect in those who profess to be his people. This was the case in Jeremiah's day. They did not plead the need of the redeemed community. All they could see were human problems, and so they sought human solutions. (It will always be this way even with us today.)

> For thus says the LORD: your affliction is incurable, your wound is severe. There is no one to plead your cause that you may be bound up; you have no healing medicines. (Jeremiah 30:12–13)

Isaiah tells us this displeases the LORD:

> Then the LORD saw it, and it displeased him that there was no justice. He saw that there was no man and wondered that there was no intercessor. (Isaiah 59:15–16)

They did not see God intricately involved in all their circumstances. God expected there to be pleaders—people in tune who could plead with God for the difficulties they faced and the healing of spiritual diseases. He expected there to be those who saw the sickness of the nation and would plead for a state of health. If there is no one who will stir himself up to go to the doctor, there will be sickness, illness, and death. They had their own solutions and so did not need God's solutions. No sense of need means no going to the physician; therefore, there will be no applied remedy or medicines.

This was a look at the nation of Israel during times of great declension, deterioration, and departure from the LORD. Forsaken by her adulterous lovers (false gods and other nations' military power), it leaves Israel without an intercessor. Why was there no intercessor who would plead for them? They had their "token" prayers but no pleading. They were looking for other solutions to their problems; they were going to manage the issue, yet there was a lot of worry deep within. There were numbers problems in their comparatively small army. Oh yes, there were money problems. They had power problems. There were political problems. They had family problems. There were social problems. They had religious problems. They had a lot of problems.

There was, however, widespread ignorance, indifference, and apathy concerning the real problem! There was no sense of the actual need, the urgent need, for a vital connection with the true and living God. They were living in denial toward the voice of their conscience. They lived, looked, and pursued safety in "a refuge of lies" and self-deception. Real prayer and pleading with God was, well, just not seen as helpful. What was their real problem? They had a problem with the LORD God Almighty! They were really serving their own kingdom, not God's kingdom and rule.

God had risen to be their enemy, and they desperately needed an intercessor. Why? Because God was their true and living accuser. Little did they know they needed an Advocate! God witnessed their numbness, declension, false reliances, and proud indifference to his pleadings with them. They had no sense of need in this area and no concern.

A sense of need leads to pleading.

> True prayer is born out of brokenness.
> (Frances J. Roberts)

They seared their conscience as with a hot iron, and they were hardhearted toward the actual issue. This is the reason God often referred to them as "hardhearted and stiff-necked." They busied themselves with their activities yet were "willingly ignorant" of the genuine need and issues in their lives. In all honesty, the actual issue demanded too much of them. The genuine issue required them to give up their control. The actual issue called for their humbling of themselves, turning from their own ways, and seeking God to turn them into his ways. His ways demanded being earnest in prayer. They needed to pray in their praying and mix repentance with their prayers. They drew their comfort from a refuge of lies and delusional denial.

There were many who would offer their "token" prayers! There were those who were carrying on their religious exercises and suggesting solutions to these problems, but where were the people who exhibited energy of soul to get to God, the true and living God? Where were the people who saw God as the first cause and only solution? Where were the people who would honestly confess their sins, hear the reproofs of the prophets speaking the Word of God's own entreaties, humble themselves before the Almighty, and plead his own words of promise to a repentant people who forsake their sins, idols, false gods, and false ways? There was no one! No wonder God says,

> Your affliction is incurable, your wound is severe. There is no one to plead your cause, so you may be bound up. (Jeremiah 30:12–13)

What horribly sad words—there is no healing for you.

> Ephraim is joined to idols. Let him alone. (Hosea 4:17)

Don't you believe it is like a loving child to pray, even to plead, "Oh, my gracious and loving Father, as your child, make me teachable and when I grow callous or willful. Make me easy to break and come to comply with your tender hand of care and leadership."

Pleading with God in prayer is essential for spiritual health.

a.   It helps us see God in everything, and now,
b.   pleading prevents spiritual sickness.

Our Savior tells us there is a condition a church can descend to which makes him nauseous and sick. This state makes God view a people as something revolting, despicable, detestable, disgusting, loathsome, offensive, and nauseating! Now there is a string of words! I would think no one would want a description of who they were to come anywhere near those words.

Think of this: would the Pharisees say they were "hypocrites," those who "devour widow's houses," or "blind guides," "whited tombs," "serpents," or a "brood of vipers"? Never! However, their view and self-estimation of themselves differed completely from Christ's view of who they really were. They had a high view of themselves. Our Lord had the "honest-before-God" view. As with Samuel's search for the Lord's anointed, "man looks on the outward appearance, but God looks on the heart."

These things may cause people to draw back and say, "But this is so negative!" Well, only if I see a cancerous condition for what it is will I seek medical treatment to heal the ugly disease. Christ did not flatter the scribes and Pharisees. He did not pronounce positive reinforcements over them to draw them to himself. However, he did them right, and if they would receive him as the great physician he was, he would lead them to undergo heart surgery for their eternal healing.

He did this for Nicodemus. The rich young ruler went away sad; however, he went away acquainted with the actual issue which separated his soul from eternal well-being. It does not tell us what he did with this new knowledge of himself and the uncovering of the disease of his soul. The Lord Jesus was faithful to him and his genuine need. Christ loves enough to be honest.

Now let's look at our Savior's words to a sick church:

> And to the angel of the church of the
> Laodiceans write, "These things says the Amen,

the Faithful and True Witness, the Beginning of the creation of God: 'I know your works, you are neither cold nor hot. I could wish you were cold or hot. So then, because you are lukewarm and neither cold nor hot, I will vomit you out of my mouth. Because you say, "I am rich, have become wealthy, and have need of nothing"—and do not know you are wretched, miserable, poor, blind, and naked—I counsel you to buy from me gold refined in the fire, so you may be rich; and white garments, so you may be clothed, so the shame of your nakedness may not be revealed; and anoint your eyes with eye salve, so you may see. As many as I love, I rebuke and chasten. Therefore, be zealous and repent.'" (Revelation 3:14–19)

As sobering as these words are, notice they come from "the Faithful and True Witness" and give due weight to the expression "as many as I love, I rebuke and chasten." These are words of restoration and come from the faithful wounds of a friend!

Their wisest course would be to embrace the truth, repent of their high view of themselves, and plead with the Lord for healing. Willful ignorance and indifference to their real and constant need was their greatest danger. Their problem was a lack of "being" as in the Beatitudes. They were not experiencing the poverty of their souls, nor did they mourn as they should. They could not yield their wills as the meek, nor were they hungering and thirsting. Christ spoke these expressed "states of being" as the marks of a healthy people who see things as they really are (the Beatitudes in Matthew 5:3–12).

The church will not plead when the church senses no real and urgent need. The individual doesn't plead when the individual doesn't sense the need of a pressing concern. When there is no strong and persevering pleading, there is sickness in the camp.

Are we ever not poor in spirit? Oh, we can be full, really full of ourselves! Do we ever need not to mourn? Christ describes his "true-hearted people"—"blessed are they that mourn"—not just one time or once in a while. Whenever they see their sin, the sins in the church, and the sins of society, a healthy soul groans and mourns. Is there ever an end to the need to be meek before our God and in our earthly sojourn? Only if we grow numb to reality! Christ sees that numbness as sickness.

The church at Corinth was a sick church. This was the malady at Corinth. There was an absence of "felt" need which humbled them and made them plead with God to come to their aid with his blood-bought provisions.

Paul tells them,

> You are already full! You are already rich! You have reigned as kings without us! (1 Corinthians 4:8)

They filled the Corinthian church with sickness and did not see the diseases plaguing the society of the saints.

This was the plague of the Old Covenant community—this state of nauseous, sickening security, produced by indifference to their genuine need. It permeated the Old Covenant setting in the days of Hosea.

> Ephraim said, "Surely I have become rich, I have found wealth for myself; in all my labors they shall find in me no iniquity which is sin.'" (Hosea 12:8)

When their true state is declared, it offended them. Such bold security creates a smugness and a greater willingness to live according to the dictates of our own hearts. "Oh, don't criticize me, just tell me good things about me."

God wants people to live in reality. Why?

> And so it may not happen, when he hears the words of this curse, he blesses himself in his

heart, saying, "I shall have peace, even though I follow the dictates of my heart"—as though the drunkard could be included with the sober. (Deuteronomy 29:19)

False teachers will say, "I just want people to go away feeling good about themselves." What about seeing themselves as God does? Deceivers lead people to self-deception. The worse thing that can happen is for people to love to have it so.

The prophets prophesy falsely, and the priests rule by their own power; and my people love to have it so. But what will you do in the end? (Jeremiah 5:31)

Think about what these people said concerning themselves (Laodicea, Corinth, and Ephraim). They were walking and living in a vain show and foolish imagination of their own righteousness and well-being. Their knowledge did not humble them and lead them to see things correctly. Having their eyes opened to "reality" would have led them to plead with God for mercy, grace, and the divine provision of pardon. They would have been importunate with God to create a clean heart within them and a change of life in their entire approach to daily living. Their own so-called advances in spiritual insight and knowledge puffed them up and removed a sense of the need to plead with God.

Perhaps the worst feature of this condition is that it conceals their true sickness and needs from themselves! Self-deception is the worst kind of deception. "You do not know!" What sad words! (Revelation 3:17). You went on with your show, your routine, and your self-protection from the true story. You placed a delicate ego in protective layers and strategically constructed moats around the castle of your heart. Your bridges and walls kept ultimate reality away. Such a condition would be common among the rich. Therefore, our Lord speaks of the greater difficulty of the wealthy entering the kingdom of heaven—not impossible but difficult.

Another sad feature of this state is others often see needs, but it only offends them if someone suggests they have a need. Why was Paul held at a distance from the people? He was honest, and they didn't like it. They became masters at calling good evil and evil good.

> O Corinthians! We have spoken openly to you, our heart is wide open. You are not restricted by us, but you are restricted by your own affections. Now in return for the same (I speak as to children), you also be open. (2 Corinthians 6:11–13)

> Open your hearts to us. We have wronged no one, we have corrupted no one, we have cheated no one. I do not say this to condemn; for I have said before that you are in our hearts, to die together and to live together. (2 Corinthians 7:2–3)

See how hard it was for them to receive the loving faithfulness of Paul who was laboring for their genuine good? Pride, an unteachable spirit, a self-protecting ego, preserves sickness and prevents healing for the soul.

To such self-sufficiency and spiritual pride, its vilest rags seem like royal robes; its filth appears to be gold and diamonds; its mercenary and proud services are holiness meriting reward and praise. "Don't tell me the truth, just say something positive" reflects their faulty value system. Their commitment is to see themselves as they want to, not as Christ does. This is a condition of self-complacency and self-confidence—all of which produces the evils of self-righteousness. All of it flows from self-deception. This state has less of the marks of genuine Christianity—or a true church as Christ would define as healthy.

As churches, where are our prayer meetings? We can soothe ourselves with music, performances, programs, and well-organized functions. We can have teaching, teaching, and more teaching, but in all this, where are we in praying and pleading? Where do we have our eyes on spiritual riches and God himself in which we stir ourselves up to take hold of God and not let him go until he comes down and blesses us? What other way is there to take the teaching and get it into our hearts and lives? There is no other way than prayer and pleading.

We must plead with God as a people who are living in reality, sensible of our need and conscious of our dependence upon God's interventions and supplies. This side of glory is one continual condition of neediness. We cannot "do" the Christian life on our own, nor can we "do church" without a present Christ who walks in our midst and gives his Spirit to minister to our souls! The presence of Christ's walking amid his lampstand is his known voice of authority and his present personal ministry to his people. One of the worst forms of spiritual sickness is to sense no urgent need of Christ. This must go beyond a formal and orthodox acknowledgement of this truth. It must move us to humility, hungerings and thirstings, and pleading with God.

Here is the equation: No pleading equals no sense of need! No sense of need means sickness has set in!

We should not be wiser than God.

—The Heidelberg Catechism

Indifference in religion is the first step to apostasy from religion.

—William Secker

It is scarcely possible in most places to get anyone to attend a meeting where the only attraction is God.

—A. W. Tozer

23

⊛

Why Pleading Is So Important (Part 2) Think and Reason Like God

His creation by God is man's only claim to dignity, importance or value.

—John Blanchard

> Now hear my reasoning, and heed the pleadings of my lips. (Job 13:6, Job entreating his friends, who lacked empathy and understanding and the correct application of wisdom)

Pleading with God is essential for spiritual health as seen in the last chapter. We now take up another important role pleading fulfills in our relationship with God.

God Is Reasonable and Expects Us to Reason with Him

Every year, my mom took a trip to Montana. She visited friends and my two brothers. Her delight was to take one of our daughters as a companion. This year, our third daughter had her heart set on going. Donna and I had concerns about whether she was ready for such a trip. While being a delightful child, her behavior and obedience were unreliable especially in our absence.

375

I took her into my office for a dad-daughter talk. I opened the conversation with this question: "Have you ever said or done something you later regretted or wished you hadn't?"

She answered, "Oh, yes."

"Well, honey, God gives parents to children to train them. Parents set boundaries for their children to protect them. The boundaries protect other people from their children's behavior—even wrong words, actions, or attitudes. When children learn to behave without the parents present, just as if the parents were there, then they are reliable and we can trust to be well-behaved."

We talked about this for a time, and I drew illustrations on a paper. Then I asked her, "Do you behave and speak the way you know Mom and Dad want you to when you are not around us?"

She looked at me with great sincerity and said, "Oh, Daddy, I can't go with my grandma this year!" There was a "matter-of-fact" resolve in her mind. She was not ready. It surprised me how completely at peace she was. She listened to my reasoning and followed it. It all made sense to her. She reasoned it through and came to a mature conclusion for such a young girl.

A. Because God made us in his image, we think and reason as he does.

God created us to be a thinking, reasoning people—first, with him as our God; second, with one another as the way of relationship; third, we are his handiwork placed in a world that displays his wisdom, power, creative skill, and majestic wonder. Everywhere we look, we see an intricate design and beauty. God's intention is for us to meditate, think, and reason about its splendor. We are to enjoy his creation. All sciences and skills arise from the way God made us to interact with the world we live in.

> The heavens declare the glory of God; and the firmament shows his handiwork. (Psalm 19:1)

Take that little conversation I had with my daughter. It was possible because we both are created in the image of God. Oh, there has been so much joy in my heart to be part of her growth and maturity as a precious individual through her younger years. Now, every time we speak, there is a delight in the things of God, fellowship, and sharing the fruits of our devotional life. We speak of guiding passages or truths which relate to real-life circumstances and how best to respond. We enjoy this. Though she is married and has five children, the joy is only richer and deeper.

What are we doing? Relating passages meditated and thought upon—these scriptural gems, reasoned through and connected with real-life circumstances, challenges, trials, or even a humorous moment. We are doing this in the context of a precious, loving, secure relationship between two people or more, who are made in the image of God.

The joy springing up in my heart from such exchanges is a small reflection of the greater joy our heavenly Father has with us. How do we carry on such exchanges with our God? Reading, meditating, and absorbing the precious truths of his Word, openly sharing your longing for the Holy Spirit's help to understand and experience his caring illumination of truth on your thoughts, communicating with him in applying what you understand to an array of circumstances, joys, challenges, obscurities, and craved wisdom to behave yourself in all well-pleasing before him. You may weep with joy in his presence, giving thanks for the glorious warmth, peace, and gladness of heart you receive from his heart expressions of loving-kindness and personal care. This indicates the atmosphere of communing with the Almighty.

He designed us to think and reason with him through the Scriptures and prayer in this way. The apostle John makes it clear our heavenly Father delights to be with us through our development as believers. That's what fathers do—born in spiritual infancy progressing to childhood, youth, and full adult maturity in the faith (1 John 2:12–14).

I hope you see that in the concepts of thinking and reasoning are the essentials for a meaningful relationship and enjoyed companionship. The relationship we have with the Father, Son, and Holy Spirit is to deepen through the years by the engagement and exercise of our thoughts, affections, and choices to embrace his communications in the Scripture and open our hearts to him in prayer. That's how we grow and mature as sons and daughters in the household of God.

God communicated his thoughts, and he reasoned with Adam in the garden as he gave him direction for life, priorities, the flow of the day and weeks, responsibilities, and more. There was harmony in mind, thought, and heart between God and man. The whole design included sharing and delighting in one another. Togetherness in the cool of the day meant relational companionship. God, the benevolent one, is worthy of all devotion, compliance to his every word, worship, and delightful allegiance. God would be guiding, teaching, and expanding the life experiences of Adam and Eve. They loved the Lord with all their hearts, all their souls, all their minds, and all their strength. Perfect joy and fulfillment resulted. They reflected the image of God.

B. The fall into sin poisoned and distorted human reasoning and thinking.

Satan, originally a gloriously created angel, through pride had fallen into a twisted insanity, enslaved in darkness, malicious drives, and infernal motives now consume him. He despises the God who gave him existence. Why? Because he wanted to be like God. Filled with his own self-importance, he felt entitled to be supreme in his own universe. Rejected, defeated, and cast out by Omnipotence, he fixates on hellish and demonic pursuits. No match for the Almighty, Satan's pitiless passion is to destroy the image of the God he hates: those created in the image of God. His enemies are the human race.

The initial tactic of the evil one was to subtly infuse suspicion about God into the thoughts of Eve and Adam!

God knows that in the day you eat of it your eyes will be opened, and you will be like God, knowing good and evil. (Genesis 3:5)

The suggestion of God hiding beneficial things from them fed more than suspicion; it grew the roots of entitlement and desirable independent thought from God.

After destroying the image of God, he worked to remake them in his own image! Lust sprouted in the soul, producing sin; and when finished, spiritual death and separation from God was the accursed accomplishment of the serpent. The diabolical accomplishment was that the human race became dead in trespasses and sins. Three spheres were engulfed in chaos, confusion, and sin's contamination: (1) Separation from God in spiritual death created suspicion, hatred, and avoidance of God. (2) Alienation between people, selfish self-seeking, and all relational conflicts arising from corrupt desires resulted. (3) Distortions within the inner world of individuals resulted. Confusion and every evil work were birthed through the fall of man.

From this death in sin, the use of reason is not just wounded and weakened; it became willful, corrupted, sinful, depraved, and wrong. A bias against God, suspicion, has spread like poison throughout humanity. Now the "understanding is darkened, being alienated from the life of God, because of the blindness of their heart" (Ephesians 4:17–18). The "light" of human reason differs little from darkness. No one can understand spiritual truth by carnal reason. If they pursue a religion, it has to be small enough to understand and so will never be big enough for the genuine need to have a remedy.

In the light of this tragic demolition of the image of God within humanity, observe this passage from Solomon:

> Truly, this only I have found; that God made man upright, but they have sought out many schemes. (Ecclesiastes 7:29)

Man's great plight was self-destruction! It still is.

God made humanity "upright," with no imperfection or corruption, conformed to his nature and will, mirroring his own likeness, straight as an arrow. God created mankind morally good, with upright reasoning ability, capable of continual joy, delight, and happiness. Man was created to be thrilled, blessed, cheerful, and over-joyed with enriching contentment. Every person in creation had the capacity for never-ending expansion of mind, heart, joy, and incredible satisfaction.

Notice the sad word *schemes*, or "devious inventions." They twisted themselves into corrupt ways of reasoning, behaving, and living. They were not content with their created condition but now study new ways of making themselves more wise and happy than God had made them, and we, as the fallen posterity, are still prone to forsake the certain rule of God's Word and the true way to happiness in order to seek our own methods of attaining the happiness everyone longs for, but all we have are fading leaves, empty hopes, delusions, and one refuge of lies after another. Now, without God, we cannot trust reason, sense, experience, intuition, or any other method offered for happiness. Everything is hollow, short-lived, turns sour, and leaves the soul craving another answer, experience, or empty hope. This is the legacy of rebelling against God.

Humanity reasons differently than their Creator. Sin is insanity. The fall distorts the reasoning of people upon the earth. In the fall of humanity, the mind became devastatingly affected. The nature of man is "dead in trespasses and sin" (Ephesians 2:1–3). Now the understanding exists in a darkened state. The mind of a fallen people is clouded with prejudice against God's authority and person. As to the true and living God, mankind is a hater of God. Romans 1:21 tells us,

> Because, although they knew God, they did not glorify him as God, nor were thankful, but became futile in their thoughts, and their foolish hearts were darkened.

All humanity knows three things: (1) God exists, (2) they are in trouble with God, and (3) they will meet God someday—face-to-face, and it will not go well! What do they do with this universal inerasable knowledge? They suppress and submerge it so they can get on with their lives, undisturbed as much as possible. This, I say, is not just rebellion, willfulness, and the securing of eternal death;

it is insanity and willful blindness. Willingly they play ignorant. (Romans 1:3)

C. The work of the Holy Spirit awakens saving reasoning or hardens human insanity.

Christ described the worldwide work of the Holy Spirit in John 16:8. He comes to influence the minds of people on earth in their fallen condition. Our Lord says, "When he (the Holy Spirit) has come, he will convict the world of sin and of righteousness and of judgment." There is a twofold result.

1. The minds of the lost have light shining into their consciousness.

Notice the word *convict*; in the original, it is to "convince." There is divine light infused into the thoughts which become "convincing" as to ultimate reality. (a) No person on earth can run from the reality of "sin." Awareness of right and wrong is woven into the moral fabric of the human race. (b) Consciousness of unacceptability before God—an absence of a needed "righteousness" or acceptability before God produces guilt. No one has this acceptance, and it is faintly known by all through subtle sensations of guilt! (c) There is an unavoidable day of appearing before God. The day of "judgment," or ultimate account, is in the fabric of the image-bearing makeup of mankind he cannot erase. All three are the same theme of Romans chapters 1–3. The Holy Spirit brings the witness of this to life in the consciences of humanity. The response of fallen people is to attempt to suppress it and put the day of their death far from them.

God is, he exists, and he is powerful, holy, and unavoidable. The witness to these truths is inside and outside of every individual. This may work to constrain human rebellion against God and not allow mankind to be as bad as they could. Left to themselves, however, man's heart is like hardened soil. It is no justification. It still leaves them without excuse before God. If they continue in their sins, they will perish. This light from the Holy Spirit may harden them in their insanity. The greatest evidence of moving toward sanity is to cry out to God that he might have mercy and acknowledge they do not deserve it.

God says to people, even in this condition, "Come, and let us reason together. Come, let us spread out our cases, and let us enter a context where each can plead his position. Come, I want to hear what you have to say. Then I want you to hear what I have to say." This tells us something of God's character and willingness to enter an actual exchange of mind and understanding with people. God is reasonable. God holds out an invitation for people to turn from their willful insanity. Sadly, many do not.

2. When this illuminating work of the Holy Spirit is accompanied with the power of the Gospel, awakening and raising a dead soul to life, an eternal change is accomplished.

A precious person, the focus of divine love, is made a new creation in Christ Jesus. God, who is rich in mercy, takes steps toward the unworthy!

D. The Spirit, through the new birth, makes new creations in Christ.

When this work of the Spirit comes upon the soul in the new birth, his activity changes the dead nature and brings life-enabling "respond-ability" to the soul. The seeds of heavenly logic and sound reasoning begins. God's compassions bring the individual closer to reality. The Holy Spirit produces a lively work convincing them of the sinfulness of their sin, their lack of acceptable standing, along with the realness of coming judgment. New reasonings emerge and progress. Their thinking changes. Without realizing it, this sets them on being renewed in the spirit of their minds.

These new believers show new life by their growth in thinking over what they read in the Bible and express it back to God in prayer. They draw their thoughts from Scripture. They communicate the formation of new thoughts in prayer to God. Spiritual growth is furthered as the engrafting of the Word of God continues.

Scripture mentions the Bible in all stages of the believer's growth:

> Of His own will He brought us forth by the
> word of truth. (James 1:18)

> As newborn babes, desire the pure milk of
> the word that you may grow thereby. (1 Peter 2:2)

> I fed you with milk and not with solid
> food; for until now you could not receive it. (1
> Corinthians 3:2)

Christ gives pastors and teachers to the church to be built up in sound doctrine. Why? To come up to the measure and stature of the fullness of Christ (Ephesians 4:11–16)! Believers must grow. Churches must be nourished in the Word of God. Mark it down: there is a great difference between a well-educated church and a well-nourished church.

Not to spiritually grow is a dangerous indicator of poor health.

> For everyone who partakes only of milk is
> unskilled in the word of righteousness, for he is a
> babe. But solid food belongs to those who are of
> full age, that is, those who, by reason of use, have
> their senses exercised to discern both good and
> evil. (Hebrews 5:13–14)

The "senses exercised to discern" is the maturing process of thinking biblically and reasoning as God would. The indication of a person's growth or a church's power is never in how much they know. Rather, it is manifested in how much truth brings a transformative influence. In reality, it is the authoritative voice of Christ in the Word, producing loving practice, obedience, and healing.

> He sent his word and healed them. (Psalm
> 107:20)

Don't underestimate the importance of this. God is not only reasonable in himself; he loves to share thought and reason with his children. In the holy Trinity, there is perfect fellowship, relational joy, love, delight, and peace. This glorious and majestic, all-sufficient, almighty, holy God devised a plan to bring back banished ones into a loving, acceptable embrace and fellowship through the atoning work of the God-Man, Christ Jesus.

As sons and daughters of the Almighty, in the household of God, we enjoy relational richness, fellowship, sharing, exchanging of thoughts, and opening our reasonings drawn from the book of God's thoughts and ways. The Scriptures are an ocean deep and wide, filled with relationally rich subject matter to take and commune with each person of the Godhead.

Remember what pleading with God is: drawing truth from Scripture, which gives a basis to argue or set out the reason for God to do or give us some desired good.

> The LORD also will be a refuge for the oppressed, a refuge in times of trouble. And those who know your name will put their trust in you; for you, LORD, have not forsaken those who seek you. (Psalm 9:9–10)

What do you find in those words? You find God's character, his names, and his promises. What does David do with the treasury of God's personal self-disclosure? He bears testimony to the LORD's reliability and trustworthiness to place one's confidence in him when oppression, trouble, or fearful circumstances arise. David is using thoughts of God's character and name to reason through the arguments to trust the Lord. They are foundational principles to press into the heart of God why he should act on behalf of one made to rely upon him.

Here is the course for personal growth, communion, spiritual development, finding peace, comfort, and God's guidance in time of need. This is learning to think and reason like God thinks and reasons. It is the pathway of walking with God and finding help on our earthly journey. We do not know what a day may bring forth. Therefore, equip ourselves with thinking and reasoning God's grand word of truth. Connect the dots of life with the truth and the self-disclosure God gave us. When trouble strikes or needs arise, plead with God his own faithful Word, character, promises, and fidelity in his relationship with you.

> Let all those rejoice who put their trust in
> you; let them ever shout for joy, because you
> defend them; let those also who love your name
> be joyful in you. For you, O LORD, will bless the
> righteous; with favor, you will surround him as
> with a shield. (Psalm 5:11–12)

So how can we grow and mature in this thinking, reasoning, and pleading with God? Here are some guidelines I trust will help:

1. Embrace the great chasm between the way we think and act with the way God thinks and acts.

Take these words found in Isaiah 55:8–9. This passage speaks of the incredible mercy of the LORD and shows how vastly contrasted God's mercies are from man's inadequate conceptions of mercy. It states the obvious to us:

> "For my thoughts are not your thoughts,
> nor are your ways my ways," says the Lord. "For
> as the heavens are higher than the earth, so are
> my ways higher than your ways, and my thoughts
> than your thoughts."

This is an amazing and an incredible display of the LORD's mercies. He invites us to learn from him and learn his thoughts and ways. God wants us to study his ways and give ourselves to meditate on his behavior. If we do, we shall develop a sweet security and humble confidence in him.

> Who is wise? Let him understand these
> things. Who is prudent? Let him know them. For

the ways of the Lord are right; the righteous walk
in them. (Hosea 14:9)

We will say, "I knew I could trust the Lord in this. I've come to
know and depend upon his character."

Because your loving-kindness is better than
life, my lips shall praise you. (Psalm 63:3)

When we experience a peaceful composure amid trials, contentment in difficult circumstances, which arises from a confidence
in the character of God, this argues wonderful maturity in the soul.
In Psalm 107, you have the record of man's erratic instability. In contrast, you have the LORD's stable displays of faithfulness and reliable
mercies.

Whoever is wise will observe these things,
and they will understand the loving-kindness of
the Lord. (Psalm 107:43)

It may be a slow process, but we must stop reading our tendencies into God. That was a monumental error of those in Psalm 50.
"You thought that I was altogether like you" (v. 21). It was ultimately
their downfall. They did not have a heart to change the way they
thought of God, but it is different with you. You want to learn the
way God thinks and acts. His pathways are peace. There is an attraction in them.

As we learn the ways of the LORD, it will rework our priorities
and values. We prize qualities, characteristics, and ways which we see
in God.

Thus says the Lord: "Let not the wise man
glory in his wisdom, let not the mighty man
glory in his might, nor let the rich man glory in
his riches; but let him who glories glory in this,
that he understands and knows me, that I am the

> Lord, exercising loving-kindness, judgment, and
> righteousness in the earth. For in these I delight,"
> says the Lord. (Jeremiah 9:23–24)

We find things so important to man in a fallen world are not attractive to God. He says, "They are an abomination." Though he is the high and lofty one who inhabits eternity, there is an attractiveness in his ways which makes us want to be imitators of God as dear children.

Genuine Christianity will elevate the character and make us less and less like the world and more "fit" for heaven.

2. Growth in thinking and reasoning like God is not optional.

Notice what God says in Amos 3:3:

> How can two walk together, unless they are
> agreed?

What does this mean? Unless they see things eye to eye, they have spoken, they have reasoned through things together and have found a companionship of mutual agreement, a togetherness in their conclusions, they are of the same mind. This is a question God puts before the community of Israel. He is using the illustration of a common experience of true-hearted companionship. The struggles Israel faced were rooted in this cause—not being in harmony with God.

God wrote these things for our learning. To not think and reason like the Lord will be our own downfall. However, let us see in these words an invitation to walk in thought and heart harmony with our God. Align our thoughts, and walk together with the Lord.

Our God both desires and expects this mind-heart harmony with us, his people. Think of it—God says, "Let us walk together in agreement as companions through your journey in life." This is essential to our growth as believers. It is vital for the development of mature Christian character. There is no walking with God without this harmony of thought. If we do not engage in this pursuit, we risk walking contrary to God and his ways (Leviticus 26). What would cause disharmony? Our stubborn will, pride, and a dislike toward his demands upon us. Then God responds, in faithfulness to our reality, to walk contrary to us in a way of correction.

The passage in Leviticus holds out promises of many blessings as we walk with God in a valued companionship described as mind/heart harmony. However, it holds out warnings should we choose a way of living described as "walking haphazardly," carelessly, thoughtlessly, and indifferent to the directing teaching of Scripture. Remember, if we will not walk "with" God, the world, the flesh, and the devil will walk with us.

Prize God's companionship, and walk with him. He longs for it with all his heart. Think like he thinks. You will not attain this without prayer. You will have many pressing occasions for needed pleading with God for it. You read pleading again and again in the Psalms. They demonstrated how much they prized this type of walking with God by their energy in prayer and pleading. "Oh, but I'm sincere." Show your sincerity by your diligence in prayer.

3. Pursue this with a principled faith in the teaching and testimony of Scripture.

Let's look at Hebrews 11:6: "But without faith." What is faith? A leap in the dark? No, such a thing is gullibility and naivety. It is nothing God takes delight in. The truth is a "leap of faith," is what the devil suggested to Christ in the temptation to leap from the temple! Such activity, Christ said, would be to tempt the LORD.

One violation of the first commandment is "vain credulity," which means a trust without reason or foundation, belief with no basis. That activity is superstition, sentimentality, or romanticism— not faith. Faith should always express sound thinking rooted in God's teachings. Genuine faith, genuine belief, is a reasonable confidence in the word and testimony of God.

Faith gives due respect to the reasonableness and truthfulness of God as he communicates to us in the Scriptures:

> Without faith it is impossible to please him, for he who comes to God must believe he is, (not only he exists, but he is approachable as a communicating Creator, Savior, and God) and he is a rewarder of those who diligently seek him.

He responds appropriately and shows himself responsive to a people who rely on his Word and take believing action upon his communications. Diligently seeking him includes the activity of prayer and pleading. This is what it is to please God.

God expects a soulful seeking of his person with energy and desire of heart. Isn't this what God intended for us to understand when he tells us to "love the LORD with all our heart, all our soul, all our mind, and all our strength?" As long as we live in this world, this activity will include pleading with God.

4. Growth in maturity is the fruit and evidence of life.

The pursuit I am describing is simply healthy Christian growth. There may be many factors which slow or hinder growth in a child of God—one's devotional life, the literature consumed, the context of life, quality of ministry they sit under, and many other considerations. However, there will be an "ache" for more in the believer's heart.

The "ache" arises from the work of the Holy Spirit and the intercession of Christ. Paul was concerned when he sought to nurture the saints to maturity but continually returned to give food to babes. Personally, I believe there are many hindrances to maturity in our day.

What I am encouraging in this book and chapter is a vital part of Christian growth. This is an important part of our maturity.

> When I was a child, I spoke as a child, I understood as a child, I thought (reasoned) as

a child; but when I became a man, I put away childish things. (1 Corinthians 13:11)

God's Word guides us to think correctly and to relate to God in a maturing fashion. It also gives us appropriate expressions and principles whereby we entreat and lay hold of him for needs arising in our lives. God teaches us how to approach him and how to reason with him in prayer. The book of Psalms is a perfect example of how to approach God with biblical reasoning. The Psalms are full of pleadings by those who longed for their soul's growth.

I believe the evil one and the forces of darkness are constantly undermining this and working a subtle conspiracy for the churches' stunted growth. The enemy of our souls will not want us to think this way, live this way, and especially pray this way. Why else would Paul conclude the passage concerning the Christian's armor with urgent entreaties for us to pray and, in praying, to pray earnestly in every manner?

> Praying always with all prayer and supplication in the Spirit, being watchful to this end with all perseverance and supplication for all the saints—and for me, that utterance may be given to me, so I may open my mouth boldly to make known the mystery of the gospel, for which I am an ambassador in chains; that in it I may speak boldly as I ought to speak. (Ephesians 6:18–20)

Paul could not say "pray" enough!

Why is it we must plead with God in a way of reasoning? Pleading honors God as being a reasonable God who listens to our thinking and communication. Do you believe God listens to your thinking and speaking to him? He is not an idol or false god. All false gods were unreasonable, unresponsive, noncommunicating, and impersonal. God must be more than just a concept!

Pleading manifests the dignity of being made in the image of God. Reasoned pleading gives evidence we are diligently seeking him in the way of his appointment. Pleading declares we are taking God at his word, which pleases God. It thrills the heart of our heavenly Father and blessed Lord Jesus just as much as any parent rejoices to see the maturity of thought and reasoning in their own children. God delights to hear his Word echoing from the hearts of his people. His Word is "truth," and God "desires truth in the inward parts" (Psalm 51:6). Pleading shows our concern for truth as the framework of our thinking and communicating. Pleading in this manner is an outworking of "having our senses exercised" to discern what is well-pleasing to our God (Hebrews 5:12–14). It is to be in harmony with Paul's entreaty:

> Do not be unwise, but understand what the
> will of the Lord is. (Ephesians 5:17)

Pleading with God is active thinking and reasoning with God as he teaches us to think and reason in the pages of Scripture. It is both how we grow and the evidence of our growth in the Christian life.

5. The last encouragement is to be determined to start, but start with small steps.

Set slow and steady as your method of progress. Put growth in this area as a goal you love and desire. Think of it as your God schooling you to think and reason. You are in his household, and you are a beginner. The Bible is your textbook. Just take one passage per week. Perhaps Psalm 62:8:

> Trust in him at all times, you people; pour
> out your heart before him; God is a refuge for us.

Take this verse to the Lord, and pray over every line. Ask him to inscribe it on your heart and memory. Bring every need or concern which arises in the week to the Lord through the lens of this verse. Ask the Lord's help to pour your soul into the words, and frame your life to be in harmony with the spirit of the passage. Ask him to make you a person that when you read these words, it is like reading a description of who you are. Look for the way of thinking and reasoning portrayed in these words to become a portrait of the way you think and reason.

Ask each Person of the Godhead to give you personal help in this effort. Humbly ask them to be colaborers with you in your maturity and advancement as a praying child of God.

> I did not say to the seed of Jacob, "Seek me in vain"; I, the Lord, speak righteousness, I declare things that are right. (Isaiah 45:19)

> You will seek me and find me when you search for me with all your heart. (Jeremiah 29:13)

These are not just some verses. These are the communications of how God thinks and reasons. They are from the heart of God to the heart of his children. They invite belief, trust, and responsive compliance. Let faith, love, obedience, responsiveness to God's kind words become the Spirit-wrought characteristic of your life.

See how many passages you can bring into this pattern of growth in a year's time. You will be overjoyed and exceedingly pleased with the fruit of your loving labors.

> *Human beings are the only creatures who are able to behave irrationally in the name of reason.*
>
> —Ashley Montagu

> *Nothing but faith will ever rectify the mistakes of reason on divine things.*
>
> —William S. Plumer

24

The root of religion is the fear of God reigning in the heart, a reverence of his majesty, a deference to his authority and a dread of his wrath.

—Matthew Henry

Why Pleading Is So Important (Part 3) Avoid Counterfeit Christianity

Pleading with God, engaged and earnest, praying in our praying, God commands this for our benefit. This quality of praying, scattered throughout our times before the LORD, is an indication we are "real" in our approach to life and prayer. The Holy Spirit uses such praying to preserve our spiritual health. Our Lord uses it to teach us to think and reason as he does, which brings precious harmony of heart and mind between us.

Another benefit of great value is the focus of this chapter. When we follow the example of our Lord Jesus, "who, in the days of his flesh, when he had offered up prayers and supplications, with vehement cries and tears," and combine this with the affectionate study of the Word of God, vital discernment weaves itself into the fabric of our souls. We mature in a way that helps avoid subtle evil and pursues precious good. This is exactly what we are told.

> Solid food (the meat of God's word, sound teaching) belongs to those who are of full age (mature), that is, those who by reason of use (habitual practice) have their senses exercised (trained) to discern both good and evil. (Hebrews 5:14)

Therefore, we come to see a third benefit and urgent reason for pleading.

Pleading Is a Safeguard against Counterfeit Christianity

When I was nine years old, I lived in Oak Run, California. After my dad left us, my mom moved us to her hometown where she grew up—a population of about 150 people. We moved into the abandoned house of the midwife to my grandmother. It was primitive living.

That summer, my cousins organized a hike to Clover Creek Falls. I had lunch in my backpack. It was a two-mile walk in a hundred-degree heat. When we arrived at the falls, we swam for hours. A few of the older boys found glittering rocks. They just knew it was gold! So they filled my backpack. The walk back was grueling. The pack was so heavy my legs and back ached, but the thought of riches made it worth it.

I made it to my uncle's. He was in the garage.

"Uncle Robert, look what I have."

He glanced at the rocks I poured out on the floor. "Oh, I see. You know what you have there? It's pyrite! Nice-looking fool's gold, but it's not worth anything." Of course, my cousins knew it all the time.

What a hard way to learn "All that glitters isn't gold." Rocks are on a low level of importance. A sore back and legs were all the damage. However, with a relationship with God and the well-being of our eternal souls, it takes on a whole new level of serious significance.

The apostle John writes of "pyrite Christianity," a "fool's gold" of religious delusion! Let these words sink in. Take them into your meditative consideration.

> You have a name you are alive, but you are
> dead. (Revelation 3:1)

"You are dead!" That is an alarming statement. It's even more sobering when we see Christ is the one speaking to a church! An unnerving subject—alive in profession and delusional activity, going on in self-deceived presumption, yet still spiritually dead in the sight of Christ. It appears more often in the Scriptures than many realize. We have seen this before:

> Not everyone who says to me, "Lord, Lord," shall enter the kingdom of heaven, but he who does the will of my Father in heaven. Many will say to me in that day, "Lord, Lord, have we not prophesied in your name, cast out demons in your name, and done many wonders in your name?" And then I will declare to them, "I never knew you; depart from me, you who practice lawlessness!" (Matthew 7:21–23)

What were these people missing? They spoke of accomplishments in the name of Christ. Impressed they were by what they had done. Why was the Lord not impressed? Our Lord spoke of genuine and personal acquaintance, which produced loving submission and obedience to him and his authoritative teaching. They spoke of activities and what "they" did. Christ spoke of intimacy in relationship and a valued attitude of heart. They never knew of this, nor did they crave, miss, or experience it.

Christ identified who they essentially were—a law unto themselves and, at heart, unattracted to him. The Christ they were familiar with was what our Lord and Paul warned—another Christ, a different Jesus.

> For if he who comes preaches another Jesus whom we have not preached, or if you receive a different spirit which you have not received, or a different gospel which you have not accepted. (2 Corinthians 11:4)

These people perverted and twisted the identity of Jesus, the spirit of Christianity, and the Gospel into what is false. Such people recast these to conform to worldly ways of thinking and satisfy the current taste for a "Christianity" without the unpleasantries the world's methods embraced, incorporated, and used so the people of the world "feel" comfortable.

There is a startling word of caution. Perhaps the word *alarm* is better. Let the force of these words settle upon your thoughts:

> Do you not know that friendship with the world is enmity with God? Whoever therefore wants to be a friend of the world makes himself an enemy of God. Or do you think the Scripture says in vain, "The Spirit who dwells in us yearns jealously"? But he gives more grace. Therefore, he says: "God resists the proud, but gives grace to the humble." (James 4:4–5)

Our Lord knew people including them. People viewed them as accomplished Christians. Christ viewed them inwardly as dead souls going about religious activity, busy with undertakings rooted in self-importance, disconnected from his authority, oblivious to his commands, and alienated from his heart, very excited with what they were doing and told Christ about it all. However, the true and living Christ was not precious to them. They were fond of a "different Christ." Christ Jesus was not a treasury of wisdom and grace to draw from. Such concepts were a foreign language, and they did not speak it. They could not discern the evil in their ways.

There may be a temptation to think, "Oh, this is so negative!" But it is Christ speaking these words! Here is another way to think of it:

> Oh Lord Jesus, in your kindness and love, help me be discerning. Beloved Holy Spirit, you know me better than I know myself. Search my heart and know my deepest state of soul. See if there is any wicked way in me and lead me in the way everlasting. (Psalm 139:23–24)

We are told to examine ourselves:

> Examine yourselves whether you are in the faith. Test yourselves. Do you not know yourselves that Jesus Christ is in you? (2 Corinthians 13:5)

The only thing threatened by examination is the counterfeit.

Notice the contrast between the Pharisees and genuine disciples in the light of Christ's honesty. When the Pharisees and scribes knew Christ spoke things which revealed the truth about them:

> They were offended. (Matthew 15:12)

Counterfeit religion despises soul honesty and heart work. These were those who trusted in themselves.

Here is the contrast. In the upper room, Christ declared one of his disciples would betray him!

> Each of them began to say to him, "Lord, is it I?" (Matthew 26:22)

The authentic lovers of Christ craved soul honesty and heart loyalty to the true and living Christ. These were those who distrusted themselves. They had come to see the hidden evils of their hearts, but they had come to confidence in their Lord's faithfulness to them. So, even with such a startling statement, *healthy* self-suspicion gripped them. They took it to Christ.

Let's look at contributing creators to "counterfeit Religion," then we will consider how pleading with God safeguards against it.

Contributing Creators of Counterfeit Christianity

1. Become familiar with three notorious enemies to your soul.

If you are not familiar with *The Pilgrim's Progress* by John Bunyan, I hope you will find it and read it more than once. You could find it in nearly every Christian home since 1680, when first written. It was required reading in high schools until the 1950s here in America. It is the story of Christian, who was born and lived in the City of Destruction, this world. Awakened by reading the best of books, the Bible, he fled to go to the Celestial City, heaven. It tells of his journey to the cross of Christ and then the Christian life. He meets helpers along the way, and he meets those who hinder him as well. Some seek to deceive him and lead him astray. Oh, it is a delightful story and still so relevant. It was standard reading for centuries until different flavors of Christianities came upon the landscape of Americanized Christian religion. It is a buried treasure, and I hope you will go dig it up!

John Bunyan tells the story as though it was a dream he had. Christian, on his journey, comes by many "religious" people in various forms of self-deception—people like Formalist and Hypocrisy. There is one Mr. Row-Both-Ways! These were names John Bunyan gave them so you could understand the prevailing qualities and characteristics of their souls. There was Talkative, who could spin your head with how much he knew of Christianity. However, he was a saint abroad and a devil at home. He knew nothing of heart religion.

There are three individuals Christian meets and tries to help. They were asleep along the pathway, just a little out of the narrow way. Each one seemed innocent enough. You can almost feel sorry for them. They are, however, enemies to your spiritual health, well-being, and eternal safety. These are enemies who live in each one of us as subtle inclinations. However, when they control one's life, they prevent genuine spiritualty from taking root in the soul. They draw back from authentic prayer and view pleading as foolish and irrelevant to their world of undisturbed ease. They may show up in churches like deadly cancers poisoning the health of the body. They are enemies within the church softly killing healthy spirituality with an innocent smile and worldly mindset. As quiet propensities, if undetected, they destroy a church's reputation in heaven and effectively remove its saltiness and light on earth. These have no heart for the purpose of Christ in redeeming his people: "who gave himself for us, that he might redeem us from every lawless deed and purify for himself his own special people, zealous for good works" (Titus 2:14). If pressed too much toward the demands and desires of Christ's heart, these counterfeit sheep grow fangs and claws.

Here is the story:

> I saw then in my dream, he went on thus, even until he came at the bottom where he saw, a little out of the way, three men fast asleep, with fetters upon their heels. The name of the one was Simple, of another Sloth, and of the third Presumption.

> Christian then seeing them lie in this case went to them, if peradventure he might awake them, and cried, "You are like them asleep on top of a mast" (Proverbs 23:34) for the Dead Sea, is under you, a gulf that has no bottom: awake, therefore, and come away; be willing also, and I will help you off with your irons. He also told them, if he who goes about like a roaring lion (1 Peter 5:8), comes by, you will certainly become a prey to his teeth. With that, they looked upon him, and replied in this sort:

(a) Simple said, "I see no danger." Simpletons take their own evaluation to be sufficient. Making themselves their own measuring line, it quite impressed them with how tall they are. They simplify their state to remove any sense of being alarmed, in need, or desperate. All is well according to their estimation. They feel no danger because they see no danger.

It is with them as in the days of Noah:

> For as in the days before the flood, they were eating and drinking, marrying and giving in marriage, until the day that Noah entered the ark. (Matthew 24:38)

Life just goes on, and they go on with no sense of urgency to be earnestly involved in their professing of faith in Christ and the Christian life. There is no warfare for them or need to be victorious through trials and challenges. They have no sense of need to get to Christ or the throne of grace to receive mercy and find grace to help in time of need. Speaking to them of these things is like an idle tale they can't relate to.

With "working out their own salvation with fear and trembling" or "be even more diligent to make your call and election sure," it makes no sense. To hear of the danger of a slighted Savior, a God to be feared, a holy day of account, and an actual hell—they see none of these things. Therefore, make no effort and give no concern to be prepared for them.

(b) Sloth said, "Yet a little more sleep." A little longer to indulge, a more convenient season will show itself. Let's not get so concerned and excited. We don't want to be moved with alarm, you know. They resent being stirred to any earnest exertion in the Christian life.

> Why, to be over zealous is to risk legalism. You know God doesn't want that. Besides, it would be "righteous overmuch" as Solomon said, and he was wise!

They desire ease in a life of dabbling with minor sins, compromise, and carnal security. Most do not think of spiritual and eternal things. If sobering thoughts intrude on their thoughts, they stifle and banish them by promising themselves to take them up in the future.

Like Felix when Paul reasoned with him:

> Now, as he reasoned about righteousness, self-control, and the judgment to come, Felix was afraid and answered, "Go away for now; when I have a convenient time I will call for you." (Acts 24:25)

Of course, that never happened.

These are people who lull their consciences to sleep.

> A little sleep, a little slumber, a little folding of the hands to rest. (Proverbs 24:33)

These live with the motto "I'll get around to it someday. No worries. No hurries. Life is good." They have a long line of worldly plans to carry out, and they flatter themselves they will live to enjoy them all. The concept of "not knowing what a day may bring forth" requires too much energy to think about.

(c) Presumption said, "Every tub must stand upon its own bottom." "You take care of what concerns you, and I'll take care of my concerns. Don't trouble yourself with my spiritual state. I'm not at all concerned. All will go well." These are the people that get provoked with any who interfere with their spiritual affairs. Their concerns are their own. They resent being told of their needs. They also resent having the demands of Christ in true discipleship brought to their thoughts or consciences.

They see themselves as sincere, they prayed God is merciful, he will not send them to hell, and there the matter ends. Now they are happy all the day.

All three have these things in common—they are out of the way. Spiritually, they are asleep. They have fetters on their feet. All three have high opinions of their opinions—a most dangerous condition. Bunyan represented their spiritual state in their names. Perhaps they have a "professional pulpitism" financed by "pew spectators" as a church. They may be active in church attendance and life. The issues are they are spiritually dead, out of the narrow way, in the broad way that leads to destruction, tethered and bound to their sins. All three have a profession which speaks of life but are dead.

2. The climate for counterfeit Christianity to flourish

For decades, the Christian church has been adopting the marketing technologies and methods of the world to attract people into churches. While there have been large churches created and increased numbers in many places, the spiritual quality of the churches has diminished. An atmosphere where it is possible to have the best of both worlds has emerged.

For this to happen, they must accommodate convenience. A shift had to take place. The offense of the cross needed to be retold. The demand for cross-bearing and self-denial had to be "lightened up some."

Prayer meetings have, mostly, vanished. Evening services had to go. The concept of the Lord's Day is extinct on a large scale. On a scale of significance, summer sports must increase and church attendance decrease. The world's major agenda—happiness trumps passion for Christ and conformity to his person. Entertainment, emotional thrills, and sentimental "feel good" songs replace worship in the beauty of holiness.

What is the bottom line of much evangelical preaching today? To be happy? To be satisfied? "Well, it is God's desire that his people be rich and feel good about themselves. Reaching the good life is a valid Christian goal." Priorities have shifted toward those shallow concerns while failing to address the sins of those who are living for themselves rather than for Christ and others. Far be it for many Christians today to preach a gospel that would expose sin and drive men and women to the Savior or demand a hard following after Jesus Christ as the only true discipleship.

We live in a therapeutic Christian age. Many churches have recast their theology in psychiatric terms. Sin has become dysfunctional behavior. Salvation is self-esteem or wholeness. Jesus is more of an example for right living than our Savior from sin and God's wrath. Sunday by Sunday, people are told how to have happy marriages and happy families and cheerful kids but not how to get right with God. The demands of discipleship may be for a select few to be taken up in private so others will not feel uncomfortable.

What does all this produce from God's vantage point?

1. Entertainment nudges out the powerful authority of God's Word.

> Indeed, you are to them as a very lovely song of one who has a pleasant voice and can play well on an instrument; for they hear your words, but they do not do them. (Ezekiel 33:32)

The same ones Christ exposed in Matthew 7:21–27.

2. The great truths of God's Word remain undiscovered.

> I have written for him the great things of my law, but they were considered a strange thing. (Hosea 8:12)

Perhaps "short shots for daily encouragement" opens the Bible. Gone are the joys and thrills of discovering the great truths of God's revelation. Coming to see the greatness and majesty of God should lead to wonder, love, and praise. Alas, they eclipse it. Being in the sensible presence of God, like Moses, Abraham, Job, Isaiah, Peter, and the apostle John, becomes unknown to many within the Christian churches.

3. No capacity to dread the right things. Simple, Sloth, and Presumption are alive and well in this environment. The rich young ruler would thrive, feeling good about his good self, and joy would fill his soul, for no one would confront him for his covetousness like Christ did (Mark 10:17–22). This man went away sad from Christ, for the Lord made it known he valued his riches more than the Savior. Who today would be faithful to such a one? Covetousness is a cancer! Proverbs 1:19 tells us it takes away the life of the one who owns it! Reality is they don't own their wealth; their wealth owns them and robs them of eternal life.

4. The fear of God, explained away and reduced, leaves no sobering influence.

    The Lord your God is a consuming fire, a jealous God. (Deuteronomy 4:24)

    Therefore, since we are receiving a kingdom which cannot be shaken, let us have grace, by which we may serve God acceptably with reverence and godly fear. For our God is a consuming fire. (Hebrews 12:28–29)

    Is this known and sensed anymore?

5. Knowledge gained remains mainly in the brain. This tendency leads to choices and behavior against the caution given in the Heidelberg Catechism. "We must not be wiser than God." Here arises the intellectual rationales to forgo corporate prayer, reducing the Lord's Day containing a mere one or two hours with a sermon and singing. The evening worship is gone! Diminishing the responsibility of family worship or devotions, personal priorities rule the remains of the day. We could go on with other important

items which are precious to the Lord and bring health to the soul, family, and church.

What is the sobering danger in all this?

> Do not be wise in your own eyes; fear the Lord and depart from evil. (Proverbs 3:7)

Reverence God's wisdom, and despise your own.

> Do not set your mind on high things, but associate with the humble. Do not be wise in your own opinion. (Romans 12:16)

There is truth in this caution:

> It is not good to know more unless we do more with what we already know. (R. K. Bergethon)

That is not absolutely true, but we sense a legitimate caution. John R. W. Stott advises,

> Knowledge is indispensable to Christian life and service. Knowledge is given us to be used, to lead us to higher worship, greater faith, deeper holiness, better service.

In these, and so many more ways, there is warfare with the forces of darkness. They work with subtlety and cater to the reigning or raging sin in the souls within churches. There is a conspiracy for delusional well-being. The evil one is working to unplug the churches from earnest pursuits of walking with God.

We are not equal to the task or the battle! Our greatest weapon is what Paul calls "all prayer!"

> The Lord takes pleasure in those who fear him,
> in those who hope in his mercy. (Psalm 147:11)

> Call upon me in the day of trouble; I will
> deliver you, and you shall glorify me. (Psalm 50:15)

A Gift from God to Help Us Live with "Judgment Day Honesty"

Psalm 50 sets a sobering scene before us. God gave this Psalm to help us live with Judgement Day honesty. The Lord will unveil all in that day, and all delusions will disappear. Paul writes of it:

> In the day when God will judge the secrets
> of men by Jesus Christ, according to my gospel.
> (Romans 2:16)

Our wisdom is to live with that day before us. Correctly used, it motivates to live life before the face of God.

The setting of the Psalm is the great and final day of account (vv. 1–3). The Omnipotent one, who is relational and gracious, though not to be disregarded, is coming to judge—just as our Lord stated in Matthew 7:21–23. This is the event recorded in Revelation 6:12–17 and Matthew 25:31–46.

This is the ultimate and unavoidable summons to appear before God. The focus in this Psalm is not the entire world but the religious community (vv. 4–6). "Those who have made a covenant with God by sacrifice," they declared themselves to be his people. He will ask them, "What right have you to declare my statutes, or take my covenant in your mouth, seeing you hate instruction and cast my words behind you?" (vv. 16–17). They were busy with religious activity, but cancer was in their soul. "Now consider this, you who forget God, lest I tear you in pieces, and there be none to deliver" (v. 22). The

Mighty One, God the LORD, is serious about people who profess to be his people! Judgement begins at the house of God (1 Peter 4:17).

God tells them the main issue he has to contend with them over is not religious performance (vv. 7–11). No religious action can ever be a substitute for heart engagement or heart longings to know and walk with the LORD.

The LORD clearly states what he desires and looks for from individuals who profess to be his people (vv. 12–15).

Negatively, it is not meeting his needs! He has none (vv. 12–13). This uncovers a problem they had. It is difficult to have clear and accurate views of God when views of ourselves obscure our perception of his revealed self. We are not to interpret God through the lens of our humanity. This was a continual problem in the nation of Israel. They continually returned to thoughts of appeasing the LORD to keep him at a distance, but they wanted him to do as they desired—a perpetual recipe for disaster.

Positively, he desires companionship with them. He longs for his people to walk with him (vv. 14–15). God clarifies he wants a genuine, meaningful relationship that is both respectful and appropriate but one that is real and rich and personal with an atmosphere of companionship. "Truly, our fellowship is with the LORD God Almighty!" As New Covenant believers, this opens more fully for us. Our fellowship is with the Godhead: the Father, the Son, and the Holy Spirit. Our one true God is glorious in holiness, fearful in praise, and doing wonders in the lives of his people. Know your God and love him. Open your hearts to him at all times. He is a precious, safe, secure, and pleasant refuge for you.

Here is what God wants with each one of us:

> Offer to God thanksgiving, and pay your
> vows to the Most High. Call upon me in the day
> of trouble; I will deliver you, and you shall glorify
> me. (Psalm 50:14–15)

This is to be our worldview, a life perspective. Receive these words and concepts from your God, meditate on them, and consciously weave them into the inner fabric of your beliefs, values, and motives in life.

What does this look like in real life? Let me open it briefly. There are five items:

1. "Offer to God thanksgiving." Live in an atmosphere of grateful acknowledgement of the Lord's kindnesses, mercies, and benefits. They are more than anyone could count (Psalm 103:1–5).

> In everything give thanks, for this is the will
> of God concerning you. (1 Thessalonians 5:18)

God wants his people to live in gratitude for the reality that all his glorious attributes are continually at work to do them good! He carries them in his heart and capable hands. This never ceases and knows no interruption! Oh, how we ought to praise the Lord with thankful hearts. How often? Now and forevermore (Romans 8:28–32; 2 Corinthians 5:6–8; Hebrews 12:3–11; Deuteronomy 8:1–6; Proverbs 13:24; 19:18; 23:13).

2. "Pay your vows to the Most High." Supremely value and embrace a loving and reverent response to God's forgivenesses, mercies, and grace. Show humble gratitude in a purposed, affectionate follow-through on your professed devotion and proclaimed willing obedience. In our baptism, we declared ourselves to no longer be our own but to walk in newness of life. With grateful hearts, out of love and thanksgiving, pay your vows to the Savior who gave his all for you. Give your all to him in loving praise and affectionate self-sacrificial devotion (Ecclesiastes 5:1–7; Romans 12:1–2, 9–21; Luke 11:28).

3. "Call upon me in the day of trouble." In the unavoidable difficulties and trials of life, whether great or small, draw near to me as your God. Run into my safe and capable hands. Take me at my word, and see me as your refuge. Look at no other. Look upon me as genuinely engaged to

be your help in every time of need. Open your heart to me as your infinitely capable LORD, friend, and king. I rule over you and will defend you. All the way to the end, I am with you. I want to do this together, and I want you to count on me. Therefore, engage in prayer, and call upon me. Call upon me in truth! (1 Peter 5:6–11; Philippians 4:6–7; Isaiah 43:2; Hebrews 4:14–16; Psalm 86:15–17).

4. "I will deliver you." I want you to have real-life, tangible experiences of my responsiveness and interventions in your life (Psalm 27:13–14; 28:6–9; 29:10–11; 2 Corinthians 12:6–10). Look for God's responsiveness and his answers to your prayers. No one will call upon me in vain! The honor of my name is there, and I will look after my reputation.

> Continue in prayer and watch in the same
> with thanksgiving. (Colossians 4:6)

5. "And you shall glorify me." Look and see, embrace and behave in harmony with the unalterable principle that everything exists and all events come to pass to bring glory to me, your God! Live with thanksgiving, and observe my ways till you burst forth in praise and exulting in my name (Romans 11:36; Revelation 4:11; Psalm 100:3–5; John 11:40).

Here are the five items God wants from you and me. We can give not one of them to the Lord without prayer! Do you see and believe we are to have a more robust prayer life? Do you see and are you convinced that to enter with these most essential and vital activities, we will need times of pleading?

> I called on the Lord in distress; the Lord
> answered me and set me in a broad place. The Lord
> is on my side; I will not fear. What can man do to
> me? The Lord is for me among those who help me;
> therefore, I shall see my desire on those who hate
> me. It is better to trust in the Lord than to put

confidence in man. It is better to trust in the Lord than to put confidence in princes. (Psalm 118:5–9)

I will keep your statutes; oh, do not forsake me utterly! (Psalm 119:8)

Hear my prayer, O Lord, and give ear to my cry; do not be silent at my tears; for I am a stranger with you. (Psalm 39:12)

My soul faints for your salvation, but I hope in your word. My eyes fail from searching your word, saying, "When will you comfort me?" (Psalm 119:81–82)

Those expressions "faint" and "fail" describe his intense longings, which had an energy-draining influence upon his soul and emotions. The psalmist blended deep longings for God's Word of help and deliverance with earnest pleadings for God's intimate responses to those longings. The psalmist had no taste for mere mental excursions in God's Word! He wanted "the real thing" of God's presence with his soul. He craved it in his walking together with his Lord.

Does it ignite love in your soul to know your God longs for this as well? I hope it does. Please know it is yours for the asking. Yet you must ask, seek, and knock with a determination to not let your God go until he gives you the blessing.

A Christian never falls asleep in the fire or in the water, but grows drowsy in the sunshine.

—John Berridge

He that is too secure is not safe.

—Thomas Fuller

25

**Why Pleading Is So Important (Part 4)
Evidence of Friendship with God**

*While all men seek after happiness, scarcely one
in a hundred looks for it in God.*

—John Calvin

*The enjoyment of God is the only happiness
with which our souls can be satisfied.*

—Jonathan Edwards

Reading the Psalms of David, we learn a basic principle in the believer's life: The way to forget our miseries is to remember the God of our mercies. David clearly expresses the only place God should have in every believer's life.

> Then I will go to the altar of God, to God
> my exceeding joy. (Psalm 43:4)

God is the believer's exceeding joy! We do not go to the Old Testament altar; we go to the "throne of grace" above and the "mercy seat" where our beloved Lord Jesus meets us. He tells us to come with humble boldness and contrite confidence to receive his sure mercies and find tangible help in the grace he gives. Here we meet with "God, our exceeding joy!"

Asaph, leader in Israel's worship, was in full agreement with David.

> Whom have I in heaven but you? And there is none upon earth that I desire besides you. My flesh and my heart fail; but God is the strength of my heart and my portion forever. (Psalm 73:25–26)

Asaph concludes this Psalm with a personal conviction every one of us should come to: "It is good for me to draw near to God!"

Believers have a relationship with God, with the Godhead, which includes the Father, the Son, and the Holy Spirit (2 Corinthians 13:14). This relationship is to be prized. To prize it, we must value it enough to pursue it. When we pursue it, confrontation with many opposing realities results. We dealt with these earlier in this book. Therefore, to enjoy this relationship, we will need to break through the barriers of the world, our own flesh, and the devil's derailing, distracting, and defeating efforts. We will face resistance from within and without. Discouragements will arise. There is no escaping this warfare.

> Walk in the Spirit, and you shall not fulfill the lust of the flesh. For the flesh lusts against the Spirit, and the Spirit against the flesh; and these are contrary to one another, so that you do not do the things that you wish. (Galatians 5:16–17)

Our communion with God will not be perfect or uninterrupted in this life. Christ reserves the fullness of life and perfect living, loving, and communing for glory.

You will experience times of deadness in your thoughts and affections. As bad as it sounds, you will get caught up in the things of life, fall into routine, and pray lifeless prayers or simply go through lists! Sin will creep in or you will fall into something. In your repentance, God will break up the fallow ground (hardened soil) of your heart and your soul will go out to the Lord with greater "realness" to connect with him and he will receive you because Christ has and is praying for you. Christ is your Advocate and Mediator. His blood is the argument for your sins being covered and paid for. You will have renewed longings and energies to go out to God in prayer, which exhibits life again.

Therefore, we will need energy of heart, importunity in prayer, and an unrelenting "praying in our praying" to enter this joy. At times there will be an ease to draw near to God. At other times, it will be a battle to get there. Sometimes we will only look with longing hearts for it—only to come short.

What is the driving force and internal motivation to stir us up to pursue this with energy? It will be that we prize and delight in God himself! We enjoy him. We love him and want to be close to him. Remember this—it is both ways! What do I mean? God wants you to want him and to prize him. He wants your closeness and presence in prayer. Our pleading with God gives clear evidence we want, prize, and love him in response. An important principle to remember: we love him because he first loved us. To stir up our love, gaze afresh upon the incomprehensible love of Christ, and remember, he displays the love of the Father and the Spirit for us. In the same way, we prize him because he first prized us! He took us into his embrace of redemptive love because he prized us. Why did he prize us? That, dear ones, is a mystery. The answer is found in God alone.

"O Lord, my God, you have called for my heart to love you and prize you. I acknowledge with David that I am poor and needy. It amazes me that you set your love and thoughts upon me. I bow with embarrassment at how feeble my love is for you and how faulty and failing I am toward you. In your loving-kindness, help me love you more. In the aggression of your affections, stir my affections for you. That you view me as a treasure and love me as you do finds no argument in me; it all rests in the mystery of your eternal purpose. It simply seemed good in your sight."

Why should we do this? Why is pleading so important? What does our pleading with God show?

Pleading Is Evidence of the Unique Friendship and Closeness We Have with God

Give serious thought to this question: how does God view his people? In the light of his eternal plan, the view of his eternal goal, how does he view and relate to his people individually and as a redeemed community? How do you personally and individually relate to God's view of you as you have fled to Jesus Christ for refuge from the wrath to come? These are important questions. They should be answered biblically.

(a) Faith must embrace God's testimony of how he views us, his genuine people.

> Moses went up to God, and the Lord called to him from the mountain, saying, "Thus you shall say to the house of Jacob, and tell the children of Israel: you have seen what I did to the Egyptians, and how I bore you on eagles' wings and brought you to myself. Now therefore, if you will indeed obey my voice and keep my covenant, then you shall be a special treasure to me above all people." (Exodus 19:3–5)

The nation of Israel was always a mixed multitude made up of some who had a heart to obey and keep God's laws and ways, but the majority did not.

> For the Lord has chosen Jacob for himself,
> Israel for his special treasure. (Psalm 135:4)

For those who came to spiritual life and loyalty to the Lord, there is no doubt how the Lord held them in his heart. Here is the genuine thought of God toward his genuine people.

414

Malachi 3:17 identifies the Lord's thoughts of his loyal people, the Israelites indeed, of the spiritual seed of Abraham:

> "They shall be mine," says the Lord of hosts, "On the day that I make them my jewels." (Malachi 3:17)

> The Lord their God will save them in that day, as the flock of his people. For they shall be like the jewels of a crown. (Zechariah 9:16)

Now, we who have come to saving faith in Christ are to represent a more pure community of devoted ones to the Lord. How are we viewed?

> You are a chosen generation, a royal priesthood, a holy nation, his own special people, that you may proclaim the praises of him who called you out of darkness into his marvelous light; who once were not a people but are now the people of God, who had not obtained mercy but now have obtained mercy. (1 Peter 2:9–10)

Whatever we face in this life arising from our loyalty to the Lord, here is how he views us: "the world was not worthy" to have us here! (Hebrews 11:38). Paul gives sweet assurances along this line:

> For I consider that the sufferings of this present time are not worthy to be compared with the glory which shall be revealed in us. (Romans 8:18)

He tells his people, which means every individual:

> I have loved you with an everlasting love; therefore, with loving-kindness I have drawn you. (Jeremiah 31:3)

My brothers and sisters,

> How deep the Father's love for us, how vast beyond all measure, that he should give his only Son to make a wretch his treasure! (Stuart Townend)

The LORD God Almighty, whose name is holy, looks upon those who have fled to Jesus for salvation and says, "Oh, my beloved, you are a special treasure to me, my precious people, and my jewels. I have made a better world for you because the world was not worthy of you. The thrill of my heart is to be together for all eternity. You are mine, my mercies and my loving-kindness is yours, and I have loved you forever and forever."

One last passage:

> The Lord your God in your midst, the Mighty One, will save; he will rejoice over you with gladness, he will quiet you with His love, he will rejoice over you with singing. (Zephaniah 3:17)

The original communicates a rush of exuberant gladness! God's love is so strong and deep, settled in his love, never to remove it. Even the words seem to dance with joy, for they reflect God's heart toward his people.

Do you see "how firm a foundation, you saints of the Lord, is laid for your faith in his excellent Word! What more can he say than to you he has said, you who unto Jesus for refuge have fled?" (Author unknown). We are to take God's testimony of how he views his genuine people and embrace it with faith. We come to the God who cannot lie.

Our sins and failings have been so adequately taken care of in the fountain opened for all sin and uncleanness.

> On the mount of crucifixion fountains opened deep and wide through the floodgates of God's mercy flowed a vast and gracious tide. Grace and love, like

mighty rivers, poured incessant from above. Heaven's peace and perfect justice kissed a guilty world in love. (Written by William Rees and translated from Welsh to English by William Edwards)

Psalm 85:10–11 speak of the kisses of Calvary!

> Mercy and truth have met together; righteousness and peace have kissed. Truth shall spring out of the earth, and righteousness shall look down from heaven.

This glorious act took place on the cross of Calvary. That is where mercy and truth met. It was the place where required righteousness kissed the accomplishment of our peace with God. Our Lord Jesus is the one who provides righteousness and (v. 13) makes his "footsteps our pathway." In Christ, we have reconciliation, peace, and friendship with God.

You may say, "But I don't feel his love." Or someone may say, "I'm afraid of presuming. What if this isn't for me?" This is what I would say:

1. Do not take your fears or your feelings for your authority or a guiding light. They are false guides and will lead you astray. There is a time—oh, I hope this doesn't offend anyone—"to spit in the eye of your feelings and say, stop it, it is God's Word I must believe." There is a time to say to your thoughts, "Quit your hellish logic and speak Scripture!" If you don't do this, you will give place for the devil to get a foothold in your soul to influence your thoughts and emotions.
2. Take special note of how David dealt with this in his situation. He talked to himself and even preached to his runaway thoughts and emotions.

> Why are you cast down, O my soul? And why are you disquieted within me? Hope in God,

for I shall yet praise him for the help of his countenance. (Psalm 42:5, 11; Psalm 43:5)

He says, "Hear this now, my soul. God has spoken in his holy Word. Settle it, put your trust in his Word. Hope in your God. It is the only safe and solid ground in an unstable world."

3.   Remember, we are not free to think whatever pops into our heads, nor to feel just any way we happen to feel. We are to bring every thought captive to the obedience to Christ (2 Corinthians 10:4–5). We are not free to just get into a worrying frame. No.

Be anxious for nothing, but in everything by prayer and supplication, with thanksgiving, let your requests be made known to God; and the peace of God, which surpasses all understanding, will guard your hearts and minds through Christ Jesus. (Philippians 4:6–7)

Paul will tell us what we are to be thinking in verses 8–9. This is part of what it is to "keep your heart with all diligence, for out if it flows the issues of life!" (Proverbs 4:23).

So, what are we to do with all this?

(b) Ask and plead with God to help you enter the relationship Christ purchased for you.

Paul communicated the closeness a believer has with God.

But now in Christ Jesus, you who once were far off have been brought near by the blood of Christ. (Ephesians 2:13)

Once alienated and enemies of God, now, in the New Covenant, because of the blood of Christ, we have all become the friends of God!

The Lord Jesus told the disciples, "I am the way, the truth, and the life. No one comes to the Father except through me" (John 14:6). The point is, we "actually come to the Father" through Christ to enjoy acceptance and an enriching relationship.

Let the words of Christ settle into your soul. "Greater love has no one than this than to lay down one's life for his friends. You are my friends if you do whatever I command you. No longer do I call you servants (slaves), for a servant (slave) does not know what his master is doing; but I have called you friends, for all things I heard from my Father I have made known to you." Christ has brought us into the private counsel of the Father and the Son. It is a privilege of the friends of God alone.

Make it a matter of personal growth. We are to mature in this privilege of being the friends of Christ and, through him, the friends of God!

You know how it is. We are most openhearted with those we are closest to. You communicate your deepest feelings to them. You reveal yourself and share thoughts then talk through things and open your reasonings. When you are in an environment where people are openhearted and tenderly honest, it produces closeness. That is what Christ was doing with the disciples. What he was sharing in the upper room was for us as well. He will pray that all his people will share in these privileges with enjoyment. To his Father, he says,

> I do not pray for these alone, but also for those who will believe in me through their word; that they all may be one, as you Father, are in me, and I in you; that they also may be one in us, that the world may believe that you sent me. (John 17:20–21)

Our Lord was praying for us! Of course, he still does.

When we give little thought to this or do not prize it as we should, it is not only our souls that suffer, our relationship suffers. It is through this intimate relationship—this friendship with the Almighty made real through Christ our Mediator—that we become a power, a witness, and a visible force in the world!

This comes through prayer; it comes through pleading prayer. Why is the church of such little consequence in the world? Why does the church appear irrelevant to our culture? It is that we are not pursuing and prizing the closeness, the friendship with God that Christ has purchased for us. We are putting information in our heads. We have good times with the brethren. Those are great, necessary, and important matters. However, it is prayer that puts the knowledge in our heads, into our hearts and lives!

In corporate prayer, we blend our souls together and come before God as one voice, one soul, one mind, and one heart to give vent to our longings and present our needs. When the church prays together, there is a concentration of belief, desire, and earnest seeking God's face.

> Wherever two or three are gathered together in my name, there I am in the midst! (Matthew 18:20)

> They continued steadfastly in the apostles' doctrine and fellowship, in the breaking of bread, and in prayers. (Acts 2:42)

When the church comes together in prayer, God's favorites gather in his presence! Things happen! They raised their voice to God with one accord and said,

> Lord, you are God, who made heaven and earth and the sea. Now, Lord look on their threats, and grant to your servants that with all boldness they may speak your words. (When they had prayed, the place where they were assembled

together was shaken; and they were all filled with
the Holy Spirit, and they spoke the word of God
with boldness.) (Acts 4:24, 29, 31)

Herod sent James on to heaven by beheading him. He put Peter
in prison.

Peter was therefore kept in prison, but constant prayer was offered to God for him by the
church. (Acts 12:5)

God sent an angel to fetch Peter out of prison; but the church
fetched the angel out of heaven through their prayers. I ask, where is
the prizing of blood-bought closeness with the Almighty in corporate
prayer? Where is it?

My brothers and sisters in Christ, these are precious privileges
God values. If we value closeness with the Father, the Son, and the
Holy Spirit, let us avail ourselves of it. Enter the enjoyment of security and purchased closeness—yes, with gratitude and thankfulness,
with reverence and amazement, but let us enter.

Therefore, brethren, having a boldness to
enter the Holiest by the blood of Jesus. (Hebrews
10:19)

Let us draw near with a true heart in full
assurance of faith, having our hearts sprinkled
from an evil conscience and our bodies washed
with pure water. (v. 22)

Our God has labored for us in tender ways to get us close to
him. Christ died to bring us close. He would have us act upon his
mercies.

Why are we so sluggish? So many talk about the difficulty of
prayer as though it is an excuse not to pursue it with diligence? Too
many people say, "Well, it is not a strong point." The Bible tells us,

"We have not because we ask not." What about faith, belief, and obedience? James tells us, "We have not because we do not ask in faith, nothing wavering."

There is an obvious reason: "We have not because we are not prizing, pursuing, and determined to get the grace of Christ and the assistance of the Holy Spirit to make us a praying people. We are not going to our Father and asking for the Holy Spirit to make a difference in our prayer life." If we wanted to make a breakthrough in our prayer life and we went to the Father to ask for the Holy Spirit, our Savior tells us, "How much more will your Father give the Holy Spirit to those who ask?" We are not pleading for what is promised. When we forgo prayer, what do we sacrifice? What is lost? The enjoyment of divine friendship! Brethren, we are forgoing God's smile and blessings being poured out on our assemblies. We have a friend in heaven who is sweetly willing to beautify our lives with his closeness and assistance in life.

(c) Ask and plead with God to help you imitate the saints who enjoyed this closeness and friendship with him.

1. Moses. "So the Lord spoke to Moses face to face, as a man speaks to his friend" (Exodus 33:11). Those who rely upon Christ's redeeming work and God's mercies through him, those who love the Lord and long to walk with God—the eternal Godhead would have you learn to plead and pray with him as Moses did! Christ died so we can come to God through him just as Moses came to God. There is no barrier. Christ has removed it. Now we are to come into a close and intimate relationship, a friendship, with the Almighty. Speak to God face-to-face as a friend speaks to his friend.

2. Abraham. The Lord Jesus and the apostle Paul tell us something vitally important concerning Abraham and us, as believers, as people who have faith in Christ.

The Lord Jesus. In John 8, our Lord is confronting the Pharisees. He tells them they were the mere physical seed of Abraham, not his spiritual seed. In fact, the devil was their father. They were the seed of the serpent, Christ states. Then he says, "If you were Abraham's children–spiritual seed–you would do the works of Abraham." Then he describes what the spiritual children of Abraham will do. (1) You will love Christ and the Father who sent him. (2) You will believe in Christ because he tells you the truth. (3) You will hear the word of God. He is describing us as believers. We are the spiritual seed of Abraham.

The apostle Paul. In Romans 4, Paul is describing the faith of faithful Abraham. He states that to all, who, like Abraham, exercise faith in the promise of God, resting in grace and not works, we are the spiritual seed of Abraham. Like Abraham, we are justified by faith. Then he lists some of the relationship blessings that flow out of this: (1) We have peace with God. (2) We have access by faith into this grace in which we stand. (3) We rejoice in hope of the glory of God—all trials build character and hope in us. (4) The Holy Spirit has poured the love of God out in our hearts.

What brought Abraham into this incredible "category" as a friend of God? (1) He believed God. (2) That belief was demonstrated and shown to be real by the priority choices Abraham made. What do I mean? Abraham loved the Lord above all other things or relations. He loved God more than Isaac, his beloved son. Nothing would or could claim more loyalty for Abraham. Are we faced with the same loyalty principle? Yes! Our Lord says, "If anyone comes to me and does not hate" (meaning as a competitor of devotion or loyalty to Christ—he is not saying we are to love them less, just no one more than him) "his father and mother, wife and children, brothers and sisters, yes, and his own life also, he cannot be my disciple" (Luke 14:26–33).

The great principles of heart religion bring their practical influence to the heart and life as loyalty, priority of devotion, and supreme love. Those people are wrong who put a mere notion of belief and prayer for the entirety of evangelical religion! Genuine faith alone is the avenue to have a part in Christ's atonement and righteousness.

This faith, through grace, saves the soul, but it produces holy fruits and is shown to be real by its effects on their acts, choices, pursuits, values, motives, priorities—i.e., works (James 2:23–24).

As Abraham was by faith, so we are now by the same faith. What is that?

> You are the descendants of Abraham my friend. (Isaiah 41:8)

> Are you not our God, who drove out the inhabitants of this land before your people Israel, and gave it to the descendants of Abraham your friend forever? (2 Chronicles 20:7)

> Abraham believed God, and it was accounted to him for righteousness. And he was called the friend of God. (James 2:23)

We have the same standing and position in faith: we are the friends of God like our (spiritual) father Abraham.

Christ died and took our sins upon himself so we could be the friends of God! Brethren, I fear we live too much in our heads or in our fears or in our unbelief or in our distractions.

Think honestly with me in this matter. Does this not point to one of the major contributing causes of the anemic nature of the church's witness in our day? Does it not speak to a major cause of the lack of saltiness and light in our communities? If we knew the LORD more intimately, as friends of the Most High, and learned to entreat, plead, and implore him to be at work in our hearts, homes, churches, and communities, would we see more of the Word of God going forth with boldness and effectiveness? I believe we would. Why? The Bible tells me so.

May the Holy Spirit use this little book, like a match, to light a fire in your soul, fueled by the grace which Christ keeps alive and the devil can't quench. May the flame ignite a holy, fervent prayer life in your soul.

Here is a precious example of prizing the relationship with God in the Edwards family:

Jonathan Edwards was a precious servant of Christ. It is a pity he is not more widely known in the churches. His spiritually rich influences remain, and he still enriches many who read his works. God, who makes no mistakes, took him home abruptly through a smallpox vaccination which went wrong. Here is how he, his wife Sarah, and his children handled it.

Jonathan's response and communications:

> After he was sensible that he could not survive that sickness, a little before his death, he called his daughter to him, who attended him in his sickness, and addressed her in a few words, which were immediately taken down in writing, as near as could be recollected, and are as follows:

> Dear Lucy,
> It seems to me to be the will of God, that I must shortly leave you; therefore give my kindest love to my dear wife, and tell her, that the uncommon union, which has so long subsisted between us, has been of such a nature, as I trust is spiritual, and therefore will continue forever: and I hope she will be supported under so great a trial, and submit cheerfully to the will of God. And as to my children, you are now like to be left fatherless; which I hope will be an inducement to you all, to seek a Father who will never fail you.

Sarah Edward's response and communications:

> Stockbridge, April 3, 1758.
> My very dear child,
> What shall I say? A holy and good God has covered us with a dark cloud. O that we may

kiss the rod, and lay our hands on our mouths! The Lord has done it. He has made me adore his goodness, that we had him so long. But my God lives: and he has my heart. O what a legacy my husband, and your father, has left us! We are all given to God; and there I am, and love to be.

Your ever affectionate mother,
Sarah Edwards

The children's response and communications:

On the same sheet was the following letter from one of her daughters.

My dear sister,

My mother wrote this with a great deal of pain in her neck, which disabled her from writing any more. She thought you would be glad of these few lines from her own hand.

O, sister, how many calls have we, one upon the back of another? O, I beg your prayers, that we, who are young in this family, may be awakened and excited to call more earnestly on God, that he would be our Father, and Friend forever.

My father took leave of all his people and family as affectionately as if he knew he should not come again. On the Sabbath afternoon he preached from these words—"We have no continuing city, therefore let us seek one to come." The chapter that he read was Acts the 20th. O, how proper; what could he have done more? When he had got out of doors he turned about—"I commit you to God"—said he. I

doubt not but God will take a fatherly care of us,
if we do not forget him.

I am your affectionate sister,
Susannah Edwards

*The knowledge of God is efficacious (effective to create a divine
influence in the soul). To know him is immediately to love him. We can
never separate love and obedience. The principle of worshipping God
is a diligent love of him. The source and cause of obedience is the love
wherewith we embrace God as our Father. A more abundant knowledge
of Christ is represented as an extraordinary reward of our love to Christ.*

—John Calvin

*The friendship of the LORD is for those who fear him,
and he makes known to then his covenant. (ESV)*

—David, in Psalm 25:14

26

The Simplicity of This Pleading

Come, my soul thy suit prepare. Jesus loves to answer prayer.

—John Newton

No one will deny the challenge of maintaining a meaningful prayer life. In this life, we experience weariness of body, mind, and heart through the demands upon us. Oh, yes, we have spiritual warfare as well. Nor can we forget temptation and sin that dogs our spiritual heels. However, prayer and pleading with God are uncomplicated.

Notice these words from God, and take in their simplicity.

> For what great nation is there that has God so near to it, as the Lord our God is to us, for whatever reason we may call upon him? (Deuteronomy 4:7)

Don't you love that! "God is near for whatever reason. We may call upon him!" This has a sweet application for us as saints. Peter tells us,

> You are a chosen generation, a royal priest-hood, a holy nation, and his own special people, that you may proclaim the praises of him who called you out of darkness into his marvelous

428

light; who once were not a people but are now
the people of God, who had not obtained mercy
but now have obtained mercy. (1 Peter 2:9–10)

Back in the Deuteronomy passage, notice verses 29–-31:

But from there you will seek the Lord your
God, and you will find him if you seek him with
all your heart and with all your soul. When you
are in distress…when you turn to the Lord your
God and obey his voice (for the Lord your God
is a merciful God), he will not forsake you nor
destroy you, nor forget the covenant of your
fathers which he swore to them.

Drawing near to God and pleading with him requires no great
revelation. What does it require? A tender heart, a believing soul,
and a sincere opening your mind to God with true reliance upon his
Word and promises. It is simple belief in what God has said, bringing
our hearts to believe him, and pressing God with his own Word and
promises to do what he has committed to do. Praying in this way
shows belief, submission to his authority, and loving trust. However,
it also includes heightened affections aroused to experience God's
activities in one's life. Think of your affections as the temperature of
your thoughts. As Paul says, "Be fervent in spirit." Let your love be
warm and hot toward the Lord as opposed to cold or lukewarm. Seek
to have this interwoven in your handling of the promises of God.

If pleading with God is this simple, what hinders us? What are the
difficulties or stumbling blocks that prevent this kind of pleading we
have been describing? Let me draw attention to a few common struggles.

1. Some struggles arise from our childhood experiences or life events.

Many with whom I have discussed pursuing a closer relationship with God have confessed they struggle to believe God is inter-

ested in them personally—at least on a deep and personal level as described in this book. They believe in Christ as the only Savior of sinners, and they trust him. However, as for God taking a personal interest in them, that's difficult to embrace. "Now that's hard," they say. "A Savior who wants an intimate relationship with me! That is beyond my ability to grasp." It is a wall they can't get over. Whether from one parent or both, they never sensed interest in them as a person. They grew up never "feeling heard" or even seen. Facing life alone and learning to "do it on their own" produced core beliefs that no one was for them. Even in coming to faith in Christ, these inner grooves of "seeing life" and their personal worth did not change.

What do you do with this? How can a healthier approach to life and relating to God happen? These core beliefs take time to change. They can only change by receiving the engrafted Word of God into the soul along with the Spirit's ministry. God's Word can change us. We must believe this. It does not happen overnight. The purpose of God's Word and the ministry of the Spirit is to realign the flow of our inner world to be in harmony with his loving thoughts toward us as his sons and daughters.

I have often thought of the demon-possessed man who had his dwelling among the tombs. Christ cast out a legion of demons from him. That day changed his life. However, the scars of a lifetime and the demon possession, most likely, followed him to the grave (Mark 5:1–20).

It would be the same with the woman at the well who had five husbands and lived with a man when Christ changed her life (John 4). Mary Magdalene, out of whom our Lord cast seven demons, had an incredible sense of gratitude for Christ's marvelous mercy and saving grace (Luke 8:2). We do not have a biography of these people. No record of the effects of years under affliction, sorrow, and pain has been preserved for us. We know they were people subject to the same afflictions and passions we are. Memories, patterns of thought, and carnal reactions did not change in a moment. When Christ ascended to heaven, they had to exercise the same spiritual disciplines given to us. They employed meditation on God's Word, prayer, and fervent prayer when needed to experience overcoming faith.

Here is counsel I have given. Take a few passages of Scripture which hold out precious promises to you and write them in a journal. As you do this, pray over every word and concept, asking God to implant or engraft his words into your mind and heart. Plead with him to give you understanding by his Spirit. Entreat him to change the thought patterns of your soul to think as he tells you to think. Confess to him your belief that while others have not given you "the time of day" with any genuine interest, you do not want to think of God according to their behaviors or treatments. Ask God to give personal attention and instruction concerning his actual character and his kind thoughts toward you.

> Let the world despise and leave me,
> They have left my Savior, too.
> Human hearts and looks deceive me;
> Thou art not, like them, untrue.
> (Henry Lyte, 1833)

Here are some helpful passages. Work them into your soul.

> Receive with meekness the engrafted word, which is able to save (deliver) your souls. (James 1:21)

God's word can deliver you from the "mind traps" of the past. Most people have patterns of thought which do not serve them well. We all must change our thinking paradigms.

> Fear not, for I am with you; be not dismayed, for I am your God. I will strengthen you, yes I will help you, I will uphold you with my righteous right hand. (Isaiah 41:10)

> I am poor and needy, yet the Lord thinks upon me. You are my help and my deliverer; do not delay, O my God. (Psalm 40:17)

> Whenever I am afraid, I will trust in you. In
> God (I will praise his word), in God I have put
> my trust. (Psalm 56:3–4)

2. *The lack of familiarity with scripture or not paying attention to the models given us in biblical history are great hindrances to many people.*

Our own unawareness of how open we can be to take our needs to God can be crippling. Our "ignorance" of the words given to us by God to help us in such praying will be debilitating. This unfamiliarity with Scripture stops us from taking the Word of God and pressing it upon our mind and heart. It will hinder us from placing them before God, pressing them upon his mind and heart with the love and respect of a humble child. This was a major problem in the nation of Israel.

> I have written for him the great things of
> my law, but they were considered a strange thing.
> (Hosea 8:12)

Look at the extent to which God goes to help the people of Israel correct this and get into genuine praying and seeking God's face.

> O Israel, return to the LORD your God, for
> you have stumbled because of your iniquity; take
> words with you, and return to the LORD. Say
> to him, "take away all iniquity; receive us gra-
> ciously." (Hosea 14:1–4)

Contrast this with faithful Abraham (here we could bring many examples). God gave Abraham and Sarah promises of their own child. They were old, and Sarah passed the childbearing years. Yet they believed in God. Faced with no present hope, they believed in the God of hope. Look at Paul's focus on Abraham in Romans 4:19–22:

> Not being weak in faith, he did not consider his own body, already dead (since he was about a hundred years old), and the deadness of Sarah's womb. He did not waver at the promise of God through unbelief, but was strengthened in faith, giving glory to God, and being fully convinced that what he had promised, he was also able to perform. And therefore it was accounted to him for righteousness.

Abraham refused to look at the problems facing him. He did not focus on the hindrances! There were impossibilities, major ones! He focused on the God who could do the impossible. Consider these passages which declare the power, greatness, and capability of God to those who call upon him.

> "Then you will call upon me and go and pray to me, and I will listen to you. And you will seek me and find me when you search for me with all your heart. I will be found by you," says the Lord. (Jeremiah 29:12–14a)

> Call to me, and I will answer you, and show you great and mighty things, which you do not know. (Jeremiah 33:3)

> Our help is in the name of the Lord, who made heaven and earth. (Psalm 124:8)

> Ah, Lord God! Behold, you have made the heavens and the earth by your great power and outstretched arm. There is nothing too hard for you. (Jeremiah 32:17)

Come back to Abraham. Years later, when the Lord told him to take Isaac to Mount Moriah and offer him as a sacrifice on the altar, he obeyed. The soul struggle Abraham had in the sacrificing of his son is hidden from our view. However, Abraham believed this was the communicated will of God and it would not cancel out the promise given. If Isaac died, God could raise him from the dead!

> By faith Abraham, when he was tested, offered up Isaac, and he who had received the promises offered up his only begotten son, of whom it was said, "In Isaac your seed shall be called," concluding that God was able to raise him up, even from the dead, from which he also received him in a figurative sense. (Hebrews 11:17–19)

3. A great hindrance is our own fear—for instance, concerns that we would be irreverent.

This is a good caution but no real excuse. Our heavenly Father looks for us to take him at his word and learn to use his own words to express our confidence and reliance upon him. Remember the illustrations Christ gave us? The neighbor who would pound on the door and not give up until he received the provisions, the widow who would not leave the unjust judge alone until he helped her. Christ says to us pray like that. Don't be overly polite. Be importunate in your praying.

God wants us to "take hold of him"! How it thrills the heart of our Father when we state his values, promises, purposes as the basis for our longed-for answers from him to our prayers. "Lord, you have made me to hope in you. O do not let me trust in you in vain!" He assures us, "I will never let my children cry to me in vain." We must drown our fears in the faithful Word of our God.

> In God (I will praise his word), in the LORD
> (I will praise his word), in God I have put my
> trust; I will not be afraid. (Psalm 56:10–11)

4. However, this fear can lead us to another reason we do not plead: unbelief.

The danger is we really do not believe the expressions given to us in Scripture. The peril is we do not take God at his Word. This, of course, speaks to a deeper problem in our relationship to God and his Word. We may say, "I fear offending," when in reality we do not have the fear of the Lord in our hearts. The tragedy is we do not exercise the obedience of faith. "If we will not believe, we will not be established."

> He did not do many mighty works there
> because of their unbelief. (Matthew 13:58)

> Let him ask in faith, with no doubting, for
> he who doubts is like a wave of the sea driven and
> tossed by the wind. For let not that man suppose
> that he will receive anything from the Lord; he is
> a double-minded man, unstable in all his ways.
> (James 1:6–8)

5. There is confusion over what your responsibility is.

There is a way of thinking that can stop us from such open-hearted pleading. This thinking will hinder us from pressing God with his words of promise. What do I mean? You have wanted to be content and not murmur. You know you ought to be very careful when it comes to many earthly things, so you become timid in asking the Lord for his involvement or interventions. Yet what we think of as timid can be a false humility and an unwillingness to put forth active faith and energy of the soul to lay hold of God for spiritual riches.

God delights when we ask for spiritual graces and blessings. He desires us to desire them with a fervency in what can be called the sacrifice of prayer. Where there is no fire, there is no sacrifice offered. It would be so much more of a healthy outlook to see this kind of praying as evidence of walking by faith and highly prizing spiritual treasure.

Early in our marriage, my wife and I would begin each year with what we called our impossible prayer list—things we looked to God to do in the coming year, which, to our abilities or understanding, were out of reach. Yet through the year, we bowed in humble thanks for the ways our God took us up and took the request as an opportunity to draw our affections out to him. He gave us occasions for praise to be lavished upon him as our God and generous benefactor.

6. A conscience that tells us things are not right between us and God.

This can be a tricky area to pinpoint. The reason it can be difficult is this. There may be actual causes for such a disturbed conscience or there can be a vague unidentified sense of guilt in our conscience.

a. For actual sins or offenses before the Lord, we will know (even if we try to play ignorant) what the problem is. You will know the area of compromise or actual sin. Those matters will nag you and stare you in the face. When you come to the Lord, they force you to deal with them or try to ignore them. You will know what you are doing. It will take a conscious effort, even if it is ever so slightly, to put it out of your mind. Indeed, this will stop you from pleading.

You sensed your hypocrisy in trying to ignore them and simply play the part in prayer. You are aware of mere stage-playing or acting the part of a person praying to God. The only course—the only safe course—is to get real with yourself and God, come clean, and make a full confession to him. In fact, you can turn this honest view of yourself into arguments for the Lord to draw near and give help to examine yourself and be honest with him and yourself.

> Blessed is he whose transgression is forgiven, whose sin is covered. Blessed is the man to whom the Lord does not impute iniquity, and in whose spirit there is no deceit. When I kept silent, my bones grew old through my groaning all the day long. For day and night, your hand was heavy upon me; my vitality was turned into the drought of summer. (Psalm 32:1–4)

b. The other condition of a troubled conscience is a bit more complex. You have a general unidentified sense of guilt, but you can't pinpoint what it is. You have no honest awareness of "regarding sin in your heart" or "making provision for the flesh to fulfill its lusts" (Psalm 66:18; Romans 13:14). There is nothing you are trying to hide or hold on to.

What do you do? Look at two passages that address this area of trouble for the people of God.

> My little children, let us not love in word or in tongue, but in deed and in truth. And by this, we know that we are of the truth, and shall assure our hearts before him. For if our heart condemns us, God is greater than our heart and knows all things. For if our heart does not condemn us, we have confidence toward God. And whatever we ask, we receive from him, because we keep his commandments and do those things that are pleasing in his sight. And this is his commandment: that we should believe on the name of his

Son Jesus Christ and love one another, as he gave
us the commandment. (1 John 3:18–23)

What John is addressing here is a child of God who is committed to walking in all, well-pleasing to the Lord, has a willingness to
love simply and purely; yet his heart, his conscience, troubles him.
He is not sure exactly what it is, but it is keeping him from confidence before his God.

John is comforting such a one with this direction: trust in and
believe in your God, who has more authority than your own conscience. Come before him with this confidence that if there is something wrong, God will let you know. He is faithful and all-knowing, so don't let general or vague feelings that things are wrong stop
you from openhearted praying. Rather, make them the argument to
come before him with a humble boldness and confidence that he will
sort it all out. The important thing is that nothing stops you from
praying and opening your heart to your caring, gracious Father.

The other passage which addresses this state of a confused conscience is Philippians 3:15. This is the counsel of the apostle Paul:

Therefore, let us, as many as are mature,
have this mind; and if in anything you think otherwise, God will reveal even this to you.

I love the wholesome practicality of the apostle Paul. You can
see there is harmony here with John. Of course, that is because the
ultimate author of both passages is the Holy Spirit, who is giving
counsel to the saints.

Paul is saying if you are mistaken or if you are amiss in your
understanding, God will be faithful and bring it to your attention so
you can correct it. Don't let vague confused worries or concerns keep
you from pressing forward. "Well, I don't know if I am mature or
well-rounded." No problem. If you aren't, God will be faithful to you
and let you know. Nothing escapes his gaze, and he knows the areas
of your needs better than you. Trust him and press on.

Two concluding illustrations:

1. An illustration from my daughter

One day, my daughter and I were painting a room. It was a delightful time to enjoy some dad-daughter conversation. As we painted, she opened her heart and expressed the perplexities of her thoughts.

"Dad, I feel frustrated and confused. I pray and ask God to save me. I really want to be his and be a Christian, but I don't sense he hears me, and I don't sense his answers. I don't know what to do. I don't have assurance that he is hearing and answering my prayers."

So I said, "Well, honey, I think we can slowly or subtlety shift our trust to our feelings and look for something within us to be confident in. You are putting your trust and faith in what God has said: 'Believe in the Lord Jesus Christ and you shall be saved.' I think you should trust that what he says is true and live on his promise. Go forth believing and know that what he says is worth being confident in. If you are mistaken, God will show you if you sincerely want him to. I think you want him to. Just don't make assurance 'the thing' you want to be confident in. If you do, you will end up putting your confidence in your 'sense of assurance.' Rather, be confident in God, the work of Christ, and what he says in his Word. Place the full weight of your faith in Christ and his invitational promise to save those who come to him."

Just recently, my daughter reminded me of this conversation and how much it helped her. Her whole approach to God, his Word, and the Christian life changed from that moment. God makes the Gospel so simple a child can understand it.

What a kindness. That was twenty-some years ago. She has walked with God ever since in a growing, loving relationship with her gracious God. She was overthinking it and making it more complicated than God wanted. We are all good at doing this. It is the same with pleading with God.

2. The Syro-Phoenician woman

Our Lord had to get away from the hypercritical Pharisees. He traveled many miles to the border of Israel near Tyre and Sidon. A Greek woman, a Syro-Phoenician by birth, had determined to find Christ. In this woman, you have the simplicity and excellence of pleading. We will go through the account with a few comments. Matthew 15:21–28:

(a) A mother with her urgent need (vv. 21–22):

> And behold, a woman of Canaan came from that region and cried out to him, saying, "Have mercy on me, O Lord, Son of David! My daughter is severely demon-possessed."

She felt need and helplessness. It gripped her mother's heart with searing pain. She shows a determination to get to Christ. This woman owned his true identity as Messiah. He came to his own, and his own received him not on a large scale. Here is one who valued the treasure of who he was. She was pleading for mercy, the very thing he delighted to give. In his mercy and power lived the solution to her miseries, and she knew it.

(b) The disciple's selfish entreaty (v. 23):

> But he answered her not a word. And his disciples came and urged him, saying, "Send her away, for she cries out after us."

> How long this went on, we are not told, but it began to annoy the disciples. There efforts to get her to go away were powerless.

Neither the disciples nor any other deterrent could stop her. She would not leave her request unaddressed. Humble boldness, contrite confidence, energy of faith kept the Savior in the crosshairs of her soul's belief, and she would not let him go without receiving the blessing desperately needed. Do not misread the Savior's silence at this point. In wisdom, he allows the appearance of an "indifferent neighbor" or an "unjust judge." We must not interpret God's delays as denials. No one knew he was drawing her faith out to break through every barrier. He determined to set her faith on display. He is preparing to give the disciples an object lesson on the power of faith they would never forget. The strength of her faith drew the power of Christ's compassion and awe-inspiring mercy with full compliance to her every wish. Here is a woman in the category of Rahab, Ruth, and the Roman Centurion—all Gentiles who possessed inner spiritual life and vibrant faith that drew the tender mercies and loving compassions of God.

The disciples were weary of her continual pleading for help. They asked Christ to send her away either by granting her request or by the denial of it. They did not like the noise, and they feared it might defeat his purpose of seclusion; and so, by their phrase "send her away," they unconsciously betrayed that what they ultimately wanted was not granting the prayer but getting rid of the petitioner. Our Savior knows the damage careless words can have upon a desperate heart. He breaks his silence with a statement of his commission. His sympathies were already welling up within. The river of his merciful love was about to burst beyond his commission to the lost sheep of the house of Israel as it had with the Centurion. Already, it was hard for so much love to be silent in the presence of so much sorrow.

(c)   The Savior's utterance of his messianic mission (vv. 24–25):

> But he answered and said, "I was not sent except to the lost sheep of the house of Israel."
> Then she came and worshiped him, saying, "Lord, help me!"

In his perfect humanity, Jesus Christ was the long-expected Servant of the LORD, Messiah come to Israel. His was a mission of mercy to remove, once and for all, the sin barrier between God and man on a worldwide scale. Perhaps there was a pause in his pace as he spoke these words. This woman takes advantage to press even nearer to the fountain of hope. She worships him. Her faith emboldens a beautiful shamelessness and repeats her prayer, but this time with great brevity. "Lord, help me!" Heart prayers are often brief prayers. Desperate prayers are not long in words but passionate in intensity. She does not call him the Son of David again, nor does she repeat her sorrow, but flings herself in desperation at his pity.

(d) Another refusal is coming which sounds harsh and hopeless. However, she now has direct communication with Christ (vv. 26–27):

> But He answered and said, "'It is not good to take the children's bread and throw it to the little dogs." And she said, "Yes, Lord, yet even the little dogs eat the crumbs which fall from their masters' table."

You wonder how much disappointment this woman can face! His refusal was a real refusal, founded on the divine commission, which he was bound to obey. As the sent one of God, the bread is the blessing for the "children" who are the "lost sheep of the house of Israel"; the "dogs" are the Gentile world. This meaning is simply the restriction of his personal activity to the chosen nation. The words had no intent to wound or insult. However, they would offend a delicate ego. They would repel a less-determined or less-sorrowful heart.

Remember where our Lord just came from. He left the scribes and Pharisees with all their pride, judgments, and hard-hearted arguments. They had no desire to know him, learn from him, and partake of his gracious provisions. He was the bread of life! The vast majority of the children of Israel would not come to his well-spread table of life-giving bread.

This woman's response is breathtaking! What incredible resilience of faith. Focused on the fountain of divine hope, she wrings hope out of a seeming discouragement. The dexterity of bold belief finds in the very arguments against her feasting on mercies needed, the substance of a powerful argument to partake of Christ's overflowing abundance! The Holy Spirit buoyed her soul up to ride victorious over the waves crashing against her soul. In humility, she embraces her unworthiness of the least of his mercies. There is no request for the children's bread. She believes the children's table is so adequately supplied that crumbs would fall off and the children would never miss them. In common households, even dogs enjoy these. "Lord, I believe there is power in the least of your mercies—even the crumbs of your mercies are adequate to meet the desperate needs I have. Oh, for the crumbs that fall from the table is all I ask. The children would never miss a crumb!"

    (e) Christ's joyful granting of her request. See Matthew 15:22–28:

> Then Jesus answered and said to her, "O woman, great is your faith! Let it be to you as you desire." And her daughter was healed from that very hour. (v. 28)

There is an exuberance, a joyful thrill in our Savior's response. "O woman, great is your faith!" The Savior could see the fingerprints of the Spirit's work all over her soul's expression of firm belief in him. Then, it is as if he takes the key to heaven's treasury and hands it to her. "Let it be to you as you desire"—as if he says, "Go in and take all you want or need. You have access to heaven's full supply. It is yours, dear soul. Yours is a faith of an overcomer."

There is simplicity in her faith. However, dogged determination is a powerful characteristic. This woman overcame all obstacles with persistent, holy arguments, and unrelenting belief. Such faith thrills the soul of our Savior. Our Lord said,

> From the days of John the Baptist until now the kingdom of heaven suffers violence, and the violent take it by force. (Matthew 11:12)

This dear sister shows that kind of prayer that stormed the gates of heaven and came back with the desired blessings. This is pleading with God.

Oh, my brothers and sisters, could we see into heaven how would Christ view our prayers? If we are a pleading people, we would see our beloved Lord Jesus looking in upon us. When he sees us pleading and praying, praying and pleading with persevering earnestness for the things which really matter, how does he respond?

"Prepare the windows of heaven! Open the floodgates of blessings! There are my dear people longing for my blood-bought riches. They long enough to plead for them and persevere in their pleading! Let them be poured out according to their desires. Give to them exceedingly, abundantly, above all they are able to ask or think! I will show them I am large hearted and openhanded. Will they rattle heaven with the force of their prayers? I will shake the earth with my response in blessing them!"

Ah! How often, Christians, has God kissed you at the beginning of prayer, and spoken peace to you in the midst of prayer, and filled you with joy and assurance upon the close of prayer.

—Thomas Brooks

ABOUT THE AUTHOR

Rick D. Bawcom has served in the pioneering work of church planting and pastoral ministry for twenty-five years. He met Donna during his first year at Bible College. They married in 1974. God blessed them with eleven wonderful children and, at present, thirty-five delightful grandchildren. Rick focuses on topics that strengthen churches, families, and individuals in their faith. As author and speaker, his passion is to build up the people of God in the power of God's truth. You may reach him at rickbawcom@gmail.com.

Printed in the USA
CPSIA information can be obtained
at www.ICGtesting.com
LVHW090353010224
770342LV00004B/57/J